# DUKEDOM LARGE ENOUGH

David A. *nton* Randall
/ / /

---

# DUKEDOM

# LARGE

# ENOUGH

*—my library*
*Was dukedom large enough—*
THE TEMPEST, Act I, Scene 2

RANDOM HOUSE   *NEW YORK*

Acknowledgment is gratefully made to the following for permission to reprint from their works:

Constable Publishers, London: from an article by John Carter in *New Paths in Book Collecting*.

E. P. Dutton & Co. Inc.: from *Highlights and Footlights,* by Crosby Gaige.

*The New York Times:* from "Adventures of Two Bibliophiles," by David Randall, 1946, and for short extracts from an article in the December 11, 1936, issue. Copyright 1936, 1946 by The New York Times Company.

Charles Scribner's Sons: from *The Letters of F. Scott Fitzgerald,* edited by Andrew Turnbull.

The Society of Authors as the literary representative of the Estate of A. E. Housman for extracts from published letters of A. E. Housman.

The Viking Press, Inc.: "Dante Gabriel Rossetti" by Dorothy Parker from *The Portable Dorothy Parker*. Copyright 1928, renewed 1956 by Dorothy Parker.

Library of Congress Catalog Card Number: 69–16418

*Manufactured in the United States of America*

*Designed by Kenneth Miyamoto*

*In Memoriam:*

*Robert M. Smith 1886–1952. Teacher*

*Max Harzof 1875–1942. Bookman*

*J. K. Lilly, Jr. 1893–1966. Collector*

# CONTENTS

# Illustrations

# Apologia

ANYONE DEALING WITH BOOKS knows that there are too many of them and apparently always have been: "Of making many books there is no end." (Ecclesiastes 12:12) At one time I took a solemn vow never to add one single grain to the sandy seashore of books. I have collaborated on and researched a fair number, but this was all part of business chores. Here I am all on my own, and with memoirs yet! Why?

I think the main reason is that I have always been sad because my betters seldom did theirs. Many were always promising but few ever produced. The stories I heard in my youth were from men who had actually known authors like Melville and Whitman, collectors like Robert Hoe and Brayton Ives (to name only two Americans who had owned Gutenberg Bibles); Dean Richmond, one of America's first prominent rare book dealers; the famed dealer George D. Smith; and scores of as interesting but less known characters in "the trade."

The stories told were of especial interest to those of an antiquarian and bookish-historical bent but are now beyond verification and accurate recall. The antiquarian, of all businesses, should be interested in recording its past, but largely it isn't.

I finally discovered that, somehow, I had become the person talking about things past and that some younger collectors, students, librarians, etc., were interested. Some looked at me and asked, "You really knew Tom Wolfe?" Or, if they were interested in bibliography, ". . . Wilberforce Eames?" I suddenly realized that these people had been dead well before the students I was talking to were born. "And did you once see Shelley plain?" The youngsters of today look back on the thirties as a Golden Age, and perhaps it was. There were heroes alive to know and good books to be gotten cheaply "in those days." Youth always idealizes, and that's good. And here I was doing exactly what I faulted my elders for: talking but not leaving any sort of record.

I entered the trade at the crest of a wave, in 1929, and left it in 1955, just as it was cresting again. The quarter-century trough I worked through spanned the Great Depression, World War II and on to the end of the Korean War. The changes in *Taste and Technique in Book Collecting,* to use the title of one of John Carter's best books, over that period had been considerable. The fields of collecting had broadened; bibliography, with the entrance of men like William Jackson and Fredson Bowers, had become more sophisticated; mechanical aids like the Hinman collating machine ("which to be hated, needs but to be seen") came into being; and public and university libraries were beginning to compete seriously with the private collector for a diminishing amount of available material. The great generals of the time, whether collectors or dealers, have left few firsthand records, so a subaltern's memoirs may serve some purpose.

My letter files from my years at Scribner's no longer exist, and a few facts had to be dredged from memory, but on the whole those recounted are verifiable. John Carter, F. B. Adams, Jr., Waller Barrett, Jake Blanck, Edward Lazare, Richard Wormser, William B. Wisdom, Virginia Warren, Philip Duschnes, Gordon Ray, Michael Papantonio and John S. Van E. Kohn have read portions of the work and made valued corrections and comments. Such errors in facts as exist are mine, just as are opinions which some of my colleagues may not share.

D. A. R.

# DUKEDOM LARGE ENOUGH

# *Apprentice Years:*
# *1929-1935*

I SPENT most of my time while at Harvard Law School in the Widener Library and attending George Parker Winship's course in bibliography, Fine Arts 5E, into which I somehow wangled myself, without credit, of course. I had decided that I wanted somehow to get into the rare book business and resigned from Harvard, thus saving Lehigh University, my undergraduate school, a black mark by not flunking, as I had been entered without examinations. Winship gave me a letter of introduction to Edgar H. Wells, a Harvard dean turned rare book dealer. He had no opening but referred me to E. Byrne Hackett, president of the Brick Row Book Shops, Inc., New Haven, New York and Princeton. I had done some small collecting of my own, but I knew so little that I was no prize, even I realized, to any bookshop, in other than a menial job. But that was all right with me—I was willing to spend six months' apprenticeship learning the whole business.

By a quirk of luck my appointment with Hackett was for 9:30 A.M. Among his employees was his married daughter, and she chose that morning, at 9:00 A.M., to inform him that she was pregnant and had to stop working. I was hired at $17.50 a week.

If anyone ever started at the peak of the business, I did. My first assignment was to attend the sale of the library formed by Jerome Kern. I sat in the last row and marked a catalogue. The first session (of ten) was held at the Anderson Galleries, Mitchell Kennerley, President, Park Avenue at 59th Street, Monday evening, January 7, 1929, and marked the end of an epoch. The 1,482 items brought $1,729,462.50—as of record—and remained the most expensive (though far from being the most valuable) single library ever sold at auction in America, until the recent, still continuing sale of the Thomas Streeter Americana.

The Kern library was typical of the collecting era in which it was formed, guided and directed by A. Edward Newton's *Amenities of Book Collecting, and Kindred Affections* (Boston, 1918). Almost entirely English literature of the eighteenth to the twentieth century, it was heavy in Johnson, Goldsmith, Lamb, Shelley, Dickens, Thackeray, the Brownings, Conrad and Hardy, with a small sprinkling of seventeenth-century English and nineteenth-century American books.

The emphasis was on association copies and manuscripts. In this Kern was following the pattern set by another popular songwriter, Harry B. Smith, who wrote the book or lyrics for over three hundred stage productions. His best-remembered song (with Victor Herbert) is "Gypsy Love Song." Smith had assembled what he described as a "Sentimental Library," which indeed it was, including the *Pickwick* Dickens gave his sister-in-law Mary Hogarth, the manuscripts of Lamb's *Dream Children* and Keats's sonnet "On First Looking into Chapman's Homer" among many others. The entire collection was purchased by Dr. A. S. W. Rosenbach in 1918 for $79,000 in what his biographers, Edwin Wolf II and John F. Fleming, describe as his first major coup.

The Kern collection contained a great number of nineteenth-century authors' first books, among them many notorious rarities. In the sale many of these achieved record prices, unsurpassed even now—and likely to remain so. The entrepreneur of the sale was the wily Mitchell Kennerley. He persuaded Kern to extend credit to purchasers much beyond what was customary at the time—up to two years, in some cases. It was boom time on the stock market, so why not? If cash wasn't available this year, it would be next, wouldn't it? Collecting in that period was not as sophisticated as it has since become, and a fair number of Kern's books turned out, after purchase, not to live up to their glowing catalogue descriptions. Especially *Tom Jones*, of which more later.

The sale was dominated by a few dealers, Dr. Rosenbach, Gabriel Wells, Alvin J. Scheuer and Barnett J. Beyer especially. And a majority of the expensive books went to a very few collectors, among them Owen D. Young, Dr. Samuel W. Bandler, Richard Gimbel and W. T. H. Howe. The libraries of Young and Howe are now in the New York Public Library, though Young had previously sold some things privately—to Scribner's, among others.

The tone of the sale was set by the eighty-fourth item, the first to reach five figures. It was Elizabeth Barrett's (Browning) first book, *The*

*Battle of Marathon* (London, 1820), written when she was just entering her teens and privately printed in an edition of fifty copies "because Papa was bent on spoiling me." It had cost Kern $1,650, and the Galleries estimated it would bring $4,000 to $7,000. Dr. Rosenbach bought it for $17,500, B. J. Beyer the underbidder. What happened was that both the Doctor and Beyer thought Young had given them his bid on it. Within a decade I was to handle two copies (of about twenty known) for under $5,000 each.

Kern's Dickenses were very nice. A *Pickwick*, in parts, which had cost him $3,500 a few years before, brought $28,000, then and still a record. It is now at Princeton. A single quarto page of the manuscript of Samuel Johnson's *Dictionary*, fewer than one hundred words, brought $11,000 from Charles Sessler of Philadelphia, bidding for Richard Gimbel of the same city. Dr. Rosenbach was the underbidder for Owen D. Young, and according to his biographers, "after the sale [he] told Young that, since he himself had sold it to Kern within the past year for $1,750, he did not have the conscience to go any higher, and his conscience on such matters had a lot of stretch."

Johnson's *Dictionary* (London, 1755) is a huge work, two volumes, folio, of twelve hundred pages. It contains a minimum of four million words. At the Kern rate the complete manuscript would be worth about $4,500,000,000—considerably more than any manuscript has brought to date. The page, the only surviving fragment, is now in the Hyde collection.

The manuscript of Goldsmith's translation of Vida's *Scacchis, or Chess* had been purchased at a London auction for Kern by Sessler a year earlier for $33,000. It brought $27,000 (one of the few losses Kern took), and was returned as not in Goldsmith's autograph. A very fine Poe letter, quoting Mrs. Browning's opinion of "The Raven," brought $19,500, the purchaser W. T. H. Howe of Cincinnati; it is now in the Berg collection at the New York Public Library. It is still the highest price ever paid for a letter of an American literary figure. And the highest-priced book in the sale was reputedly Shelley's own annotated copy of *Queen Mab*, which made $68,000 but was of questionable authenticity.

Dr. Rosenbach purchased, for stock, the autograph manuscript of the first three books of Pope's *Essay on Man* for $29,000 and, for exactly the same price, a first edition (London, 1749) of Fielding's *Tom Jones*, reputedly the only copy known in original binding, all edges uncut. This led to a *cause célèbre* in which I played a minor part, which epitomizes the times and the *caveat emptor* attitude of collectors and dealers alike.

The Doctor later sold both of these, for cost plus 10 percent, to Owen D. Young. The story of what happened next is partially told in Wolf-Fleming's *Rosenbach*, more fully in John Hayward's *The History of Tom Jones, a Changeling*, privately printed for Lord Rothschild in 1951. Young had seriously overextended himself in book purchases and his General Electric stock was not what it once had been. He began to dispose of some of his books to pay his bills. Just about this time Lord Victor Rothschild was forming his famous eighteenth-century collection of printed books and manuscripts, which he eventually presented to Trinity College, Cambridge. His principal source was the London firm of W. H. Robinson, located in Pall Mall. Gabriel Wells, when in London, occupied a flat next to Robinson's and did considerable business with them.

Wells, who was selling some of Young's books, persuaded him in 1937 to part with two of his Kern purchases, the *Essay on Man* manuscript and the unique *Tom Jones*, and sold them both to Rothschild in a package deal for £3,500—some slight indication of the drastic drop prices took in post-Depression times.

Just at that time I was collaborating with John T. Winterich on a series of bio-bibliographical articles based on A. Edward Newton's famed list of "One Hundred Good Novels," which he had first published in his *This Book-Collecting Game* (Boston, 1928). This had great influence in its time and became a sort of collector's vade mecum. Winterich did notes on the books in his inimitable style—akin to his sketches gathered in *Twenty-three Books and the Stories Behind Them*, to which I supplied bibliographical collations. The articles were printed in *Publishers' Weekly*.

Eventually we came to do *The History of Tom Jones, a Foundling* (London, 1749), issued in six duodecimo volumes. It was a bibliographically complex book and had never been accurately described. It was reissued in the year of publication without change of title pages, in a page-for-page but not line-for-line reprint. In the first edition there are errata for the first five volumes. In the second edition the errata are removed and the errors corrected, making identification simple. I discovered hitherto unnoted variants in Volume VI. In collating J. K. Lilly's copy, from which I was working, I noticed several canceled leaves, some of which bibliographers had not recorded in any descriptions I could find. In my dilemma I turned to my London colleague, John Carter. The late John Hayward records what happened next, in his *The History of Tom Jones, a Changeling:*

Early in 1939, when war appeared to be imminent, Lord Rothschild, realizing the risk to which my lameness might expose me if I remained in London during air-raids, invited me to make my home for the duration at Merton Hall, Cambridge. I arrived there, on his advice, a few days before the outbreak of war and have been permanently resident there up to the present time.

Shortly after war was declared Lord Rothschild's library was moved, for greater safety, from Merton Hall, Cambridge, to Rushbrooke Hall, Suffolk, a house which he had recently acquired but which was still being prepared for occupation. Work on the renovation and furnishing of the house was broken off when the greater part of the mansion was handed over to the Red Cross for use as a hospital. But before this, a week-end party was invited to Rushbrooke Hall early in the New Year of 1940, the exact date of which I cannot recall, having made no particular record of this visit among the several I paid to Rushbrooke Hall at that time. I motored over from Cambridge with Lord Rothschild and, the Sunday morning being wet, I decided to spend part of it in the library. I had in mind a request made to me by my friend John Carter, a well-known bibliographer, to check a bibliographical point in the first edition of *Tom Jones*. It is unnecessary to say more than that it was a technical matter, connected with "cancel" leaves which are common but often puzzling features of eighteenth-century publishing. Mr Carter knew that Lord Rothschild possessed the unique Jerome Kern copy of *Tom Jones*. Such a copy, in original boards with the leaves untrimmed, might be presumed to present the earliest state of the text and possibly to preserve, as sometimes happens in such conditions, leaves in uncancelled form. It was in the hope that this copy of *Tom Jones* might throw light on this matter that Mr Carter had asked me to examine it, if and when I had an opportunity of doing so.

For the purposes of comparison, Lord Rothschild brought out for me, in addition to the Jerome Kern copy of *Tom Jones*, two other copies of the first edition—the so-called Dillon and Belhaven copies—bound in contemporary calf with the leaves trimmed.

My first impulse was to examine the Jerome Kern copy from the collector's or connoisseur's point of view, and to postpone the bibliographical investigation until I had appreciated its unique quality. I recognized in each volume the (to me) familiar small book label of its former owner, Jerome Kern, at the auction of whose library in 1929 this copy of *Tom Jones* had been bought by Dr Rosenbach for the astonishing sum of $29,000. I noticed also, in each volume, the signature of an earlier owner, "Martha Erthigg Moore." I also noticed, on the inner cover of the first volume, a pencilled note, the exact wording of which escapes me—I did not pay attention to it at the time—but it was to the effect that the copy was a first edition of *Tom Jones*, "Extremely rare" (or words to that effect) on account of its being in original boards, uncut. This note was afterwards identified for me as indicating that the volumes had once passed through the hands of the London firm of F. Sabin and

Co. at some period antecedent to their ownership by Jerome Kern. At a later date they were, I understand, in the hands of the Philadelphia firm of Sessler, from whom Mr Kern purchased them.

While I was casually turning over the leaves of one of the volumes I was suddenly aware of a slight difference in the feel (between thumb and forefinger) and (to an eye familiar with the type and paper of books of the period) the appearance of one of the leaves. A doubt immediately entered my mind as to the authenticity of the leaf in question and consequently of the whole set of volumes.

Accordingly, I proceeded to make a very careful examination of the six volumes of *Tom Jones,* and in the result I was convinced that they did not, as a whole, constitute an authentic copy of the first edition.

At this point things became complicated. Briefly, Rothschild attempted to return the *Tom Jones* to Wells. He refused to take it back alone, though he would take back *both* items and cancel the transaction. But Rothschild was loath to part with the *Essay on Man*. A lawsuit was begun by Rothschild against Wells and Owen D. Young for having sold him a fake copy. This put everyone involved, particularly "Dr. R.," in an indefensible position. He had to admit either (a) that he had never examined the books and was, hence, pretty careless about $29,000 purchases and had sold the books without collating them, or (b) that he had examined and collated them without detecting the fraud.

Wells seemed on sounder ground. He claimed that what he sold Rothschild was the Kern copy of *Tom Jones* and that was exactly what he delivered. It was not his fault that it turned out to be a fake. Kern, by the way, had purchased the book from Sessler of Philadelphia for $3,500, and they, in turn, had bought it from the well-known London dealer Sabin.

John Carter and Percy Muir, writing in *The Bookseller*, neatly summed up the dilemma:

> If this book is half as bad as Lord Rothschild's complaint alleges, might it not be held to have been somebody's duty to uncover its defects during the past thirteen years? The newspaper reports make no reference to its provenance before 1929, though it is understood that Mr. Kern purchased it from a Philadelphia dealer who, in turn, had acquired it from a prominent dealer in London. But wherever Mr. Kern got it, it has since passed under a battery of expert eyes. It was a star item in the most publicized sale of our generation. It was catalogued by a famous auction house, the Anderson Galleries. It was purchased by the most prominent rare book dealer in America, Dr. Rosenbach, for a prominent collector, Mr. Young. On his behalf it was sold by a hardly less prominent dealer, Mr. Wells, to Lord Rothschild, who apparently had it on his fastidious shelves for three years before its alleged faults

were detected. It is true that "pedigree" books are customarily collated with less care than windfalls. Dealers and collectors love (and perhaps are insufficiently suspicious of) "the Smith-Jones-Brown-Robinson copy" of such-and-such. But seldom has so publicised a book passed through such a succession of distinguished hands, to be accused of such glaring imperfections at the end.

Trial was set in New York and the books were shipped to Rothschild's lawyers, Spencer, Ordway and Wierum, who retained me as an expert witness on his behalf. I was to make a separate examination and report on the volumes. It took me all of an hour and a half to come up with exactly the same conclusion Hayward (whose report had not been shown to me) had reached; i.e., that twelve leaves (twenty-four pages) had been inserted from a second edition. As I mentioned earlier, the second edition was a page-for-page but not line-for-line reprint of the first. Hence anyone counting the pages only, or collating by signature marks only, could easily assume its completeness. But catchwords did not match and there were other variants.

Rosenbach testified at preliminary hearings that the book "had the full complement of pages" and that was all he knew about it. A colloquy between Rothschild's lawyer and Dr. Rosenbach went like this:

*Q* How long do you estimate it would take you to compare the defects alleged in that bill of particulars with the books themselves, which are there on the table, and tell us whether or not the defects alleged are the true defects?

*A* Why should I do that and spend a week?
  *By Mr. Kaufman:* That is not the question. The question is how long it would take you to do it.
  *By the witness:* I haven't the slightest idea.

*Q* (*Mr. Marden*): Couldn't you tell on quite a casual examination whether the texture of a certain page was the same as the pages preceding?

*A* You have to look at the watermarks. You have no idea. This fellow at Cambridge took weeks to give the report to Rothschild. Why, they used everything—X-rays, everything. You have no idea of the amount of time it would take to go over a book.

The case never came to trial. The Rosenbach biography says: "As the two dealers involved most inextricably, Sessler's who had sold the set to Kern and the Rosenbachs who had sold it to Young, each put up $4500, Young paid $2500, Wells $1500, and the tarnished books went to the Rosenbachs as a reminder of human fallibility." Owen Young ended the episode with a generous statement: "There was no 'fraud' or bad faith on the part of anyone involved. All four parties recognized that they were jointly the victims of handling a volume which, after many years, had been found by a bibliographical expert to be incorrect and they tried to apportion the loss equitably between them by a settlement of the suit."

Rothschild's Introduction to Hayward's account is:

> A number of my book-collecting friends have suggested that the details of this lawsuit would interest book collectors (even, perhaps, booksellers) and should be published. The same friends were really responsible for the lawsuit itself. They told me that few book collectors would dare to bring a lawsuit against a bookseller, however good the grounds; that I should be doing a service to bibliophiles if I were to do so; that I was one of the few collectors who could afford such an action; and that they were sure I would never take their advice. I did, and the reader will be able to judge whether their advice was good or bad, though he will not be able to imagine my feelings in the witness box, nor when I found that my friend Dr. A. S. W. Rosenbach was to become involved in the action.
>
> I learnt two things from this case, which took place at a time when it was difficult to concentrate on book collecting and its hazards. First, that if you are a collector and people like John Hayward or John Carter are your friends, you are bound to have some unpleasant surprises when they have "had a look" at your library. Secondly, that the law is very complicated and if you try and understand it, you will never buy a barrel of glue, a stallion or a valuable old book again.
>
> The case was settled out of court, on terms which, from my point of view, were entirely satisfactory.
>
> R.

*Cambridge, 1951*

The book was later purchased by Lou Silver and is now in Chicago's Newberry Library.

Gabriel Wells was a good friend to me. I wrote the following piece about him in *The Book Collector* in the Spring, 1961, issue:

> In his "Further Reminiscences" in the Autumn Number, 1960, P. H. Muir does less than justice to the memory of the late Gabriel Wells —"a dear, pathetic, ridiculous little man." In his opinion "brash, unjust" Dr. Rosenbach was by far the greater bookseller and he adds that "to treat 'G. W.' and 'Dr. R.' on the same level is an injustice to the latter." With this I thoroughly disagree. Mr. Muir did not know them on their home grounds and even in London "we in the booktrade saw much less of 'Rosie' than of Gabriel. Rosie bought almost exclusively in the sale room or privately. Gabriel was in and out of bookshops all the time."
>
> There is the nub. Admittedly "The Doctor" was the more scholarly and better educated person and the more skilful manipulator, but in the period I knew them best, the decade and a half following 1930, G. W.

was by far the greater and more wholesome influence on the entire antiquarian book-world.

They worked on diametrically opposite principles. The Doctor, a lone wolf, collaborated with no one in the trade and did absolutely nothing during the Depression to support the auction market or his fellow dealers. G. W. desired nothing more than to sell books to the trade and was a constant buyer for stock both from the trade and at auction.

It may interest Mr. Muir, and others, to know that over these years G. W.'s auction bills were consistently much higher than the Doctor's. And, I emphasize, his purchases were usually for stock. The public had a contrary impression, simply because of the Doctor's absurdly simple, but efficacious technique, which was "to grab the headlines." This he generally succeeded in doing by purchasing the most expensive item in a sale—invariably with someone else's money. G. W. would purchase much more at any given sale, consistently underbid what he didn't purchase, and yet end up the forgotten man.

The Doctor refused absolutely to work with the trade; he would not allow them to draw on his stock, sometimes even as an outright purchase. Those of his employees who worked on commission, got none if an item was sold to a competitor, nor, as a general rule, would he buy from the trade.

G. W. loved nothing better than to have his stock on someone else's shelves. And if a dealer had an opportunity to purchase something he couldn't finance, G. W. was always there to aid him. A fair few dealers are now in business because G. W. helped them over rough going. The late Max Harzof, of the G. A. Baker Company, the finest all-around bookman I have ever known, supported me, for example, and Edward Lazare and Jacob Blanck when we were starting—and G. W. supported *him*.

A personal experience may illustrate their difference. In the early 1930s when I was on my own, I stumbled across a quite important collection of Count Zinzendorf material, including Benjamin Franklin imprints. I had no funds to purchase it and no customer for it, so I approached the Doctor whose reaction was: "Tell me where it is and I'll buy it. If, after I've sold it, there is a profit I'll let you know." G. W. advanced the purchase price, allowed me to keep the material for sale and asked only a share of the profits after I had made a sale.

Instances could be multiplied indefinitely. Sufficient to say that in the years of the Depression G. W. was the strong right arm of the small (and some not so small) dealers and of the American auction market. His death, at that time, would have been a shattering blow to the antiquarian trade, Dr. R.'s, merely a matter for gossip.

Many people took cruel advantage of G. W.'s ignorance and vanity. Mr. Muir's reminiscence of Shelley forgeries brings to mind the Jerome Kern copy of *Queen Mab*, supposedly Shelley's own copy with his annotations—suspect in some quarters even at the time of the sale. G. W. bought it for $68,000, the highest price in the Kern sale and for a long time to come the second highest American auction record for a book. It remained in his stock till his death and sold, eventually, for less than an eighth of what he had paid for it.

When Scribner's were publishing Dr. Robert Smith's *The Shelley Legend* (New York, 1945), I made an effort to find out something of the circumstances of the sale and tried to discover the underbidder.

Wily Mitchell Kennerley, promoter of the Kern sale, clarified matters to me. The evening of the sale containing this particular item, he took G. W. to dinner. During conversation he emphasized the fact that the Doctor had been getting most of the publicity and suggested that G. W. do something spectacular, such as purchasing *Queen Mab*. This he did. Kennerley gently explained to me that the day of the sale was G. W.'s sixty-eighth birthday and that "some of us conspired to help him celebrate it appropriately."

G. W. could be very generous—a character flaw the Doctor never exhibited to me. He gave the New York Public Library such missing leaves from its Gutenberg Bible as he possessed. He bought the original manuscript of Thomas Wolfe's *Look Homeward, Angel* at a charity auction and presented it to Harvard. At his death a number of libraries were allowed first choice of what they wanted from his stock. And he helped many lame dogs over stiles—myself included.

If the Doctor was Achilles, sulking in his Depression-ridden tent, G. W. was Patroclus, always in the thick of the fight. Unquestionably the Doctor sold greater books, but this does not, to me, mean that he was the greater bookseller.

After the exhilaration of the Kern sale I settled down to prosaic tasks. My immediate boss was Michael Papantonio, who had worked at the shop for several years and was a little younger than I (he still is) and knew a lot more (he still does). I first found favor in his eyes by being punctual—he never was, and I don't believe is, to this day. Hackett, who lived in Brooklyn, was even worse. Mike used to arrive about 10:15, the boss at 10:30, or, occasionally, vice versa. This had caused friction. But I was there at 8:30 and had everything nicely under way for whoever arrived first.

Mike undertook to teach me the rudiments of the business. I remember at the time resenting the fact that I had wasted five good years on "higher education" which would have been more profitably spent clerking in a good antiquarian bookstore.

An antiquarian business—any, not only the rare book business—cannot be taught, it must be lived, I am convinced. Let me have a small roll call of some of those I have worked with. Mike started at the Brick Row at the age of fifteen and, with John S. Van E. Kohn, now operates the distinguished Seven Gables Bookshop in New York, which boasts a better stock of English literature than any shop in London. Edward Lazare, who for years has edited *American Book Prices Current* with a passion and ability which draw paeans of praise from such as the *London Times Literary Supplement,* and from whom I learned a lot when he was Max Harzof's right hand, once told me he spent his fifteenth birthday in an Army stockade for underage enlistment. Jacob Blanck is a Bostonian born, but he is not a Harvard College (or any other college) graduate. He edits the *Bibliography of American Literature . . . for the Bibliographical Society of America* (Yale University Press, 1955–      ). This carries on the great tradition of Joseph Sabin and Charles Evans in American bibliography and is the greatest single American bibliographical project of our era. The late Charles Retz, associated with me at Scribner's and later head of the book department at the Parke-Bernet Galleries, began his career as a butcher. Josiah Quincy Bennett, of a distinguished Boston family, who succeeded Retz at Scribner's and went on to become chief book cataloguer for the Parke-Bernet Galleries and now for the Lilly Library, was a high school dropout.

In my ten years of academic associations I have found very few graduates of library schools who were competent rare bookmen or who could pull their weight with a good bookstore clerk. The late great Randolph Adams, of the Clements Library in Ann Arbor, Michigan, summed this all up in a provocative essay, *Librarians As Enemies of Books.* I couldn't agree more, except that, as I once told him, the title should be *Librarians (from Library Schools) As Enemies of Books.*

Libraries have had to dig deeply into the "trade" or recruit collectors to get sophisticated and knowledgeable direction. Edwin Wolf II, who heads the venerable Library Company of Philadelphia, the oldest library of its kind in America, began working for Rosenbach at the age of eighteen. Ellen Schaffer of the Free Library of Philadelphia was rare book expert of Dawson's in Los Angeles for years. John S. Mayfield of Syracuse University was a collector prior to turning librarian; so was Fritz Liebert of Yale's Beinecke Library and Frederick B. Adams, Jr., of The Pierpont Morgan Library. The late William A. Jackson of Harvard's Houghton, the greatest librarian of our time, had no Library Science degree—indeed, like myself, all he ever earned was a B.A., though he was posthumously awarded the Gold Medal of the London Bibliographical Society, a distinction also achieved by the late Wilberforce Eames, perhaps our greatest bibliographer, who began his career in a bookstore at the age of thirteen.

What it all adds up to is that a proper appreciation of the value of this type of books is an emotional and not an intellectual process, like love. And that can't be taught in schools. But, unfortunately, the union badge of graduate school degrees as a prerequisite to a library career is a growing, cancerous thing. Thus endeth the lesson.

But to return to Hackett. I will always be grateful to him for giving me my first job. He was an Irishman who could charm the birds from the trees when he chose to. He was such a fine salesman that he hypnotized himself. I remember once when he acquired a beauty of a copy of an eighteenth-century novel. Only, it lacked the half-titles. He forgot to mention this slight defect when he sold it, simply because he had actually forgotten it.

After six months I told him that I was about to be married and that a small increase in salary would be welcome. He agreed and I was advanced $5 per week. He solicitously inquired if my wife-to-be was wealthy. When I replied negatively his airy comment was, "Well, of course, your first wife doesn't need money. That's not what you marry her for." I made the mistake of repeating this *bon mot* to my bride. Hackett had done all right for himself—though it took him four marriages to achieve financial security.

I learned from him one very important lesson (besides how not to run a bookshop): this was to avoid systematically underestimating your clients' intelligence. Hackett did this consistently with eventually fatal results.

I vividly remember one chore he sent me on. Morris L. Parrish of Philadelphia was assembling his wonderful nineteenth-century fiction collection, now at Princeton. Hackett had a beautiful *Vanity Fair* in parts and sent me off to show it to Parrish with the instructions: "The price is $5,000. If he will pay cash he can have it for $4,500." The Kern copy had just fetched $7,750.

Seated in Parrish's office, we examined together the book, plates, advertisements, points of issue, etc. He then asked the price, and when I mentioned $5,000, he thought a while and said, "That's quite a sum, isn't it?" I answered immediately and forcefully, "God, yes." And he commented, "You know, young man, you are in the wrong business. You seem to have a liking for books—why don't you become a librarian? You will never be a salesman." I didn't sell him this book, but he later became one of the delights of my life and one of my very best customers.

A society matron was a favored customer of the Brick Row. She was always buying medieval manuscripts as wedding presents, Christmas gifts and so on. I remember her hesitating over which of two to give as a wedding gift; one was priced at $5,000, the other at $8,500. After much though she finally purchased the lower-priced one, explaining, "After all, I don't really know them well." We received a letter one day stating that she would be in town that weekend and wanted something very special in the way of manuscripts for a gift to someone she knew very well. Not having anything important in stock, I scurried around town and got a fine collection "on consignment." On Saturday afternoon she arrived.

There was a certain protocol to be observed in approaching Hackett. The door to his office was always closed. One approached it, knocked, was bidden to enter, closed it, announced the visitor's name, reopened it and admitted the favored one. Which is exactly what I did on this occasion, except that I forgot to close the door after me. Hackett was seated at his desk, his back to the door, when I knocked, was admitted and announced who awaited without. "Fine," said Hackett, "you bring her in and sit her on my lap and I'll diddle her again." I turned to do so, and there she was, right behind me. She looked at the boss, looked at me, turned and disappeared forever.

On Christmas Eve, 1931, Hackett told me that he would no longer need my services after the first of January. He really didn't, of course. The Depression was getting into swing, he had heavily overbought at the Kern sale, and he was dropping his branch office at 30 Broad Street, which I was then managing, etc. I thought at the time that he could have waited until the day after Christmas to make this announcement, and I think so now.

This posed an evident crisis. My father had died earlier in the year, leaving most of what funds he had in bank stocks—not a good thing at that particular time—and there was only enough to care for my mother. My wife was pregnant with our first child, and the only thing to do, it seemed, was to return to the Pennsylvania coal mines. The dilemma was solved by my wife, who firmly stated that I was difficult enough to get along with when I was doing what I liked and would be completely intolerable otherwise. So I decided to stay in the rare book business, if I could.

In my two years with the Brick Row I had developed some acquaintances in "the trade." But everyone was retrenching; Scribner's, for example, always the great caterer to the carriage trade, had even dropped their doorman. Putnam's, Dutton's, Brentano's, all the well-known New York bookstores were hiring no one. Other smaller businesses were usually family affairs. Two prominent dealers offered me employment on a commission basis, I doing the selling and they doing the billing. Naïve as I was, I saw through this: what they wanted me for was to tip them off to

Hackett's customers—few though they were at that time, he had some important ones. After that I would have been through.

I decided to become a book scout, working from my home on East 10th Street, just off Fourth Avenue, which, from 8th to 14th then was solid with secondhand bookshops. Booksellers' Row it was called, but now, alas, they have almost all gone, along with the adjoining burlesque houses. A scout's function was to know all dealers, their specialties and requirements, the books they had, the prices they asked and—most important—what they were likely to give for what they needed. Then he combed bookshops from Harlem to Brooklyn seeking bargains. By that I mean he would spot something he could get for ninety-five cents and sell to a specialist dealer for $2.25. If the dealer got triple that price, or more, there were no hard feelings. One watched *Publishers' Weekly* for "books wanted" ads, attended local warehouse auctions of unwanted goods, dreamed of, and occasionally heard of, others finding a fabulous "sleeper," and so on. Many scouts were knowledgeable, informed people—one famous for his accurate bibliographical information was Russian-born I. R. Brussel of Brooklyn, author of important source books on the priority of English versus American first editions, *Anglo-American First Editions, 1826–1900: East to West* and *Anglo-American First Editions, 1786–1930 West to East.* Published by Constable of London, 1935–36, they are still useful. Brussel signs his letters LOGS—"Last of the Great Scouts," which he well may be.

I vividly remember my first "find." I was working for the Brick Row and we had a W. H. Hudson enthusiast. I became familiar with his works and bibliography. I was browsing one day in the shop of Frank Walters, who specialized in ornithology, when, among some pamphlets, I spotted "No. 3 of the Publications for the Society for the Protection of Birds." Walters had priced it $5, on the basis of the going price for similar items, which was about what it was worth to an ornithologist. But to a Hudson fan it was invaluable. It was his fifth publication, subtitled *Osprey; Or, Egrets and Aigrettes* (London, 1891), and his official bibliographer, G. F. Wilson, recorded that he "has not been able to secure a sight of the original edition of this pamphlet so the necessary particulars relating to the second edition are supplied." This was the first edition! Hackett immediately sold it to his customer for a price undisclosed to me, blandly taking credit for its "discovery." That bothered me not a whit. I later uncovered many more valuable books (though none rarer, as the pamphlet is still, I believe, unique), but I never got a greater thrill from a discovery.

I was slightly suspect around some secondhand shops at the beginning of my scouting from having worked "uptown" (then anything north of 23rd Street, where Alfred Goldsmith, the Walt Whitman specialist, had his famous shop "At the Sign of the Sparrow"). I was early taught a lesson (which I never fully digested), which was when to keep my big mouth shut. P. Stammer was the king of Fourth Avenue. He had a four-story building crammed with books, and in the center of the first floor, where he had his desk, a veritable mountain of books—piled higgledy-piggledy on the floor, most of them having obviously been there for at least a decade. And he had nickel-dime-quarter stands outside.

One day I spotted a book on the quarter stand. It was a minor Whittier item, but a presentation copy with a verse in his hand, all written on the back flyleaf of the book—hence escaping Stammer's notice when he put it out. It was worth, uptown, at least $25 wholesale. I promptly took it in to him, produced my quarter and then proudly showed him the inscription. He jerked the book from my hands, ripped out the inscribed flyleaf, tore it into shreds, dropped them on the floor and handed the book back, growling, "No goddamn youngster is going to make me look a fool. Now the book's worth what I priced it." He later repented to the degree of hiring me part-time for a few months. I also got part-time work with various minor auction galleries cataloguing, running errands, etc. It was a living and a reasonably good one by Depression standards, and I was, at any rate, doing what I wanted.

I also came to know a few private collectors, notably Morris Parrish, Carroll A. Wilson, who was then a Trollope, Hardy, and Gilbert and Sullivan enthusiast in addition to the New Englanders, and H. Bacon Collamore of Hartford, Connecticut, then collecting English and American literature, mostly nineteenth and twentieth century, though with a marked liking for Laurence Sterne, Henry James and A. E. Housman. I think I sold him his first Beatrix Potter, the privately printed *Peter Rabbit*, the keystone of his famous collection, which he recently presented to the Philadelphia Free Public Library.

Wilson once mentioned to me that he badly wanted a copy of the American edition of Trollope's *The Struggles of Brown, Jones and Robinson, by One of the Firm*, issued by Harper's in New York in 1862. It was then and is now an obscure book and scarcely worth the reading. Within a week of his mentioning it I found a pristine copy in a Fourth Avenue shop marked fifty cents. I purchased it and hied me to his office at 120 Broadway (he was chief counsel for the Guggenheims) via a nickel subway ride, debating what to price it.

I finally decided on a $25 asking price—you could always go down. Wilson examined it carefully, asked the price and said, "Well, Randall, I never thought I'd see this. Even Parrish doesn't have a copy." (I supplied him one later.) "It completes my American Trollopes. I think we can do future business together, and as this is our first transaction, I don't want to take unfair advantage of your ignorance. Remember this in the future." With that he wrote me a check for $250. When I purchased his library for Scribner's a decade and a half later for over $100,000, there it was, catalogued in his neat hand:

> One of the outstanding Trollope rarities; I know of three other copies in wrappers. Eight years before the English first edition. This was No. 220 of Harper's Library of Select Fiction. With a preliminary leaf and two terminal leaves of advertisements of the series, ending at No. 220.

I remembered: and from there on Carroll could usually place his own price on anything I ever had. In point of fact the book was worth that kind of money only to an ardent Trollope collector. Today it probably wouldn't bring any more. But Wilson wanted it, which is the nub of the matter, and he also wanted to do me a kindness. It is now in the collection of Robert H. Taylor, whose collection of Trollope is unrivaled. I introduced him to both Wilson and Parrish, never dreaming at the time (nor did he) that his Trollopes would far outstrip theirs. He eventually purchased most of Wilson's, at least those he didn't have, and has presented them all to Princeton, which was also given Parrish's collection. Wilson's smallish penthouse apartment eventually became so crowded with books that he was forced to keep his Trollopes in the bathroom.

About this time I was doing some little business with Max Harzof, owner of the G. A. Baker & Company, Inc., Booksellers, then with a huge shop on the fifth floor of 480 Lexington Avenue. He was a great bear of a man, about 275 pounds, irreverent, profane in speech, sloppy in dress, ill-at-ease with a necktie on, pugnacious on occasion—and withal the finest all-around bookman I have been privileged to know.

Rosenbach laughed at him but respected him; Harzof laughed back and respected *him* not at all. He had, surprisingly, a much higher opinion of George D. Smith as a bookseller. I recall one story he told of the latter. They were called in on some estate to consider purchasing the books. It was a bitterly cold winter day, so they kept their overcoats on. Negotiations with the lawyer or whoever was in charge went badly. Harzof noticed that "George D." kept stumbling against him while going over the library but thought nothing of it at the time. After they left the home and were around the corner, Smith stopped and pulled several books from Harzof's pockets, remarking, "We deserved something for our time, didn't we?" Smith, the chief architect of the famed Henry E. Huntington library, pulled some rather unethical tricks on his patron. When Huntington was informed of the double crossing by those who hoped to supplant Smith as Huntington's agent, the latter is said to have listened carefully, then remarked, "Well, gentlemen, he got me the books. I wouldn't have a library without him, would I?" and kept right on dealing with him. Smith died of apoplexy at the age of fifty. Harzof's summary of his career was, "It's a lot better to be an honest crook than a pimp, like some dealers I could name." He also said the most knowledgeable dealer he ever knew was Wilfried Voynich.

Scholars like Chauncey Brewster Tinker, bookmen like William A. Jackson, and collectors like Carroll A. Wilson delighted in Harzof's company and valued his advice. He was never well known outside the trade, nor cared to be, but it was he who appraised the Folger Library (Edward Lazare doing the legwork) and many others of lesser fame.

Harzof was born in Vienna in 1875. His father decided to emigrate to America after some soldiers swaggered down a sidewalk and forced him and his family into a gutter. The Harzofs arrived in New York in 1881. Max Harzof attended grade school in New York City until he was twelve years old; he then got a job as errand boy and general office boy and packer with the firm of F. W. Christern & Company, one of New York City's better bookshops, on Fifth Avenue near 23rd Street. He remained in the book trade until his death in 1942.

He used to delight in telling how he managed to get to work on the first day of the blizzard of 1888 (March 11) by hitching a ride on a milk sleigh down Second Avenue from 51st Street to 23rd Street. He arrived at 7:30, only a half hour late, but he was second: the firm's old bookkeeper, who lived in Greenpoint across the East River from Manhattan, had arrived on time, a feat he could accomplish because, the river not being frozen, the ferries were running.

In 1905 Harzof went into business for himself as a dealer in out-of-print books. His first shop was at 730 Lexington Avenue and was named the Lexington Bookshop. Book auctioneers announced his purchases as "Lex" to the day of his death, even though the shop name and address changed several times after 1910 (C. Gerhardt & Company; G. A. Baker & Company, Inc.; etc.).

He had a passion for anonymity long before that phrase became popular. Of the scholars he helped, many wished to dedicate books to him: he

wouldn't allow it. In fact, he wouldn't even permit his name to be used in
the usual acknowledgments. He urged and aided Milton Waldman to do
his excellent *Americana: The Literature of American History*. Most of
the research on this was done in Harzof's shop on books he had handled.
Yet Waldman could do nothing, after thanking most of the greats in the
libraries of New York, Boston, London, Paris and Milan for their aid,
except to add, "The heartiest of all my debts is due to one who will not
permit his name to be mentioned, and to him my gratitude must remain
anonymous, though no less heartfelt for that." He was a kindhearted man,
and it seemed that at one time or another practically everyone in the
business had worked for him while he trained them and eventually sent
them along. William Hobart Royce, the Balzac scholar, was one. "Gabriel
Wells," Harzof recalled (no one called him "Max" except G.W.),
"needed an assistant—an honest one—much harder to find than a bright
one. I gave him Royce, then working for me, whose main virtue was that
he could be implicitly trusted with bags of uncounted gold."

When I recounted my plight to Harzof—that I had no money, no
books, nothing except an ambition to stay in the business—he reacted as
he so often had to stray souls. He offered me free desk space in his shop,
access to his books "on sale" and whatever else he could do. In exchange I
helped out with occasional cataloguing, errand running, attending minor
auctions and other chores. But not in packing books. That he did himself.
He could get more books into less space than ever seemed possible—a
trick learned from his boyhood days at Christern & Company.

It was a beginner's paradise. I worked harder, earned less and learned
more in the three years I spent with him than any other comparable
period.

Harzof had a sideline to his book business. He made appraisals of books
and manuscripts for those seeking insurance policies, or in the case of
estates, for tax purposes. He also served as adjudicator, for one side or the
other, in various cases of loss by fire, theft, etc. His inventory lists described each item or lot and gave the current market value of each entry.
In the 1920's insurance companies became stricter about fine-arts policies
insuring personal property, and appraised inventory lists compiled by
"disinterested third parties" had to be submitted to obtain a policy of size.
These appraisal lists for owners (more often for their lawyers or brokers)
were made by various appraisal firms, the largest number being located in
New York City. The appraisal companies had on their staffs, or on call,
appraisers who knew how to describe and evaluate properties found in
the homes of the well-to-do up to the richest—furniture, rugs, paintings,
art objects, silver, glass, etc. However, no appraisal firm had on its staff a

bookman. When firms would contract to make appraisals of properties which included books and manuscripts of special quality, seven out of ten would call on Harzof to do the books. For about ten years after World War I, it was Frank Walters, Harzof's associate and cataloguer (and dealer in natural history books), who compiled the descriptive lists. From 1929 on, these lists were compiled on the job, variously, by three of Harzof's employees: Edward Lazare, Bernard G. Otto and John S. Kebabian. Harzof did the evaluating.

Certainly there were those who knew more than he did about their specialties: Rosenbach on early English literature, Harper on the classics, Walters on ornithology, Sessler on Dickens, Eberstadt or Goodspeed on Americana, and so on. But set them all to doing an evaluation of, let us say, the entire contents of the New York Public Library, and they would be lost. Not Harzof. He would have come up with a sounder valuation of what was there, what was needed, where to get it and what to pay for it than all of them combined. And among his admirable qualities was his imagination.

"Read, read," he used to exhort me. "There are millions of things to be collected. Don't degenerate into a one-author enthusiast—or a one-subject one, either." He liked the (then) obscurities: Beaumont on the gastric juice, Bowditch on navigation, Holt on children (when these were $10 books). It was he who urged me to read the entire *Dictionary of American Biography*—a task I have not yet fully completed, alas. He was a bookman.

In his "early" days one of Harzof's solo appraisals was that of the library of Mrs. Gertrude Vanderbilt Whitney. While he was on the job, Mrs. Whitney asked him what he thought her copy of *The Bay Psalm Book* was worth. He looked out the windows of the library of her house on upper Fifth Avenue and waved his hand at Central Park. "What is that worth, madame?" he asked.

Another dowager complained that he had undervalued some of her books because they were badly worm-eaten. "You are not an authority in these matters," she stormed. "You are not accustomed to handling treasures of such value—you are a mere junk dealer." "Madame," he retorted equably, "that could be, but I have never heard it said that a bookworm made any distinction between a ten-thousand-dollar book and a ten-cent one."

In 1931 Harzof was sole agent for the sale of the Herndon-Weik collection of legal papers of Abraham Lincoln, a collection which contained, in addition to 734 legal documents in the hand of Lincoln from 1836 to 1858, many other pieces of Lincolniana collected by both Herndon and

Weik. Jesse W. Weik, who had collaborated with William H. Herndon, Lincoln's last law partner, in the writing of *Herndon's Lincoln: The True Story of a Great Life* [*1889*], had inherited the collection from Herndon. Weik died in 1929, and less than two years after his death his heirs turned the collection over to Harzof for sale. After he agreed to act as agent, the collection was stored in his office safe, ready for show to anyone interested in purchasing. He had few bites, the Depression being in full swing.

One day two elderly ladies came into the shop. The taller one was dressed in black, in the style of the 1880's. She was Mrs. Wadsworth (of the Geneseo Wadsworths), an old customer of Harzof's. Her friend, who was unknown to him, was queenly, stylishly dressed, richly bejeweled. The bejeweled lady sat herself near one of the flat-top showcases and looked past them at the quartos shelved nearby across the aisle. Mrs. Wadsworth sat herself in a chair near Harzof's desk and bent his ear about a recent dreadful happening: somebody had stolen her copy of Stanley Weyman's *Under the Red Robe*. Harzof, who couldn't keep his eyes off the bejeweled lady, assured Mrs. Wadsworth he would get her a copy within two days, and for free. Then he stood and moved toward the jewels. The lady wearing them waved, in her queenly style, at a set of Harry T. Peter's *Currier & Ives*, two volumes, quarto.

"How much is that?" she asked. Harzof put on his most enticing grin and said, "That's marked one hundred and twenty dollars, but I'll let *you* have it for one hundred."

"Hmmph," she hmmphed, "it's a good work, but it does not give any prices."

"Ah, if you want prices," said Harzof, "this is the book you should have," and he hauled down Jane Cooper Bland's *Currier & Ives*. "I'll let you have that for thirty-five dollars."

The bejeweled one opened the book to the title page, then looked at the reproduction in color of the Currier & Ives print "Skating in Central Park."

"Hmmph," she hmmphed again, "*I* own that."

Harzof's eyes bugged. He pointed at her across the showcases. "You, you are Mrs. Whitney" [Helen Hay Whitney, daughter of John Hay, who married Payne Whitney in 1902]. Then he said quickly, "I have something for you."

She stood up. Her eyes had a wary look in them.

Harzof continued, "I have something for you . . . I have a great collection of Lincolniana. . . ."

"I haven't got a penny!" she said, and started for the door, which was a hundred feet away.

"Wait!" he said. "This is a great collection!" He lowered his voice to the level of reverence. "Besides the Lincoln manuscripts, there are many additional pieces, and among these is a letter, written by your father, *John Hay*, in which he compares Abraham Lincoln to *Jesus Christ!*" He paused. "Buy the collection and give it to Yale! It's yours for one hundred thousand dollars."

Mrs. Whitney had escaped up the aisle toward the exit door. She turned on Harzof and snapped, "I've just given Yale two million dollars for a new gymnasium, and they haven't even thanked me."

"For Christ's sake, woman," said Harzof, "you might wait until they lay the cornerstone."

"I haven't got a penny," she said, and moved swiftly toward the door, and reached it.

Harzof, who could not move with speed, was still standing near the showcases.

"What the hell do you do with all your money?" he asked amiably. "Buy diamond-studded toilet seats?"

"I haven't got a penny," she yelled back, and vanished.

Mrs. Wadsworth, appalled, just shrugged and followed her friend. Harzof waddled up the aisle, slammed the door after them and turned to Edward Lazare: "How's that for telling the old biddy, huh?" he said with a lot of satisfaction in his voice. He took a messy-looking wad of bills from his pants pocket and handed him a dollar bill. "Get me a ham sandwich on gluten bread, and an apple and a glass of milk."

Once when Eddie Lazare and I returned from lunch with him we found in the shop a wealthy collector he had no use for. "Throw that g-d-b out," he commanded us, sailing on to sit at his desk without glancing back. When he once charged his friend Wells $1,040 for a book he had just bought, and Wells asked about the odd price, Harzof answered (truthfully), "I wanted to make a thousand dollars today." When the well-known writer Edward Laroque Tinker managed to incur his wrath, Harzof ever after included his books in his catalogue—under STINKER. Anecdotes are endless.

It was at Harzof's that I first began reviewing bibliographies (with his aid) for *Publishers' Weekly* and *The New York Times* and met John T. Winterich, then helping to found the book collector's magazine, *The Colophon*, and William Mitchell Van Winkle, collector of sporting books. Eventually I collaborated with Winterich on revising his *A Primer of Book Collecting* and with Van Winkle on a *Bibliography of the Works of Henry William Herbert* (Frank Forester).

And it was at Harzof's that I issued my only two catalogues as an independent bookdealer—slim volumes, printed by Peter Beilenson, and consisting mostly of Harzof's stock and duplicate or unwanted volumes supplied by Wilson and Winterich. It was also there that I met Fred Adams, Bill Jackson, John Carter, H. Bacon Collamore and, especially, J. K. Lilly, Jr.

Appraisals were sometimes interesting assignments. I recall one I was sent on, a matter of fire damage. The wife of a rather prominent New York social figure became annoyed with her spouse, for what reason I don't know, but nothing he could possibly have done would have justified her retaliation. She went into his library and tried to demolish it. Tearing up the books, cutting out pages, ripping off bindings, she piled the debris on the floor, spilled lighter fluid over it, set a match to it and left. Fortunately the husband had been an indiscriminate kind of collector of expensive and gaudy sets, etc., and few books of any real importance (as against price) were destroyed. He got his divorce—and damn well he should have—and promptly resumed collecting, though I never heard of his remarriage.

The damage was not as great as I thought at first sight—books are tough objects and difficult to burn (water is what usually ruins them), and the blaze quickly went out. I reminded the owner that he was extremely lucky not to have collected porcelain, and he replied he hoped his wife remarried someone who did.

One day an insurance adjuster came in with a claim he wished me to look over. A collector had sent a shipment of rare books from New York to a friend in New Orleans and it hadn't arrived—that much was certain. All he wanted us to do was to validate the value of the missing items.

The list he presented was clear and detailed and obviously done by someone who knew his business. There were first editions, some presentation copies, books from the Doves and Ashendene presses, all fairly priced at the current market and accurately described.

But the more I looked at the list the more puzzled I became. It was heterogeneous, not the sort of thing a collector would be likely to have; it was too diversified. It seemed to me more like a bookseller's stock. I suddenly remembered a catalogue I had received about a year before, looked it up, and there were the books—all of them—described and priced on the bill of lading as in that catalogue.

It was one issued by Phil and Fanny Duschnes when they were first established in tiny (as compared to current) quarters at 507 Fifth Avenue. Some of the very books supposedly lost *en route* to New Orleans had among them easily identifiable unique items, presentations, etc. It required only legwork from there on. I gathered all of the books together (borrowing many from Phil), in the editions specified, and found that they could not possibly fit into the weight and size of the boxes specified in the bill of lading.

The officials then took over, and it was all very simple. A small gang had been successfully practicing this particular racket for some time. They shipped insured goods out of New York, via sea, to other ports, and a confederate in the ring with access to the shipping room conveniently dumped the packages out a porthole. They had been very careful not to overestimate the values they put upon such items: in this case they were too careful. One of the gang must have been somewhat of a bibliophile (I trust he got off with a light sentence), and figured the Duschnes catalogue was a perfect "cover" for descriptions and values, which it almost was.

The same insurance company once paid off on the theft of a first edition of Mary Baker Eddy's *Science and Health* (Boston, 1875), a book of some scarcity, though not nearly as rare as the second edition. A collector claimed it had been stolen from his library and that was that. An appraisal was made, the claim paid and the collector bought another copy. Over a year later he appeared, a little shamefaced, with *both* copies, asking what to do. It seems he had gone into his kitchen (where he rarely made an appearance) and found the missing volume. His cook, a Christian Scientist, had spotted it in the library and had borrowed it for her private reading!

And then there was the lad who required two separate appraisals—one for his insurance company and another, at a tenth that amount, to show his wife, and also a fine library which had dealers' descriptions, letters and so on, placed in the relevant volumes, only in every case the price had been cut out.

Most dealers have private cost marks and sometimes selling prices penciled in volumes they have handled, usually a simple ten-letter word with no repeating letter; the Brick Row's was CHRYSOLITE. But some had more complex forms, Greek letters, symbols, etc. Harzof had broken every single one of those, which was a great advantage in appraisal work. I foolishly never kept a record of them.

# Scribner's

THERE WERE a number of bookstores in New York in the 1930's which for decades had been associated with publishing houses—among them Dutton's, Putnam's, Brentano's and Scribner's, all on or just off Fifth Avenue and all catering to the carriage trade. Mostly this meant selling sets in elaborate (and expensive) bindings, sporting books, as Orme's *British Field Sports*, *The Sporting Magazine* (1792–1870) in 156 volumes, plus the scarce *Index*, and other works always found in "a gentleman's library." And a very profitable business it was. Long Island and Westchester homes were designed by architects who had in mind, on the ground floor, first a drawing room, then a dining room, then a library, and lastly a billiard room. Not so now.

The Fifth Avenue shops carried small selections of "old and rare" for the snob value this was supposed to bring—bound firsts of *Pickwick Papers, Jorrocks' Jaunts and Jollities*, Boswell's *Johnson*, Chesterfield's *Letters*, extra-illustrated sets of Irving's *Life of Washington*, fore-edge paintings, jeweled bindings, etc. (And frequently a carefully hidden bit of pornography.)

It was by no means uncommon for elaborately bound sets, "done on Japan vellum," to sell for $250 a volume upwards. One of the gaudiest libraries in New York was that of the late Colonel Jake Ruppert, owner of the New York Yankees, whole herds of goats being sacrificed to secure the bound sets in his library—"Morocco bound, or adrift among books," one wag observed on seeing it. It was all a hangover from the Gilded Age, and it is a shame that no firsthand account of it survives. It is no legend that the libraries of many people were furnished by their interior decorators who ordered yards of Balzac, Dumas, Stevenson or Ainsworth because the color of the bindings matched the drapes. All this is pretty well gone now, at least in the East. The average library in an apartment house is scarcely suitable to anything other than a collection of paper-backs.

Not that it was entirely reprehensible. A great many collectors began buying unread sets of books and gradually became more sophisticated—J. P. Morgan, I am told, J. K. Lilly, Jr. and Henry E. Huntington, among others.

All of the upper Fifth Avenue shops were in trouble in the Depression: Dutton's and Putnam's eventually disappeared, Brentano's were in one of their innumerable bankruptcies, and even Scribner's were taking a grave look at things.

Scribner's had always taken more serious interest in rare books than their competitors, probably because most of the family had been collectors themselves in a desultory kind of way—rather akin to Lamb, of whom Charles Scribner had a very respectable collection. And at this point, when competing firms were retrenching, Scribner's decided to expand—within limits. Or, rather, in the current jargon, to "change the image" of the rare book section of the bookstore. Less emphasis was to be put on the conventional, traditional and standard works and more on modern aspects of collecting. The main idea was to attract the young collector with little money but some imagination.

All this was the doing of John Carter, who had joined the London branch of Scribner's in 1927, as the buyer of rare books for the New York shop. He was frustrated by the staid bookstore management there and was pushing for a change. He had already made a reputation in collecting circles as a lad to watch—and was about to publish, with Graham Pollard, the bibliographical sensation of the century, *An Enquiry into the Nature of Certain 19th Century Pamphlets* (London, Constable; New York, Scribner's, 1934), the exposé of Thomas James Wise, the century's most famed fabricator.

I had met Carter on one of his New York business trips at G. A. Baker's and had contributed an article on "American First Editions, 1900–1933" to a symposium, *New Paths in Book Collecting*, which he edited in 1934. This was intended to, and did, point out neglected collecting fields: Carter contributing "Detective Fiction"; Michael Sadleir, "Yellow-Backs"; C. B. Oldman, "Musical First Editions"; P. H. Muir, "War Books"; etc.

Carter was urging Scribner's to follow this path, and he succeeded, with the help of George McKay Schieffelin, Scribner's nephew, who was enthusiastic and skeptical in equal proportions. George later signified his approval by presenting me with a monkey, escaped from a nunnery near his Far Hills home, he claimed. We promptly named it Pal Joey, and it loved all the family but me. It was a rhesus and bit me whenever and wherever possible. For months people would ask, "What in the world is wrong with your hands?" and I'd answer, truthfully, "My monkey bit me." Further explanations got me nowhere, as truth usually does.

The idea was for Scribner's not to try to compete with Dr. Rosenbach in Elizabethan literature, Lathrop Harper in incunabula, and other dealers in the expensive, traditional and stodgy. Anyone with money could buy these museum pieces. New ideas and enthusiasms needed to be cultivated and the young (but not too *non*-affluent) collectors attracted.

My association with Scribner's was entirely John Carter's and Wilmarth Lewis's doing. I knew "Lefty" Lewis slightly, having met him at Harzof's when he was beginning to form his incomparable Walpole collection. He was a friend of Scribner's and actually began his Walpole collection there, as he records in his delightful *Collector's Progress*. I had made some slighting and inaccurate comment on Walpole in print and he came into Harzof's shop to correct me. He recently wrote me, "I really did have something to do with your going to Scribner's because when John Carter asked me to recommend 'a young bookseller' I mentioned you. I remember clearly our first meeting. I went into Harzof's and there you were at a desk in a little alcove to the left of the entrance." He was kind enough to add, "I wish all my recommendations had turned out so well."

I remember my first interview with Charles Scribner, which was lunch at the Racquet and Tennis Club on Park Avenue. I had decided ahead of time that I wasn't ready for the Big League (even second division) but thought I'd take a chance at it if I could get a contract; I had figured out it would take them six months to discover my complete incompetence and I also remembered Hackett. When Charles offered me the job I accepted "if I could get a two-year contract." He responded gently that in the last forty-five years at Scribner's only two gentlemen had held my proposed post and added, "If I thought you would be with us only two years, I wouldn't consider hiring you in the first place." He then added, a little tartly, "I realize that I am paying you for what you are reputed to know, not how you dress, but it is customary, really, for my employees to wear shoes which match." I glanced and saw I had on one brown shoe and one black one. In the R & T, of all places! Properly abashed, I took the job, at $70 a week, and stayed twenty-one years without contract. And I may add that at that time I was among the highest-priced employees in the rare book business. Others, working on commission, "finder's fees," etc., made much more, but for a salaried employee that was about tops.

I took the job for two reasons: the first was financial. I had no capital nor prospects of getting any. My children were young, and an accident to me would have been catastrophic. If that happened while at Scribner's, I had no worries. In other words, I settled for security. But beyond that was the intriguing prospect of having the resources behind me to implement *ideas*, to experiment a bit with Carter, Percy Muir, Carroll A. Wilson, Michael Sadleir, and other forward lookers in and out of the trade. I have never regretted it. Financially, as things turned out, it was a first-water error (I never, in my years at Scribner's, made a five-figure salary), but in the more important aspects I had a lovely time.

The going was not easy. It amuses me today to hear dealers complain that it's simple to sell books, but where to get them? And of their hiding at home, instead of exposing for sale in their shops, anything reasonably desirable. Three decades ago it was quite different—a main reason being that university libraries had not yet gone completely berserk in their sudden frantic attempts to achieve "status," or something, by appallingly ignorant mass purchasing of rare books. In my particular field in the past decade, in my opinion (paraphrasing Churchill), "Never has so much been spent by so many for so little in so short a time."

We had an imaginative stock at Scribner's, but we were ahead of our time and it was slow in moving. So I "beat the bushes" with exhibitions at Marshall Field's in Chicago, bookshops in Dallas, Detroit, Los Angeles, Washington, D.C., and elsewhere, sometimes alone, sometimes with Carter. Sales usually amounted to practically nothing and expenses were written off to "institutional advertising," except that occasionally a customer of potentials would appear and a seed was sown. Today, with the stocks we exhibited, one could issue a mimeographed list from Ascension Island and have it sold by cable within a week, or at least those items not snapped up by buyers who chartered planes to fly in for personal examination.

Scribner's was always (and still is) the best general bookstore in New York, yet it was somewhat overshadowed by Brentano's. Their publicity, based on their Paris shop, shouted "Booksellers to the World"—an admirable ad and as untrue as most slogans are.

It was easy then (and for all I know still is) to get competent, intelligent bookstore clerks for the asking—and damn little pay. This was because there was always some kid fresh out of Radcliffe, Vassar or, preferably, Bryn Mawr, who wanted to see New York after graduation and before marriage. Worried parents subsidized them and were only too happy to have them work in as cultured, refined and genteel an atmosphere as a Fifth Avenue bookstore represented. There they would meet only nice people, like authors and those who purchased their books, and be safe from nasty things like liquor, wild parties and the assorted sins which prevailed in Greenwich Village. Ha!

The chief salesman at Scribner's was Charles Wilcox, a small one-eyed man with marked simian features which he delighted to exploit. He was a fabulous salesman with a wide acquaintance among all sorts of people from Edna Millay and Walter Winchell to Ernest Hemingway. If he liked a book, a sale of at least a hundred—no small number then—was assured. He simply mailed it to his customers with a bill—and few dared do other than accept it. I remember one who did: Charley had sent him some avant-garde novel, and when he returned it, complaining that he couldn't understand it, Charley commiserated, "That's not your fault, or the author's or mine." "Whose is it then?" queried the customer. "God's," sighed Charley, turning away.

He was widely read in the lives of the eccentrics of the eighteenth and nineteenth centuries—George Selwyn, Beau Brummell, the Chevalier d'Eon and their like, and vastly admired the Duke of Queensberry, who dislocated London's milk supply by bathing in it, and the Countess-Duchess of Kingston, who attended a ball in a gauze dress and vamped the Pope of Rome. A modern Miniver Cheevy, he had an oratorical style and a philosophy based on Sam Johnson, and he delighted in quoting the opening lines of *The Prince of Abissinia:*

> Ye who listen with credulity to the whispers of fancy, and pursue with eagerness the phantoms of hope; who expect that age will perform the promises of youth, and that the deficiencies of the present day will be supplied by the morrow; attend to the history of Rasselas prince of Abissinia.

When someone asked how he liked the novel, he snorted, "My God, sir, I never read further. Who but a clod would go beyond an opening paragraph like that?"

His touch with dowagers was usually faultless. When one came into the store after an absence of some little time (spent, Charley knew, in a Manhattan hospital getting her face lifted), he greeted her with a courtly bow and, "How nice to see you! Back from Paris and lovelier than ever!" She ravaged the shop buying sets. He once came a cropper. Someone published a book on how to grow vegetables in water, spiced with a few assorted chemicals, etc. We had a display of the book in the shop, complete with a live fountain and a half dozen goldfish bowls with watercress, etc., to show how it was done. Charley disapproved of all this, and when someone approached him and inquired how the book was selling, he confided that he was doing everything possible to suppress its sale. "I am a Rhode Islander," he loudly proclaimed, "descended from a long line of poor but proud farmers who fled that fascist bastard, Cromwell. My ancestry traces back to agriculturists of Richard the Third's time and I can assure you, gracious lady, that nothing will grow edible plants but shit." It turned out he was talking to the author of the book. "A toothsome wench," he once observed on another occasion of a striking-looking gal at a cocktail party, "handsome as a fiddler's bitch, she could double for Amber." As indeed she could, being Kathleen Winsor—they got along famously.

Though I missed the gilded days of the trade—the Scribner Fifth Avenue doorman was gone before I appeared, as was the salesman who arrived and left in his chauffeur-driven car (he had a bit of money on the side)—I got some of the backwash. One favored customer would phone in an order for books every Monday morning (after reading the Sunday reviews) from his summer home at Pride's Crossing. His private plane would fly to Newark, be met there by his chauffeur, who would pull up to the curb at 48th and Fifth, take the bundle of books requested and deliver them to Newark to be flown home for his evening perusal. When he was shown Arthur Rackham's illustrations for *The Night Before Christmas*, he had us cable an order for the originals, price unspecified: "Just get them."

One afternoon he purchased a first edition of Keats's *Poems* for several thousand dollars simply because he liked Riviere's rather gaudy binding. The next morning he was back asking me to get him another. Rather puzzled, I asked why, and he replied that on the way home he had stopped at some party and met someone who had admired the book, so he gave it to her. He had no idea who she was.

A Tuxedo Park matron—whose debutante daughter, whom I knew quite well, had just married—stopped in to purchase something, and I politely inquired as to how the newlyweds were doing. "Badly," she proclaimed. "You know my daughter: I brought her up to know right from wrong and did the best I could for her. And do you know what's happened?" I didn't, though I could imagine quite a few things she couldn't. "There she is with her husband, living on Long Island like a couple of pigs! They don't even have a butler!"

I happened to be at a soiree in Boston a short while later and repeated this story, at the end of which my hostess looked up and said, "I sympathize with your friend. The servant problem is really getting difficult, even here."

I always got along very well with butlers. I was once sent to do an appraisal of a library, a two-week job, while the owners would be absent. I had a gracious drink at about five with the owner, who then explained to the butler that I would be working in the library for the next few weeks and that if I wished refreshments at that time, I should ring for them. For the next two or three days I did, and then, getting tired and lonesome, I asked George, when he appeared with the heavy silver service for one, if he wouldn't join me. "Indeed I will," he replied brightly, picking up the decanter, and remarking as he left the room, "and in that case, we'll drink the master's private stock." It was prewar bourbon such as I have never had before or since and the pleasantest appraisal I ever made.

# Scribner's Files

ARLY IN THE 1940's Scribner's were approaching their centenary. Something had to be done about it, and the obvious thing was to commission a history. I was assigned the task of assembling, or rather reassembling, the surviving correspondence, records, files and whatnot to be used in this project. It proved to be a difficult, frustrating, baffling and altogether enjoyable chore. The Scribner files are in my experience by far the most comprehensive of those of any comparable American publishing house, over its hundred-year (in 1946) existence.

One reason is that the firm remained in the control of the descendants of the original founder, had not been merged and remerged with other firms: "efficiency experts" in these cases usually discard old files and records. Scribner's discarded nothing, though one disastrous fire in the 1880's destroyed some records.

But a vast amount of things remained, stacked and stored in the most implausible places. Some anonymous soul (blessed be he!) had decreed that nothing be destroyed, only filed. The great cache was in a sizable cubbyhole on the third floor of the building at 597 Fifth Avenue into which, for a period of thirty years, things had been crammed. This was the Comstock Lode. Dust was thick over everything and there was much dross but also much silver and gold.

Here in bales, boxes, packages tied with twine, in no order at all, were records and correspondences of Scribner authors from the 1870's onward. Sorting these out, arranging them, reading them, was sheer delight. There were not only the publishing house's own files but a part (though only a part, alas) of the magazine files.

And this was only the start. On other floors and in other buildings were other files, and there were desks to be rifled, often with surprising results. To a natural prier-into other people's papers this was absolute heaven— and I was being paid to do it!

There was an enormous sorting task, to begin with, and I enlisted the aid of an able bookman, "Doc" Roberts, who had worked at one time or another for several New York dealers and was to work for others later. "Doc" had a good eye and knew wheat from chaff. I thought for a while he could do the book himself, but it wasn't to be.

The Scribner firm was established in 1846 by the first Charles, who had graduated from the College of New Jersey (Princeton) and studied law, but because of ill health gave up practice and turned to publishing. He married Emma Elizabeth Blair, the daughter of John Insley Blair, famed capitalist and philanthropist.

J. Insley was quite a person. Born in 1802, he lived to be ninety-seven, and his school instruction, obtained during a few brief months in the winters, ceased when he was eleven years old and went to work in a country store. It is said he then exclaimed to his mother, "I have seven brothers and three sisters, all educated. I am going to get rich." And so he did, via the Union Pacific Railroad, among other operations. His estate at his death was estimated at over $70,000,000.

In any case, Roberts insisted that his projected history of the firm begin with the sentence opening his first chapter (as I remember it): "The smartest thing any Scribner ever did was the original Charles's marrying the daughter of the then richest man in America." When I protested that this was not exactly the way to open a house history, he remained unconvinced. Now I hasten to point out that Scribner's placed no strings whatsoever on the use of their files in the writing of their history, but, after all, fun's fun. Eventually Roger Burlingame, the son of Scribner's famed editor of the turn of the century, produced *Of Making Many Books. A Hundred Years of Reading, Writing and Publishing* (New York, 1946). It is competent but not inspired, considering the incredibly rich source material at his command. Rereading it, I sometimes wish Roberts had continued past his first chapter. However, my job was not to criticize but to organize, and I can here only list some high spots.

In a drawer of one abandoned desk were a bunch of Scribner copyright issues, that is, books printed in a very few copies prior to their English publication, to secure copyright in America. This included two copies of Stevenson's *The Master of Ballantrae*, Author's Edition, 1888, of which only ten copies were printed a year before its English publication. There was Barrie's *The Wedding Guest* (New York, 1900), one of six copies only, some copyright Merediths and books of other English authors the firm was publishing in America. All speedily found suitable homes.

And there was also the reverse of the coin, a copyright of an English book sent over for Scribner's consideration. In 1897 *The Nigger of the 'Narcissus,' A Tale of the Sea* was serialized in the English magazine *The New Review*. The English publisher, William Heinemann, in order to assure copyright, had a few copies, probably seven, struck off from the magazine setting. It is the most important, though not the rarest, of such Conrad copyrights. One was sent to Scribner's, and I found it in the abandoned desk. It was a quarto, in gray printed wrappers with an autograph note by the publishers on the upper-left-hand corner: "Serial setting only. Book form will be ordinary sized paper." Scribner's turned it down because "our fall list is already full of cheap fiction"! It was eventually published by Dodd, Mead with the title changed to *The Children of the Sea. A Tale of the Forecastle*, because it was thought the American public would not buy a book with the word "nigger" in the title. It was listed in one of our rare book catalogues at $1,650 and now is part of the splendid collection of Conrad's works formed by Nicholas Cooper.

Scribner's had ill luck, or showed bad judgment with Conrad, though editor Burlingame was a great admirer of his work. Later on when the magazine was offered *Typhoon* he declined it because it could not be put into one issue. "An account of a single storm written with such tenseness as this, cannot make its adequate impression if cut into two or three parts with a month between readings," he wrote Conrad's agent at the time. Later, commenting to its English publisher, he said that "artistically it would be nearly ruined by division, for it was of all things one that should have been read in a breath," and he was right. The handling of such long short stories had long been a problem to magazines, though *Lippincott's* had run Oscar Wilde's *The Picture of Dorian Gray* in a single issue, as well as Kipling's *The Light That Failed;* and *Beetons*, to its immortal glory, had so published Conan Doyle's first Holmes novel, *A Study in Scarlet*. But these were unusual ventures scarcely to be duplicated until decades later when *The New Yorker* devoted an entire issue to John Hersey's *Hiroshima,* and *Life* to Hemingway's *The Old Man and the Sea*.

I tried to persuade my superiors to establish an "archive" of some sort to preserve this material together with all their publishing records, file copies and the like. I also envisioned having tape recordings made of sales meetings where forthcoming books are dispassionately dissected and discussed by those on whom in the long run their fate depends. Nothing, of course, ever came of this. It is curious that publishers, of all people, are so uninterested in their own history. Not a single one of them has done a damn thing about it, in America at least, when it would be so easy. Almost to a man they distrust antiquarianism and erect roadblocks against it wherever possible. Probably this is because, as I have said elsewhere but repeat for emphasis, they are so concerned and worried about their future they don't care for their past. It's all a pity.

This being so, and I being a believer in putting things where they belong and can be properly used, I persuaded Charles Scribner to allow me to sell some of the files I had uncovered (retaining photocopies, of course).

The Stevenson material went to Ed Beinecke, a friend since my Brick Row days. It was quite a haul—thirty-two letters to Charles Scribner between March, 1885, and January, 1889, and sixty-three letters to Burlingame written mostly from the South Seas, some extending to five folio pages. There was also considerable manuscript material, including a portion of *The Master of Ballantrae*, proof of *The Wrong Box* corrected by Stevenson, proving just how much he had to do with it, many of the original poems from *Songs of Travel* and so on. These are duly listed in the six-volume catalogue of Beinecke's Stevenson collection issued by the Yale University Press. They cost a modest $5,000 (the manuscripts, not the catalogue).

When I delivered the loot to him at Greenwich, Connecticut (the home, incidentally, of a surprising number of book collectors), he asked me to take anything I wished as a souvenir, and I chose the original manuscript of my favorite of all Stevenson's poems, the poignant "Over the Sea to Skye," which opens:

> Sing me a song of a lad that is gone,
>   Say, could that lad be I?
> Merry of soul, he sailed on a day
>   Over the sea to Skye

and ends:

> All that was good, all that was fair,
>   All that was me, is gone.

It hangs in my library now, and I may add that although as usually printed the first two lines of the second stanza read:

> Mull was astern, Rum on the port,
>   Egg on the starboard bow:

RLS wrote:

> Mull was astern, Egg on the port,
>   Rum on the starboard bow:

Waller Barrett got the Henry Adams correspondence. Scribner's had published his famous *History of the United States,* of which six or twelve (records are unclear) copies were done on special paper for the author's personal use—try and find them! Adams was forever having his books privately published at his own expense and never made, or expected to make, money from his histories. He wrote Scribner an amusingly snobbish letter about this:

> First, I wish you to understand my position as you would regard it in a business point of view. If I were offering this book for sale, I should, on publisher's estimates, capitalize twelve years of unbroken labor, at (say) $5000 a year, and $20,000 in money spent in traveling, collecting materials, copying, printing, etc.; in all, $80,000, without charging that additional interest, insurance, or security per-centage which every business-man has to exact. This book, therefore, costs me $80,000; and on business principles I should make a very bad affair if I did not expect to get ten per cent per annum from it for ever. If I bargained according to publishers' rules, I should demand eight thousand dollars a year secured to me; and if I get it, I should still get less than I could probably have acquired in any other successful business.
>
> As I am not a publisher, but an author, and the most unpractical kind of an author, a historian, this business view is mere imagination. In truth the historian gives his work to the public and publisher; he means to give it; and he wishes to give it. History has always been, for this reason, the most aristocratic of all literary pursuits, because it obliges the historian to be rich as well as educated. I should be sorry to think that you could give me eight thousand a year for my investment, because I should feel sure that whenever such a rate of profit could be realized on history, history would soon become as popular a pursuit as magazine-writing, and the luxury of its social distinction would vanish.

In 1890 he wrote Charles Scribner:

> In regard to the battle of New Orleans, I have been profuse of maps. This course is not due to the importance of the battle, which was really of little importance, military or political; but for some reason, probably sectional, the Battle of New Orleans has always held an undue place in popular interest. I regard any concession to popular illusions as a blemish; but just as I abandoned so large a space to Burr—a mere Jeremy Diddler—because the public felt an undue interest in him, so I think it best to give the public a full dose of General Jackson.

Adams is possibly the most difficult of all American writers (certainly of historians) to collect because of his penchant for anonymity and private printing. His anonymous *Democracy an American Novel* (New York, 1880) is known in first edition, first state, only by the Lilly Library copy and one privately owned copy, and his pseudonymous *Esther A Novel* by Frances Snow Compton (New York, 1884) is not easily come by. He even went so far as to allow his work to be presented as by others. The speech "Recognition of Cuban Independence" delivered in the Senate on December 21, 1896, by Senator Don Cameron of Pennsylvania is entirely Adams'. Adams always appealed to me, though, and I have had at one time or another every book of his except the 1893 privately printed and anonymous edition of *Memoirs of Marau Taaroa Last Queen of Tahiti*, though I have had that in its revised edition printed in Paris in 1901 as *Memoirs of Arii Tainai E Marama of Eimeo Terriirere of Tooaria Teriinui of Tahiti Tauraatua I Amo*.

Scribner's were the major publishers of Theodore Roosevelt, who persuaded Robert Bridges, long-time editor of the magazine, to publish an obscure poet, Edwin Arlington Robinson, whose work they had already turned down. Thus came about the Scribner edition of *The Children of the Night* (New York, 1910). Though TR promoted his literary friends as a private citizen wherever possible, he did not allow his position as President to be used in any manner, an admirable attitude.

Robinson is a case in point. On October 13, 1905, on White House stationery, Roosevelt's secretary, William Loeb, Jr., wrote Bridges:

> The President is in receipt of the volume of Edwin Arlington Robinson's poems "The Children of the Night." On the paper wrapper of the cover is printed a quotation of the President. This is rather embarrassing as the President is continually asked for permission to be quoted in the advertisement of books, and the requests are invariably declined. Will you therefore discontinue the use of the President's name in any way in connection with the book?

This was done by issuing the book without a dust wrapper—or at least I've never seen one.

Bridges must have been a remarkable man to keep the devoted friendship of both TR and his Princeton roommate, "Tommy" Woodrow Wilson. In 1914 a restless Roosevelt decided on one more expedition. It was to be financed partly through articles to be published in *Scribner's* magazine. Visiting the republics of La Plata, he plunged into the blank spaces of the map, as told in *Through the Brazilian Wilderness*, where he found the "River of Doubt," barely escaped with his life and never fully recovered from consequent tropical infections.

But his copy came through on time. It was written from the jungle, and to assure arrival in New York he wrote in pencil on a pad with two carbons; hence three copies were sent, each by a different messenger and by a different route. Some did not get through, though no single installment failed to appear in some form, original or carbon. Bridges carefully saved these in his rooms at the University Club and used to show them occasionally, pointing to a blot or spot of blood on some of them, explaining, "That's where Teddy swatted a mosquito."

I was charged with the liquidation of Bridges' literary effects after his death. After various misadventures his Wilson correspondence ended up at Princeton. There was enough material to form two sets of the Brazilian adventure. These were offered to the New York Historical Society and the Museum of Natural History, where they properly belonged and were turned down, for what reason I cannot conceive. Eventually one manuscript went to Waller Barrett, the other to Dr. W. W. Boyd of Washington, D.C.

Scribner's files have been deposited at Princeton, and a healthy group of Ph.D. aspirants they should serve. As I had no hand in their disposal, they have no proper place in these memoirs, but I do remember one envelope vividly: it contained numerous versions of a single sentence in Hemingway's hand, the final one of *A Farewell to Arms:* "After a while I went out and left the hospital and walked back to the hotel in the rain." And I remember a letter from Edith Wharton to Charles Scribner about Henry James. Her relationship was not always easy with Scribner's, and I recall one letter in which she loosed a tirade against the firm because a friend of hers had not been able to obtain a copy of *Ethan Frome* at Brentano's—Paris branch. But this time she wrote that James had just received his year's royalty account from Scribner's (this was around 1912) and was violently depressed, not because of the money but because of the evident lack of interest in his books. Would Scribner's, therefore, deduct a considerable sum from her next royalty report and transfer it to his? Absolute secrecy was to be observed and no one but CS himself was to handle the matter.

Despite what I think are inadequacies (and I may be judging it unfairly), *Of Making Many Books* is the best account of an American publishing house I know of and should be required reading for all aspiring writers and graduate students in English, along with Maxwell Perkins' letters, *Editor to Author*. They are not, of course.

# Scribner's Catalogues

S OMEONE HAS REMARKED, in fact many someones, that the
most pleasurable of all desultory reading is the perusing of secondhand book dealers' catalogues. The quote is usually attributed to
Lamb, probably with complete inaccuracy. Of course, part of the fun involved relates to the date of the catalogue at the time one is reading it. If
it is current, perhaps advance proofs sent by a bookseller to a favored few,
that horrible thought, "Can I afford this, and should I cable or phone for
it?" is inevitable. If it is years or decades old, one muses over opportunities
lost, or, sometimes luckily, not taken.

There are many dealers who have never (or seldom) issued catalogues
at all—Gabriel Wells, Sessler, Hamill & Barker, among recent Americans
to come to mind. Some, such as Lathrop Harper, A. S. W. Rosenbach,
The Seven Gables, Goodspeed, Kraus, to name only a few, have issued
magnificent series which are of solid scholarly importance, glorying in
advertising what they had.

There are many reasons for this. In Gabriel Wells's case, for one
example, he dealt largely through agents and didn't want their imagination to be limited by his price list. Other dealers, other reasons. Incidentally, many dealers' catalogues to this day are numbered but not
dated. There is some validity behind this. If, for example, a catalogue is
dated 1967 and is sent out in 1968, the recipient is likely to assume
everything in it has been sold, which is often not the case.

Not too many decades ago there were many pleasant tricks played by
dealers smaller than those I have mentioned in the catalogue racket. One
ploy was for a dealer to catalogue a book well beneath its market value—
the "loss leader" theory—and actually sell it at the quoted price, thereafter loudly trumpeting to all customers how cheaply he sold books.
Another was for a dealer to catalogue attractive books he didn't have,

again at bargain prices. If this led to an order, he simply replied that the item had already been sold—but he had a new customer and a line on his wants. The most brazen effrontery in my experience was when I broke up and catalogued an imperfect folio Audubon. A small secondhand dealer simply reprinted the list (which cannot be copyrighted) over his own name, raised Scribner's prices 50 percent and got more orders for plates than I did! My own unwitting inclusion of a "ghost" book by Robert Frost in my very first catalogue led to a lifetime friendship with H. Bacon Collamore.

When John Carter and I became associates at Scribner's in 1935, we determined to issue catalogues of "different" books and break with the rather rigid convention which apparently insisted that a catalogue begin with "à Becket" and end with "Zangwill." For one thing, the Depression was still on, and we saw a chance of a healthy development of a modest sort of book collecting involving new types, new patterns and new frameworks, which, thank goodness, is always true of young dealers, and properly so. As Carter wrote in his introduction to *New Paths in Book Collecting*, which he edited (London, Constable, 1934):

> The enterprising novice must be made to realize how infinite are the possible variations on the book collecting theme. A collection of "high spots" may sound the chord of C major, which is indeed a fine and resounding noise; yet there are other and more subtle harmonies, the pleasantest are those which we evolve for ourselves. These are composed of notes which anyone can use and many have used, but by our own arrangement of them we can achieve a sound never before heard. So it is with books. By rearranging familiar books according to some constructive plan, a new significance is added to them, and, which is more, the unfamiliar, the neglected books, will acquire significance by their context.

I believed in this thoroughly. The day of the really high-priced book was gone and would never return. But the lure of collecting would remain and the solution was to stimulate the imagination and enthusiasm of those of modest means to collect books whose acquisition might mean the forgoing of a Brooks Brothers suit but not the purchase of a Greenwich, Connecticut, estate. It was a lovely theory and a lot of fun doing, but we suffered, alas, the fate of most pioneers: reality eventually violently outstripped imagination (or, I really suppose, our lack of it).

It was Charles Lamb—the perfect instance of a great book lover with little money to spend on them—who observed that first editions were not as rare as tenth editions. I once contemplated a rare book catalogue of tenth editions only but was never able to find enough.

I have recently been reviewing the Scribner catalogues Carter and I issued over two decades and it has been an instructive, sometimes saddening, but generally amusing experience.

The first catalogue I was responsible for at Scribner's was *Familiar Quotations in Their Earliest Appearances*. Carroll Wilson, an indefatigable (and accurate) quoter, had for years been gathering in their earliest appearances quotations familiar to him. It was virgin territory then and great exploring fun. There were few bibliographical guides: John Bartlett and Burton Stevenson's *Familiar Quotations*, for instance, Julian's *Dictionary of Hymnology*, Merle Johnson's *You Know These Lines* (American only), about did it. You had the *New English Dictionary* and other guides, but most of the research had to be done by yourself. It was intriguing also to discover how often these standard sources were wrong. It was also fascinating to find that the first printing of a favorite line of a poem came, not in an expensive first edition, but in a completely neglected later printing, to be found for 2s. 6d. or twenty-five cents if at all. And also how often "familiar quotations" are quoted out of context and completely distorted.

It is only very recently that a U.S. Supreme Court judge quoted Edmund Burke as saying, "You cannot indict an whole people." This common misquotation did not surprise me, but what did was that no commentator, among the seeming thousands we have, faulted him. What Burke actually said in his *Speach—on Moving His Resolution for Conciliation with the Colonies*, March 22, 1775 (London, Dodsley, 1775), page 28, was, "I do not know the method of drawing up an indictment against an whole people."

He was not speaking as a philosopher or a moralizer, but simply as a practical lawyer expounding a technical legal problem. What Burke was driving at is that an indictment *can only be charged against a definite person or persons* and is a legal device operating under technical restrictions, while a people is an abstract entity composed of an unspecified number of indefinite persons, whom it is thus impossible, legally, to indict. This is about as much as I remember from my Harvard Law School career, but I managed to sell the book to a lawyer for $75 on the basis of this description.

I think of familiar quotations in terms of Tennyson's lines in *The Princess* (London, 1847):

> Jewels five-words-long
> That on the stretch'd forefinger of all Time
> Sparkle for ever.

My Introduction to *Familiar Quotations in Their Earliest Appearances* read:

> The present catalogue is an attempt to present a "new path in book-collecting." We have gathered here a group of books, some familiar, more that are unfamiliar, but all notable as containing the first appearance in print of some remembered poem, phrase, or quotation. The emphasis is thus placed upon the actual content of the book itself, and only incidentally upon its rarity or authorship.
>
> Most of the quotations are, naturally, poetry, as it is the smooth, rhythmic beat which best fixes phrases in memory, and yet many of the great poets of the English language are not represented: Browning, Swinburne, Landor, and Milton, for example, "though they charm the soul in the warmth of the study, do not spring from the little red school house, to remain fixed forever in the recesses of the brain." For it is familiar lines, not great poetry, with which we are concerned, though to be sure, on certain happy occasions the two are synonymous.
>
> Still, a great number of familiar sayings and poems are unknown, by author, to the schoolboy and savant alike. The small thick dust of oblivion has fallen on the names of T. H. Palmer, S. J. Hale, Augustus Toplady, and John Byrom, yet "every schoolboy knows" as well as every college president: "If at first you don't succeed," "Mary had a little lamb," "Rock of Ages," and "Strange this difference should be, twixt Tweedle-dum and Tweedle-dee," which were written by these authors, respectively, and of which the first appearances in print are included in the present catalogue. Thomas Morton's play "Speed the Plough" has no revivals but it makes a real appeal when it is remembered that in its pages there makes her first appearance that paragon of respectability, *Mrs. Grundy*, who, appropriately enough, does not appear in the play at all, but only in the mouths of the characters pondering her probable reactions: "What will Mrs. Grundy say? What will Mrs. Grundy think?"
>
> Nor is the present catalogue, strictly speaking, a "first edition" catalogue (collectors and dealers have long been too snobbish about first editions), for it contains many second, fifth, or seventh editions, as it is often in these later issues that the authors incorporated their now familiar sayings. It is the seventh edition of Campbell's "Pleasures of Hope" which first contains "Coming events cast their shadows before" —the third edition of Harry Carey's "Poems" which has "Sally in Our Alley"—and the fifth edition of Bryant's Poems in which we find "Truth crushed to earth shall rise again."

In rereading the catalogue I found I had completely forgotten not only that John Byrom made his living teaching shorthand, but that the musical "Epigram on the Feuds Between Handel and Bononcinc" first appeared in his *Miscellaneous Poems* (Manchester, 1773) and contained:

> Some say, compar'd to Bononcinc,
> That Meynheer Handel's but a ninny;
> Others aver that he to Handel
> Is scarcely fit to hold a candle:
> Strange all this Difference should be,
> Twixt Tweedle-dum and Tweedle-dee!

Three of my own favorite poems were included in their first appearances in print: O. W. Holmes's "The Chambered Nautilus" (in *The Atlantic Monthly*, February, 1858) and J. H. Newman's "Lead, Kindly Light" (in *Lyra Apostolica*, Derby, 1836); it has been said of both poems that their complicated metrical schemes were invented by their authors and never successfully imitated. The other was "The Bridge of Sighs," in Thomas Hood's *Poems* (London, Moxon, 2 volumes, 1846).

> Take her up tenderly,
> Lift her with care;
> Fashion'd so slenderly,
> Young, and so fair!

This is the only dignified example of trisyllabic rhyme in English known to me.

Leigh Hunt's "Abou Ben Adhem," by the way, was *Abon* Ben Adhem when it first appeared in *The Amulet* in 1834 and was so written in the original manuscript, which I once owned.

I was responsible for a few catalogues of American interest, of course. An early catalogue was, naturally, *Scribner Firsts, 1846–1936*. This was crammed with useful information regarding issue points, publication dates, number of copies printed, etc., but its chief charm, as I look it over now, is the frontispiece representing the interior of the Scribner Book Store, sometime in the 1880's, at 743 Broadway when Astor Place was way uptown. Another catalogue listed Cooper's own copy of *The Prairie* (Philadelphia, 1827), interleaved and completely revised for English publication in Bentley's *Standard Novel Series* of 1834, $750; the complete original manuscript of Henry James's *Confidence*, which first appeared in six monthly installments in *Scribner's* from August, 1879, to January, 1880, and is I believe the only James manuscript of a major novel ever to appear on the open market, $1,650. Bill Jackson reluctantly eventually purchased it for Harvard, but only after I had reduced the price.

This catalogue also had the original manuscript, typescript and drawings for Rockwell Kent's *Voyaging Southward from the Strait of Magellan*. All I remember about this is that I bought it from his daughter, who was pregnant at the time and badly needed funds. I don't know what I gave her for it, but it couldn't have been much, as it was catalogued at $500 and hung around for ages.

Another catalogue was devoted to *Juvenile Fiction*, issued in 1936. It had some pleasant books in it, including a fine copy of the correct issue of Horatio Alger's *Ragged Dick; or, Street Life in New York with the Bootblacks* (Loring, Boston, 1868), $7.50. I catalogued it as "Alger's most successful work which so aroused public opinion on behalf of the helpless child bootblacks in New York as to be directly responsible for the abolition of the vicious 'padrone system.' " I didn't realize that within a decade it would be listed in the Grolier Club's *One Hundred Influential American Books* and its price moved some decimal points to the right.

The catalogue had another unexpected result. I had listed "Harry Castlemon's" (Charles Austin Fosdick's) *Frank on the Lower Mississippi* (Cincinnati, Carroll, 1867) at $6, noting that it was by one of America's most successful juvenile writers and that, as part of his *Gun-Boat* series, it was based largely upon his own experiences in the Mississippi Squadron before Vicksburg.

When he got the catalogue J. K. Lilly called in high excitement from Indianapolis to ask if it were still available. When I replied that it was, he said, "Get it and bring it to the phone. I haven't read that book in nearly forty years but I think I can still quote the first paragraph," which he proceeded to do. He then explained that in his childhood most novels in his home were forbidden reading—but not Castlemon's. These were patriotic history, hence allowable: they were also high adventure and accurate at that.

After rereading the book Lilly casually wrote that he wanted everything Castlemon had written (there were some sixty titles) in every available edition. Now there is nothing more difficult to get than the first editions of an outdated and forgotten juvenile author—stand-books, thirty-five cents to $5 top (and then only if inscribed).

Yet five years later Lilly had acquired by his own techniques, described elsewhere, some three hundred copies of this author's works, and Jacob Blanck had compiled from them *Harry Castlemon. Boys' Own Author. Appreciation and Bibliography* (New York, Bowker, 1941), dedicated to Lilly with an amusing Foreword by Franklin P. Adams, and a revealing Portrait by the author's nephew, Raymond B. Fosdick, who discreetly revealed that his uncle had "one or two rather conspicuous human frailties which shocked the pious—for one thing he refused to go to church. As I recall him after all these years, I think perhaps he was the most human specimen our family has produced." Lilly once remarked to me that he had spent less money and had more fun with this collection than any other he ever made.

Another catalogue I had a great deal of pleasure doing was *American Historical Novels, Fifteenth to Nineteenth Century*. These were arranged chronologically by subject matter, not publication date, and included information on place, time, characters, etc. Its completion required reading (or at least skimming) some hundreds of novels, mostly bad. Item Number 1 in the catalogue was:

> Cooper, James Fenimore. *Mercedes of Castile; or, The Voyage to Cathay*. Philadelphia: Lea and Blanchard, 1840. 12 mo, First Edition, 2 volumes, original red cloth, paper labels. In a red cloth slip case. Foxed. $20. 1496. The discovery of America. Spain and the West Indies. Columbus, Ferdinand, Isabella.

The final item, Number 228, was:

> Munroe, Kirk. *Forward March*. New York: Harper, 1899. 12 mo, First Edition, original green cloth. Illustrated. $2.00. 1898. The Spanish-American War. Santiago, San Juan Hill. Roosevelt, Hobson.

Between these, though, were some very good books, many now sadly neglected. Jane G. Austin's *Standish of Standish* (New York, 1889) is to my mind the best tale of the Plymouth Colony ever written. John Neal's *Rachel Dyer* (Boston, 1828) is a bitter, unrelieved tragedy of New England witchcraft, making no compromise with romanticism. Hawthorne was a great admirer of Neal. I find that I characterized *The Scarlet Letter* (Boston, 1850) as "a philosophical handling of a problem of sin and remorse. A famous novel, this is historical only in its atmosphere."

My disillusionment with that vivid and scarlet *A* came when, for some completely forgotten reason, I had occasion while at Harvard Law School to look up the punishment for adultery about that time. It was pretty rough, believe me, but there was nothing about a *scarlet* letter. What the *Acts and Laws Passed by the Great and General Court of the Province of the Massachusetts-Bay in New England—the Thirtieth Day of May, 1694* said among other things was:

> That people convicted of Adultery, "shall be set upon the Gallows by the space of an Hour, with a rope around their neck, and the other end cast over the Gallows. And in the way from thence to the Common Gaol, shall be severely Whipt, not exceeding *Forty Strikes* each: Also every person or persons so Offending, shall for ever after wear a capital A of two inches long, and proportionable bigness, cut out of cloth of a contrary colour to their Cloaths, and sewed upon their upper Garments,

on the outside of their arm, or on their Back, in open view. And if any person or persons, having been Convicted and Sentenced to such Offence, shall at any time be found without their Letter so worn, during their abode in this Province; they shall by Warrent from a Justice of the Peace, be forthwith apprehended. and ordered to be publickly Whip'd, not exceeding *Fifteen Strikes;* and so from time to time *toties quoties.*

I have always had a great deal of sympathy for Henry Ford's opinion: "History is bunk"; and the more history I read the more I applaud his dictum.

One surprising result of my American fiction catalogue was an order from the Huntington Library for almost every item printed before 1850. Though I did not know it at the time, this was the beginning of Lyle Wright's famous series of checklists of American fiction.

One of the rarest books in the catalogue was George Lippard's *Herbert Tracy; or, The Legend of the Black Rangers. A Romance of the Battle-Field of Germantown* (Philadelphia, Berford, 1844), $175. Lippard was quite a lad, among the leading beatniks of his time—a century and a half ago when conduct such as his often led to tar and feathering and being ridden out of town on a rail—not subject to sympathetic editorials. He was against marriage as an institution, for example, so he coupled with his wife, Rose Newman, on May 14, 1847, by swimming with her at dawn, both naked, to a high rock in the romantic Wissahickon Creek, there plighting their troth before God and some onlookers and then swimming back to Philadelphia, as, they considered, man and wife. He developed a solid Marxian theory while Marx was still a schoolboy, organized a potent Brotherhood of the Union which eventually became the Odd Fellows, and just might have accomplished much had he not died of consumption at the age of thirty-two.

He was a literary hack most of his life from necessity, and *Herbert Tracy* is especially important because the last two pages print a letter to him by Poe, dated "Philadelphia Feb. 18, 1844," in which Poe attacks "the literary animalcula" who were criticizing Lippard. That's one book I wish I had back.

Our main concentration at this time, however, was beginning to be in English literature, music and science. In 1938 Carter and I issued what was one of the first deluxe dealers' catalogues done by an American firm up to that time: such catalogues are commonplace now. This was a folio, hardbound volume of *50 Books, Manuscripts, Music.* Each item was illustrated on the right-hand page, and opposite it were a description and price. I list here only a few of my favorites: a flawless copy of Browning's *Pauline* (London, 1833), immaculate in original boards and inscribed to Comte Amédée de Ripert Monclar, a young nobleman who met Browning in 1834 when visiting England on a Carlist mission, and to whom Browning dedicated his second book, *Paracelsus*, in 1835. This was priced at $12,500—on the basis of the poorish and uninscribed Kern copy, which had brought $16,000 a few years previously.

It is by far the finest known copy. There was for many years a tremendous Browning cult in America, and innumerable women's reading clubs were devoted wholly to a study of his (though not Elizabeth's) poetry. The most considerable collection of his works was at Baylor University at Waco, Texas. Its librarian had once told me, "If you ever find *Pauline*" (the only first the collection lacked), "bring it to me with a blank check." I did, and the only thing I remember about that episode was that funds were not available for its purchase and that Waco had bells, not lights, as traffic signals. I was at a hotel on what we now call, I suppose, a four-way stop, and was awake all night. But the book eventually went, as a gift from his host of admiring students, to Chauncey Brewster Tinker, on his retirement, which was just where it belonged.

Other nice literature included the copyright issue of Conrad's *Some Reminiscences* (New York, Paul R. Reynolds, 1908), $175, one of only two known copies; John Donne's *Poems* bound with *Juvenilia* (London, 1633), J. R. Lowell's annotated copies, $500; John Henry Newman's *The Dream of Gerontius* (London, 1866), one of the rarest books of the nineteenth or any other century, immaculate in green glazed boards, $475; the English edition (London, 1838) of Poe's *Narrative of Arthur Gordon Pym*, then and now the only recorded copy in original boards, paper label, $300; Walpole's autograph manuscript of *The Duchess of Wrexe* (1,438 pages), $550; the complete manuscript collection of Mary Webb's *Poems*, 1928, $875.

Science included Agricola's *De Re Metallica* (Basel, 1556) and *De Ortu et Causis Subterraneorum Libri V* (Basel, 1546): together $225; Vesalius' *De Humani Corporis Fabrica Libri Septem*, both the Basel 1543 and the 1555 editions, $900; Robert Boyle's *The Sceptical Chymist*, both the first (London, 1661) and the second (Oxford, 1680), in original bindings, together $1,250. I got in some real trouble on these as the first proved to have been stolen from the library of Geoffrey Keynes, no less. He had seen the description in the catalogue, went to his shelves to check his copy—and found it missing. Matters were eventually straightened out.

The music in this catalogue is discussed elsewhere. Every book of the fifty listed was eventually sold—except one. After Merle Johnson's death,

Jake Blanck was attempting to settle his rather muddled affairs. One day he called me and asked me to drop around. It seemed that Mrs. Johnson was unable to pay Jake his salary and owed him about $50. "Sell something," she advised him, "and keep the proceeds." There were pretty slim pickings left at that point but I spotted a rather beat-up copy of Donald G. Mitchell's ("Ik Marvel's") sentimental essays *Reveries of a Bachelor: or a Book of the Heart* (New York, Scribner, 1850). It was not in its accustomed blue cloth but in original half morocco with sprinkled edges. This I recognized as one of a very few especially bound for the author for presentation, and surely enough it was inscribed on the flyleaf: "G. P. R. James, Esq., with the compliments of the Author." I purchased it for $50 and catalogued it with a full-dress description for $175. When I left Scribner's twenty-odd years later it was marked down to $25 and was still unsold. I bought it for sentimental reasons and still have it.

A spate of other catalogues followed, and rereading them, I come across many favorites. In one I catalogued the "original autograph manuscript, nineteen folio pages, entirely in the author's autograph, of an early draft of the opening six chapters of Hawthorne's posthumously published *Dr. Grimshaw's Secret*." I priced the manuscript at $1,500 and immediately sold it to the Pierpont Morgan Library. I had purchased it, incidentally, from the widow of Hawthorne's son, Julian, who had edited the book. It was an embarrassment to discover eventually that the manuscript draft was in Hawthorne's hand—only Julian's, not Nathaniel's.

And I once, only, had a complete copy of Edward Lear's *Book of Nonsense, by Derry Down Derry* (London, Thos. McLean, February 10, 1846), with the full complement of seventy-two leaves, each containing a picture and a limerick, lithographed on the recto (all versos are blank)— the text being in the regular rough sloped capitals and *arranged in three lines* (later, always five), $650.

Other pleasant books were Anne Brontë's own copy of *The Tenant of Wildfell Hall* (London, 1848), with corrections in her hand, presented by herself and her sisters to Mary Brown, sister of Tabitha, the faithful servant of the family, on the occasion of her marriage to a man named Jopling. Among great association copies was that of *The Moonstone* (3 volumes, original cloth, London, 1868) which Collins gave Dickens, $2,250. Of numerous Oscar Wildes I regret now not having is the dedication copy of *The Importance of Being Earnest* (London, 1899, one of twelve on vellum) to Robert Ross ($1,000), and at the same price a superb first of *Salomé* (Paris, 1893) with nine pages of exquisitely amusing original and wicked pen-and-ink drawings by Beerbohm.

We never did much with incunabula or early English literature, leaving these to the specialist dealers, Rosenbach, Harper, Quaritch and the like. In fact, I never sold a Shakespeare First Folio in my life, which must be some sort of record for so common a book for someone as long in business as I was. But I do recall with pleasure selling a very good copy of the infinitely rarer Third Folio edition (with the *1663*, not the 1664, title page) for $2,600 to a pleasant young couple, newly married and living in a modest apartment in Detroit, to whom I had been introduced by Randolph Adams. It was a major investment for them at that time and it took considerable persuasion on my part to convince the husband that his wife really wanted it. It was the first important rarity Don and Mary Hyde ever purchased. They went far from there.

Scribner's did publish one catalogue of *English Books Printed Prior to 1700*. I had somehow acquired a few very nice things, chief among them the A. Edward Newton copy of *Comus* (London, 1637), which I priced $10,500; a magnificent copy, in original limp vellum, of that great Elizabethan anthology of lyric poetry, John Bodenham's *England's Helicon* (London, 1600), $3,750; Herman Melville's copy of the Beaumont and Fletcher *Tragedies* (second collected edition, London, 1679), crammed with his notes, $300, and like material.

But I didn't have enough for a substantial catalogue. At this point Bill Jackson suggested that the Houghton Library had a fair number of duplicates he was willing to give me, on sale (he setting the prices), and Scribner's paying for the catalogue and taking a modest commission on items sold. It was pretty much of a disaster, as I recall it now. Many of the books were on the whole second-rate and repaired copies. One could then, one thought, await perfect copies: I recall a nice copy of Thomas Nash's *Lenten Stuff* (London, 1599), priced $250, that was returned because "one word and a numeral were in facsimile" (and thus described in the catalogue). The latest copy to appear at public auction, a pretty inferior one, brought £450.

Anyway, when adjustment was finally made, the Houghton Library received a substantial check for what had been sold (at their prices), plus the return of everything unsold, and I discovered that the commission I had made from their books, together with the profit on our own books sold, didn't together pay for the cost of printing, illustrating and distributing the catalogue. Bill should have been a bookseller.

But I did sell Milton's *Comus* to the University of Illinois. They were then forming their incomparable Milton collection. *Comus* is not a really uncommon book—perhaps twenty-five copies are known in all—but the trouble was that most of them are locked up in institutions (the British

Museum has four) or privately owned by individuals unlikely to part with them. It seemed like now or never for Illinois, but the librarian was reluctant to spend a five-figure sum for a single volume. Awkward questions might be asked by legislators, etc. In a suddenly enlightened moment I asked if there would be any objections to their buying a collection of Milton. It seemed there wouldn't, so I scurried around secondhand bookstalls in town, assembled a number of "cripples," odd volumes, old theses, etc., for an outlay of perhaps $50 at most, raised the price by perhaps a thousand, and Illinois had their *Comus*—which, alas, my own university's considerable Milton collection still lacks.

One Chicago collector of moderate means but abundant enthusiasm and considerable knowledge plucked many plums—Harold Greenhill, most of whose small but choice library is now in H. Bradley Martin's collection.

We took swings at many other catalogues of specialized (for American dealers) material. "Rare Book Bulletin Number 1" was *Continental First Editions*. Item Number 3 remains one of my favorites:

"Balzac, Honoré de. *Le Cent Contes Drolatiques.. . . Par Le Sieur de Balzac, Pour L'Esbattement Des Pantagruelistes Et Non Autres* (Paris, 1832–1837). Three volumes; original printed wrappers, $1,500." A little high for the times, perhaps, but not excessively so when it is considered that these were the copies he gave his mother, inscribed "À mon bonne mère chérie, Honoré."

Another of my favorite books was a copy I found for nothing of Louis Hémon's *Maria Chapdelaine* (Montreal, 1916) which I priced $75. First published in 1914 in *Le Temps* (Paris), and then in French in Canada as above, it created no stir at the time. But in 1921 the French critic M. Daniel Halévy revived it as the initial number of the famous *Cahiers Verts*, since when its success has been phenomenal. The author never knew of it. He died tragically and unnecessarily, making the error, being deaf, of walking down a railway track, never having heard the engine's whistle.

Perhaps the most interesting catalogue we did at that time was Number 117 in 1938: *Scribner's Present The Modern Library in First Editions*. I persuaded Bennett Cerf and Donald Klopfer to allow us to do this and furthermore to bind it in an exact imitation of their famous series. The spine is lettered merely MODERN LIBRARY SCRIBNER'S. The Introduction (by John Carter), an able summary of what we were attempting, in a rather juvenile way, read:

> Every book collector has a "want list." The stamp collector, poring over the pages of his album, is as sharply aware of the empty squares as of the occupied, and frets that the design is incomplete for some such

trifling desideratum as a Blue Mauritius. So, on his (as we think) higher plane, the Trollope collector's eye often seeks—not the ordered ranks of his Barchester Chronicles, but the place at the end of the shelf which *The McDermots of Ballycloran* (in original boards, uncut) has yet to fill. The nature of the collector's want list will depend on many things: the type of collection, the length of his purse, the degree of his determination: but be sure he has one, in his head if not on paper.

Why does John Ford's tragedy, *The Broken Heart*, bring so unexpectedly high a price—a price quite out of line with those commanded by his other works? Because it is one of the Grolier Club's *One Hundred Books Famous in English Literature*. Why does *East Lynne* do the same? For the beaux yeux of Miss Ann Harding? No, but because Mr. Newton tipped it as one of *A Hundred Good Novels*. And whether it is the collector's pleasure to follow someone else's good advice or his own sweet will, there will always be certain books without which his chosen scheme remains incomplete.

At one time and another in the past, Scribner's have issued subject catalogues which represented, however imperfectly, attempts to round out a selected list of our own making. *Adventure Stories, Classics of Discovery and Exploration, Detective Fiction, American Historical Novels*, and so forth. Our purpose was not in any sense dogmatic, even to ourselves. But booksellers, like collectors, need something to steer by, and often have to make their own charts. The results of these catalogues proved that our soundings were on the whole approved by our customers (indeed the *Detective Fiction* catalogue was purchased en bloc), and we have felt encouraged to proceed.

We decided, however, that this time we would steer by someone else's map for a change—if a sufficiently attractive and unspoilt prospect, adequately charted, could be found. So, turning also from the particular to the general, we began to look for a select list of books, of all kinds, which enjoy not only the accolade of fame but the solid testimony of steady sales—books that the world both admires *and reads*. We wanted, moreover, a list catholic in subject and in date; something which would take in Shelley and Schopenhauer, Chaucer and Caldwell, Plutarch and Lewis Carroll.

In The Modern Library we found just such a list. It does not contain all the world's masterpieces: but then there are many masterpieces which the world seldom reads. It contains a number of books which are not masterpieces: but many such books have some living quality which ensures that, whatever the professors may say, the world goes on reading them. The Modern Library is the result of a keen sense of what the general reader wants, crossed with a sound, catholic and sensitive (but in no way magisterial) taste for what is good in literature and what is important in history, philosophy and thought.

Imitation being the sincerest form of flattery, the Scribner Rare Book Department thereupon set out to reproduce the Modern Library list in terms of first editions. And in the following pages will be found a representative, in first edition, first translation, first edition of the translation used or whatever, of every title in the list. We believe that many collectors prefer live literature to dead (however infallibly canonised), and read the books they collect. We believe that many collectors already operating on a wide scale will appreciate the special qualities of such a list as this. And we believe that many regular Modern Library readers— perhaps desultory collectors, perhaps not collectors at all—may be inspired, by the sight of so many of their favorites in first edition form, to try the taste of a new pleasure.

It was not a bad catalogue and was very successful. Among some of the books in it I would like to have back is Richard Carlile's *What Is Love?* in its original magazine appearance in *The Republican*, Volume XI, Number 18, May 6, 1825, priced $22.50. This remarkable essay, the first English treatment of contraception in its medical, economic and social aspect, was later expanded into that fabulous rarity *Every Woman's Book*, of the first and second editions of which no copies are known. Carlile's radical opinions caused many of his articles to be written, like this, from Dorchester Gaol.

Dr. Sigmund Freud's *Die Traumdeutung* (Leipzig and Vienna, 1900) was modestly priced at $45, while all that exists of the original manuscript of Joyce's *A Portrait of the Artist As a Young Man* was daringly priced at $500, and purchased, after much heart-searching, by H. B. Collamore.

A later effort presenting *The Limited Edition Club Books in First Editions* was less successful. There were many other catalogues, but a listing of them would be tedious: a few important ones on science and music are described later.

The last major effort of the Carter-Randall Scribner axis was, again, *Fifty Distinguished Books and Manuscripts*. This was issued in 1952, just before the current "collecting explosion" occurred. It was the only dealer's catalogue in our century, I believe, to list a Gutenberg Bible—or likely to, for that matter. Here is a brief listing of some works unmentioned elsewhere. Pietro Bembo's *De Aetna* (Venice, Aldus, 1495)—a milestone in the history of type design and of the very first importance in the development of Roman type, $950, now at Harvard. Charlotte Brontë's original manuscript of *Emma* (now in Robert Taylor's collection), on which she was working when she died. It was catalogued:

BRONTË, CHARLOTTE. The original manuscript of Emma. 20 pages written in pencil in the author's minuscule hand. Dated, on the first page, Nov. 27, 1853. 8vo, bound in blue levant. About 7,000 words.　　$3,500

The finest Brontë manuscript which has come on the market in many years. It was on this manuscript that the author was working when she died. It was published posthumously in the *Cornhill Magazine,* April, 1860, with an introduction by Thackeray which reads in part: "I can fancy many readers turning to these—the last pages which were traced by Charlotte Brontë's hand. . . . As I read this little fragmentary sketch, I think of the rest. And where is it? Will not the leaf be turned some day, and the story be told? Shall the deviser of the tale somewhere perfect the history of little Emma's griefs and troubles? . . . Hundreds of those who, like myself, recognized and admired the master-work of a great genius, will look with mournful interest and regard and curiosity upon this, the last fragmentary sketch from the noble hand which wrote Jane Eyre."

I underestimated the desirability of Sir Richard F. Burton, or, perhaps, *The Arabian Nights.* I had the most important of his surviving manuscripts (most having been burnt by his wife after his death.) This was a manuscript on 177 folio leaves, dated at the end "Athenaeum Club, August 1, '86." It occupies pages 63–602 of Volume X of the *Nights* and develops in great detail his revolutionary theories. Though today this famous "Terminal Essay," which caused a fantastic stir upon publication, pales beside the vivid investigations of Freud, Krafft-Ebing, Kinsey, et al., it preceded them all by many years, it is more catholic, and it is literature. It was priced at $1,850, and Ed Hanley's order was first among many received. It is now, I assume, at Texas.

I thought much more highly of a collection of drawings by James Wells Champney, catalogued as follows:

[CHAMPNEY, JAMES WELLS.] A collection of over 250 original illustrations in wash, pencil, and pen and ink, for The Great South, done by James Wells Champney for the famous series of articles by Edward Smith King, which were commissioned for and published by *Scribner's Magazine* in the decade following the Civil War.         $4,000

No small part of the success and enormous influence of these articles was due to the sketches, scenes, characters, etc., drawn from all parts and conditions of the South, executed by Champney. Born in Boston in 1843, Champney studied in France and was one of the first American painters to understand and apply the theory of "values" developed by the French impressionists Manet and Monet. He was a very talented artist and pastellist and ranked among his contemporaries with Whistler and Robert Blum.

When *Scribner's Magazine* was founded in 1870, it was with the determination to make it truly national, and not sectional, as its current rivals were: *Harper's* (New York), *Atlantic* (Boston), and *Lippincott's* (Philadelphia). The South had absolutely no possible outlet whatsoever for its budding creative artists.

*Scribner's,* determined to bind up bloody wounds, sent the brilliant

journalist Edward King, and the equally able artist Champney, on a two
year, 25,000 mile tour, by carriage, stagecoach and saddle, of the South
to gather material for a series of articles on the effects of the Civil War,
the economic promise of Southern development and interesting features
of its landscape and social life.

*Scribner's* noted, at the end of this vastly successful tour, that "it is
with no ordinary pride and satisfaction that we record the completion
of a task undertaken with the desire to enlighten our country concerning
itself, and to spread before the nation the wonderful natural resources,
the social condition and political complications of a region which needs
but just, wise and generous legislation with responding good-will and
industry to make it a garden of happiness and prosperity."

Indeed Albert Tassin in his *The Magazine in America* states in part:
"the first Northern magazine which was open to Southerns was *Scribners*, both in stories which represented their life, and articles which
stated their point of view. . . . All this change of attitude, North and
South, had been brought about by *Scribners*. It had not only opened
its doors to the Southern writers, but it had gone to them and invited
them in. . . . *Scribners* in providing Southern writers with an approved
and profitable Northern vehicle created a new *national* attitude in both
North and South and so shaped a literature it had gone far toward
creating."

As a by-result of this series, *Scribner's* became the publishers of
Lanier, Cable, Harris, Fox and a still continuing list of Southern authors, as Freeman, among numerous others, testifies. These illustrations,
a first-hand view of a vanished South, are of very considerable historical
value, aside from their artistic qualities.

These invoked no interest whatsoever from anyone. To me they were,
and are, fascinating—to the extent that I purchased them for the Lilly
Library when I became its librarian.

Another collection of letters related to the genesis of the *Monitor*. In
today's frantic rush to reach the moon or dig ten miles down beneath our
own crust, we are apt to forget epic achievements of other decades. Smith
is a common name, as Holmes declared in his famous poem. Who knows,
today, the name of Commander Joseph Smith, U.S.N.? Ask any Civil
War buff at any Round Table and you will get, perhaps, one in a
hundred who will know that he was given "one hundred days—and they
short ones" to save the Union. He entered the Navy in 1809 at the age of
nineteen and served in the battles at Lake Champlain in 1812, where his
heroism was so conspicuous that he was voted a silver medal by Congress.
Years later he served on the frigate *Constellation* in the Algerian affair.
He later became chief of the Bureau of Navy Yards and Docks, full of
honors and due for retirement.

Suddenly the Civil War began and the South set afloat the ironclad *Merrimac*. Lincoln, on August 8, 1861, authorized Smith to examine plans for an ironclad vessel for the North. In defiance of his own board, naval tradition and other expert naval opinion, he chose the plan submitted by John Ericsson for the *Monitor*. I had much of the correspondence relating to its building: "a hundred days—they short ones, are few enough to do all that has to be done," he wrote. The *Monitor*'s subsequent duel with the *Merrimac* went far to save the North, created the profoundest sensation in the court of every maritime nation and was the greatest development in naval history up to its time. Ironically, one of Smith's sons commanded the *Congress* when she was attacked by the *Merrimac* in March, 1862, and was killed in the battle.

The price of the collection was $650.

Another item of prime American importance was the originals of General Ross's maps detailing the march of the British Army from August 19–29, 1814, which period included the Battle of Bladensburg, the burning of Washington and the composition of "The Star-Spangled Banner."

These maps were done explicitly for the Duke of Wellington, who was in supreme command of all British forces at that time, and from a descendant of whom Scribner's purchased them. I remember them as among the most exciting Americana I ever had. These were catalogued as comprising:

(a) A carefully drawn and tinted plan, on a scale of just over two miles to the inch, of the advance of General Ross' army on Washington and its return after the Battle of Bladensburg, and the burning of the public buildings of Washington. On the same sheet is a set of five plans (scale three inches to one mile) of the positions of the army on various dates during this operation.

(b) A very detailed sketch of the Battle of Bladensburg, August 24th, 1814 (on the scale of four inches to one mile), showing the various dispositions of the British forces, the American loss of three successive defense lines and subsequent retreat towards Washington, etc. These excellent military maps (none of which have ever been seen by any historian) were executed by Lieut. Robert Smith of the British 44th Regiment.

(c) The well-known Ellicott map of Washington with the burned buildings delineated (suitably enough) in red, with a manuscript note, probably by General Ross, to this effect, in the margin. These included: the Capitol (and Library); the President's House; Dockyard; Rope Walk; Arsenal; Green Leaf Point, all bridges, etc.

A superb American historical collection. The story of Bladensburg and its aftermath need only the briefest recapitulation. In August, 1814, a British fleet sailed into the Chesapeake and landed an army under the command of General Ross, one of Wellington's most trusted and distinguished commanders (he had just been awarded a gold medal for his gallantry in the bloody Battle of Vittoria, where he had two horses shot from under him). He marched on Washington and put to torch the public buildings, destroying among others, the President's House and the Library of Congress (the latter an irreplaceable loss) and such naval stores as could be reached. The curious, whose memory of the War of 1812 has dimmed since high school days, could profitably read Neil Swanson's stirring account of these perilous times in his recent excellent novel, *The Perilous Flight*.

After burning Washington the British, at North Point, east of Baltimore, again defeated the Americans, though General Ross was killed (the British had bad luck with their commanding generals, Packenham being killed a few months later at New Orleans). But, while the battle at North Point was going on, the British fleet was bombarding Fort M'Henry, whose defense inspired a young lawyer to write "The Star-Spangled Banner."

It is not common knowledge, incidentally, that the line in our national anthem, "the rockets' red glare," meant just that. The British did use rockets as artillery, and the positions of the "Rocket Brigades" are clearly marked upon the map Lieut. Smith did for General Ross. Because of their erratic action (they blew up friends and foes indiscriminately) rockets went out of fashion, in warfare, until our generation.

The Collection: $7,500

Neither of these items ended where they obviously belonged: in the Naval Academy, Library of Congress, National Archives or some similar institution. And why not? Simply because we have never supported these admirable institutions financially. Nobody in Congress seems to give a damn (or ever has) about preserving our national heritage so far as historical records, printed or otherwise, go. There are some signs of a change in attitude about all this, but I retain grave doubts that anything intelligent is going to be done about it. All that ever has been done is government harassment of private individuals or institutions who have searched for, bought, treasured, described, loved and taken care of material which else would long since have disappeared.

John Carter and my predecessor at Scribner's, John Champion, shared one enthusiasm—music. Scribner's had issued several successful catalogues in the specialized field of the printed first editions of classical music, a completely new and unexplored field of collecting in America. I was appreciative but completely unknowledgeable about it all: my musical background was limited to the mandolin, Gilbert and Sullivan, Cole Porter, etc. In fact, I'm strictly a lyric lad: if there are no words, I'm lost.

This did not prevent me from recognizing that when first printings of *Erlkönig*, or the "Moonlight" or "Kreutzer" sonatas and scores of others could be had for a tenth of what comparable literature was bringing, they were bargains indeed.

Music had been collected on the Continent for a long time, but rarely as first editions. What was sought was the costly collected editions of the great masters: Bach, Handel, Mozart, etc. Early music—its incunabula, so to speak—the works of Genson, Gafeerius and Luys Milan, were eagerly sought for, but not eighteenth- and nineteenth-century material. Here the interest was confined almost wholly to manuscripts, those of Beethoven, Haydn or Schubert, for example; I decided to stay away from this as much as possible unless guaranteed an impeccable provenance, particularly because forgery in this field had been rampant for years.

Now the whole idea of equating the collecting of printed masterpieces of music, well-known songs and the like, with their literary peers, first occurred to Percy Muir in the early thirties, as he relates in *Minding My Own Business* (London, 1956). As his Elkin Mathews book business was at a really low tide at this time, Muir approached Carter with his idea. He heartily approved and Scribner's financed Muir on a trip to Germany to scout out possibilities.

It was all extremely successful, but it is Muir's and Carter's story, not mine. Carter did the buying and cataloguing, a tricky business because the bibliographies then available were not plentiful or invariably accurate, and because music published from lithograph plates presents different problems from printed books.

Most of our sales were to institutions at first, but gradually the idea caught on with individual collectors, especially the late Mrs. George A. Martin of Cleveland, Charles J. Rosenbloom of Pittsburgh, and a few others. Carl Haverlin, then president of Broadcast Music, Inc., was entirely responsible for its very fine collection.

We always had, I remember, fine Richard Wagners, for whom I have an admiration based, I suppose, on my early Arthurian interests. In one catalogue alone there is listed *Lohengrin* (Leipzig, 1851), piano and vocal score, a presentation copy, $225; the full score of *Parsifal* (Mainz, 1883), one of fifty copies only, $385. A complete set of the full score of *Der Ring des Nibelungen* (Mainz, 1873–76) was priced $950 and had belonged to Camille Saint-Saëns, the famous French composer, at that. Probably the most interesting association copy of *Der Ring* was a first edition of the libretto (Leipzig, 1853), of which only about thirty copies were printed for private distribution among Wagner's friends. This one was given Schopenhauer with the composer's inscription: "In veneration and gratitude." Schopenhauer annotated it somewhat caustically and expressed his disapproval of the love scene between Siegmund and Sieglinde in *Die Walküre:* "One may *forget* morality but one must not slap it in the face." And at the end of the same scene beneath a stage direction reading, "With a cry she sinks on his breast—the curtain quickly falls," Schopenhauer observes: "and high time, too!" The Oesterlein catalogue remarks that this is the greatest rarity in the whole range of Wagner literature.

One particularly nice item was catalogued as:

*A Relic of High American Interest.* *$120*

This is the Baton with which Wagner himself conducted the first (private) performance in Europe of his *Grosse Festmarsch,* written to celebrate the centenary of the Declaration of Independence. This performance took place in the Festspielhaus at Bayreuth on July 2, 1876; the march having been previously played on May 10 at the World Exhibition at Philadelphia.

Wagner gave the baton to Herman Ritter, a member of the Festspielhaus orchestra, after the performance. Ritter gave it to Dr. A. Mays, of Heidelberg, in whose possession it remained until 1931, when it passed to his daughter.

The relic is authenticated by autograph signed notes of both Ritter and Mays, and a letter from the Curator of the Museum at Wagner's house, Wahnfried, Bayreuth, written to Frau Gaum-Mays in 1935.

Though concentrating largely on printed material, we did have one tremendous manuscript which had a romantic story behind it. This, certainly one of the greatest musical treasures to appear in my time, was the original of Wolfgang Amadeus Mozart's Haffner Symphony. It comprised thirty leaves and was contained in an elaborate velvet and silver case with King Ludwig II's arms. Muir has told the fascinating story of its acquisition, complete with tangled finances, smuggling (the manuscript went out one way, the case another) and complications worthy of Ian Fleming. It is a chilling story Muir has to tell, and worth remembering. Briefly, the owner of the manuscript was Max Pinette, "Pino" to his intimates, owner of the Lengfeld'sche Buchhandlung in Cologne, a specialist in music and close friend of Percy's. He had decided that the Nazis had come to stay for a long time and was liquidating his holdings in Germany as fast as he could, as any day a party official might arrive to tell him that his business had been passed to an "Aryan." If he could salvage twenty-five pfennigs of every mark, he would be doing tremendously well. Pinette and his wife eventually escaped to Brussels and then Paris, and Muir ends his account: "He had to flee southwards when Paris was occupied; but the Nazis caught up with him at last when they finally overran the south of France. He and his wife were brought back to Paris, en route presumably for some nameless and horrible fate in Germany or Poland. Perhaps mercifully, neither of them survived the journey."

The price of the manuscript was £2,400 (when the pound was $3.20); Scribner's purchased a half interest and it duly arrived in America. I recorded it in my *Fifty Books Manuscript Music Catalogue*, with the case as frontispiece and another full-page illustration, as follows:

> This is the original holograph manuscript, in Mozart's hand, of the full orchestral score of the Symphony in D major (the so-called Haffner Symphony), Köchel-Verzeichniss No. 385. The superscription is by Leopold Mozart, the father of Wolfgang. It reads:—Synfonia/di/Amadeo Wolfgango/Mozart a Viena nel mese di/Juglio 1782/.

> The Manuscript comprises thirty leaves, in the customary oblong folio, of which fifty-seven pages contain the manuscript. Each page has twelve music staves and is uncut except at the top edge. It is contained in a superb satin-lined, pale blue velvet case, with corners of beaten silver, on the upper side of which is the italic letter "L" (Ludwig II) and an emblem with the Bavarian arms in silver.

> The Haffner symphony is the first of the seven composed in Vienna by Mozart. It was written at the end of July and the beginning of August, 1782, shortly after the first performance of *Die Entführung aus dem Serail*. Its origin is due to the wish of his father, Leopold, to grace the festivities in the house of the Salzburg merchant and Burgomeister, Sigmund Haffner (for whom Wolfgang had already, in 1776, written the exquisite *Haffner Serenade*) with an orchestral piece by his son. According to his letter to his father, Mozart, already deeply engaged in other work, undertook to carry out the proposal in the greatest haste, sending each movement separately to his father as it was completed.

> The manuscript was one of those bequeathed to Mozart's widow, Konstanze. It was acquired from her in 1800 by Johann André, inherited in 1841 by his son Julius, from whom King Ludwig II of Bavaria, the patron of Wagner, acquired it. He accounted it the most precious of his musical possessions.                         $20,000.

There were no takers and only one serious inquiry. This was from Charles J. Rosenbloom of Pittsburgh, to whom I had been selling a few books (*A Communist Manifesto*, London, 1848, in original wrappers, for $750, among others), and a lot of music. His main interest, however, was etchings, which he was buying from Charles Sessler of Philadelphia. I took Mozart to Pittsburgh.

After a pleasant dinner, during which my host, who is very knowledgeable musically, expounded at length on nineteenth-century music, he suddenly exclaimed, "I want Haffner badly but I can't give you a decision until eleven o'clock. I have to wait for a phone call." It came in due course. He answered and after a brief conversation hung up, turned to me and said, "Sorry, I can't take the Haffner. I've just become the owner of the Read first folio at twenty-eight thousand dollars, and I can't afford both."

Years later I told this story to Dick Sessler, who then briefed me on the background. The elder Sessler had recently died, and there was gossip that the firm would go out of the book business, Dick's primary interest being prints. He said, "I told Mabel [Zahn, long-time Sessler's right arm, and now the whole body] that the only way to put a stop to this talk was by buying the most expensive book that next came up at auction, regardless of what it was and regardless of what it cost."

It just happened to have been the William A. Read copy of the first folio, sold January 9, 1936, and he bought it, in the Philadelphia tradition, with someone else's money. It's a nice book, to be sure, and today would bring several times what Rosenbloom paid for it. But the bidding for the Haffner, were it to come on the market, would probably *open* at five times my asking price, and I venture no prophecy where it would close.

So it stayed in stock for a number of years despite some attempts to sell it. Marcia Davenport, whose famed biography of Mozart, Scribner's had published, was entranced by it and brought Toscanini around to see it; he was also entranced, though not to the point of purchase. He did intimate, however, that he would accept it as a gift. This led to its being put on display at Radio City during a Toscanini-conducted NBC broadcast of the Haffner, complete with Pinkerton guards and the whole bit. All the brass, in white tie and tails, looked at it, and, just perhaps, one or two may have appreciated what they were seeing. But no sale.

Eventually a mysterious person whose name I cannot recall announced he wished to purchase it and that he was acting for an anonymous, but solvent, buyer. Things went well until one tiny grain of sand got into the gears. The learned musicologist Dr. Georg Kinsky, Muir's great friend, had made a description of it, which accompanied the manuscript. Only, it wasn't signed!

Percy Muir's account follows:

> John [Carter] went into the Ministry of Information—a misnomer if ever there was one, for his job was to censor news. In between times he was able to fit in an occasional visit to his office at Scribner's; and I would sometimes come up from the country to lunch with him.
>
> It was over the lunch table that he told me that the Mozart was as

good as sold—and for \$20,000 withal, and the £ sterling worth \$3.20.
All that was needed to complete the deal was the original of Dr. Kinsky's
description of it. This I protested that I had already handed over; but
John said that all they had was a rather badly typewritten copy. This,
I pointed out, was the original that Kinsky had typed before my eyes
in the Lengfeld'sche at Cologne, signed on the typewriter. An exchange
of messages across the Atlantic showed that the purchaser was adamant
—no document signed by Kinsky, no sale!

This was really carrying the fetish of a signature to absurdity; and
I cursed myself for having (a) accepted and (b) passed on Kinsky's
entirely superfluous authentication. At the head of the first page
of the manuscript the composer's father had written: Syn-
fonia/di/Amadeo Wolfgango/Mozart a Viena nel mese di/Juglio
1782/, beneath which G. N. von Nissen, who married Mozart's widow,
had added "und seine Handschrift." It was known to have been among
the manuscripts acquired in 1800 from the widow by Johann André,
the music publisher in Offenbach, who published it; and the satin
lining of its royal case recited its acquisition by King Ludwig from
Johann's son Julius. Any competent musicologist could have checked
these facts, and have verified the various handwritings, not least the
unmistakable music script of Mozart himself. It was all of no avail.
Unless we could produce Kinsky's signed attestation, the sale was off.

It was as though the manuscript of one of Shakespeare's plays could
have survived, the manuscript from which it was known to have been
first printed, the history of which could be traced at every point from
the moment of its completion; and then someone should say that all this
counted for nothing without A. W. Pollard's opinion that it was indeed
by Shakespeare.

It was a tantalizing, infuriating situation, with Kinsky completely
inaccessible at Bonn. The instigation to forgery was almost irresistible,
and if I had had an original of Kinsky's signature I might have been
tempted. But it was not very long before I hit upon another possible
solution. Pino was in Brussels; and Belgium was not at war with
Germany. I sent him a copy of the Kinsky text and asked him to do all
he could to get it signed. Within two weeks the signed document was
in my hands; and the sale went through.

I had not done what I should have, which was to tell the purchaser to
go buy a Mozart symphony somewhere else. I wish I had. Or, Scribner's
should have purchased Muir's interest and awaited a proper buyer.

In any event the whole Haffner saga ended with an episode which I
recall with distaste. One afternoon after the transaction had been completed a true Brunhilde type came in the store and asked to see the
manuscript. I explained that we no longer owned it and she then asked
where it could be seen. I said truthfully that I had no idea and was sorry I
couldn't be of more help. She turned on me in a sudden fury, screamed in

German, "You've sold it to some Jewish swindler. You American swine don't deserve such a treasure," spat full in my face and stalked out.

Though uninterested, sometimes to the point of boredom, in classical music, I was entranced by the possibility of selling first editions of American songs. Eli Lilly, J.K.'s father, had become interested in Stephen Foster and was forming his incomparable collection, which eventually was given to Pittsburgh.

He did this partially with the help of a remarkable man, Joseph Muller, whom I met at Harzof's. He was world-traveled, having been for years major-domo on J. P. Morgan's yacht, *The Corsair*. He had compiled a fascinating bibliography, which Harzof issued in 1935, of *The Star Spangled Banner, Words and Music Issued between 1814–1864*. (Note that "Star Spangled" is often printed thus, and not hyphenated as it is in the original manuscript.)

First-edition material of Francis Scott Key was of some interest at that time, and I supplied Mr. Lilly with all printed versions of "The Star-Spangled Banner." But aside from Key and Stephen Foster, there was no general interest in American music, except for a very few institutions and specialized collectors, and they wanted, usually, early eighteenth-century material. I saw a chance to parallel in America in popular music what Carter and Muir had done in classical works.

Joe Muller had an enormous collection of such material, and he allowed me to make a selection of his duplicates, which I eventually issued in an early Scribner catalogue as *First Editions of Famous American Songs*, with a Preface:

> The present catalogue is, we believe, the first extensive catalogue of American Songs which has been issued, and was prompted by the enthusiastic response to our previous catalogues of music issued in 1933 and 1935.
>
> There has been, to date, too little collecting of American Songs, though their importance and appeal are obvious. The greatest drawback to such collecting has been, no doubt, the scantiness of bibliographical knowledge available about the various publishers and the difficulty of determining points of issue. The research instituted, however, by Mr. J. K. Lilly of Indianapolis, in forming his famous Stephen Foster collect-tion, has resulted in great advances in American musical bibliographical technique, and thrown much light on publishers' methods.
>
> The items in the present catalogue have been carefully checked against all available records, including those of the Library of Congress, and we have every confidence in the accuracy of the descriptions attached. Especial thanks are due Mr. Joseph Muller, of the Music Department of the New York Public Library, and author of the recent

*Bibliography of Francis Scott Key's "The Star Spangled Banner,"* for his advice and assistance in various bibliographical problems.

I look back on the catalogue with nostalgia. Included were: "Tenting on the Old Camp Ground" (Boston, 1864), with an autograph transcript, $20. "Silver Threads Among the Gold" (New York, 1873), "Words by Eben E. Rexford. Music by H. P. Danks," was daringly priced at $75. But in justification I may add that it was accompanied by a three-page folio transcript of the poem by Rexford, on the last page of which he wrote:

> The above is a copy of the song as it first appeared, when issued by C. W. Harris, owner of the copyright. Since then, singers have abridged it somewhat. Mr. Danks died some years ago in Philadelphia, poor, and alone. He had long been estranged from his family and I have never been able to get into communication with any of his relatives, or any one who knew much about the man.

"The Wearing of the Green" was first published in Philadelphia in 1865, "As Sung by J. E. McDonough in E. H. House and Dion Boucicault's celebrated Irish Drama Arrah Na Pogue." This wonderful street song, the melody dating back to the days of the French Revolution, was an instant hit when produced in America. It was suppressed when the play was produced in England.

But consider Epis Sargent's "A Life on the Ocean Wave" (New York, 1838), $10. This became so very popular in England that in 1889 it was made the official march of the Royal Marines. At least this is an easier tune than that of "To Anacreon in Heaven," so the British got the better of that exchange.

There were "Civil War Songs, Northern." George Root's "The Battle-Cry of Freedom" (Chicago, 1861), priced $7.50, the rallying song of the North, was written on Lincoln's second call for troops. It is reputed to have become famous when, during the Battle of the Wilderness in May, 1864, a brigade of the Ninth Corps broke the enemy's lines by assault, became exposed to flank attack and were almost routed. A soldier in the Forty-Fifth Pennsylvania rallied the lines with this song.

The catalogue included "Southern Civil War Songs" (they clearly outclassed the North), "Minstrel Songs," broken down into "Bryant's Minstrels," "Campbell's," "Christy's," "Congo's," "New Orleans," etc., and others.

My experiment in attempting to popularize American music collecting was a complete and abysmal flop. The majority of the items were priced under $10, and even if all had been sold, which certainly didn't happen, the net profit would scarcely have justified the expense of the catalogue plus a Fifth Avenue rent. My experience in this paralleled Percy's attempt to popularize English songs. There was nothing wrong with either of our ideas. The main trouble was that the timing was wrong and the prices too cheap.

The collecting of American music, the interest of a small group of enthusiasts, has only begun its upward climb and will never, I believe, equal the dizzying climb of science. I don't personally really care, as I have secured for my library one of the most substantial collections extant, formed by a knowledgeable collector and guided to Lilly by Dick Wolfe, a former associate. This includes historical pieces, pop and folk music, jazz, rock-'n'-roll, country music and musical comedy. The lithograph covers alone are exciting viewing, and there are about 100,000 of them.

Three very substantial and very good books in their own ways have been published in the past few years: David Ewen's *American Popular Songs: From the Revolutionary War to the Present* (New York, 1966); J. J. Fuld's *Book of World-Famous Music, Classical, Popular and Folk* (New York, 1966); and Lester S. Levy's *Grace Notes in American History. Popular Sheet Music from 1820 to 1900* (University of Oklahoma Press, 1967). These will certainly stimulate interest in a field in which I modestly claim a bit of pioneering.

At the same time they were experimenting with music, the Carter-Muir axis was becoming deeply involved in another project: the development of an interest among collectors of literature in the classics of medicine and science. I had much more fun with this than I had with classical music, mainly, I suppose, because I knew more about it.

Medical and scientific books had always been collected by specialists, mostly doctors and notably Sir William Osler. As guides there were the massive *Bibliotheca Osleriana*, Garrison and Morton's *Medical Bibliography*, Sotheran's famous series of catalogues, *Bibliotheca Chemico-Mathematica*, and others.

Our ideas went beyond these specialized lists, however. We wanted to make scientific works as popular among collectors as was literary material. So we issued what I think was the first catalogue of its kind done in America: *Science and Thought in the 19th Century* (1938). The catalogue's half-title bore the quotation from Benjamin Rush's *On the Diseases of the Mind* (Philadelphia, 1812): "The frequent and rapid transition of the mind from one subject to another. It is said booksellers have sometimes become deranged from this cause." The Introduction to the catalogue was by Carter, who had assembled and annotated most of its contents.

Of recent years, discriminating collectors have turned their attention increasingly to the first editions of those books which have in one way or another influenced the progress of science or the development of thought and human behavior. And what more natural and proper? The names of Volta and Ampère, of Faraday and Kelvin, commemorate by their everyday use the services of their owners to civilization. Darwin and Freud have added adjectives to the language. And Karl Marx is more powerful today than when *Das Kapital* was first published.

The incurious and the hasty do not stop to ask why a *volt* is so called. The thoughtful man wonders, and finds out. The book collector goes further: he searches for the first appearance of Volta's epoch-making paper, from which every electric battery in the world today derives, and he treasures it for what it is—a cardinal document in the history of Progress.

Many of the great names, the historic books, in the history of science and thought are indeed sufficiently familiar. Any schoolboy will connect the atomic theory with the name of Dalton, the theory of the conservation of energy with that of Helmholtz; antiseptic surgery with Lister, Positivism with Comte, X-Rays with Röntgen, short-hand with Pitman, finger prints with Galton, or Zarathustra with Nietzsche. But there are many less obvious, though equally important landmarks; and others besides schoolboys might well be puzzled to say when was the first recorded case of appendicitis, what is the origin of the square root of minus one or the coefficient of friction, or who first distinguished proteins. Why is *Plimsoll's Line* so called? Who inaugurated modern methods of contraception? Who discovered Neanderthal Man, or the infra-red rays of the spectrum? Who coined such words as *fluorescence* and *electron?* Who was responsible for the modern system of food-canning, or the higher criticism, or the ticker-tape, or colloidal chemistry?

No one who has not dabbled in this kind of collecting can have any idea of the fascination of the search for facts and achievements, and their printed origins; the tracking down of a pregnant idea or train of philosophic thought to the mind that first conceived it. Hilaire Belloc once said of a favorite work that it was "a book like a decisive battle"; but this phrase, a fine hyperbole when used of a piece of pure literature, might be applied with absolute literalness to dozens of books listed in the following pages.

We have endeavored to assemble here a representative selection of books and pamphlets illustrating the progress of science and thought in the nineteenth century. There are certain gaps, where some clew to the crucial book has eluded our researches, or where some desired item has proved unobtainable; but we believe that everything offered is significant in its field, whether by its direct relation to the world today or its influence upon the thought of its own and subsequent generations. This material is of a character, we believe, to attract the collector of vision, and to command the attention of those libraries and institutions which take the history of science and of thought for their province.

Such catalogues on such subjects are commonplace now, but not at Scribner prices—firsts of Freud's *Die Traumdeutung* (Leipzig and Vienna, 1900), $45; Turgenev's *Un Dernier Mot sur l'Emancipation des Serfs en Russie* (Paris, 1860), a presentation from the author, $25; Bowditch's *New American Practical Navigator* (Newburyport, Mass., 1802), $50; an original print of the first x-ray ever made, with related material, $27.50; Thompson's first announcement of Dalton's atomic theory (Edinburgh, 1807), $25; Gray's *Anatomy, Descriptive and Surgical* (London, 1858), $12 (the latest copy I have seen catalogued was £140); Koch's *Die Aetiologie der Tuberculose* (Berlin, 1882), $14; and Klebs's *Verhandlungen des Congresses* (Wiesbaden, 1883), first reporting the diphtheria bacillus, $8. One of the few expensive books in the catalogue was listed thus:

> Nietzsche, Friedrich. *Also Sprach Zarathustra.* Chemnitz: Schmeitzner, 1883–84; and Leipzig, Naumann, 1891, $185.
>
> 8vo, the four parts in one volume, all first editions, modern half cloth, gilt. Portrait to part 4. A clean copy. Very rare.
> The first three parts of Nietzsche's celebrated work, when found in first edition at all, are almost always of the second issue. Naumann, the publisher of part 4, took over the remainder of Schmeitzner's stock and furnished cancel titles of his own, dated 1891.

None of my American customers cared enough to buy it (Lilly turned it down because it was rebound). Martin Bodmer cabled for it from Switzerland. In thirty-five years I have never heard of another copy's being offered for sale.

There were a few dealers in America who were beginning to deal in such material at this time. Henry Schuman in Detroit was specializing in medicine, and Jake Zeitlin in Los Angeles was beginning to toy with science, and that was about it. And there were not many more collectors. Robert Honeyman was well on his way to his amazing collection, and Drs. Laurence Reynold of Detroit and W. W. Boyd of Washington, D.C., were beginning to be interested, as were David Wheatland of Cambridge, Massachusetts, Ian Fleming of London and a few others. The notable collections of Harrison Horblit and Bern Dibner were not even in their formative stages. In 1964 Horblit published *One Hundred Books Famous in Science* (New York, The Grolier Club), and in April, 1964, at Norwalk, Connecticut, the Burndy Library, "Founded to serve scholarship in the history of science and technology," was dedicated.

My early struggles to learn something about scientific books, their comparative rarities, values and so on, were immensely aided by that great scientist, scholar and book collector: the engaging, delightful, irritating and wholly knowledgeable Dr. Herbert M. Evans of Berkeley, California.

He had just, in 1934, put on at the University of California a pioneer show, an *Exhibition of First Editions of Epochal Achievements in the History of Science*. The final paragraph to his brief Introduction reads:

> The collection of first editions, one of the chief cults of bibliomania, is perhaps more justifiable in the realm of scientific "first" than in any other territory invaded by the hobby. The precise form of an achievement in *belles lettres* is of course the very reason for its being, and it is preserved in the abundant reprints by means of which man reverentially multiplies these ministers to his spirit. Now as Sarton has well said, knowledge, as opposed to beauty, is cumulative and progressive. Reprints of scientific works, as originally enunciated, are rare. Yet it is only by consulting the first form of a scientific achievement that one can hope to observe the origin and change of ideas. But, more than this, it may be maintained that one cannot adequately understand any scientific subject without knowledge of the manner in which our present conceptions were established. Enriques has said: "Si la signification même d'une théorie consiste dans les liens qui la rattachent au développement des théories qui la précèdent et de celles qui en vont sortir, on ne comprendra vraiment la science, en une acception élevée, que par son évolution historique."

This little pamphlet, costing thirty cents, was my Bible for a long time. Of the hundred and fourteen works it listed—in Mathematics, Astronomy, Physics, Chemistry, Geology, Botany and Zoology (Medicine, Applied Science and Invention were not included)—I was eventually to handle at least one copy (and sometimes many) of all but one. This was item thirteen, usually my lucky number:

> 13. Bólyai, János, 1802–1860.
>      . . . Scientiam spatii absolute veram exhibens: a veritate aut falsitate axiomatis XI Euclidei (a priori haud unquam decidenda) independentem; adjecta ad casum falsitatis, quadratura circuli geometrica. . . . [Maros Vásárhelyini, J. et S. Kali, 1832]     *
>      2 prelim. 1., [3]–26, [2] p.   23 diagrs. on 1 fold. pl.      23½ cm.
>      "Appendix" to: Bólyai, Farkas. *Tentamen juventutem studiosam in elementa matheseos purae.*  1832–33.   vol. 1.
>
> This famous appendix created non-Euclidean geometry, which was independently achieved by Lobachevski. Halsted [its English translator] speaks of it as "the most extraordinary two dozen pages in the history of thought."

I never had a chance, either, to obtain Lobachevski's famous work (Kazan, 1829–30), but aside from such *introuvables* I have had at one time or another most of the key books of science. Though the great books were not then as available and as cheap as they had been a generation before, still they had not anywhere reached their present rarity, popularity and price.

I find in the early twenties, to give just two examples, fine copies, offered by reputable dealers, of Sir Isaac Newton's *Philosophiae Naturalis Principia Mathematica* (London, 1687), for £18 18s, and Nicolaus Copernicus's *De Revolutionibus Orbium Coelestium* (Nuremberg, 1543), for £21. When the Lilly Library disposed of their duplicates of these books at auction at the Parke-Bernet Galleries in the fall of 1962, they brought $5,500 and $11,000, respectively, and have now advanced from those plateaus.

As an example of what could be done at that time, consider the collection then being formed at the Buffalo Museum of Science, Humboldt Park, Buffalo, New York. The director in the thirties was a remarkable man, Chauncey J. Hamlin, who decided to add rare books to his museum's holdings and went after them in a decidedly original way. When a Copernicus became available and funds were not, he organized a dance of Buffalo's Polish population, appealed to their pride and passed the hat. He got his book, as he did many others by similar methods. He put on an exhibition of "Milestones of Science" in 1938 and issued a small catalogue listing over one hundred and fifty books, including a great number of rarities, all collected (many from Scribner's) in less than five years and with a very restricted budget.

But the most important result of our catalogue was that it sparked J. K. Lilly's imagination. In all his vast collecting career he had been, above all, a "collector of vision." Fascination with books which had influenced thought and the mind of man grew upon him as his interest in literature lessened and the history of science became the last of his book collecting ventures.

# Modern Manuscripts

ALL THROUGH my bookselling career I was always interested in authors' manuscripts and managed to handle quite a few of them. For some reason it was not a field which attracted the individual collector as much as first editions, and on the whole it still doesn't. Of course, collectors would buy individual manuscripts of authors in whom they were particularly interested, but no one set out to do this on a comprehensive scale except Ed Hanley, and, in a minor way, Crosby Gaige. Nor was much attention then paid to publishers' records and suchlike material by collectors or librarians.

I attended a conference sponsored by the University of Texas, in 1956, on "Materials for Research in American Culture." I pointed out publishers' records as an important neglected source of such material, as were those of authors' agents, etc. This is no longer true (especially at Texas), and all I can say is someone down there must have been listening.

Among other headaches I handed Charles Scribner was *l'affaire Peter Pan*. I had just begun working for Scribner's when I was offered the manuscript of the play's original version, so original, in fact, that it hadn't even a title. It was simply headed *Anon. A Play*, and in this form it never yet has been published. It had a romantic association because it was owned by Maude Adams, no less, having been given to her by Sir James Barrie.

This, of course, simply could not be passed up at practically any price—I happened to be asked $7,500 for it. I fell in love with it on sight and purchased it on the spot.

The whole transaction was over before Bert Cross, Scribner's treasurer, became aware of it. Then he felt the firm had been double-crossed and something should be done about it. It seems that years before we had given Miss Adams the exact sum of $7,500 as advance royalties against her

*Memoirs*, which were first to be published serially in the magazine and later as a book. And not a smidgen had that shy one ever delivered.

Just at this time I was about to issue a catalogue devoted to modern manuscripts and included this item. Its description read:

> The manuscript comprises 84 leaves, 8vo, written on the recto only, in the author's minute handwriting. It is entirely in the author's autograph, and is enclosed in a full blue morocco case. The first leaf bears the date Nov. 1903, and the last leaf the date March 1, 1904. On the upper left hand corner of the first leaf is the inscription:
>
> "To Maude Adams this, the MS of *Peter Pan*, from her humble servant and affectionate friend, J. M. Barrie."
>
> The manuscript is titled "Anon. A Play," Barrie apparently not having decided upon a title when he started writing it. It contains *a third more material*, thousands of deletions and corrections, and several startling variations from the published text, which was not issued until 1928. A full transcription accompanies the manuscript.
>
> In the preface to the published text of the play, Sir James wrote, "This brings us back to my uncomfortable admission that I have no recollection of writing the play of *Peter Pan*, now being published for the first time so long after he made his bow upon the stage. . . . It does seem almost suspicious, especially as I have not the original MS of *Peter Pan* (except a few stray pages) with which to support my claim. . . . I know not whether I lost that original MS or destroyed it, or happily gave it away."
>
> *Peter Pan* is of the immortals. It is difficult to imagine a modern manuscript of greater appeal than this: and its provenance makes perfection more perfect, for Miss Maude Adams created the part of Peter Pan in America and her name will always be associated with it. $15,000

Thinking that Barrie would be pleased to know of its recovery, I wrote him a full account. I should have known better. He was interested all right, but not in the way I had anticipated. Back came a cable: DELAY BECAUSE UNWELL. GREATLY INTERESTED ABOUT DISCOVERY OF LONG LOST MANUSCRIPT. STOP. THOUGHT I MIGHT HAVE GIVEN ADAMS BUT UNCERTAIN. STOP. WANT TO BUY IT BACK FROM YOU. STOP. KINDLY CABLE SUGGESTING TERMS. STOP. BEST REGARDS. BARRIE.

By 1928, when Barrie was ready to publish the text of the play for the first time, he was, as he says, unable to remember what he had done with the manuscript and wrote Dion Boucicault (the son of the famous playwright), the first American producer of the play in 1905, about it. He knew nothing either. At this point Barrie prepared another manuscript, the last leaf of which is dated July, 1928. This is in the fine Barrie collection formed by Walter Beinecke, Jr., now at the family-named library at

Yale. I supplied him with all of Scribner's correspondence with Barrie, which was extensive.

A crisis impended with the arrival of the cablegram because I was in negotiations with Lilly about it, and collectors, like children, resent being tempted with something only to have it snatched away. Charles Scribner felt we were obligated to offer it to Barrie at $10,000, which we did and which he then, fortunately, turned down. Lilly got it after all. He was, at this time, financially supporting a Library of Congress project to do a bibliography of American juveniles, which came to naught. The rare book librarian there was then one V. Valta Parma. He was a small person, given to wearing high heels, and it was just after the purchase of *Peter Pan* that he visited Indianapolis for the first time to discuss the juvenile problem.

They lunched at Lilly's club, and the next day Lilly was presented with a document from his fellow members stating, in general terms, that it was all right with them if he purchased *Peter Pan*, but did he have to bring him to the club for lunch?

Parma (né Houghton) had changed his name by numerology and spent most of his time at this particular lunch describing to Mr. Lilly certain Indian medicinal recipes which would make his firm's fortune if he could only market them. I once had dinner with V. Valta in his Washington apartment, and a distinctive feature was that individual tables were set up in corners, facing the wall. The theory was, I gathered, that conversation facing a blank wall was more stimulating than face to face. Less distraction.

Charles Scribner and Maxwell Perkins let me down only once. One of the best catalogues I issued from Scribner's was *Literary Manuscripts and Autograph Letters of Eminent Authors*. This had some high-powered stuff. Among the important manuscripts was that of Barrie's *Mary Rose*, here in a first draft entitled *Poor Barbara Lucy Joan*, with an interesting note by Barrie explaining why it was written with his left hand (he had developed "writer's cramp"), $2,250; also the original manuscript of the earliest known version of "Auld Lang Syne" (now in the Lilly Library), $7,500; a collection of Dickens' letters to his publisher, Richard Bentley, $12,500; de la Mare's *Songs of Childhood*, $2,000; A. E. Housman manuscript material, $5,500; Irving's *The Sketch Book*, $35,000; seventeen letters of John Keats to B. R. Haydon, $35,000; the original autograph manuscript and drawings for *Old Mother Hubbard*, $5,000; and material of that ilk.

*Old Mother Hubbard* is not, as most people imagine, one of the Mother

Goose rhymes, or indeed of very great antiquity. It was written by Sarah Catherine Martin in 1804 when she was staying at the house of her brother-in-law, John Pollenfex Bastard, M.P. of Kitley, Devon. The character, if not the story, is believed to have been based on the housekeeper of the Bastard family. Very little is known of the author except that she was a young and very lovely girl, daughter of Sir Thomas Byam Martin, later admiral of the fleet, under whose orders young Prince William, afterward William IV, was serving. The young prince became enamored of her and wished to marry her. It was to break up this affair that she was sent to stay with her brother-in-law, and to this broken love affair we owe this juvenile classic.

I acquired it in the simplest way possible. After its early printing the manuscript disappeared and was recovered in the 1930's, among a number of old family pictures and drawings, by the author's great-grand niece, Miss May, of Stubbington, Hampshire. Shortly after the manuscript came to light it was exhibited by the Bodleian Library at Oxford; recognizing its tremendous sentimental appeal and historical interest, the Oxford University Press issued a collotype facsimile of it for general circulation, recounting these facts. Five minutes after I saw one an airmail letter was on its way to Miss May, asking if she might care to part with it, for a consideration. I was sure that the Bodleian already had the manuscript firmly in its clutches, but there was always a chance. Back came Miss May's air-mail reply; she would be delighted to part with it, nobody had ever asked her for it before.

Well, with material of this kind I wanted some interesting but less expensive things to bulk out the catalogue, and just at this time Paul Palmer got in touch with me. He had been for years connected with the *Reader's Digest,* and before that with H. L. Mencken's *American Mercury,* in various editorial capacities. He was retiring, he explained, moving West, and had a lot of miscellaneous literary things to dispose of. Did I want them? After I saw them, I certainly did. There was nothing spectacular in a monetary way, but there were the kinds of things I liked: early manuscripts of stories by authors now becoming known, bits and pieces of this and that, some good letters and so on. Sometimes even the first appearance of an author in print, at least so far as I could find out.

Palmer explained to me that during his years of editorial chores he had made a habit of keeping things that otherwise, in normal business procedure, would have gone into the wastebasket. Not everything by any means, just stuff he personally liked. I took it all and put some into the catalogue.

These included the dramatic version of *The Green Hat* (New York, 1925), $17.50 (remember Katharine Cornell and Leslie Howard in the principal parts, and later Greta Garbo as Iris March?); Floyd Dell's *Love in Greenwich Village* (New York, 1926), including on eleven autograph pages the original manuscript of "The Ballad of Christopher Street," $125 (the highest priced of the Palmer lot); William Faulkner's "Hair," one of the first of his short stories to be published, in *Mercury*, May, 1931, $45; Scott Fitzgerald's "Crazy Sunday," in *Mercury*, October, 1932, $55, the story Edmund Wilson considered his finest achievement; Saroyan's "Aspirin is a Member of the N.R.A.," probably his earliest appearance in print, in *Mercury*, May, 1934—as a notation of the manuscript showed he had been paid $45 for it, that's what I priced it; fourteen of Jesse E. Stuart's earliest sonnets, in *Mercury*, October, 1933, which later appeared in his first book, *Man with a Bull-Tongue Plow*, $50. Many of these had various editorial emendations and so on in the autograph of H. L. Mencken.

And I also included, quite casually and only because it was his first story to appear in print, at least in a national magazine, James M. Cain's "The Baby Was in the Icebox," *Mercury*, January, 1933, $35. That did it! Cain got a copy of the catalogue from a Hollywood collector friend of mine who thought he would be pleased to see himself in fast company. I got an initial polite letter from him, destined to be the last polite one of several, asking how Scribner's had gotten hold of the manuscript. I answered truthfully and with equal politeness. The second time the postman rang, James really raised Cain. He informed me in no uncertain terms that he wanted it back and unless he got it—and anything else we had of his—he would sue, and that I and all other book dealers and publishers were literary scavengers. I paraphrase from memory as the original correspondence is not available and probably no longer exists.

I replied, in effect, nuts to you, and settled my brains for a long winter's fight. I hadn't had one for a while and things were very dull. I had the manuscript—luckily there was no embarrassment in having sold it to a customer—but I saw no reason that Cain should get it.

For one thing, if I gave in to him, what in the world would happen in principle to the rest of such things I had—and not only those from Palmer. Not only to me, but other dealers? My stand was that I had bought the manuscript in good faith from a person who hadn't stolen it but rescued it from certain destruction. Furthermore, Palmer had a perfect right to it as he was the editor of the publication to which it had been submitted, it had been duly published and paid for, and, anyhow, the magazine had changed hands and gone out of business long since. Also,

Scribner's could scarcely be charged with profiteering, as the marked price, $35, didn't even cover the cost of cataloguing—which was quite true. If Cain wanted to sue anyone, let it be Palmer. I was willing to return the manuscript to Palmer, to let him do just that. And who the hell did he think he was, anyway? An Irving or Keats? Their material was removed from his by three decimal points to the right, and he ought to be grateful to be seen in their company, let alone be in a manuscript catalogue at all.

Cain also took his stand on moral grounds. What he had sold to *Mercury* was merely, and only, the publication rights to a story. That was all they had paid for and were entitled to, legally, ethically or any other way. The physical manuscript and such value as it had was his in perpetuity. The fact that it had survived sheerly by accident made no matter. It was still his and he was entitled to whatever market value it commanded—$1 or $1,000. And the fact that if *Mercury* had rejected it, it wouldn't be worth ten cents, was also immaterial.

I began to like the guy. He had a point I didn't agree with but he was damn well willing to fight for it. I discussed the whole matter with several dealer friends, Dave Kirschenbaum among them, who had autographic interests, and opinions were divided. Lawyers were consulted, and here again there was no agreement. It seems that this exact case had no precedent. In fact, the whole matter of the legal ownership of literary manuscripts, if not stipulated in an original contract, was moot. Suppose a publisher got a manuscript, properly published it, didn't return it to the author—who never asked for it back anyway—and a few years later its author was offered a considerable fortune for it, only to find the publisher, considering it worthless, had destroyed it? Could he recover? Or what if the publisher had given it away as a souvenir (as has happened)? Or an editor rescued it for sentimental reasons and later lost it? There were all sorts of combinations and permutations.

I couldn't have been more pleased, and excitedly dumped the whole matter in Maxwell Perkins' and Scribner's laps. This was a real goodie, a chance to have a friendly lawsuit over an inconsequential item and get some ruling—no matter what—which would finally decide an important literary problem. Scribner's *vs.* MGM, whose lawyers, as I recall, Cain had summoned to his aid.

Incredibly, they turned down my invitation, politely but firmly. They wanted no part of lawsuits over such matters. For one thing, think of what might happen if we lost. The right of Scribner's, as publishers, defending the right of editors to sell authors' manuscripts might offend, and hordes of authors would come scrambling for their no longer existing manuscripts, or the assumed value thereof. It was letting the wolf loose on the fold.

When I pointed out to Charley that this was a good fight and that, win or lose, we would be entitled to at least a footnote in literary history, and reminded him of Random House's valiant battle over *Ulysses*, he remained unimpressed—to the point of reminding me that he was responsible for Scribner's literary reputation, in the long view, and that I could best serve the firm by, if not producing some profits, at least by staying out of expensive lawsuits over $35 manuscripts. Perkins agreed. Before this united front, unjust and unreasonable as it seemed to me, I had to surrender.

Cain won his point, to this extent: the Writers' Guild, or whatever organization he was putting up his fight for, got into their contracts a clause obliging the publisher to return to the authors their original manuscripts after publication. For which point he had started the fun in the first place. Legally, however, I am told the whole matter has never been cleared. I still wish we had our lawsuit. That would have been a real baby!

I was always fond of Max Beerbohm and carried as large a stock as I could. I have often thought *Zuleika Dobson* would make a wonderful movie—only who could play Zuleika?

I once had an exhibition of his books, original caricatures, etc., in the Scribner window which attracted some attention. A man named Smith, from his accent obviously a Southerner, came in one day and began to discuss Beerbohm, about whom he was exceedingly well informed. After some conversation it developed that he was not interested in purchasing anything but that he did have a considerable Beerbohm collection he could be persuaded to part with. "Such as?" I inquired. "Well, the most important, I suppose, is the original manuscript of *Zuleika Dobson*." He had told me he was from Atlanta, Georgia, and I simply could not imagine Oxford's *Zuleika* there. Surprises are common enough in this business, but I found this one hard to believe.

He went on to explain that his sister, the actress Florence Kahn of Tennessee, had been Beerbohm's first wife and that he had inherited her effects after her death. *Zuleika*, he assured me, was in Atlanta all right, safely wrapped up in waxed paper and stored in a breadbox to be safe from silverfish. *Zuleika* in a breadbox! Imagination boggles. Yet, there she was, and delivered to Scribner's thus. Not only was there the first draft in pencil with many sketches, some not relating to the text, but also the manuscript sent to the printer, heavily revised with canceled lines, wholly obliterated in India ink, in Beerbohm's infuriating manner. The manuscripts duly passed for about $3,500 to Bob Taylor, together with the breadbox.

I am a great admirer of Edgar Lee Masters' *Spoon River Anthology*. Scribner's had published many of his books, though not this. I once asked him about the manuscript and he replied that it simply didn't exist. Many of the poems had originally appeared in *Reedy's Mirror*, and the copy sent to the printer consisted mainly of clipped printed material. He would be glad, however, to copy the manuscript on good bond paper for $1,000. This he proceeded to do and, as I discovered later when trying to sell it, had done a number of other times.

One day Gabriel Wells appeared at Harzof's with a treasure, the original manuscript of Richard Brinsley Sheridan's *The School for Scandal*. This is probably the earliest important surviving manuscript of a famous English play. Sheridan's *The Rivals* was destroyed when the new Drury Lane Theatre, in which Sheridan had tied up all his capital, was burned in 1809. Harzof vetted the manuscript but advised Gabriel to go slowly as he felt it was probably entailed. This turned out to be so, and it is still somewhat of a mystery how it reached America from its home in Frampton Court.

In any event the Philadelphia collector Barton Currie, then editor of *The Saturday Evening Post*, purchased it for, newspapers had it, $75,000 —actually the sum was considerably less. He has recounted the whole story in his *Fishers of Books* (Boston, 1931). Years later, when I was selling many of Currie's books, including many Dickens presentations, Conrad manuscripts, etc., I wanted this, but it was one thing his wife particularly liked and she wouldn't let him part with it. Actually, he had given it to her along with other of his books. By the time I had about persuaded her to part with it, I left Scribner's, and the manuscript eventually wound up in Bob Taylor's collection, where I had planned it to go in the first place.

I was particularly interested in *The School for Scandal* because I had discovered that the *authentic* text had first been published in America. This I catalogued (and sold to Chauncey Brewster Tinker). The whole story is a complex one, as I recounted in my catalogue description of Scribner's copy—still, I think, one of only two known. It is now at Yale.

SHERIDAN (RICHARD BRINSLEY). *The School for Scandal*. A Comedy by Richard Brinsley Sheridan, Esq., performed with universal applause at the theatre in New York, from a manuscript copy in the possession of John Henry, Esq., joint manager of the American Company, given him by the author. New York: Printed by Hugh Gaine, at the Bible in Hanover Square, 1786. The first printing of the authentic text, full calf, antique.                                                                                          Sold

One of only two known copies, the other being in the Library of Congress; not listed in Paul Leicester Ford's *Hugh Gaine Bibliography*.

Of all the problems of theatrical bibliography, those of *The School for Scandal* are the prettiest. While Sheridan lived, numerous editions were published, none of them authorized, and all but one following the same corrupt and pirated text. The edition until recently regarded as the earliest was the undated Dublin edition, with the imprint, "J. Ewling." This has now been disproved (see R. Crompton Rhodes, *Plays and Poems of Richard Brinsley Sheridan*, New York: 1929, Volume II), and the true FIRST EDITION is recognized as being the one published in Dublin and dated 1780.

This, however, and all subsequent editions until 1799, were pirated from the same corrupt version; and they are very inaccurate. In 1799 an edition was issued in Dublin, printed from the prompt-book of the Theatre-Royal, which Sheridan had given his sister, and which she sold for £100, and this is called by Rhodes "the editio princeps of the authentic text" (*op. cit.* p. 161).

The present American edition, however, prints the authentic text eleven years before the Theatre-Royal prompt-book saw light, and is indisputably the earliest version of the authentic text.

There remains the problem of how the text could have been printed in America a decade before it appeared abroad. The answer lies in the printed title-page, where it is stated that the play is printed from "a manuscript copy in the possession of John Henry, Esq., joint manager of the American Company, given him by the Author."

John Henry (see *Dictionary of American Biography*, Vol. VIII, p. 548) was reputed to have been trained under Sheridan's father and he certainly played at Drury Lane while Sheridan, himself, was manager, and knew him then. So what more natural than, when coming to America, to get from Sheridan a manuscript of the famous London hit, to stage abroad.

That Henry knew the texts being circulated (including the Philadelphia, Bell, 1782, First American Edition, a reprint of the Dublin pirated edition), were incorrect, witness his advertisement on page 5:

"So many spurious copies of *The School for Scandal* having been obtruded on the Publick has induced the Editor to lay before them in its proper garb, this most excellent comedy presented to him by Richard Brinsley Sheridan, Esq., the justly admired Congreve of the present times."

Other manuscripts I recall with pleasure are Kipling's *Mandalay*, first published in book form in America two years before it appeared in England. I had this twice, priced $750, and the second purchaser was the wife of the famed tenor John Charles Thomas. She bought it as a Christmas present for him because it was a song he was continually singing in the shower.

Don Emmett's transcription of "Dixie," which I sold Lilly for $250, bears a note in Emmett's hand about its composition for Bryant's Minstrels in New York, in 1859. It differs somewhat from even the earliest printed versions, which do not reproduce the dialect correctly, and none I have ever seen prints the second or the fourth verse, which Emmett has carefully written out:

II
Will run away-Missus took a decline,
Her face was the color ob bacon-rhine;
When she libbed, she libbed in cloaber,
When she died, she died all oaber.

IV
In Dix-ie Lann de darkies grow,
If white foax only plant darr toe;
Day wet de groun wid bak-ka smoke,
Den up de darkies head will poke.

The song became famous when it was used on February 18, 1861, at the inauguration of Jefferson Davis as President of the Confederacy at Montgomery, Alabama, simply because it "had a pretty, catchy air." Theodore Roosevelt at one time campaigned for it as our national anthem. It was only in another Roosevelt's administration, Franklin D.'s, that "The Star-Spangled Banner" was officially so designated.

I have mentioned some manuscripts elsewhere in these records. Others I recall with pleasure include Lee's General Order No. 9, the surrender at Appomattox, April 10, 1865. This was catalogued as:

One sheet, quarto, written in faded ink in an unknown hand, but signed in full "R. E. Lee, Genl." $450

Hdqrs. Army of No. Va.
10th April, 1865.

General Order
No. 9
After four years of arduous service marked by unsurpassed courage and fortitude, the Army of Northern Virginia has been compelled to yield to overwhelming numbers and resources.

I need not tell the brave survivors of so many hard fought battles who have remained steadfast to the last that I have consented to this result from no distrust of them; but feeling that valour and devotion could accomplish nothing that would compensate for the loss that would attend the continuance of the contest, I determined to avoid the useless sacrifice of those whose past services have endeared them to their countrymen.

By the terms of the Agreement Officers and men can return to their homes and remain there until exchanged.

You will take with you the Satisfaction that proceeds from the Consciousness of duty faithfully performed, and I earnestly pray that a Merciful God will extend to you his blessing and protection.

With an unceasing admiration of your Constancy and devotion to your Country and a grateful remembrance of your kind and generous consideration for myself I bid you all an affectionate farewell.

R. E. Lee
Genl.

These were sent to commanders in the field. Surviving copies, signed by Lee, are very rare.

It ranks, to me, among American documents with the Gettysburg Address and is even shorter. I discovered this in, of all improbable places, a home in Rye, New York, hanging over a fireplace between crossed Northern and Confederate flags. Its appearance so deep in Yankee-land was explained to me by its owner, whose mother was the daughter of Lee's adjutant. During the war she fell in love with a Yankee, later married him and moved North, taking this precious document with her. I sold it to a lad who was not a collector of anything. When I asked why he was purchasing it he replied that he was constantly engaged in losing battles with his wife and was buying this to hang on his library wall to remind himself "how to surrender with dignity." He eventually lost not only the battles but the war, as, after his divorce, I repurchased it from him.

I particularly like Robert Burns, of whose works I have had quite a bit at one time or another. One day Mrs. Robert Woods Bliss of Dumbarton Oaks, Washington, D.C., phoned me to ask what I could suggest as a gift for the departing Ambassador from the Court of St. James. As he was a Scotsman, something by Burns would be suitable. I explained I did indeed have something, an unpublished version of "Green Grow the Rushes O." Only the catch was that the reason it was unpublished was that it was somewhat ribald "in the muse's manner"! "Send it along anyway," she said, "and let me be the judge of that."

It was untitled, headed merely "A Fragment," and was

written at the most critical point in Burns' life. After the verses are the words, "Multa desunt," the date—Sept. 3rd, and the sentence: "Armour has just now brought me a fine boy and girl at one throw—God bless them, poor little dears. R.B." This refers to the birth of his twin children by Jean Armour, afterwards his wife, and dates the letters as 1786, exactly at the time the Kilmarnock edition of his poems was being published.

It was, Mrs. Bliss told me later, an unqualified success, sung loudly and several times at the farewell party.

The earliest of the several extant versions of "Auld Lang Syne" is in the Lilly Library after having bounced around considerably. It was sold by Goodspeed's of Boston to Frank J. Hogan for $8,750. I purchased it at his sale for $3,900 and promptly catalogued it:

The original autograph manuscript of the earliest known version of *Auld Lang Syne* in Burns' autograph. 1 leaf, 4to, written on both sides in ink. In a full red morocco case.                    $7,500

This early version, of the best loved of all Scottish songs, comprises six stanzas and the chorus, and differs somewhat from Burns' later revisions. The first stanza and chorus are:

> Should auld acquaintance be forgot,
>     And never thought upon?
> Let's hae a waught o' malaga,
>     For auld lang syne.

Chorus:

> For auld lang syne, my jo,
>     For auld lang syne.
> Let's hae a waught o' malaga,
>     For auld lang sye [sic].

The last stanza reads:

> And there's a han', my trusty fiere,
>     And gie's a han' O' thine!
> And we'll tak a right gudewilly waught,
>     For auld lang syne.

Following this stanza is Burns' note: "Light be the turf on the breast of the heaven-inspired Poet who composed this glorious Fragment. There is more of native genius in it than in half a dozen of modern Bacchanalians . . . Now I am on my hobby-horse I cannot help inserting two other old stanzas which please me mightily." He then transcribes the first four lines of *My Bonie Mary,* beginning, "Go fetch to me a pint o' wine," etc.

This leaf containing the song was originally part of a very long letter Burns wrote to his old friend, Mrs. Dunlop, from Ellisland, December 7, 1788.

The major portion of the letter is now in The Pierpont Morgan Library, New York City, and the final leaf is in the Observatory Museum in Dumfries.

This manuscript was once in the possession of J. V. L. Pruyn of Albany, and the letter of the famous bookseller Henry Stevens, of Vermont, explaining its provenance when selling it to him on the centenary of the poet's birth (1859), is present:

> "This autograph of Auld Lang Syne was for many years in the possession of my late friend William Pickering, the Publisher, and after his death it fell under Sotheby's hammer in 1855 to me, at a price which I dare not name, but which would have gladdened the hearts of the poet and his poor Jean had they in time reaped the benefit. 'For America' were the only words of the auctioneer that accompanied the fall of the hammer, and as I pocketed the precious relic, 'for America' was many times repeated by the poets and scholars present . . ."

In parting with the manuscript Stevens tells the purchaser of his own pleasure in having possessed it and his gratitude over its remaining in this country, "where Burns is more read, more admired, and more universally appreciated than elsewhere, aye than even in his native Scotland."

There are three other, and later, transcripts of this song by Burns, one done in 1793, in The Pierpont Morgan Library; and another, written by Burns in the Laird of Glenriddle's interleaved copy of Johnson's *Musical Museum*, Gribbel sale (New York, 1941) and another privately owned.

Examples of Burns manuscripts are not especially uncommon. But *Auld Lang Syne* is one of the half dozen best known and best loved poems in the world: and it is only three times in 157 years that a manuscript copy has appeared, of which the present is the earliest and finest.

It was around quite a while before I sold it to Mary Benjamin. It next appeared at the sale of Charles C. Hart and brought $5,250. I let it go because I had had trouble selling it before. Goodspeed's purchased it and promptly sold it to Lilly at a price considerably more than that at which I had once offered it to him. So I have custody of it again.

A few years back, at least it seems like a few years, a reporter friend of mine was assigned to travel with a presidential candidate on his barnstorming cross-country tour. When he told of his forthcoming, to him dismal, chore, I was ecstatic; both our fortunes were made. I explained to him the ready market for presidential autographs, which are avidly sought for, and that here was a chance to corner the market. I alerted him to take every chance he had to save every scrap of the future President's autograph which came his way. Search wastebaskets, I counseled, pick up the bits and pieces wherever you can: save everything! This was better than a money tree, I told him, and we would, by judiciously letting this out on the market, be able eventually to retire wealthy.

He enthusiastically agreed, and for the trip took along one small suitcase for his clothes and two large empty ones for the loot. I followed his reports and itinerary carefully and was reassured by telephone calls and letters that he was following instructions carefully. He had even rescued, signed, a dinner menu entirely in the great one's hand, besides scads of lesser notes on speeches made or projected, etc.

We foregathered at Larchmont for the victory celebration on election eve, and quite an event it was. We were not only going to be rich, we had preserved for posterity vital documents of national importance which would otherwise have been irretrievably destroyed.

All went well. The witching hour of twelve passed, drinks were passed, and then, slowly, came dawn and doom. At 6 A.M. or so we were tossing the manuscripts into the fireplace, singing, "Throw another Tom on the fire." By the time Dewey conceded, nothing was left of the historical hoard.

I'd also had another newspaper acquaintance who was simultaneously traveling with "Give 'em hell" Harry Truman but hadn't had sense enough to have him do the same thing. Why bother with an also-ran?

# Collections

THE *en bloc* purchase of entire collections was a keynote in the great success story of Dr. A. S. W. Rosenbach. His biographers relate how, time after time, he was able to acquire collections, sell some of the rarities for enough to cover the purchase price, and have a superb stock left—all eventual profit. The classic example of this technique, of course, is the acquisition of the famed Phillipps collection of manuscripts by the Robinson brothers of London, the greatest rare book coup of at least our century.

I managed to purchase a few collections for Scribner's but on a much lower level. Those I usually acquired, I felt, should be kept together; in fact, often that was where their value lay: the whole was worth more than the sum of its parts. And when I did obtain collections which were eventually dispersed, these usually contained no few fine nuggets which would recoup the purchase price and leave a further rich vein to be mined. Or perhaps, come to think of it, I just paid too much for them.

The first collection I was ever offered was also the largest, though far from the most valuable. Carroll Wilson asked me one summer day in 1934 if I would care to spend a weekend with him visiting the widow of a book dealer, Thomas J. Taylor of Taunton, Massachusetts. Taylor, a dealer for forty years, had been a source of supply of New England literature to Wilson, P. K. Foley, the famous Boston bookseller, and many others. He dealt primarily in "soft-covers": pamphlets, almanacs, periodicals of all sorts, newspapers and the like.

Wilson confided that there was probably not much left of individual value as separate items, but thought he ought to take a look, as Taylor specifically instructed his wife to consult Wilson about the disposal of his stock after his death. We set off in Wilson's seven-passenger Packard, a monster of a car which he loved dearly, and duly arrived in Taunton.

We were greeted with a sight I have never seen before or since—literally a house full of books. It was a typical New England house with cellar and attic, which we could not explore as the stairways were crammed with books. The Taylors lived in three rooms, as I recall, which included the kitchen. Everything else was simply jammed with books. One room only had been shelved, but it was virtually impossible to see what these contained, as mountainous material was piled before them. Books were under the beds, in the closets, everywhere.

Any kind of search was hopeless. To please the widow, Wilson and I each bought something, which we discarded on the way home. On this return trip we discussed what to do. It was obvious I couldn't and didn't want to handle it. Eventually I came up with the name of a lad who had recently gone into business in a small office in a building on West 48th Street, Richard S. Wormser.

I thought him a far cut above most of his contemporaries and one who would inevitably succeed. In this I was right, as he eventually became, among many other things, president of the Antiquarian Booksellers Association of America.

We had something in common, besides our birthdays, and were doing considerable business back and forth—running, in a good month, to perhaps $250. Dick had an eye for the unusual (and still does) and was just the boy, I thought, to winnow the wheat, if there was any, from this mountain of chaff. The only stipulation attached to alerting him to the trove was that he offer Wilson first, and myself second, the choice of anything we might desire, a condition strictly observed.

As Dick recently recounted the story, "On a June morning in 1934 Professor David A. Randall, then Mister, rushed into my office, proclaiming, 'I've just seen more ... ... ... God-damned books than you've seen in your whole life.' When he had comfortably seated himself with his feet on my desk he told me the story. He said, in one of his most remarkable understatements, 'There must be a hundred thousand of them!' "

That's all of my part of the story, except that the sequel shows the close interdependence of collector, dealer and librarian at its best. Dick, through that very fine and unfortunate bookman Robert J. Lingel, then of the New York Public Library, arranged for that institution to finance the purchase and house the books in return for the opportunity to acquire such material as it did not have, the duplicates being delivered to Wormser. An entire floor of the warehouse was filled with the collection, which eventually proved to be about 450,000 pieces and weighed thirty-

nine tons, and every week for eight years the library truck delivered a
load of duplicates to Dick's office. It was an imaginative and profitable
partnership of which we see too little.

Sometime in the early forties I was at a dull cocktail party and got
backed into a corner with a pleasant gentleman whose name I didn't
catch. A brief chat about books revealed that he was remarkably well
informed on current literature, and well he should have been—he was
Harry Scherman, founder of the Book-of-the-Month Club in 1926.

I had and have an admiration for this particular organization. I never
subscribed to it but I know very well its enormous value in spreading
books to small communities where bookshops are not available within a
hundred-mile radius or more. It was making something besides magazine
reading available to book-starved individuals, and I approved. Friends of
mine, some of whom worked for the organization, didn't, but then they
were ones who prided themselves on never buying books: they were
supplied with review copies or borrowed them from those who were. But
purchase—never!

It was just at this time that the Book-of-the-Month was attempting,
rumor said, to exercise editorial control over its selections. Whether this
was so I simply don't know. Several of the judges, including Chris
Morley, were acquaintances of mine, and I knew of their procedure of
submitting reports, etc., on the books which were under consideration.
These were supplied them, of course, in prepublication form, galley
proof, etc. I asked Scherman what happened to all this material and he
just didn't know. Every six months or so employees were allowed to take
anything they wanted from what had been submitted. The reports were
probably burned. I went to the club's offices with him and discovered
that little indeed remained there except the necessary copyright and
financial records.

This appalled me. I explained to him that this was all source material of
the kind future historians of our era would find invaluable—and search
for in vain unless someone preserved it. What if we had this kind of
publishing record for the eighteenth or nineteenth centuries? How many
plaguing questions would be answered. And so on and on. Scribner's
wanted nothing out of this, I assured him. All I wanted was to stop
unnecessary destruction of vital documents and put them where they
would be preserved. Scribner's would get credit for a good deed from
whoever acquired it, the BOM a tax deduction, and all would be well.

I had an immediate convert and was told to go ahead, subject to the
single stipulation that Scherman's alma mater, the University of Pennsyl-

vania, be given first refusal. And refuse it they did! As did the Library of Congress, the New York Public Library, and assorted university libraries, including all of the Ivy League. It was "too much bulk," "too contemporary," "we like to make our own selections," "we get copyright copies," the Library of Congress replied, while others said it was too expensive to catalogue, etc.

All missed the point, it seemed to me, which was that here they would be getting the original versions of popular novels before editing, reader's reports on contemporary sales possibilities reflecting the mores of the times, and much else. And for free! No one was forcing them to catalogue all this. They could use what they thought important and crate or destroy the rest.

The weeks went by with refusal mounting on refusal and Scherman zealously advising everyone to save everything and at monthly luncheons asking me embarrassing questions about where it was all going. It is frustrating enough for any salesman not to be able to sell, but when he can't even give his product away . . . !

Eventually I persuded Yale to take what everyone else obviously regarded as a white elephant, and twenty-five years later they are still getting the files. Scherman was pleased, and though a little shaken by my near-miss on the project, so was I. When I recently made an inquiry at Yale for some details on the transaction, no one could remember anything about it. Ah, well.

One fine collection of modern literature I did acquire was that formed by Crosby Gaige, famed theatrical producer of the 1920's and among other things a book collector and proprietor of a private press which printed, in limited editions, much of the trivia of well-known authors and occasionally a good book. He had made so much money in the twenties that he didn't know what to do with it. Among his successive hits had been the still memorable *Broadway, Charlot's Review, Smilin' Through, The Circle, Why Marry?* (Pulitzer Prize), *Coquette* (with Helen Hayes), among others, including Channing Pollock's *The House Beautiful*, which Dorothy Parker dismissed in a one-line review, "*The House Beautiful* is the play lousy."

Gaige was born in Skunk Hollow, New York, a descendant of the famed Enoch Crosby, of revolutionary fame, hero of Cooper's *The Spy*. He has told his theatrical story interestingly in a twenty-two-chapter book, *Footlights and Highlights* (New York, 1948). I never knew him in his glory days when he was collecting books and running his private press. He tells the story of these in one chapter, fourteen pages, of an over-three-hundred-page book. He writes, concerning his library:

> I was engaged at this time in forming a collection, as complete as possible, of the works of contemporaries, authors of my generation who in my opinion, mistaken or not, might stand the years. The collection started with Thomas Hardy and ended with Virginia Woolf. It was rich in personalized items: manuscripts, correspondence, corrected proof sheets, autographed copies, and the minutiae that seldom come the way of the average collector.
>
> Each item was protected by a Morocco-bound slip case; the slip cases of individual authors were of the same color design. The collection was housed in a large pine-paneled room in my apartment on upper Fifth Avenue. There was a large fireplace, and all of the available wall space was devoted to books. Long shelves of richly colored bindings gave the room great dignity and beauty.
>
> A detailed description of the collection would be too lengthy, but let it be said that I had plenty of money to spend on my hobby, and I spent it gladly. There was, for example, a mint copy of Hardy's *Desperate Remedies,* his first book, which he published at his own expense. This one I bought from Mrs. James Stillman of "Indian Guide" fame. There were manuscripts of Kipling, Bennett and Lafcadio Hearn, and many others. When I abandoned New York as a place of residence, and sold my apartment to Bruce Barton, I did not feel it safe to take the books with me because my house in the country was not fireproof, and there was much irreplaceable material on my shelves. The books were packed in large wooden cases and stored in a warehouse, where they remained for nearly twenty years, finally emerging to become the property of the house of Scribner, to be dispersed and give pleasure to other collectors. As a comment on the soundness of the collection, it may be added that the great college and university libraries were eager bidders for much of the material. Occasionally I drop into Scribner's resplendent store on Fifth Avenue and buy one of my former treasures, if only as a reminder of friendship with an author.

This is an accurate enough statement, except that the reason Gaige stored his library was to keep this asset from his creditors, as I found out when I tried to sell it. Everyone in New York, it seemed, thought they had a lien against it. And there were other troubles. He had known Siegfried Sassoon, and the first book to bear Gaige's name as publisher was his volume of poems, *The Heart's Journey* (New York, 1928). He also had a nice collection of Sassoon's manuscripts, but after I acquired them, S. N. Behrman, whom Gaige claims to have put on the road to fame, showed up in the bookstore and claimed they were his own property. There were other similar fusses about who owned some of the material I had acquired from Gaige's private press enterprise, "The Watch Hill," named for his farm in upper Westchester, where he moved after leaving New York.

I was unable to sell the collection intact—it was too heterogeneous—but I did manage to peddle its parts. As Gaige noted, every single book in the collection, and there were several thousand of them, had its own morocco slipcase, and I purchased the entire collection for little more than the cost of the slipcases plus storage charges over the years. Investing (which is really what Gaige was doing) in modern first editions especially is not always a winning venture. I remember one collection in particular, a fine lot of Richard Aldington's works, many privately printed and very hard to come by. Gaige had published Aldington's *Fifty Romantic Lyric Poets* (New York, 1928), and the author had given him many of his own books. This collection went to Yale. Gaige also had some fine Irish things, O'Flaherty, Joyce, Stephens and Yeats among them. One of the Yeats books I remember especially well. It was his first book and is the most desirable copy I ever heard of. I catalogued it:

Yeats, William Butler. *Mosada. A Dramatic Poem*. With a Frontispiece Portrait of the Author. Dublin: Printed by Sealy, Bryers, and Walker, 1886. 8vo, First edition, original printed wrappers. In a green morocco solander case. $500

The author's first book. Inscribed on the inside of the front wrapper: "The first copy that I have seen in many years. The play was published in the Dublin University Review & from that reprinted in the present form & had of course no success of any kind. It was my father who insisted on the portrait . . . it was also his insistence that kept me bearded. W. B. Yeats, Nov. 10, 1923."

On the last page the author has further noted: "I read this through for the first time since it was first published. I wrote it when I was twenty-one & think rather sadly that when young men of that age send in like work I am not able to foresee his future or his talent. W. B. Yeats."

Certainly one of the most desirable copies of this great rarity to appear in many years.

I sold this to Ed Hanley (who ever had an eye for a bargain), and it is now with his collections at Texas. The last copy to come on the market, uninscribed, brought $3,700.

Early in 1950 or so John Carter wrote that he had just spent a weekend with Major J. R. Abbey at Greyfriars, Storrington, Sussex, advising him in the printing of a catalogue of his library, the first volume of which was due shortly, with others to follow. They were to be sumptuous volumes, large quartos privately printed at the Curwen Press and lavishly illustrated. They were the culmination of a quarter century's collecting, and John felt sure that, their publication achieved, the Major could be persuaded to part with his books; already Abbey had his collector's eye fixed elsewhere, and, many of the books being folios, he was being crowded out of even his spacious quarters. His wife agreed and I imagine instigated the idea.

The first volume of the collection was devoted to *Scenery of Great Britain and Ireland in Aquatint and Lithography 1770–1860* and was issued in 1952. It was followed by a second volume in 1953 subtitled *Architecture, Drawing Books, Art Collections, Magazines, Navy and Army, Panoramas*, etc. Two similar volumes followed, *Travel in Aquatint and Lithography 1770–1860*, Volume I, *World, Europe, Africa* (1956); Volume II, *Asia, Oceania, Antarctica, America* (1957). All continued to be beautifully printed and illustrated. There were full bibliographical descriptions of the more than 2,500 individual titles (many in multi-parts) which comprised the collection.

Carter impressed on me that the condition of the books was superb and that Abbey had insisted wherever possible on getting the books, many of which were issued "in parts," in original wrappers. This was important, as much valuable information is lost when the parts are rebound and wrappers discarded.

The term "scenery" was not strictly confined to landscape but included architecture, urban and social scenes such as coronations, etc. Abbey omitted general sporting books as he considered these adequately treated in C. F. G. R. Schwerdt's three-volume catalogue of his collection, *Hunting, Hawking and Shooting* (1928).

All this was interesting, but I didn't know quite what to do about it. I knew in a general way the rarity of many of the works, created because a great number were broken up for individual framing of the plates, and I recognized their vast importance as vivid records of a past glory. The famous firm of Ackermann published many notable works and employed at wretched pay as many as seventy-five girls or more who executed the hand coloring of the copper plates which sometimes sold for as much as ninety-five guineas a volume, no inconsiderable sum for those days.

Still, it was a field in which I really knew little and cared less. I had inherited oodles of color-plate books at Scribner's when I first went there—Alken's, Rowlandson's, Cruikshank's, etc., and was never much attracted to them. Libraries on Philadelphia's Main Line, in Westchester, Long Island and New Jersey were jammed with them.

I did recognize, however, that Major Abbey's collection was duplicated nowhere in America and very few places in England, perhaps none, considering their remarkable condition, and that after all a decent respect for the country of our origin seemed to require some such collection on our shores. I made tentative inquiries of several libraries, museums and the like, with no enthusiastic response from anyone. This only increased my determination to place them somewhere, as the more I studied the collections the more I came to appreciate their importance and the fact that if this chance were missed another such was not going to come along.

Suddenly I remembered an episode of a dozen years back. There had been a sale coming up at the Parke-Bernet Galleries, including, as I recall, some special copies of either Malton's or Ackermann's famous views of Oxford and Cambridge, in which I had no interest whatsoever. Just before the sale I received a call from Bill Gannon, from Boston. He explained that he was snowbound and couldn't get to the sale and asked me to execute his bids for him. I agreed, of course, and he later told me that he was particularly exercised because the bids were from Paul Mellon, who had attended Cambridge and wanted these books badly. I knew in a general way of Mellon's interests, but I had never thought of him in connection with the Abbey collection until this recollection. Once it was pointed out to him it stimulated his imagination and enthusiasm not only for acquiring it, but for adding to it, which is being successfully done. So briefly, the Abbey collection came to Virginia simply because of a snowstorm.

My original sight of one book in the first Abbey collection really stunned me, and whenever I visit Brick House I always reexamine it. Twenty years in the making (1821–1841), it has been said to be the most sumptuous work ever printed, that none but itself can be its parallel, and I cannot from my own experience fault this claim.

Done in two elephant folio volumes in this single copy only (though a "popular" edition was later published), it cost upward of 2,000 guineas to produce and was intended for his Majesty King George IV, but was not finished before his death. This unique book is painted, enameled, gilded, bejeweled and printed on vellum and satin. The portraits of royalty are all full length, dressed in their coronation robes, heightened with gold and silver and painted on satin. The coronets placed at the top of these plates are adorned with brilliants and precious stones set in gold. Ornately bound, it is enclosed in two especially constructed rosewood tables.

Ordinary methods of description pale when one is faced with the task of describing it. Its description occupies four double-spaced pages in the Abbey catalogue, the first paragraph of which is:

> CORONATION OF HIS MOST SACRED MAJESTY, KING GEORGE THE FOURTH, solemnized in Westminster Abbey, July 19, 1821. A series of Seventy large and most magnificent Paintings of the Procession, Ceremonial and Banquet, comprehending faithful Portraits of many of the distinguished Individuals who were present, in their Robes of Estate, by Sir T. Lawrence, Chalon, Stephanoff, Pugin, Wild, and other eminent artists; all exquisitely finished in colours, like Miniatures; several of them most brilliantly executed upon Vellum or White Satin, surmounted by Coronets set with BRILLIANTS, RUBIES, AND OTHER PRECIOUS STONES.
>
> With descriptive letter-press printed in Letters of Gold. The back of every painting lined with white silk. Superbly bound in two very large volumes, elephant folio, crimson turkey morocco, with broad and beautifully tooled borders of gold, the sides ornamented with a representation of the Abbey Altar, with the Regalia, inlaid with morocco of various colours; blue morocco linings and morocco fly-leaves, covered with elaborate gold tooling, with treble gold borders, &c. the Royal Arms in the centres.

I have never been able to reconstruct what happened to the book, except that it was never acquired by the royalty for whom it was intended. It is recorded that "Mr. Whittaker received an indemnification of several hundred pounds from the Privy Purse but his own death soon followed, and his valuable collections were sold at a considerable loss." This must be an understatement, as the work appears in Henry G. Bohn's rare book catalogue for 1841 priced £250, Bohn recounting that "he has bestowed upon it a binding which alone cost upwards of One Hundred Guineas." Which doesn't indicate he could have paid much for it. It then disappeared from sight until it appeared in the Abbey collection.

Other collections are described elsewhere in these pages, but none contained a book like this.

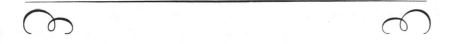

# My Two Ventures in Modern Publishing

I HAD, during my majority at Scribner's, a rough working agreement with the management. If they wouldn't putter around with my cherished "old and rare," I wouldn't interfere with their current publishing. It worked reasonably well. But there were exceptions.

Max Perkins once asked me for support in his effort to get Alden Brooks's *Will Shakespeare and the Dyer's Hand* published. It was, I gathered, a mania with him. At every editorial conference he would bring up the book and it would unanimously be voted down. So, being a man of infinite patience, he would reintroduce his suggestion at the next conference, with the same result.

What charmed Perkins about the book, I eventually discerned, was that it credited Dyer, an editor, for Shakespeare's success. This he approved of, and eventually his colleagues published it simply to please him. Scholars universally rent it. One of these was Dr. Robert Metcalf Smith, the Shakespearean authority of Lehigh University.

It was Robert Smith who took a fancy to me in my freshman year at Lehigh and got me through school and into my first job. He was a terrific teacher and an enthusiastic though not always accurate scholar. He had done a pioneer job on the bibliography of the Second Folio of Shakespeare, and it was in his course that I added my first, and only, drop in the enormous sea of Shakespearean research.

Years later Smith switched from Shakespeare to Shelley and became entranced by the still unsolved mysteries of the forgery and fraudulence which pervade the poet's biography. With three associates, including a handwriting expert employed as Consultant Document Examiner by the

New York State Police Laboratory in Albany, New York, Smith set out
to unravel them.

When fairly well advanced, the manuscript was submitted to Scribner's,
and I arranged a lunch with Smith and Perkins. Both reticent New
Englanders, it was mutual admiration on sight. One tie was Thomas
Hardy, whose theology they would discuss for hours. It always curiouses
me how literate New Englanders invariably love Hardy. There is something about his Jobness which appeals to them. From then on the
publication of the book was assured. It was the first work I had ever
brought to Scribner's, and because of its antiquarian background and my
friendship with Smith, I was assigned to editorial chores concerning it.

A crucial point in *The Shelley Legend* (New York, 1945), as the book
was titled, and in fact in Shelley biography, is the December 16, 1816,
letter in which Shelley accuses Harriet Westbrook, his first wife, of being
a prostitute, and her sister Eliza of being a murderess. The trouble is that
there are four versions of this letter. Some, at least, are forgeries. Shelley
biography is bedeviled by them—many done by a Major Byron (born de
Gibler) who claimed to be Byron's illegitimate son and to have lived in
my family's hometown, Wilkes-Barre, Pennsylvania.

Smith and Company were convinced that the British Museum's copy of
this letter, then unavailable for examination (this was 1942), was a Major
Byron forgery. If this were so, it would be strong evidence that Shelley
never made these charges and that his second wife, Mary, could be convicted of complicity in their manufacture and dissemination. The fact
that the letter had been owned by Thomas J. Wise before the British
Museum acquired his library didn't help its case, though Wise has never
been to this day, I believe, accused of invention or forgeries of manuscripts. We all, of course, have our standards.

Most of *The Shelley Legend*'s arguments rested on this one letter, as
did the intricate handwriting analysis. Part II, "Problems in Handwriting
of the Shelley Circle," is exhaustive. No fewer than eighteen plates are
devoted to reproductions, some of Shelley's writing of the word "which"
and Mary's writing of the same word; others of "The Forger's Natural
Hand" and "The Forger's Disguised Hand"; "Forged Leigh Hunt At-
testations"; "Same Words as Written by Leigh Hunt"; etc. It is all very
difficult to follow and, perhaps for that reason, very impressive.

Despite the learned arguments, the fact remained that the authors were
working only from photo-facsimiles of the crucial letter. I knew there
was no substitute for actual examination of the original letter and hotly
protested against any irrevocable limb-climbing. To no effect.

It is a very complicated matter. The authors regretted their "inability to examine the paper, the postmarks, and seals directly." They flatly stated, however, that "what has happened is that a letter purchased by the Shelley heirs, exposed as a forgery in 1852, discovered by them to be a forgery and twice declared by them to be a forgery, once in 1852, and again in 1867, has on its transfer from Forman to Wise regained respectability and re-entered Shelley biography in good standing wholly through the equivocal and erroneous statements of Messrs. Wise and De Ricci."

The authors also condemned another famous Shelley letter, that written to Byron on January 17, 1817, and owned by Carl Pforzheimer, as a forgery, again without seeing it. They stated that "when the present owner, who now refuses, permits the holograph itself to be submitted to unbiased examination and publication it will be found to be a product of Major Byron's pen."

After the war one of the collaborators, Theodore G. Ersham, visited the British Museum and came to the conclusion, duly published in the London *Times Literary Supplement*, that the December 16 letter was genuine and that only the signature was a forgery! He came to this conclusion largely on the basis of postmarks: "Byron was chronically unable to forge convincing postmarks; those on the letter at the British Museum are unquestionably authentic."

Ersham went on to do an interesting study of Major Byron, and when the January 17, 1817, Byron letter was made available for his examination, he again "became convinced that the handwriting is unquestionably genuine throughout."

These findings dealt a mortal blow to *The Shelley Legend*'s scholarly pretentions, which is a pity, as, when dealing with printed material, it has a great deal of merit. It had been written, however, with a great deal of peevishness and without any of the objective calm of a Carter-Pollard *Enquiry*. The following paragraphs are typical.

> The understandable desire of dealers and owners of manuscript allegedly written by famous persons to wish to believe their items authentic has resulted in a gradual infiltration of a mass of bogus material into the literary remains of many of our famous men. In a recent periodical issued by a well-known autograph dealer, equipped with more confidence than discretion, we read:
>
> > An *immediate* appraisal of the *genuineness* and approximate value of a manuscript may seem miraculous to a novice who does not realize all of the quick mental processes, some subconscious, involved in a judgment— paper, ink, condition, provenance, the writing itself and various other

factors. There is really no magic but only long years of broad experience, in the development of a virtual "sixth sense" which can deduce with fairly exact approximation during what period an undated manuscript or letter was written, and in what country.

We are led to wonder after reading such a claim that forgeries are not more widely accepted. "An immediate appraisal of the genuineness" would seem "miraculous," indeed, not only to a novice, but to any one of the leading handwriting experts. It smacks too much of Hitler's military "intuitions."

May I add here that it is not only cupidity which causes people to hold, or deny, the genuineness of literary or historical property. There is also the scholarly desire to make discoveries and to twist, sometimes unconsciously, evidence to favor their thesis. Smith and Company fell into this trap, unwittingly, I am sure. Personally I will take any experienced dealer's autographic judgment on an author or a period he is familiar with, over that of a battery of handwriting experts or professional scholars.

After Ersham's announcements I remembered something. At one time Charles Scribner had given me an unusual Shelley letter he had inherited, to sell for him. It was to Ollier, Shelley's publisher, dated sometime in 1818 and mainly concerned with publishing arrangements for *Laon and Cythna*, issued that year. It seemed to me to throw doubt that the accepted first issue, "only twelve copies," was what it purported to be. The letter had a double appeal from a very touching and sentimental postscript: "What do you hear said of Frankenstein?" One can just see Mary, whose book had recently been published, breathing over her husband's shoulder and asking the author's universal question.

I had sold the letter to Robert Taylor and later borrowed it to show Smith and Company, who promptly pronounced it a forgery. I sadly related their decision to Robert Taylor, who as sadly returned it to me, as I did to Scribner.

As events turned out, I thought I'd better have another look at it. Perhaps it wasn't a forgery after all. When I asked Charles for it he said, "When you told me it was a forgery I tore it up and threw it in the wastebasket. Wasn't it?" We will never know. As a sad epilogue to *The Shelley Legend* it must be mentioned that Professor Smith died by his own hand, a copy of Seneca's *Of Old Age* by his side. He had a lot of the old Roman in him.

My final adventure into the modern publishing world also had a tragic ending. After two years at the Shamokin, Pennsylvania, high school I was shipped off to prep at the Harrisburg Academy before entering Lehigh to study engineering.

There my closest friend, a form below me, was a frail, shy, bright-eyed, agile kid named Morton Thompson. He was good at languages and lousy at math. I, vice-versa. So, naturally, we did each other's work. A vivid remembrance is my sitting on a ledge outside the headmaster's office, three stories up, legs dangling, while Morty slipped his exam papers in trig out the window to me. In return for which he would "trot" me in Latin and French—of which I knew, and know, little. Mort wound up teaching celestial navigation during the war, the only proof I ever had that I was a good instructor.

It never occurred to either of us, till years later, that our teachers might wonder why we had made marks of 30 percent in class and 99 percent in exams. But they were tolerant and we had an honor system.

Mort came from a rather strange background. His Jewish parents were separated and he was farmed out between them during various vacations. On occasion I would go home with him or he would come home with me.

His were the more exciting expeditions. His father owned a bunch of hotels in New York, and Mort had free run of the kitchens. And the game rooms. It was here he tried to teach me the finer techniques of pool. Being naturally nondexterous I was not an apt pupil, which annoyed him. He was just plain good, as are gifted people, at many things; his superiority stuck out like goose pimples.

One of the things I remember best about him was his laundry. He never had any. Everything was always brand new. This, he eventually confided in me, was one way of getting even with his parents for their neglect of him. He was given no money—we were all limited to a $1.50 weekly spending allowance anyway—but he had unlimited credit. The bills were sent to a clearing house or someplace where they were paid. Mort would simply wear underwear, shirts, socks and so on until they were dirty, then give them away and go to the local haberdasher and get new ones. So far as I know, this practice was never questioned by anyone—least of all the haberdasher! In later years Mort was the best dressed, or at least had the most clothes, of any person I knew, with the possible exception of Grover Whalen, whose house in Washington Mews, New York City, I occupied for a number of years. This had clothes closets fifteen feet high, operated by pulleys, to accommodate Whalen's wardrobe, and the risers in the stairs were fitted to contain his shoes.

After graduation I completely lost touch with Mort, though I often wondered what happened to him. I found out twenty-odd years later. One day a rotund one wandered into Scribner's with one of my rare book catalogues. He was interested in some Humbert Wolfe firsts I had and in other books I had acquired with the Crosby Gaige collection.

Recognition was by voice, not sight. Mort (without even graduating from the Academy and never attending college) had become, somehow, a journalist and writer. He had written a column—"North Northwest"—about seven years, for *The Hollywood Citizen News*. He actively disliked most of the movie world and his column was about little things that fascinated him: books, horse races, the little stores, people and recipes. He had been, from childhood, accustomed to the best cooking and had the run of his father's hotels' kitchens. He once cooked a turkey for me. It took twelve hours.

He never had much money, nor cared. He lived as extravagantly beyond his means as he was able, without actually gypping anyone. For example, he enthusiastically bought over $1,000 worth of first editions the day we met at Scribner's—most of which I eventually took back because he simply couldn't pay for them. If he really had had to pay, he'd have done so, somehow. When once he hit it big with his short story "My Brother Who Talks to Horses," sold as a movie, he bought a racer and a plane. And loved them.

Some of this he has written about in one of my favorite books—one of those somethings with a rare flavor about it—*Joe, the Wounded Tennis Player*. My copy is inscribed "For Dave—who was practically an august statue down the hall and one of my schoolhood demi-gods—one of three bright names in the whole of my memory. On meeting him again, thank God. April 19, 1945." It is in this book that Thompson is found at his best. It is long out of print but has a few faithful friends, and like a great favorite of his, *Miss Lonelyhearts*, it will, I suspect, be rediscovered come another decade or so. It is dedicated to his younger brother "Lewis Marshall Thompson, II. Air Cadet. Killed at Kingman, Arizona, on the seventh of January, 1944." This was the brother "who talked to horses," which Mort passionately insisted was so. I have no doubt of it. They were a strangely gifted pair.

Mort had been hurt during the war and spent a good deal of time in hospitals. It was here that his interest in surgery (they did a lot on him) and in medicine generally was quickened.

He had seen much of needless suffering and had all of sorrowing humanity heavy in his heart. His horror of war was so intense that he literally went through days with a pistol in his pocket, just plain willing to shoot anyone who was against peace. This he explained (nobody listened) in his second book, *How to Be a Civilian*, dedicated "To the Unknown Baby who will become the Man who will become the Unknown Soldier of World War III."

I saw a lot of him when I was in Hollywood for a while just after the war. He had found a hero in the tragic Ignaz Semmelweis, the conqueror of puerperal fever through antisepsis in obstetrics. Semmelweis was one of medicine's far-shining names, and Mort found in him another martyr, another Crucifixion. He had projected a Life, but it was turning into a fictionized biography. Mort had never been to Europe but he taught himself German to read Semmelweis in the originals, most of which I supplied him. He studied contemporary maps of Budapest till he knew its streets and alleys as he knew those of Harrisburg, Hollywood or New York. The resulting *The Cry and the Covenant* (New York, 1949), dedicated to Bella Pindyck, is to my mind the finest medical novel ever written. My copy is inscribed: "For Dave, twenty-six years later and a lot earlier than anyone might expect. Fondly, gratefully and clinging hard. Mort."

It was well reviewed and sold a fair number for a first novel. But Mort wasn't satisfied, nor was Bella, who had been a literary agent and became his second wife. He was inclined to blame his publishers for bad advertising (a common literary complaint) and to some extent himself for his vivid descriptions of the horrors of childbirth and the callousness of doctors and hospitals at the time. Women, it seemed, couldn't or wouldn't stomach it. And they bought books; but not this one.

He was already at work on his next novel. This was to be the story of the making of a doctor, a small-town general practitioner. Of a strange childhood, shaken by the conflict between his parents, but of a man whose central purpose, more than to heal or relieve suffering, was simply to fight for life.

Mort at this time was again fighting for his own, with Bella's devoted help. She once took him across the continent in a car, alone, a three-week trip, while he lay helpless in a stretcher in the back.

Mort had another idea about the book. It was to be serious, true enough, but it was to sell. It was to make money, and lots of it, enough to take him and Bella around the world and give him time and freedom to write his opus—a life of St. Luke.

To do this he deliberately planned to load the book with selling sex. The women, by God, would buy this one and so would Hollywood. It was to have plenty of purple patches—though he complained about the difficulty of writing them and was afraid of them. It was very tough to recall youth faithfully. Incidentally, he considered Booth Tarkington's *Seventeen* the finest story of adolescence ever written.

I read a little of what he had done and recognized the setting. It was Seiler Hall at the Harrisburg Academy and had a lot of our youth in it.

He also wanted to change publishers. I was reluctant to push Scribner's —no surer way of losing a friend than to publish his book. And at first he wasn't enthusiastic, nor was Bella. For one thing he was stoney and would need a considerable advance against royalties to get through the year, a minimum, till the work could be finished. And my house was not noted for large cash advances—few are, as a matter of fact, who are still in business. And I have little interest in or knowledge of the worth of contemporary novels—except to realize the enormous odds against Mort's becoming the terrific best seller he envisioned.

But I gave Charles Scribner copies of *Joe* and *The Cry*, and both he and his editors were impressed. Eventually there was a conference on the fifth floor with Charley, Mort, Bella and myself. Mort was advanced what he thought he needed, found an old farm in Connecticut and worked. He converted a barn into a workshop and tacked pages of his manuscript on the walls. There he would flit around like a mosquito adding a touch of dialogue to this page, a description to that. And complain of interruptions because twice a day, at six in the morning and six at night, a farmer passed by. For relaxation he would do some shooting—he had a fine collection of guns and a good eye—or wood working, at which he was extremely skillful, and self-taught. And cook.

He had a cookbook planned, entitled *The Naked Countess*, to which Robert Benchley was to write an introduction. Benchley explains all this in his Introduction to *Joe*, which concludes, "Just as viands of the first order need no vintage wine, so *Joe, the Wounded Tennis Player* needs no first-class introduction, which is exactly what it isn't getting."

Finally the book was finished and came the great day when we found out it was to be a Book-of-the-Month selection. Not only that, but the Reader's Digest Condensed Books took it also—the only novel to be a simultaneous selection of two book clubs up to that time. All other indications were of a runaway success. It had already been sold to Hollywood. But the most sanguine expectations faded before what actually happened—two solid years of best-sellerdom, mostly as Number One. And the tremendous paperback editions. Mort was in, but good. Boy, what plans were made. Mexico, after publication, for a rest, then Hollywood for the movie—then the world.

Two weeks after Mort found out of his success and before the book was published, he suddenly died as the result of war injuries. Bella wanted none of a world without him. Two days following his death she killed herself with his Navy .45. It was a doom-ridden family. As these words are being written, the Los Angeles papers report, "The former wife of the late Morton Thompson, author of the best-seller, *Not As a Stranger,* was stabbed to death by her son while she worked a cross-word puzzle in her home."

*Not As a Stranger* is dedicated "To Bella Pindyck Thompson, to whom this book and this author are dedicated." It became, of course, one of the great best sellers and moneymakers of our generation. The sadness is that Mort didn't have, and without him Bella didn't want, even a little time to enjoy what they had done. And we shall never have, as only he could have interpreted it, the life of Luke.

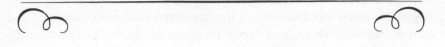

# The Permanent Questionnaire

ALONG IN 1935 *Vanity Fair*, then tottering toward extinction, published a literary quiz, which they called "The Permanent Questionnaire," with a twist, and a first prize of $50. When I think of this episode I recognize it as a sort of character test which I failed miserably. I was never asked to go on any of the modern quiz shows, but I'm sure that if I had, and I'd been propositioned, I'd have accepted. For what I had already done was just as bad, morally, if not as profitable.

The quiz came out in the July issue and contestants were given about two months—and they proved to be short ones—to get in their answers. Twenty-five well-known American literary lights asked two questions each, which they thought would puzzle readers. Some were silly but some were dillies. This, I thought, is my meat—only to be really baffled by a good lot of them.

The old and rare (they have now sissified it into antiquarian) business was dull then, so I had lots of time. I got the best two bibliographical brains I could think of, also reasonably at leisure, to help me. In fact we formed a syndicate, the three of us, and really went to work. Finally, reeling from exhaustion, we mailed in our composite answers under my name, a privilege I had won by a coin toss.

One beautiful day came a telegram: PLEASE ACCEPT FORMAL FELICITA- TIONS ON WINNING FIRST PRIZE IN OUR QUESTIONNAIRE. STOP. VERY SLIGHT REWARD FOLLOWS WITH ADMIRING WISHES FROM THE EDITORS OF VANITY FAIR.

*Vanity Fair* sent around a photographer and I even got my picture in it—something much better men have not. Of course, Jacob Blanck and Edward Lazare both shared the prize with me, which really didn't amount to much split three ways. But my employers were impressed and even a customer or so, and I calmly accepted all the kudos: "It was nothing, really nothing. I knocked it off over a dull weekend." But I carried a heavy weight on my conscience since and I'm glad now I've told all.

As the questionnaire was rather typical of its times, I give it here for the gentle reader to try on himself. There are some members of the English department at one large university, I may add, who couldn't even identify all the authors asking the questions. Such is literary fame.

One reason I never dreamed the televised quiz shows were rigged was that the questions asked were so simple—compared to the horror we had mastered—that there seemed no point to fixing them. So don't feel badly if you do ill on this. And if you aren't nearing fifty, don't attempt it at all.

The questions lead off with a paragraph as follows:

No man is living who can answer all of the questions on these two pages. There are fifty questions—each a literary humdinger—, and the test is to see how many you can master by dint of much brainwracking in the quiet of your August cabaña. All except one of the queries pertain to English or American literature, between 1600 and the present time. If one (or more) of them looks answer-proof, don't blame *Vanity Fair,* because we didn't ask them. They were maliciously hatched by twenty-five distinguished writers, columnists, educators, and critics. When the dead and missing are counted, three prizes will be awarded. $50 in cash to the contestant who turns in the greatest number of correct answers; $25, as second prize; and a copy of *Vanity Fair's Portfolio of Modern French Art,* as third prize. Contenders must have their answers in our hands not later than August 21st, next. The correct answers, as well as the names of the winners, will be announced in the October issue.

## THE PERMANENT QUESTIONNAIRE

*Sinclair Lewis*
  1. Who was the first author to use the realistic-policeman-Hammett type of detective, in contrast to the Poe-Doyle school of amateur detectives?
  2. What is the most popular literary work of Theodore Dreiser?

*Damon Runyon*
  3. What American baseball reporter wrote a poem which had nothing to do with sport, but is one of the best-known pieces of verse in the English language and is almost rated as a classic?

4. What English poet was patron, pal, and pupil of a famous heavy-weight fighter of his time, and mentions his boxing lessons in his works?

*Edmund Pearson*

5. Which two heroines of English literature suffered death by hanging?

6. What is the name of the English authoress of whom it can be said: her parents were literary people; her husband was an illustrious author; she took part in a celebrated elopement; her fame rests on one novel—her first; she once had a mild flirtation with a celebrated New York author; and her work, after more than a century, is still, in this present year, inspiring Hollywood?

*Joseph Hergesheimer*

7. What two heroic legends of the Civil War, celebrated in American verse and history, were actually inglorious?

8. What minor poet was employed by the United States government to cover the attack of a new deal of Federal sanctity?

*H. L. Mencken*

9. To the funeral of which American metaphysician did the Elks of Boston send a floral piece in the form of a book four feet high, made of carnations, daisies, and tea-roses?

10. Which eminent American poet is buried in the red-light district of a great American city?

*Aldous Huxley*

11. What American poet wrote: "You are the living cuspidors of day"?

12. What Poet Laureate of England translated into heroic couplets a Latin poem on venereal disease?

*Carl Van Doren*

13. What episode of what famous American novel is a backwoods version of the story of *Romeo and Juliet?*

14. Who wrote the novel and who the play about Serena Blandish?

*John Van Druten*

15. What happened to Barnes' Gander and when?

16. Who, upon hearing someone say that he was a member of the Church of England, asked what the subscription was?

*Manuel Komroff*

17. What was the source of Hearn's first name, Lafcadio?

18. A great many books have been written about Napoleon, but how many would you imagine?

*Henry Seidel Canby*

19. What great American writer liked pie for breakfast?

20. What great American war story was written by a man who had never seen a battle?

*Harry Hansen*

21. In what book and in what year did Sherlock Holmes arrive on the scene?

22. What famous story by an English author was used as the theme for an orchestral suite by a living American composer?

*Clifton Fadiman*

23. What have the following literary figures in common: Stirling, Simple, Grimm, Bell, Whiffle, Paltock, Fleming, Wimsey, Quince, Belloc, and Rabbit?

24. Name two authors both of whom wrote *The City of Dreadful Night*.

*George Jean Nathan*

25. Who wrote the *Belle of Bowling Green?*

26. What American writer was arrested as a spy during the early days of the late war and lodged briefly in the hoosegow because he had been seen lounging about a mile and a half from an Atlantic seaboard light-house?

*William Lyon Phelps*

27. What American historian is buried in the Protestant Cemetery in Florence, Italy?

28. Where did the late William De Morgan obtain the title for his novel, *Somehow Good?*

*Booth Tarkington*

29. In what book by what American writer is a "solitary oesophagus seen floating high in the air"?

30. In what American book is a slave fattened for use as an ottoman?

*Edmund Wilson*

31. What extremely improper scene did Shakespeare write in French?

32. What famous quotations, from one of Shakespeare's plays, are really interpolations by someone else?

*Stark Young*

33. What celebrated author was said by the wife of what author to be always within sound of her dinner bell?

34. What famous author complicated his financial budget through the urge he felt to dig for buried treasure?

*Charles Hanson Towne*

35. What American literary society expelled a member for his alleged pro-German sympathies during the World War, and what was the member's name?

36. What magazine, in 1915, made certain editorial changes in the last installment of what American author's serial, and was forced by the author to print, in the following issue, his own version of the manuscript?

*Charles T. Copeland*

37. Truth resides in the statement, which I quote from memory: "A little dinner, not more than the Muses, with all the guests clever and some of them pretty, offers human life and human nature under very favorable circumstances." Who first made the statement?

38. What celebrated English poet and letter-writer wrote the story of *The Three Bears,* commonly placed among the anonymous classics of the nursery?

*John Erskine*

39. How many days before the Battle of Lexington did Paul Revere really make his famous ride?

40. Who gave Longfellow the plot of *Evangeline?*

*Robert Cantwell*

41. From what religious writer did Stephen Dedalus quote—without giving proper credit—when he characterized Shakespeare's London life: "Twenty years he dallied there between conjugal love and its chaste delights and scortatory love and its foul pleasures?"

42. Who was the first American novelist to try a sympathetic portrait of a revolutionary terrorist?

*Corey Ford*

43. Who said that who was only a part of whose dream, and if he woke up ". . . you'd go out—bang!—just like a candle!"

44. Who put salt in her tea and what did the lady from Philadelphia do to help her out of her difficulties?

*S.S. Van Dine*

45. Of what American detective novel was a "memorial" edition published—fifty-six years after its initial appearance—during the author's lifetime?

46. And who (solemnly believing the publishers' report that the author was dead) wrote the introduction to this "memorial" edition?

*Tess Slesinger*

47. Who wrote *The Portrait of The Artist as an American?*

48. What great American short-story writer went to Mexico, disappeared, and was never heard of again?

*John Held, Junior*

49. What author was a prize-fighter in Galveston, Texas, known as "Nig"?

50. What author used a pair of strange spectacles in order to translate part of a famous book?

The following paragraphs and the answers came in the October issue. How did you make out? Second place in the contest went to Manter Q. Hall, Cambridge, Massachusetts; third, to Betsy M. Fleet, Richmond, Virginia. Betsy was the real winner. It didn't occur to me till years later—and it never occurred to the editors of *Vanity Fair*—that "Manter Q. Hall" was a dormitory at Harvard!

Here, on this page, are the long-awaited answers to *Vanity Fair's Permanent Literary Questionnaire,* which has broken the hearts and destroyed the homes of many Americans during the past two months. Most of our foremost citizens—editors, publishers, bankers, and housewives—gave up their summer to this inquisition, and have now been put away for the fall.

We print the answers exactly as we got them from the renowned writers who hatched the questions originally. On this page, each writer's name appears after his two questions and answers. Fidelty to *these* answers is all that counted in the final reckoning; but even so, the judges have left town. Little did they think, last August, that they were in for hundreds of responses to this questionnaire—from Paducah, Ky. (Irvin Cobb's town), New Palestine, Ind., and Eau Gallie, Fla. Even Samuel Chew, who perpetrated our *Ultimate Horror in Questionnaires* eight years ago, did his part. One victim, Rachel Biggs, wrote from Atlantic City: "It has been hideous."

The Editor himself was able to answer only six of the queries. And the winner, after weeks of research, mastered not many more than two-thirds of them. But the difficulty of the questions has not kept this from being the most successful questionnaire in *Vanity Fair's* history. . . .

## ANSWERS

1. Charles Dickens, with Inspector Bucket, in *Bleak House.*
2. His lyric for the song, *The Banks of the Wabash.*
3. "Denver" Langdon Smith, who wrote *Evolution.*
4. Lord Byron, who mentions, in the 11th Canto of *Don Juan,* "My friend and corporeal pastor and master, John Jackson, Esquire, Professor of Pugilism. . . ."
5. Cordelia in *King Lear* and Tess of the D'Urbervilles.
6. Mary Godwin, daughter of William Godwin and Mary Wollstonecraft; wife of Shelley, with whom she eloped; she had a tender friendship, when a young widow, with Washington Irving; and she was the author of *Frankenstein.*
7. Sheridan's Ride and Pickett's Charge.
8. Philip Freneau.
9. Ralph Waldo Emerson.
10. Edgar Allan Poe, in Baltimore.
11. Maxwell Bodenheim.
12. Nahum Tate, who translated Fracastoro's poem, *Syphilis, sive morbi Gallici.*
13. The Shepherdson–Grangerford feud in *Huckleberry Finn.*
14. Enid Bagnold and S. N. Behrman.
15. "When we lived at Henley, Barnes' gander was stole by tinkers," said Mrs. F's aunt in *Little Dorrit.*
16. Dolly Clandon, in Act II of *You Never Can Tell.*
17. Lafcadio comes from Leucadia (pronounced Lefcadia), which is the name of the Greek-Ionian island where he was born.
18. A bibliography by F. M. Kircheisen (1911) lists 100,000 titles. It is by no means complete, and since, many more thousands have appeared.

19. Ralph Waldo Emerson.
20. Stephen Crane's *The Red Badge of Courage.*
21. *A Study in Scarlet*, 1887.
22. *Through the Looking Glass,* by Lewis Carroll, for Deems Taylor's *Through the Looking Glass.*
23. The name Peter.
24. James Thomson and Rudyard Kipling.
25. Amelia Barr.
26. Eugene O'Neill.
27. Richard Hildreth.
28. Tennyson's *In Memoriam,* stanza LIV.
29. In Mark Twain's *A Double-Barreled Detective Story.*
30. In Herman Melville's *Moby Dick.*
31. *Henry V,* Act III, Scene iv.
32. "Off with his head! So much for Buckingham!", and "Richard is himself again!", in the last act of *Richard III*—lines which Colley Cibber wrote into his acting version of the play.
33. Mrs. Emerson said this of Thoreau.
34. O. Henry.
35. The Poetry Society of America; George Sylvester Viereck.
36. *Everybody's Magazine;* Owen Johnson's *Making Money.*
37. Disraeli in *Coningsby.*
38. Robert Southey.
39. The Battle of Lexington happened on a Wednesday morning, and Paul Revere rode through all the towns on the preceding Sunday, warned them, and promised to ride out Tuesday night to say whether the British were coming by river or by road. He had advance information, but, unluckily, so had the British, and when he started on the Tuesday ride he was promptly arrested. He got to Lexington on foot after the battle was over. He told all this in a letter which ought to be famous. It is published in the *Old South Leaflets.*
40. Nathaniel Hawthorne. The plot is published in Hawthorne's *Notebooks.*
41. Swedenborg, who wrote, "Deliciae sapientiae de amore conjugiali; voluptates insaniae de amore scortatorio."
42. Henry James.
43. Tweedledee said that Alice was part of the Red King's dream, in *Through the Looking Glass.* Tweedledum said that if he woke up, Alice would go out like a candle.
44. Mrs. Peterkin of *The Peterkin Papers.* The lady from Philadelphia suggested that she pour herself a new cup of tea. (The hard part about this question is that it was not tea, but coffee.—The Eds.)
45. *The Leavenworth Case,* by Anna Katherine Green.
46. S. S. Van Dine.

47. Matthew Josephson.
48. Ambrose Bierce.
49. Roark Bradford.
50. Joseph Smith. The spectacles were the Urim and Thummim. The famous book: *The Book of Mormon.*

# Gutenberg and the Book of Books

GUTENBERG REMAINS a very special name for bookmen. There is no book that is studied more than the Bible. And there is no Bible that has been studied more than the Gutenberg Bible, generally considered the first large book printed from movable metal type. Every letter of every line on every page has been subjected to analysis. And no one yet knows for sure that it was printed by Gutenberg. Or who invented printing. Or what book was first printed. Or where. Or when. Claims, counterclaims, lawsuits and the paralyzing apparatus of scholarship smog all.

Yet there is left, for all of us to see, one of the most beautiful books the world has managed to create. As Seymour de Ricci has said:

> The quiet dignity of those twelve hundred and odd pages of dark stately type, the deep black ink, the broadness of the margins, the fine texture of the paper, may have been equaled, but they have never been surpassed; and in its very cradle, the printer's art, thanks to the Gutenberg Bible, shines indeed as an art much more than as a craft. . . . Last but not least, the Gutenberg Bible is the first edition of the Book of Books. The mere fact that in the Rhine Valley in 1450 the first book to be printed should be the Bible, tells its own story. Did Gutenberg realize that by setting up the Holy Text in type he was heralding one of the greatest movements of human thought in the history of the civilized world?

Of the second copy of the Gutenberg Bible ever to cross the Atlantic, Henry Stevens of Vermont, the Yankee turned London bookseller, wrote thus in 1870 to George Brinley of Hartford, Connecticut:

Pray, Sir, ponder for a moment and appreciate the rarity and importance of this precious consignment from the old world to the new. Not only is it the first Bible, but it is the first book ever printed. It was read in Europe half a century before America was discovered. Therefore, in view of these considerations please to suggest to your Deputy at the Customs to uncover his head while in the presence of this first book and never for a moment to turn his back upon it while the case is open. Let no ungodly or thieving politician lay eyes or hands upon it. The sight can *now* give him no good, while the Bible may suffer. Let none of Uncle Samuel's Custom House officials, or other men in or out of authority, see it without first reverentially lifting their hats.

The original of Stevens' letter is now with the Scheide copy of this Bible in Princeton, New Jersey.

It is every bookdealer's dream to discover a Gutenberg Bible, or failing that, to figure in some transaction involving one. There are many dealers in many countries and very few Gutenbergs, so most dreams concerning them must remain just dreams. When Edward Lazare did his first census of known copies in 1950 for the *Antiquarian Bookman,* he located forty-five on vellum and paper and in various states of completeness, fewer than half perfect: twelve in the United States, eleven in Germany, nine in Great Britain, four in France, two in Italy, two in Spain, and one each in Austria, Denmark, Poland, Portugal and Switzerland. This last had formerly been in the Imperial Library at St. Petersburg and was sold by the Soviet Government in 1931; it is now owned by the great collector Martin Bodmer. One volume was privately owned in England by Sir Philip Frere. This, the most recent copy to have changed hands, Volume I only, was the Dyson Perrins copy and had brought £22,000 at Sotheby's in 1947.

Of the twelve American copies one was on the West Coast—at Huntington. Others were at Harvard, Yale, three at the Pierpont Morgan Library (though not all perfect), the New York Public Library, the General Theological Seminary in New York and the Library of Congress. Three were privately owned: Carl H. Pforzheimer of New York, the John H. Scheide Library in Titusville, Pennsylvania, and (Volume II only) Arthur A. Houghton, Jr., of Queenstown, Maryland. The late great dealer Dr. Rosenbach had handled all three. In 1923 he bought, at the Earl of Carysfort's sale in London, a perfect copy in a contemporary binding for £8,500 for Carl Pforzheimer. The following year he sold the James II. Ellsworth, of Chicago, copy (then lacking seventeen leaves) to John H. Scheide for $46,000. In 1926 he purchased at auction in New

York the perfect copy owned for centuries by the Benedictine Monastery of Melk, Austria, for $106,000. This was the highest price ever paid at public auction for a printed book at that time. Mrs. Edward S. Harkness purchased it and presented it to Yale University. Finally, in 1937, Rosenbach acquired at auction in London an imperfect Volume II (250 of 317 leaves) for Arthur A. Houghton, Jr., for £8,000. Much more of this later.

It was assumed that any possible relocations would of necessity center around the five privately owned copies. There was always the possibility of a new copy's being discovered, though this had not happened in our century—the last copy uncovered was in a monastery in Spain in 1874. And even if a new one did appear, the chances of its coming on the open market were extremely remote.

Such was the Gutenberg situation in 1949, when I was visiting Mrs. Edward Doheny in Los Angeles with some rare books of Scribner's, by whom I was employed. An ardent book collector, she had established at Camarillo, California, the Edward L. Doheny Memorial Library, featuring among its treasures a substantial collection of early Bibles, both printed and manuscript. During one conversation she mentioned casually how very much, for personal reasons, she wanted a Gutenberg Bible and how unlikely she was ever to get one. She revealed that she had been the underbidder for the Dyson Perrins copy and regretted having lost it. I laughingly promised to offer her the very next copy Scribner's obtained.

Back in New York I got to thinking. Here I was with a customer for THE BOOK and I ought, by golly, to try and do something about it. I made inquiries of all private owners as to the possibilities of purchasing their copies and received a universal "no." "After all," said Carl Pforzheimer, "I wouldn't have a library without it, would I?" Martin Bodmer replied, on one of his typical postcards, "If I didn't have mine I'd go out and buy it, if I could." And so on. The Pierpont Morgan Library with their three copies (how grand can you get?) politely informed me they had every intention of keeping them. No public or university library or state institution could conceivably part with theirs. So that left the copy at the General Theological Seminary, 175 Ninth Avenue, New York City. Imagine, the Bible on the *West* Side!

I knew this copy very well and had even been privileged to handle it on occasion. This came about because a small number of my fellow students at Lehigh University eventually went into the ministry ("angel makers," we used to call them), and of these some always went directly from Bethlehem to the General Theological for their graduate studies. Living at the time on Tenth Street, at St. Mark's-in-the-Bouwerie, I would run into old friends from there fairly often. Inevitably, of course, our talk would get to their Bible, and I remembered one classmate of mine, since become a bishop, who used to argue the uselessness of the book in its current habitat. "Nobody ever sees it, nobody ever uses it, it's just put away in an old safe in the library which isn't even locked most of the time. And anyway, there are a half dozen copies in New York if anyone must consult it. What good is it doing here?" He was all for selling it and using the proceeds for good works—and so was I. But this was in the early thirties when even the Bible probably wasn't salable. So nothing was done, even about abortive plans to swipe it. These fell through, because what are you going to do with it after you have it? Our thinking did not, at that time, reach the ransom level.

Suddenly, twenty years later, remembrance of all this popped into my head. I still had friends at the Seminary. Furthermore, Charles Scribner's daughter had married a lad who was resident and teaching there. And I was told upon excellent authority that the Seminary needed funds at that particular time rather more than they usually did. The money provided by the sale of the Gutenberg would serve for some very useful scholarships and other worthy projects.

There followed the usual meetings with theological VIP's and so on. I pointed out that the transfer would be absolutely without publicity of any kind. Everyone seemed enthusiastic about the prospect except, appropriately enough, the librarian. A price was fixed which was, quite properly, the highest at which this book, or indeed any printed book, had ever been sold, $150,000. Scribner's were acting merely as broker in the transaction. The purchaser was to pay the Seminary directly, and they were to pay Scribner's a commission. It's always better this way, I have found. "Europeans," to paraphrase Sterne, "order things differently." But this, after all, was a reputable hundred-year-old publishing establishment dealing directly with a somewhat older, but equally respectable, institution. No documents were signed. None were needed. The Bible was taken to the Pierpont Morgan Library to be properly packed and shipped to Los Angeles. I could not help imagining, of course, what Gutenberg, active exactly five hundred years earlier, would have thought of all this. Here was one single copy of his baby (imperfect, at that, as will appear) which was being transported three thousand miles over a continent he had never heard of, and valued at a price which would have settled all his sad lawsuits with money left over.

And Gutenberg, though he never heard of America, had enormous influence upon its history. Had his invention followed Columbus's discovery by as many years as it preceded it, history would be quite different. Others, we know now, had made the trip; none had a printing press to report it. Columbus could have joined them in myth and legend instead of in cold, clear type.

The copy owned by the General Theological can be traced to about 1830, when the English collector Sir John Thorold bought it for his Syston Park Library. Its provenance before then is uncertain, but it may have belonged at one time to the church at Offenburg, Germany. At the sale of Thorold's library in 1884 it was bought by Bernard Quaritch for £3,900 and sold to the Reverend William Makellar of Edinburgh, a Scottish Presbyterian cleric.

At the sale of Makellar's library in 1898, Quaritch, acting for the Very Reverend Dr. Eugene Augustus Hoffman, then Dean of General Theological, purchased it for £2,950. Thus, there came to New York's *West Side* THE BOOK. One trusts the Makellar heirs forgave him his investment.

In all accounts of this copy it had been listed as perfect. Not until my negotiations with the Seminary were well advanced was I told that it was imperfect. Leaf III of Volume II, Ezekiel, chapters 14–16, was in pen-and-ink facsimile. This fact was discovered in 1916 by the expert Dr. Joseph Martini, who was methodically collating it with a magnifying glass. The mystery of when or by whom this was done remains unexplained to this day. Most volumes of any ancient work, or modern one, for that matter, if imperfect, lack leaves either at the beginning or the end. Normal usage accounts for this. The legendary Shuckburgh copy, as will appear, was thus defective. And so with others which were not totally dismembered.

Somewhere along the centuries this leaf was torn out, or conceivably never bound in to begin with. Dr. Martini was of the opinion, as I am, that the facsimile "probably was done by the well-known Harris about 1835 or 1840." Harris was so skillful in book restoration and pen-and-ink facsimile that he eventually had to initial his own work to enable himself to distinguish it from the printed page. His eyes failed him and he died blind.

Quaritch thought the leaf predated Harris, largely on the question of binding. The leaf was probably present when the book was rebound in blue morocco, gilt-tooled, early in the nineteenth century. The flyleaves of the binding bear watermarks of 1815. But this gives only a *terminus ad quem*. The problem remains. To supply the missing leaf seemed impossible. The traditional search for the haystack needle was simple in comparison. When the defect was discovered the Seminary attempted to

*To W Wordsworth with the author's sincere Reverence —*

# Poems,

BY

## JOHN KEATS.

" What more felicity can fall to creature,
" Than to enjoy delight with liberty."
*Fate of the Butterfly.*—SPENSER.

## LONDON:

PRINTED FOR

C. & J. OLLIER, 3, WELBECK STREET,

CAVENDISH SQUARE.

1817.

*Title page of the copy of Keats's* Poems *with the author's inscription to William Wordsworth*

*Rip Van Winkle.*

a posthumous writing of Diedrich Knickerbocker

By Woden, God of Saxons,
From whence comes wensday. that is Wodensday,
Truth is a thing that ever I will keep
Unto thylke day in which I creep into
My sepulchre ——
                                        Cartwright.

Whoever has made a voyage up the
Hudson ~~since~~ must remember the ~~Kat~~
Kaatskill mountains. They are a dismembered branch of the great Appala-
chian family, and are seen away to the
west of the river swelling up to a noble
height and lording it over the surrounding country. Every change of season,
every change of weather, indeed every hour
of the day, produces some change in the
magical hues and shapes of these mountains, and they are regarded by all the

*Manuscript page of Washington Irving's* Rip Van Winkle, *America's first international literary success*

*(Opposite, above) Manuscript page of* Old Mother Hubbard *(1804), by Sarah Catherine Martin*

*(Opposite, below) Manuscript of the earliest known version of Robert Burns's "Auld Lang Syne"*

She took a clean dish
To get him some tripe;
When she came back
He was smoaking his pipe.

Auld lang Syne ————

Should auld acquaintance be forgot,
 And never thought upon;
Let's hae a waught o' Malaga,
 For auld lang syne.

 Chorus.
 For auld lang syne, my jo,
 For auld lang syne;
Let's hae a waught o' Malaga,
 For auld lang syne.

And surely ye'll be your pint-stoup!
 And surely I'll be mine!
And we'll tak a cup o' kindness yet,
 For auld lang syne.
 For auld &c.

We twa hae run about the braes,
 And pou't the gowans fine;
But we've wander'd mony a weary foot
 Sin auld lang syne.
 For auld &c.

*To Mrs Banyar, from her Humble Servant the Author. This first copy that has been issued, is Respectfully Presented*

THE SPY;

A TALE OF

THE NEUTRAL GROUND.

"Breathes there a man with soul so dead,
Who never to himself hath said,
This is my own, my native land.—"

BY

THE AUTHOR OF "PRECAUTION."

IN TWO VOLUMES.

VOL. I.

NEW-YORK:

WILEY & HALSTED, 3, WALL-STREET.
::::::::::
Wm. Grattan, Printer.

1821.

*Title page of the only known inscribed copy of* The Spy, *by James Fenimore Cooper*

*(Opposite) Manuscript page of early version of Edgar Allan Poe's "The Bells"*

# The Bells

## By Mrs. M. L. Shew.

The bells! — ah, — the bells!
The little silver bells!
How fairy-like a melody there floats
From their throats —
From their merry little throats —
From the silver, tinkling throats

Of the bells, bells, bells —
Of the bells!

———

The bells! — ah, the bells!
The heavy iron bells!
How horrible a monody there floats
From their throats —
From their deep-toned throats —
From their melancholy throats!
How I shudder at the notes

Of the bells, bells, bells —
Of the bells!

V

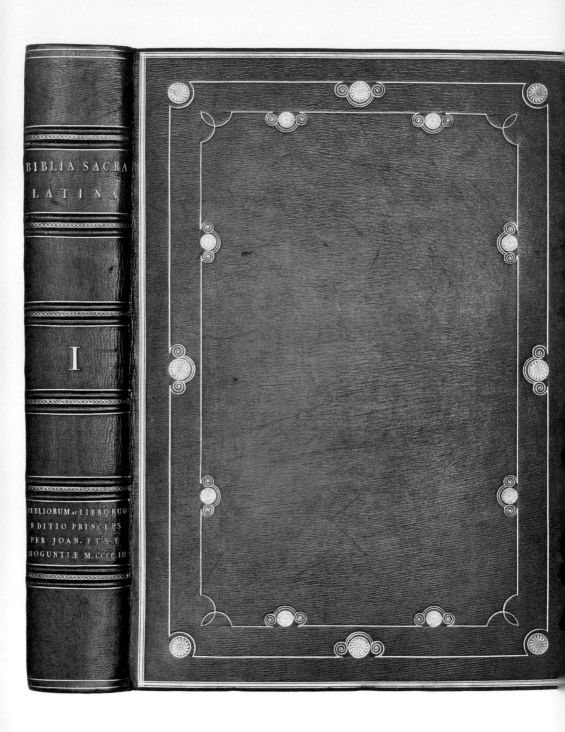

*Binding and front endpaper of the Shuckburgh copy of the Gutenberg Bible*

VII

in not closing with terms greatly inferior to those upon which our previous negotiations have proceeded. ——— Besides, — if you please, Mr Bentley — let bygones be bygones; let those previous books, for the present, take care of themselves. For here now we have a new book, and what shall we say about this? If nothing has been made on the old books, may not something be made out of the new? — At any rate, herewith you have it. Look at it and see whether it will suit you to purchase at the terms I shall state below. It is a larger book, by 150 pages & more, than I thought it would be, at the date of my first writing you about it. Other things being equal, this circumstance, in your mode of publication — must of course augment its value to you.

——— I can not but believe, that as the overtures you made me in your last note were based upon an almost entire ignorance as to the character of the new book (because you could have no means of knowing what it was going to be) now that you see it before you, you will, upon a reconsideration, be induced not to decline the ultimate terms which I here submit, as follows: ——— £100 (you buying the book — for England — out-&-out) to be drawn for by me at thirty days' sight, immediately upon my being apprised of your acquiescence. — I trust that our connection will thus be made to continue, and that on the new field of productions upon which I embark in the present work, you & I shall hereafter participate in many not unprofitable business adventures.

Very Truly Yours
Herman Melville.

*Two pages of Herman Melville's melancholy letter to his English publisher, Richard Bentley*

P.S. If, Mr Bentley, you accede to the before-mentioned terms, you might then go on and publish without further hearing from me. For the book will reach you, I think, in the prime of the season. At all events, I shall suspend the publication at the Harpers' till I have concluded some satisfactory negotiation in London. So you may be sure that if you undertake the book, your publication will not be anticipated here by the Harpers. I send you the proofs from the type instead of the plates, for which I should have to wait some few days.

I presume that ere this sheet comes to your hand, Mr Lemuel Shaw will have arrived in London. I furnished him with a letter to you. And would here again invoke for him any attentions you may be able to bestow. —— H. M.

One more P.S. — I have thought that, on several accounts, (one of which is, the rapid succession in which my works have lately been published) it might not prove unadvisable to publish this present book anonymously, or under an assumed name: — * "By a Vermonter" say. I beg you to consider the propriety of this suggestion, but defer the final decision to your own better experience in such matters, since I am prompted in throwing out the idea, merely in regard to your advantage as publisher.
H. M.

* or "By Guy Winthrop."

IX

Mr. Lamb presents his respects to Mr Munden, and begs his acceptance of a Volume, at the end of which he has ventured a faint description of the pleasure he has received from Mr. Munden's acting.

20 Great Russell Street
Covent Garden.

*Inscription to Joseph Shepherd Munden in a copy of Charles Lamb's* Elia, *perhaps the dedication copy*

*(Opposite)* Page *from Percy Bysshe Shelley's notes on* Frankenstein

Frankenstein & the being on the sea of ice ~~~~~
es of almost approaches in effect to the recep
to labours of Caleb Williams with his ~several~
Falkland. It amints us indeed somewhat the
style & character of that admirable author, ~writer~
~of which indeed this author~ up to whom the
author has dedicated his work, & of whose
productions he seems to have studied. ~At t~
There is only one instance however ~in which~
we detect the least approach to imitation
& that is, ~in~ Frankensteins landing ~& that~
in Ireland. ~HOW~ ~~~~ ~~~~
death of Elisabeth, the ~story~ the general
character of the tale indeed resembles ~on~
~~~ precedes it. After the death of Elisabeth
the story, like a theme which grows at
once more rapid & profound as it proceeds,
assumes an irresistible solemnity, and the

<u>Private.</u>                 22nd. February, 1929.

Dear Professor Housman

By command of the King I beg leave
to inform you that it is His Majesty's wish
to confer upon you the Order of Merit, in
recognition of your valuable work as a
Classical Scholar and in the ranks of literature.
Will you kindly let me know whether it will
be agreeable to you to receive this Honour.

Yours very truly
Stamfordham

Professor A.E. Housman,
    Trinity College,
        Cambridge.

With all gratitude for His Majesty's most kind and flattering
wish to confer upon me the Order of Merit I humbly beg
permission to decline this high honour. I hope to escape
the reproach of thanklessness or churlish behaviour by
borrowing the words in which an equally loyal subject,
Admiral Cornwallis, declined a similar mark of the
Royal favour: "I am, unhappily, of a turn of mind
that would make my receiving that honour the most
unpleasant thing imaginable".

XIII.

"Over the Sea to Skye"

Sing me a song of a lad that is gone,
    Say, could that lad be I?
Merry of soul, he sailed on a day
        Over the sea to Skye.

        Mull was astern, Egg on the port,
            Rum on the Starboard bow:
        Glory of youth glowed in his soul:
            Where is that glory now.
Sing me a song of a lad that is gone,
        Say, could that lad be I?

                8

Merry of soul he sailed on a day
    Over the sea to Skye.
        Give me again, all that was there,
            Give me the sun that shone:
        Give me the eyes, give me the soul,
            Give me the lad that's gone.
        Billow and breeze, islands and seas,
            Mountains of rain and sun,
        All that was good, all that was fair,
            All that was me is gone.

*Manuscript of Robert Louis Stevenson's "Over the Sea to Skye"*

*(Opposite) George V's offer of the Order of Merit and A. E. Housman's gracious refusal, written on the reverse side*

I

II

III

(Opposite) First page of manuscript of Mozart's Symphony in D Major (K. 385) and the elaborate case in which the manuscript is kept

Manuscript of Mark Twain's Preface to Tom Sawyer

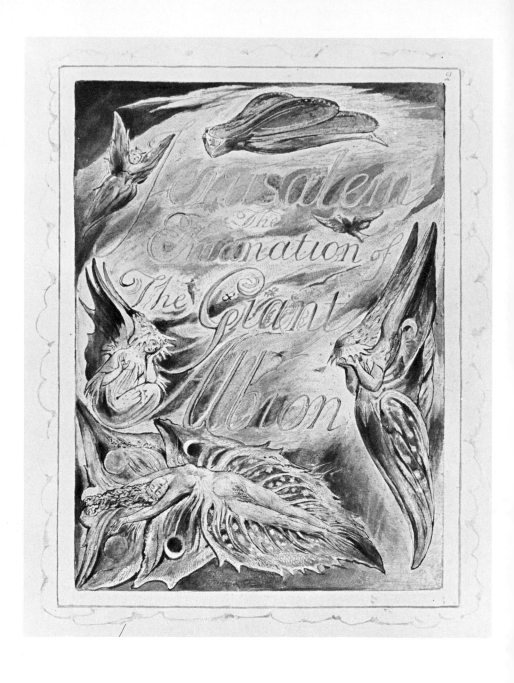

*Title page of William Blake's* Jerusalem—*"Not only a great Blake, the great Blake"*

return the Bible, luckily without success, the book having been sold "with all faults."

I did not tell Mrs. Doheny of the flaw until I saw her. She had insisted that the whole transaction be kept secret. Even in her own home the book was referred to in code—"commode" was the word.

The great day arrived. I was met at my hotel by a chauffeur, driven to Mrs. Doheny's estate in the center of Los Angeles, stopped at the gate by guards, as usual, etc., and found myself, after lunch, with the "Countess," as some knew her, or "Ma," as others did, THE BOOK, and some assorted characters, gathered around a small table in the library.

The confession came first: the gem had a flaw. This disconcerted "Ma" not a whit. But her counselors, none of whom, I immediately perceived, wished her to buy the book, saw a quick out. She was reminded on the one hand of the new wing the children's hospital needed, on another that the tax situation was tough (she had just disposed of, according to the Los Angeles papers, some stray oil lands for $40,000,000), and on still another that, being imperfect, THE BOOK wasn't worthy of her, etc., *ad nauseam.*

It was a curious conference. All of her advisers—financial, religious, legal (with the honorable exception of Miss Lucille Miller, her librarian)—agreed that this was not for her. "Back to New York, son, and take your bait with you—go fishing elsewhere," I was advised (not quite in those terms).

The "Countess" listened carefully and then spoke. "I remember 1912 when the Robert Hoe copy of the Gutenberg Bible sold for fifty thousand dollars to Henry Huntington. Ed and I were having breakfast when I read of it in the paper, and I said, 'Will you, some day, buy me a Gutenberg Bible, dear?' He said, 'I promise you I will.' It was an impossible promise for him, in those days. Gentlemen, I am buying this book as a present from him to me."

End of discussion.

I flew back to New York with cheerful news for everyone concerned. To this point the Seminary had not known the eventual disposition of their Bible. When I had a conference with their directors, jubilantly reporting "mission accomplished," a freeze occurred. Finally Mrs. Doheny and Scribner's were informed that the Seminary would not part with the Bible. Before starting this venture I had naturally explored all possibilities—the legal right of the Seminary to dispose of this gift, their willingness to do so (evidenced, obviously, by their granting me permission to take it to California), and so forth.

I was never informed of the reason for this decision. Frank P. Leslie, in his enthusiastic essay on "The 46th Gutenberg" (Wisconsin, 1960), states:

> The General Theological Seminary decided to sell their great copy in order to provide higher salaries for the faculty. I am indebted to Professor William Jackson of the Houghton Library at Harvard for this priceless story. The faculty, fully conscious of the desire of the Trustees to improve their incomes, voted down the proposal in a display of devotion to academic ideals that lifted the spirits of all who knew of it. Mr. Jackson dryly wondered how safe it would be to submit such a proposal to other faculties.

The nearest I came to understanding the trustees' action was information that Dr. Rosenbach, putting on his usual dog-in-the-manger act after he learned of the negotiations, persuaded them for his own private reasons that they weren't getting enough for it. "Goodness," as Mae West has said, "had nothing to do with it."

It was all terribly embarrassing. I felt that I had let Mrs. Doheny down and the Seminary had let Scribner's down, and a very gracious lady had been needlessly hurt.

In any event, here I was with a customer for THE BOOK, and no book. I wrote my "opposite number" in Scribner's London branch, John Carter, the well-known bibliographer and nemesis of the forger Thomas J. Wise. In a matter of months the miracle happened. On January 4, 1951, Carter wrote:

> I took Dring of Quaritch's into my confidence about your abortive negotiations last year, on the theory that they were the most likely firm in England to hear of any other that might come on the market. And by a most surprising coincidence he reported to me very shortly thereafter that he had heard of the existence of a copy, the possibility of buying which would depend on his being able to mention in fairly firm terms a pretty substantial price. At this stage, of course, we both thought the thing was probably a mirage; but on the chance it was not, I thought the only thing to do was to put our cards on the table, tell him the price we had successfully put on the Seminary's copy and work back from that. The price we decided to offer was £40,000, profits to be divided 50/50. Is Mrs. Doheny still in the market?

I answered:

> I sent you an enthusiastic cable and talked the matter over with Charlie and George Schieffelin, and though neither of them are dancing in the streets at the prospect of so substantial an investment in a single book, neither are they altogether against it.
>
> You say in your letter that it would cost us approximately $116,000 with Quaritch getting a fifty-fifty split in the profits when sold. I think

I could persuade myself, granting of course that the copy is a really fine one, to do one of two things—either we buy this jointly with Quaritch, they putting up half the capital purchase and taking half the profits when sold, or, which indeed I would prefer, we buy the book outright from them, give them a profit of ten or twelve thousand and control the whole show ourselves, i.e., if it could be delivered here at a price of say around $125,000 free and clear to us, more if they felt they wanted it. After all, when you get in water this deep a few extra thousands don't matter much.

I can tell you this confidentially about the main reason we didn't get the General Theological copy last year. Although ostensibly Mrs. Doheny's offer was turned down as a matter of principle and not on a matter of price, the chairman of the board, Mr. Givens, told me confidentially later that they had several outside opinions as to the book's value and the consensus was that the offer was considerably too low, and I don't think they would have accepted anything less than $200,000 for the book. Of course I felt all along that they treated me rather shabbily in the whole transaction, and I simply refused to have anything to do with any further negotiations. Anyway there was still a strong undercurrent among the faculty against selling the book at any price, and I strongly doubt that it will ever come on the market, during our time at any rate. But now that this astonishing piece of luck has come along with this unrecorded and so far unseen copy cropping up, I'll be damned if I'm going to let it go without a good healthy whack at it.

There is not as you realize much possibility of making any substantial profit over a $125,000 investment. We can make twenty percent or so for a quick turnover, perhaps more if we're lucky, but what the Hell's the use of working for capitalists if you don't make them use their capital occasionally, and it would be fun to handle a Gutenberg. Anyway, that's how I happen to feel after a very good lunch and three Martinis. Let me know how things eventuate.

Neither Quaritch nor Carter had seen the book at this time, and both were working through an intermediary (Sir Sydney Cockerell) who alone knew the book and its owner. When it was finally available, it turned out to be defective, lacking the first leaf of each volume and the last three of Volume II. This was partially offset by the fact that of the eighty-two leaves known to have been reprinted in course of production, every one was present in first state—a rare and much-prized distinction. Informed of the defect, the owner refused to adjust the price, and THE BOOK was purchased as agreed.

After the purchase had been completed I wrote "Ma" about this new "commode."

Had it not been for your interest it is extremely unlikely that this copy would have been uncovered. You were so generous and gracious to me last fall that I was even more disappointed than you when the Seminary decided not to sell. (I remember particularly your story of the Huntington copy.) I feel morally committed, therefore, to give you the first refusal of this copy. And as I told Miss Miller, I was determined not to approach you until I had complete rights to sell you the volume on the spot if you decided you wanted it.

She declined, explaining that, since I had seen her a few months before, she had acquired a copy! Sir Philip Frere's copy, to be exact. We had previously, of course, discussed this copy, the latest to have changed hands. It was Volume I only, but a very fine copy bound in contemporary calf over wooden boards. It had formerly belonged to the Earl of Gosford, whose entire library was purchased by Toovey, a London book dealer, in 1878. In 1884 he sold the library at auction, buying in the Bible at £500. It was sold shortly afterward to Lord Amherst of Hackney for £600. At the sale of his library in 1908 it was purchased by Bernard Quaritch for £2,050 for C. W. Dyson Perrins. At the Dyson Perrins sale, March 10–11, 1947, it was bought by Maggs Brothers for £22,000 with Mrs. Doheny the underbidder, and wound up in Sir Philip's possession. I had made some inquiry as to its possible availability, with negative results.

The redoubtable Countess eventually acquired it. She had been hurt by the Seminary's withdrawal of their copy, and the possession of THE BOOK became an emotional necessity when she remembered her husband's promise. Or so I think. So two Gutenbergs came to America's West Coast—one at Huntington, the other at Camarillo. I was happy, of course, for Mrs. Doheny and offered to take the volume in part exchange for Scribner's set, but she was satisfied with the status quo. According to Lucille V. Miller, in her Introduction to Part III of the *Catalogue of Books & Manuscripts in the Estelle Doheny Library* (Los Angeles, 1955), by a happy coincidence the Frere copy was delivered to her on October 14, 1950, the tenth anniversary of the dedication of the Edward S. Doheny Memorial Library, and during Holy Year. So within a few months I found myself no longer with a customer for THE BOOK and no book, but exactly the reverse.

At this point Quaritch offered to sell their interest outright for £2,500. Charles Scribner and I discussed this over lunch at the Racquet and Tennis Club. I knew that this was my only chance ever to own a copy of THE BOOK and felt that the Carter-Randall axis, having uncovered it, deserved it. Charles listened to all this and finally rather plaintively inquired if there wasn't something else a little cheaper that he could buy to keep me happy. Then he added—sadly, prophetically—"I'll probably die possessed of it, but, at that, it will be a star in my crown when I face St. Peter."

Except for the missing leaves, the book turned out to be a very good one, comfortably larger than the George III and Grenville copies in the British Museum, and bound with restrained elegance in crimson morocco, signed and dated 1789, by Henry Walther, one of the several German binders then working in London.

One feature was curious. Below the main title and volume numbers on the back of each volume are the words: *Bibliorum ac Librorum Editio Princeps Per Joan. Fust Moguntiae MCCCCLII.* (The first Bible and the first book by Johann Fust, Mainz, 1452.) Thus the binder, or whoever instructed him, attributed the work not to Gutenberg, but to his partner, Fust, and at a date three years earlier than that generally ascribed. Thus was the forty-sixth copy restored to the known hierarchy.

As to the history and discovery of Scribner's lost legendary copy: The first census of Gutenbergs in England was made by the famous antiquarian Thomas Frognall Dibdin, in Volume II of his *Library Companion* (London, 1824) in a footnote on page 13, where he lists twelve copies. Among those in private collections were mentioned "the King, the Duke of Sussex, the Duke of Devonshire, Earl Spencer, Sir G. Shuckboro', Sir M. M. Sykes." This is the only nineteenth-century reference to the "Shuckboro'" copy. In 1911 Seymour de Ricci in his *Catalogue Raisonné*, prepared for the Gutenberg Gesellschaft, listed it among the "exemplaires disparus." All the other copies in England were accounted for.

Book dealers, collectors and librarians form a very small, tight and generally gossipy group, and it seemed unlikely indeed that a copy of THE BOOK could be privately owned in England for a century and a quarter without someone's knowing about it. Yet it turns out that it was just this that happened—or very nearly. And had not inquiries been made on Mrs. Doheny's behalf just at the time they were, it is quite possible that the copy would still be residing in Dorset in complete obscurity so far as censuses or public knowledge of its existence goes.

There was much interest, especially in the British press, as to the Bible's owner. Through agreement this was not mentioned. The announcement said "it was known as the Shuckburgh copy from Sir George Shuckburgh, who had it in his library in the 1800's, and it was found in the possession of an unnamed collateral descendant." That was all, but it was more than enough. Within a matter of a few days one English newsman, armed with *Burke's Peerage* and other genealogics, knew the owner—

Lady Christian Martin, daughter of the fifth Earl of Portarlington, whose first husband had been the Honorable Fergus Bowes-Lyon, brother of the Queen of England.

Presumably Sir George Augustus Shuckburgh, sixth baronet, bought the book when he made the Grand Tour in the early 1780's. He died in 1804 without male issue, and the book descended through the female line. It was, at one time or another, in the libraries of half a dozen noble families in the peerage of England. It seems incredible that someone, sometime, would not see it and remark in print upon it. At any rate, old Dibdin (who clearly never saw it) excepted, no one did. Dr. Rosenbach was especially chagrined when he heard of its provenance, as Lady Martin had been an especially close friend of his brother Philip, who had frequently visited her. But Philip was never much interested in books, as the Wolf-Fleming biography makes abundantly clear.

John Carter flew the Bible across the Atlantic. He arrived at Idlewild on a Saturday, only to find that some pre-entry forms had not been complied with and that the book would have to remain in a wire cage till Monday. A receipt was given by Customs "for one suitcase said to contain a Gutenberg Bible."

On Monday, February 4, 1951, its acquisition was jointly announced in New York and London and put on the wire by the Associated Press, among others. In addition the volumes were shown on television, mentioned on radio, subjected to accounts in *The New Yorker, Time, The Saturday Evening Post*, etc. No book, certainly, ever received such widespread publicity, both in America and abroad. This resulted in a veritable deluge of letters offering "old Bibles," none of which, regrettably, proved of the slightest interest. But the publicity led me three years later to the discovery in the south of France of the only existing manuscript of James II's *Memoirs*. But that's another story.

Following Mrs. Doheny's rejection there was a decision to be made as to what to price the volumes. With payment to Quaritch and the intermediary and various expenses, the cost to Scribner's was just under $125,000. Dealer David Kirschenbaum had appeared with an offer of $150,000, the price at which it had been offered to Mrs. Doheny. He was acting, I later discovered, for H. Bradley Martin, Jr. We decided to turn the offer down and raise the price. As reported in *The New Yorker*'s "Talk of the Town" department on February 17, 1951:

> "The Shuckburgh Bible will bring more than the record price paid for *any* book—to wit, the hundred and fifty-one thousand dollars that Dr. Rosenbach, acting for Yale, paid for the Bay Psalm Book," said

Mr. Carter. "After all this is a period of inflation, and Scribner's isn't in business for its health."

However, we underestimated the seriousness of the defects, from a salesman's point of view. In the best of times it is difficult enough, believe me, to sell, let us say, the Hope diamond—perfect as it is; imperfect, the problem becomes formidable. It presents the prospective purchaser with too easy an out. Popular conception to the contrary, buyers do not come running with negotiables in their hot little hands to buy even the most romantic of books—or gems. Every conceivable defect is magnified by the prospective purchaser to avoid his fate. And reasonably so, I presume. In the present case, if one were going to pay a world record price, one wished the world's finest copy of what one got. Which this wasn't. Even though it was a question of "this, or nothing," it still left the quarry with an obvious excuse. Mr. Lilly turned the offer down for this reason and lived to regret it. Lou Silver, whose famed collection is now at the Newberry Library in Chicago, having been purchased by them for $2,750,000, wanted to buy it very much but was dissuaded by his amiable wife and fellow bibliophile, Amy, who simply didn't want the publicity she knew would result.

At this point my old friend, the imaginative librarian Lawrence Powell, of the University of California at Los Angeles, had an idea for a circulating copy of the Gutenberg Bible. This, in his own words,

> was for the State of California to buy it, to be circulated annually between the State Library in Sacramento and the University Libraries in Berkeley and Los Angeles. In changing location, the Bible would have been consigned to the State Highway Patrol, with parade stops at public schools en route. The education and inspirational benefits would have been enormous, particularly in the Far West.

He details this in his *A Passion for Books*, in the chapter, "My Biggest Flop."

Meanwhile the Chicago Bible Society expressed interest in purchasing the book, and much as I liked Larry's idea, I could not give him an option for the length of time needed for the California legislature to move, if they ever did. And in all honesty I much preferred to have the Bible in the Midwest if it were at all possible. There were, after all, two copies already in California, and the rest were in the East, all but one being on the Atlantic Coast (and that one is there now). It seemed only proper that one should be somewhere between. The Society's then secretary, the Reverend Don C. Norman, was just beginning his career as a Gutenberg enthusiast and was extremely optimistic over the possibilities of Chicago's acquiring it. Norman eventually compiled a *Pictorial Census of the Gutenberg Bible*, personally examining every known copy except two reputedly "liberated" by the Russians and currently unavailable. No one else can make this claim; I have only seen slightly over half.

The Chicago Bible Society was putting on a drive for new quarters, a building on North Michigan Avenue. What better tie-in than a building to house their collections, featured by THE BOOK? The Bible went to Chicago for a month's exhibition at the Field Museum while a fund-raising campaign got under way.

The book is in two volumes, and as I write I have before me the receipt of the Field Museum officials acknowledging the loan from Scribner's, for exhibition purposes, of *two* Gutenberg Bibles. I never held them to this when I took the book away. The campaign finally failed, as I should have known it would in the first place. These things seldom succeed. I decided at this point to peddle it no longer but to put it in the bank vault and wait until someone came along—which would eventually happen. (The Chicago Bible Society, by the way, got its building. But somehow there wasn't enough left over to buy the Bible *and* put up a building. My opinion of the Church's attitude toward THE BOOK became, at this point, a bit too brittle to print.)

It is curious, but no religious institution possessing a copy can trace its provenance to its origin. The copies in the Vatican Library (both imperfect), as a case in point, were acquired by them only in the twentieth century. Nor has any religious institution, to my knowledge, ever purchased a copy. As with almost all other institutions, they were acquired as gifts. The only American exceptions that come to mind are the Library of Congress and Indiana University. This is a rousing tribute to the vision, love, affection and generosity of private collectors who have the wisdom to put first things first.

The Bible was still in the bank vault when Charles Scribner died unexpectedly. The new regime decided that even though the Bible was just as good as money in the bank, they would prefer the money there and not the book. I had said that it could be broken up and sold profitably. In fact, in this case the whole was worth much less than the sum of its parts. Over six hundred leaves at an average of $500 per leaf was at least $300,000. Many of the important leaves—for example, the Sermon on the Mount, the Twenty-third Psalm, and so on—were readily salable at considerably more, and the book had been priced merely $200,000. So I was told to consider breaking it up.

I retired to the University Club for a few quiet drinks and to review the situation. I then dropped in on Arthur A. Houghton, Jr., whose Corning Glass offices were just up the avenue. It would be a sin to break up a nearly perfect copy, and furthermore, I didn't feel too happy about going down in book history as the only dealer who ever bought a Gutenberg and couldn't sell it!

Agreement was reached in a matter of minutes. Houghton purchased the Bible, part payment being his imperfect Volume II and (which I did not know he owned) the Reverend Roderick Terry copy of the Book of Genesis (twenty-four leaves, lacking the last leaf) from the Baroness de la Zouche copy broken up by Gabriel Wells. It had fetched $5,000 in Terry's sale on May 2, 1934.

I delivered THE BOOK to Houghton's summer home at Wye Plantation, Queenstown, Maryland, on a weekend. Sunday afternoon I was driven to Washington, D.C. to stay overnight at a hotel and return to New York by train Monday morning. The car pulled away and I went to the desk to register and suddenly realized that I was absolutely penniless. I had left my wallet on the dressing table. I didn't even have a dime for a phone call! All I had was an overnight bag and a battered valise with a Gutenberg Bible inside. I finally induced an incredulous clerk to put it in a safe while I trudged out seeking some friend who would advance me enough cash to pay the hotel bill and return me to New York.

I finally succeeded and returned to the hotel, exhausted, retrieved THE BOOK and retreated to my room. I curled up with it in a double bed and slept soundly.

The Houghton copy had a romantic history. It was found in 1828 in a peasant's home in Oelwig, near Trier (French, Trèves; ancient Augusta Trevirorum), a small city in the Rhineland about six miles from the Luxembourg border; Trier is reported as pleasantly situated in a small valley surrounded by hills, on the right bank of the Moselle about sixty miles southwest of its confluence with the Rhine at Koblenz. It was a cathedral town, the seat of an archbishop and elector of the Holy Roman Empire who held third place in the electoral college after the archbishops of Mainz and Cologne. This connection between Mainz and Trier, existing in the fifteenth century, can lead to interesting (though unprovable) speculations on the early arrival of this copy in that city.

It was found by Wyttenbach, the Trier Stadtbibliothek librarian, in a pitiable state; one story has it that the farm children had used some of the leaves to cover their schoolbooks. A note by him in German on the inside front flyleaf reads in part: "This second volume of the Biblia, printed by

Gutenberg, I rescued in September, 1818, when this very rare printing was at the point of being utterly destroyed." All homage to him!

The book must have originally belonged to some local church. How it passed from there to a farmhouse will forever remain unknown but may be speculated on. Although Trier was taken once by the Spanish and twice by the French in the seventeenth century, both armies were Catholic, and it seems improbable, though not impossible, that either would have deprived a cloister of a Bible; and, if they had, that it would have survived into the nineteenth century. However, in 1794 the Rhineland was overrun by another type of French army, that of the Revolution, which was then rising to a pinnacle of anticlericalism and terror. During this period the Bible may well have been looted and then abandoned in the murky triumphs and reverses of war.

The Trier Stadtbibliothek had, in 1931, three portions of the Gutenberg Bible. Volume I had been purchased in 1803 from a neighboring Benedictine monastery and is still in the library. Volume II had, as recounted, been discovered by Wyttenbach and placed in the library in 1828. And there was also a third fragment of sixty-three Old Testament leaves, origin unknown.

In the early 1930's a decision was made to sell the latter two portions. In December, 1931, the firm of Hiersemann in Leipzig purchased the Old Testament leaves. These are now in Austria, owned by Viscount von Seilern, according to Don Norman's census.

Negotiations were then entered into for the sale of the imperfect Volume II. The same Leipzig firm apparently had it on consignment at one time, since an inscription on the first preliminary leaf notes that it was collated in 1933 "after its return from the firm of Hiersemann." The city of Trier was asking a price of 130,000 to 135,000 reichsmarks ($52,-390 to $54,405), when E. W. H. Mitscherlich, Continental representative of Sotheby's, arrived at Trier in August of 1936 with a firm offer of 125,000 reichsmarks ($50,375). According to Dr. Schiel of the Stadtbibliothek, Mr. Mitscherlich "acquired" the volume at that time, although he probably did not personally become its owner.

When it was offered for sale at Sotheby's on June 21, 1937, as "The Property of a Gentleman," the consignor of record was, according to Mr. Anthony Hobson, a Dr. Wiernick. Dr. Wiernick was fleeing the anti-Semitic persecution in Germany and, being unable to export any capital, selected this method of obtaining funds abroad. Although no evidence can be offered, it is possible that the Bible left Germany as technically the property of somebody else. Dr. Wiernick claimed to have paid 155,000 reichsmarks ($62,500) for it; it was sold at Sotheby's for £8,000 ($39,520, with the pound at $4.94). His financial loss on the transaction may not have been as great as appears, considering the buying power of the pound in England. In any case, it is reported that his receipts from the sale enabled him to found a small business and prosper.

When I acquired the Houghton copy for Scribner's I knew that two of the leaves present in it were missing in Volume II of the Shuckburgh and that with these leaves, Shuckburgh would lack but three leaves, not five. I knew, furthermore, which no one else did, that one of the leaves present in the Houghton copy was the very one lacking in the General Theological's! There was fun in sight. Furthermore, in breaking up the Houghton copy and selling separate leaves, and whole books where possible, it was feasible to keep together the New Testament, nearly complete (116 out of 128 leaves). After all, Matthew, Mark, Luke and John are, to many, the heart of the matter.

No copy of a Gutenberg Bible had ever been perfected. What was the value of a single leaf which would make one so? I knew from experience what price-differential a missing leaf makes. One could practically write one's own ticket if one could perfect a copy. A consensus of informed opinion was that $20,000 would be a bargain. Charles Scribner, who succeeded his father as head of the firm, thereupon *presented* it to the General Theological Seminary as a gift. The missing leaf, miraculously restored, carried parts of Chapters 14 and 16 and all of Chapter 15 of Ezekiel. ("And I put a jewel on Thy forehead," Ezekiel 16:12.)

The volume was broken up into books where possible (occasionally one book will end and another begin on the same leaf) and into separate leaves. The New Testament was kept as a unit in its original binding. Through the good offices of Dr. Frederick B. Adams, Jr., director of the Pierpont Morgan Library, George A. Poole, Jr., of Chicago, a notable collector of incunabula, of whom at that time I had never heard, purchased it for $36,000.

The largest other unit preserved was thirty-one consecutive leaves comprising the books of Jeremiah and Lamentations complete, and one leaf of Baruch. This passed, through Philip Duschnes, to John M. Crawford of New York for $11,500. The second largest unit preserved was the Books of Maccabees, twenty-eight leaves. These passed to H. P. Kraus of New York. It appeared as item 3 of his catalogue 69, "The Cradle of Printing," priced $11,800. Its present location is unknown to me, although I am told it is probably owned by a European collector.

Individual leaves were priced according to content, condition and general desirability (whether or not, for example, a watermark was present), and ranged from $350 up. Their going price today is around $2,000. In the final results Scribner's got "very much" change over $200,000, rather than the "little" Carter had estimated.

The Book of Genesis was sold to the Robinson brothers of London for $8,000. It eventually turned up in the late Louis Rabinowitz's collection. When his books (those which were not given to Yale) were being dispersed by the firm of Charles Stonehill, New Haven, Connecticut, Genesis was generously offered to me first by Robert Barry for $25,000. Incredibly, I refused to repurchase it: why, I can't to this day understand. It was a perfect match to my New Testament, it had several leaves in their earliest printed state, and it was priced merely three times what I had sold it for a few years before. At the time my budget simply wouldn't allow it, and to my everlasting sorrow I failed to follow my stern injunction to book buyers (when I was a dealer): "There is no more ridiculous reason in the world for not buying a *great* book than the feeble excuse that you can't afford it." In any event, the Midwest got it and it is now at the University of Illinois.

Mr. Poole's collection in Chicago, one of the finest ever formed, contained other Gutenberg printing: the only proof sheet of the forty-two-line Bible in existence; one of the few known leaves of the thirty-six-line Bible in America; a beautiful copy of the 1460 *Catholicon*, and a leaf each of the controversial Constance Missal and of the 1457 and 1459 Psalters. And a dazzling display of other incunabula.

A few years after the Gutenberg sale I switched careers, though not interests, and became (much to my own amazement) curator of rare books and professor of bibliography at Indiana University, in charge of the famed J. K. Lilly Library there. I deeply regretted that I had been unsuccessful in tempting Mr. Lilly with the Shuckburgh copy when Scribner's had it. He had turned it down because of its imperfection (how high can your standards get?), not because of its price.

I had kept in touch with Poole over the years—less frequently since I left the trade—and knew something of the importance and growth of his library. In the late fall of 1958 I was in Chicago and stopped as usual at the St. Clair Hotel. Quite by chance I ran into its owner, Lou Silver, famed book collector, and an acquaintance of Poole's. "Did you know that Bill [as he is called] has sold his library?" "Good Lord, no! When, where, and to whom?" "Just a day or so ago. To the girls. I don't know what they intend to do with it, but I understand it is to stay in Chicago."

"The girls," Frances Hamill and Marjorie Barker, were old friends of my bookselling days. Working very quietly and very hard, they had become eminently successful dealers in rare books and manuscripts. Miss Hamill indeed is a past president of the Antiquarian Booksellers' Association of America, the only woman ever so honored. They are among the very few women who have been conspicuously able in this difficult field. As long ago as 1934, when I first joined Scribner's, they had given a tea for me and John Carter in their new bookshop, and we had been friendly ever since.

Well, it was Sunday, and I couldn't get in touch with them. All I could do was send a special-delivery congratulatory letter on their foresight and courage, reminding them that if there was any possibility of prying the Bible loose not to forget Indiana. When I finally saw the library I realized that I had to have it *en bloc,* if possible. It fitted perfectly with Lilly's gift. Though he had some choice incunabula, they had been acquired to support other interests: literature, science, exploration, books which had influenced thought, etc. He had never been attracted to early printing as such, or to the graphic arts, or to medieval texts, illuminated manuscripts and the like—all of which the Poole library had in abundance. This, I knew, was IT. I could see no possible chance, during my lifetime, at least, for Indiana to acquire so choice and vital a collection, one which would plug our weakest gap. It would not be possible again to go into the open market and get works of this stature. For one thing, the competition would be too tough for most state universities to buck.

But "the outlook wasn't bright, that day." I was informed by Miss Hamill that Poole had expressed a desire for the collection to remain in Chicago, if at all possible, and that an option had been extended to the University of Chicago. That does it, I thought. Among Poole's enthusiasms, dating from his college days at Yale, had been Chaucer. And his collection contained a noble array of Chaucers: the first Caxton edition of *The Canterbury Tales* (1477), the second (and first illustrated, 1484), the third, printed by Pynson (1491), the first collected edition (1532) among them. And the University of Chicago had a notable Chaucer collection. But not these. And just behind me by a matter of hours, breathing hard, was Texas.

All the girls could do was to promise me first refusal in the unlikely event that the University of Chicago didn't purchase the collection. I agreed to take it—without ever asking the price or, more important, knowing where or if I could raise the money to pay for it. I didn't know what the girls paid for it and don't to this day. It doesn't matter, and I never asked. I knew my dealers and I knew the quality of the material they had. Any price they put on it would not be an unreasonable one. As it turned out, the price was $410,000, perhaps the finest bargain I ever acquired. Collections of books of quality of this vital period simply do not exist in quantities any more.

I needn't have worried so about Chicago: the University never even came around to look over the treasures. So I had my chance.

My Indiana colleagues, Robert Miller and Cecil Byrd, bubbled. A brief session with President Herman B. Wells clinched matters: a collector himself, he knew "there is a tide in the affairs of men." So a Gutenberg New Testament came to Indiana.

When negotiations for the purchase of the Shuckburgh forty-two-line Bible were advanced in 1951, I received news from Carter even more startling than his original announcement. It was that the same source also had a thirty-six-line Bible!

Only thirteen copies of this fabulous book are extant, not all perfect. There is no copy in America, and in point of fact only six owners here possess individual leaves, several of these fragmentary. No copy, perfect or imperfect, has been offered for sale in over a century. The identity of the printer of this book and the place and time of its production remain controversial. For many years it was believed to have been done by Gutenberg at Mainz earlier than the forty-two-line Bible. In 1890, however, Karl Dziatzko proved that it must have come after the completion of the forty-two-liner but before the year 1461, when the copy in the Bibliothèque Nationale was rubricated. Current opinion tends to credit Bamberg as the place of origin and perhaps Albrecht Pfister as the printer, or the unknown Mainz printer of the "Turkenkalender," etc.

It turned out that this was nowhere near a complete copy—perhaps two thirds. And that, because of tax complications, it would not be sold with the forty-two-liner but might be available later. The strictest secrecy was enjoined. Its very existence was to be mentioned to no one. Nor was it.

Lady Christian Martin was annoyed when her ownership and sale of the forty-two-liner was (through no fault of Scribner's) heralded in the world's press, and declined further overtures for any other purchases from her library. No one, to my knowledge (with the exception, now, of Christie's), knows to this day what it actually contains. The people of bookish interests who have visited Cam House, Dorchester, have had only furtive glimpses of its library, if any. Just recently a portion was sold in London at Christie's. But not this Bible.

When I was in England in 1956, after "turning my coat," I received an invitation to visit Lady Christian Martin, canceled by illness. And in 1959 when I was again to be in England she graciously and unexpectedly wrote me that on this visit (I have the letter before me), she would bring the thirty-six-line Bible to London, to Quaritch, for my examination and possible purchase. When I reached there, I learned she had died a few days before my arrival.

So though I never owned a thirty-six-liner, I came closer to it than perhaps any other person in a century or so. Indiana's Lilly Library contents itself (for the present) with Poole's fragmentary leaf, a portion containing Sap. 7:25–9:17.

I am somehow reminded of what happened to the west corner of 48th Street and Fifth Avenue within my recent memory. A few years ago, on the southwest corner, was a jewelry firm, Black, Starr, and Frost (would I were steadfast as thou art!), until recently, Black, Starr, and Gorham. On the northwest, just across from Scribner's bookstore, was a church. Specifically, an Episcopalian church. It was the one the Scribners attended, and one day, looking across the street as the church was being demolished, Charles remarked to me, "If God can't afford one corner on Fifth Avenue, how can I afford the other?" I read this as an omen of no raises next year. And I was right.

I mentioned this later to a member of B. S. & G., who informed me that many years ago they had decided to build there for just one reason— north light. That was needed for examination of gems. And across the street, to their north, was the church. Protection triple proof. No one ever would pull down a church on Fifth Avenue. Their north light was forever safe. Well, a very few decades later, Sinclair Oil shed lots of light on lots of places, but from its building on 48th and Fifth where the church used to be, its skyscraper cut off the north light of B. S. & G. So much for city planning—and so much for the deep-laid plans of booksellers! Had any one of innumerable permutations and combinations come to pass, I never would have had second and third chances at THE BOOK and large fragments thereof. Though I regret my library does not have the Shuckburgh copy, still we do have the Trier-Houghton-Poole New Testament. It was first put on display only occasionally, but so many requests to see it were received that, to save wear and tear on the personnel and the book, it was put on permanent display. It is the only copy recorded in the census to be seen between the East and West coasts of the nation. Many of the books at Lilly are rarer, but none is more prized.

# William Blake

I HAVE NEVER BEEN very fond of William Blake's prose, poetry or painting, which diminishes me, but I have had over the years some very choice things. One was the most nearly complete copy of his first color-etched book (no perfect one is known), *There Is No Natural Religion* (London, 1788). This brief philosophical treatise enunciates Blake's belief in the mystic character of matter as opposed to the deification of nature and the denial of supernaturalism propounded by the Deists, among them his friends Tom Paine and William Godwin.

It is the first of his works entirely printed from engraved plates, and it shows the defects of a new and unfamiliar medium, crudity and lack of freedom. The principle of Blake's method, printing from relief-etching or stereotyping, was his own innovation; that which was to form the white space was eaten or cut away, while that which remained formed the text and design. Blake drew on copper plates with an acid-resisting mixture, the exact composition of which is still unknown, bathed the plates in aqua fortis, touched up the highlights with a brush dipped in acid or with a graver, and then printed the plate in whatever color or combination of colors fitted his scheme. Often he or his wife illuminated the printed page, usually with watercolors or opaque pigments, sometimes adding gold.

Blake's best-known poems are in his *Songs of Innocence* and *Songs of Experience* "Shewing the Two Contrary States of the Human Soul" (London, 1789–1794), "done in Illuminated Printing," his contemporary advertisement for them states. They are very rare books indeed and bibliographically complex. Since copies were made up on demand and over a period of some years, Blake's momentary fancy governed the arrangement and coloring of the plates. Also, his wife, Catherine, did some, and, after his death, some third person, so no two copies are alike.

The most striking array of them I ever saw was that of twelve, side by side, in the famed Blake exhibition held at the Philadelphia Museum of Art in 1939, "Selected from Collections in the United States." Only nine are known to have been done by 1794, though twenty complete copies are known in all.

Just after this exhibition Scribner's obtained what are probably the finest known copies of these books, once the property of George Cumberland, engraver, inventor of a relief printing process and an early friend of Blake's. They were sold at Sotheby's in 1929 without any mention of their unique qualities for £1,900 and even so achieved the highest price ever paid for the books in the open market at that time.

There were plates in proof state, double- and treble-color printing, in fact, every kind of experimental treatment both in the printing and in the application of additional pigment and wash, Blake occasionally using his peculiar opaque medium, the exact composition of which remains unknown. These remarkable copies became the property of Edison Dick of Chicago, from whom I repurchased them, and they eventually wound up in Paul Mellon's unrivaled collection.

In 1928 there was discovered in Auckland, New Zealand, a complete set of Blake's twenty-one designs, in watercolors, for his *Illustrations of the Book of Job* (London, 1826). This New Zealand set belonged originally to an artist, a pupil of John Linnell named Albin Martin, who emigrated to New Zealand the middle of the nineteenth century. The drawings are all carefully finished and painted with bright watercolors. Since their discovery was not upheld with fully documented provenance, there has been some discussion of their position in the Job cycle. Laurence Binyon, writing on the *Place of the New Zealand Set*, concludes with these words: "Judging them simply by themselves, I myself cannot believe that any other hand than Blake's could have caught so intimately his manner and his spirit, as do the best of these water-colors, such as that for No. 12, where the figure of Elihu shews a manifestly finer conception and execution than in any of the preceding sets." These were purchased by Philip Hofer, who, when he decided not to concentrate on Blake, sold them to Scribner's. They are now Mellon's. I had purchased some Blakes from Mrs. William Emerson of Cambridge, who had Blake's commonplace notebook, known as the *Rossetti Manuscript* from the fact that it once belonged to D. G. Rossetti, who penciled a note on the verso of the flyleaf: "I purchased this original manuscript of Palmer, an attendant in the Antique Gallery at the British Museum, on the 30th April, 1847. Palmer knew Blake personally, and it was from the artist's wife that he had the present manuscript which he sold me for 10s. Among the sketches there are one or two profiles of Blake himself." Mrs. Emerson once offered this to me for $40,000, but while I was trying to make up my mind she changed hers and I missed a great bargain. The manuscript is now in the British Museum, where it properly belongs.

Sometime in the early fifties I saw a brief note in the London *Times Literary Supplement* that there was to be reproduced for the Blake Trust the only known copy of the greatest book of Blake's maturity, colored throughout in his own hand, *Jerusalem. The Emanation of the Giant Albion* (London, 1804). This is Blake's longest and most unreadable poem, full of strange symbolism and absolutely beyond my comprehension, and I daresay I am one of the few people who ever finished reading it. The designs, however, make it the finest of all the prophetic books. It has been said that the coloring of the many plates was so unprofitable that Blake painted only one or two copies. Perhaps John Ruskin had one, but he had the bad habit of cutting up manuscripts for scrapbooks. In any event, the only known colored copy (four are known in black and white) was obtained by Frederick Tate, among other books, after the death of Blake's wife in 1832. It was not merely a great Blake book but *the* great Blake book, and I thought it would be nice to have. It belonged to a collection formed by General Archibald Stirling of Keir, who purchased it in 1887, and had the choicest Blake collection in private hands in the British Isles.

Describing this book, Geoffrey Keynes wrote in his Introduction to the facsimile edition (London, 1951):

> The splendour of this extraordinary book is difficult to describe in a few words. The text and illustrations were etched on a hundred copper plates. The unique copy here reproduced in a rich orange ink was then illuminated by Blake in water colours and gold, with varying elaboration on the different plates. The illustrations were printed with a degree of magnificence unusual even for Blake. The whole book is a continuous delight to the eye; at the same time it is impossible for the observer to ignore the striking symbolism of the illustrations which inevitably present a challenge to the intellect. [This was] the culmination of his genius as artist, prophet and poet. He was not making a mere picturebook to amuse an idle hour. He was embodying in these pages his final attempt to present in poetic form the message which he hoped would help others to resolve the mental conflicts he himself had suffered—and so to pass on to others the spiritual freedom he had won.

I wrote Carter about it without really expecting anything to happen. As I thought, the Stirlings of Keir would not part with the book but countered, unexpectedly, with an offer to sell the entire collection, including five paintings. Three of these were done in tempera on canvas, one in tempera on copper and one in watercolor on paper. The latter, *The Fall of Man*, had the following explanation written by Blake on the back:

> The Father indignant at the fall: the Saviour, while the evil angels are driven, gently conducts our first parents out of Eden through a guard of weeping angels. Satan now awakes Sin and Death and Hell to celebrate with him the birth of war and misery; while the Lion seizes the bull; the tiger, the horse; the vulture and the eagle contend over the Lamb.

The symbols of the Passion are seen amid the flames which surround the throne; and the sun, moon and planets have each within them a distraught mourning figure, representing the sorrow of the universe. The Holy Spirit in the likeness of a dove hovers over the Saviour's head. An elaborately composed and consciously balanced drawing, pale in color; the circle of flames and angels about the throne has a rose-like appearance, standing out against the starry sky.

Carter was as startled as I at this development. The price was not unreasonable, but he thought (and he was very nearly right) that we would be denied an export license on the grounds of its being a national treasure. It took most delicate and dexterous diplomacy on his part to get it to New York, and then only at the cost of having the paintings remain in England at the Victoria and Albert Museum. It became part of Mellon's collection and it is pleasant to recall that he was able to show it to that great lover of Blake, Chauncey Brewster Tinker, just before his death.

John Hayward commented in *The Book Collector* issue of Spring, 1953:

> As we go to press we learn that Lt. Col. William Stirling of Keir has sold to an American collector the unique coloured copy of Blake's *Jerusalem* (illuminated by Blake himself) which was recently reproduced in facsimile by the pochoir process for the Blake Memorial Trust. The price—£30,000—is the second highest ever paid in this country for a printed book. The news that this precious volume has crossed the Atlantic will be, or will already have been, received with mixed feelings. But those who regret its loss to this country have the consolation of knowing that the nation has acquired (for the Victoria and Albert Museum) as a direct result of its sale five Blake paintings of the first quality (formerly at Keir), the finest of them, a Madonna and Child, as a generous gift from the anonymous purchaser of the *Jerusalem,* the

others at a price well below their current value in the international market. Nevertheless the Reviewing Committee on the Exports of Works of Art, appointed by Mr. R. A. Butler after the issue of the Waverley Report, in reaching this, their first major decision, must have found it extremely difficult to balance conflicting claims to such a valuable collection. The long and difficult negotiations were conducted by Mr. John Carter, London director of Charles Scribner's Sons of New York, who is to be congratulated on a transaction even more remarkable perhaps than his purchase of the Shuckburgh copy of the 42-line *Bible* in 1951. Like the *Bible*, the *Jerusalem* was flown to New York in his personal charge.

# *Scott*

**M**Y EARLIEST EXPERIENCE with old books came when I was about eight and an aunt died in Pennsylvania. I was allowed to take my pick of the library when the house was being closed. The books were mainly theological, but I managed to find several Hentys, a long run of early American editions of Sir Walter Scott and a few Coopers. I have remained faithful to these authors all my life, and in a way have been repaid by more than the reading pleasure they gave me. At one time I possessed, though briefly, the finest Scott collection ever assembled (of which more later), and Indiana University now has the most complete collection of first and other editions of G. A. Henty it is possible to assemble, many of them the author's own copies. And I have handled unusual Coopers.

The Scotts were wretchedly printed American editions, but I loved them more than Henty or Cooper, I believe. My favorite, perhaps because it was the first one I read, and the next to the last, I found out later, Scott wrote, was *Count Robert of Paris*. I currently reread at least two Scott novels a year and can, if pressed, recite most of *Marmion*. What I did not know at the time—and neither did anyone else, in fact few do now—was that in reading these early editions published in America, I was actually reading Scott's text as it was originally published, something his Scottish and British audiences were not able to do.

Hereby hangs a bibliographical puzzle I was to unravel many years later to my own satisfaction and that of John T. Winterich, an editor of the American book collectors' quarterly, *The Colophon*, who printed my technical findings in the Summer, 1935, issue. They made no considerable stir then and haven't since, but I had fun doing the research and Winterich once praised it to my own ears as "solid stuff." So let us consider that article *Waverley in America*.

The novels of Scott were America's first sensational fictional best sellers. It is not now generally realized just how avidly our fathers read and reread them or how vast his influence was.

John Hay, speaking at the unveiling of the bust of Sir Walter Scott in Westminster Abbey, May 21, 1897, said: "I have heard from my father—a pioneer of Kentucky—that in the early days of this century men would saddle their horses and ride from all the neighboring counties to the principal post-town of the region when a new novel by the Author of *Waverley* was expected." William Edward Dodd says: "Few men ever had greater influence over the cotton planters than the beloved Scottish bard and novelist." Influence indeed! One is used to hearing Harriet Beecher Stowe blamed for helping foment the Civil War with *Uncle Tom's Cabin*, but the same charge has been brought against Scott, and by no other than Mark Twain: "Sir Walter Scott had so large a hand in making Southern character as it existed before the war, that he is in great measure responsible for the war."

It is probable that, though Scott's American popularity was not confined to the South, it waxed strongest there. The Richmond *Enquirer* of November 20, 1832, edged its columns in black on receiving news of his death, and probably the original Ku Klux Klan owed its origin in part to the influence of *Anne of Geierstein*. His influence was felt over the whole nation, and so large were the sales of his novels that entire editions of a new work would be sold out on the day of publication, and their printing and distribution became a hectic, cutthroat game, with booksellers and publishers striving for every advantage. It is startlingly parallel to the present "high fashion" competition between Continental and American designers. Thus it came about that America, though it probably did not have the honor of reading Scott's novels before any other nation, did have the opportunity of reading them more nearly as the author originally wrote them than did even his most ardent Scottish and English admirers.

Following the startling success of *Waverley*, succeeding Scott novels were reprinted in America as soon after receipt of British copies as possible. But with every increasing success—almost every new novel outsold its precursor—competition became keener. J. and J. Harper and C. S. Van Winkle of New York, Lilly of Boston, Mathew Carey of Philadelphia and numerous others battled for the books, and it became apparent that even a few days' advantage by anyone of them over his competitors would enable the enterprising publisher to reap a small, if not well-merited, fortune on each publication.

Mathew Carey in particular saw his chance, and not being a man to hesitate, he took it. Carey, a Dubliner born, had fled from Ireland to

Paris, pursued by a vengeful government that charged him with publishing seditious literature, and while in Paris he met and admired Franklin and Lafayette. He returned, unwisely, to Dublin and soon found himself in prison with ample time to think about Franklin's land of the free. At any rate, Carey appeared in 1785 in Philadelphia with $400 lent him by Lafayette and immediately embarked on a vigorous and distinguished publishing career.

Carey saw the advantage to be gained by being the first to put Scott's new novels on the market and set out to devise some scheme for doing so. The question, obviously, was how to get copy ahead of his competitors. For if he could get it first, and have his books on the market before his rivals even began to set type, he would have perhaps a week's advantage; the competitors would immediately print from his copies, of course, without waiting for exemplars of the British edition to arrive. But with a hungry South and a scarcely less eager North ready to buy from the first to offer, a week's start would be enough. It would not do to wait, as Carey and others had been waiting, for finished copies of the novels to arrive from abroad, as that was already causing a stalemate. Carey could possibly have dealt with Scott directly, but Scott was receiving such enormous sums for his work that his rates would probably have been prohibitive, and besides, why pay substantial money for what could be had without much of it? Carey planned to secure advance sheets, or, better, galley proofs, and set type from these; with his transatlantic experience and friendships he could get them, and did get them.

The above and the following observations were sparked by researches inspired by a letter I came across from Scott's publisher, Archibald Constable:

25 April, 1822

Wm Kerr Esq.
GPO Edinb
   Having reason to believe that one or more of the workmen in Mr. Ballantyne's Printing Office are in the Practice of Abstracting sheets of works in the progress of Printing—more especially those of the Author of Waverley, and forwarding said Sheets by means of the Post Office to America, more particularly to Philadelphia, we beg to know if it is consistent with the rules of the Post Office to stop any such Sheets so transmitted in order to effect the detection of the person abstracting our property in this manner.

It is obvious that Carey succeeded in planting a workman in Ballantyne's printing office, or more probably in bribing a workman already there, to send him galleys, or sheets, of the novels as they came off the press. Indeed, he may have had a secret agreement with Ballantyne for the purchase of such advance material, for Ballantyne was exceedingly Machiavellian, and though Scott had implicit faith in him, others, as Constable and Blackwood, seem just as thoroughly to have mistrusted him. However that may be, someone, apparently before 1822, began to send advance sheets or galleys to Carey and continued to do so until the last of Scott's works were published.

Carey worked fiendishly when he received them. Edward Bradley says that the copy, when received, was apportioned to every printing house in Philadelphia, and the complete novel put in type in three days.

> It was necessary to keep relays of compositors working over the early sheets night and day. When the binder had finished his work a stage coach had been chartered and a young employee, William A. Blanchard, later to become a partner, would gallop off to New York with the supplies. Mounted gallantly on a huge pile of *Waverley,* he would ride night and day, ferrying his precious cargo of romance across the North River to the waiting booksellers.

All this may be, perhaps, interesting as the first example of American literary piracy on a large scale; the phenomenon was to be duplicated again and again until the present imperfect copyright law was enacted. But it has an important bibliographical phase. Scott was a meticulous workman, forever revising, correcting and furbishing his novels until the moment of publication, and, ardent antiquarian that he was, intolerant of even the slightest error. Many of his manuscripts and proofsheets have disappeared, but we have tangible and tantalizing proof of the extent of his revisions by the presence in his English first editions of numerous canceled leaves. Of the twenty-three titles of his *Waverley* novels, twelve have canceled leaves in first edition.

A canceled leaf is proof positive of some last-minute textual change. There are, of course, other means of correcting errors—errata lists, primarily, but they disclose what was to be corrected and why. A cancel, on the other hand, is a challenge. It shows that a change has been made without giving any hint as to what the change was or the reason for it, and the conscientious editor, literary student or admirer of the author's work, who would not have a single word unrecorded, is faced generally with an insoluble puzzle unless a copy of the work turns up with the original leaf intended to be excised and replaced still intact—and it rarely does.

If the original leaf is not found, all sorts of vain imaginings arise to plague one's waking moments. The knowledge that a leaf has been canceled, instead of being superfluous knowledge, becomes dangerous knowledge. If, when found, the reason for the cancellation proves to be trifling, at least its discovery has removed a source of irritation. And just what is "trifling"? That is a problem for the literary critic, historian and biographer; as the late R. W. Chapman, the authority on the subject, puts it, "It is not for the bibliographer to decide what is of value to his betters; his business is to record the facts."

We have, then, the facts that Mathew Carey, Philadelphia printer, late of Dublin and Paris, through chicanery or otherwise secured advance sheets of Sir Walter Scott's *Waverley* novels from the shop of Ballantyne, the Edinburgh printer; that he generally secured *uncorrected sheets;* that, therefore, textual examination of these sheets, read against the English, will show the changes made. As to their interpretation, following Mr. Chapman's advice, I leave that to my betters.

Once recognized, through the Archibald Constable letter, the problem was simple. Greville Worthington had done, in 1931, an exhaustive bibliography of *The Waverley Novels,* listing all of the canceled leaves. One needed only to compare the British text with the American to reconstruct the original text.

Let us now for a moment switch scenes to William C. Van Antwerp of San Francisco, California, who formed a remarkable collection of Scott, recorded in his *A Collector's Comments on His First Editions of the Works of Sir Walter Scott* (1932). He had attempted (and with marked success) to reconstruct the original text of the novels by comparison with the original manuscript where this was known to exist. He realized, however, that "tracing cancels from manuscript alone is not the dependable method, because the really important clues are often found only in the uncanceled leaves or in the proofs."

This is perfectly true, for it is only when an error is not caught until the final stages of printing that such expensive and drastic surgery as cancellation is resorted to. And errors in transcription, in Scott's case, were sure to creep in. It should be remembered that so great was his desire for anonymity that neither his original manuscript nor corrected proof sheets ever reached the printer—George Huntly Gordon, his secretary, or James Ballantyne copied everything he wrote. So some of the errors which necessitated last-minute changes may have been copyists', not Scott's.

The variant readings need not be detailed here—they can be found in my *Colophon* article—but as one example, in the *Chronicles of the Canongate* (London, 1827; Philadelphia, 1827), of which Van Antwerp says, correctly, "the bibliographical problems are nowhere more baffling," the American edition reads: "Zilia de Moncada heard the question; and it seemed as if," etc. The English edition reads, "Zilia de Moncada heard the question (which being addressed to the father, Grey had inconsiderately uttered in French), and it seemed as if," etc. The error in this sentence, which Scott caught and corrected in proof in the English edition, lies in the fact that a few paragraphs earlier it had been stated that Zilia de Moncada "understands no English." There are many such.

I think Scott's excessive care with proofs may have come from his political experience with *Marmion*, published in 1808. This poem, with those lines every schoolchild knows (or should): "O, young Lochinvar is come out of the west"; "dar'st thou then/ To beard the lion in his den"; "O what a tangled web we weave/ When first we practice to deceive"; "o, Woman! in our hours of ease,/ Uncertain, coy, and hard to please," etc., has cancel problems.

Van Antwerp was the first to discover this. He wrote (in the March, 1934, issue of *The Colophon*):

> Another prize I have not been able to find is the first issue of *Marmion*, and here I make a modest claim to pioneering because neither the bibliographers nor the booksellers have ever, to my knowledge, referred to it. Lockhart distinctly tells us that when Scott was revising *Marmion* proofs he decided to enlarge the tribute to Fox by adding two lines to page 10 (B$_1$), but that Ballantyne, without waiting for these revised proofs, went ahead with the printing and thus "some copies got abroad in which the additional couplets were omitted." When this was discovered the press was stopped. Sig. B$_1$ was cancelled, and a new leaf containing the additional lines was inserted on the stub. But the harm was done: *The Morning Chronicle* got hold of both issues, and after comparing them, charged Scott with playing politics by printing one issue for the Whigs and another for the Tories, whereupon Scott found it necessary to defend himself in letters to the Press. I have never seen or heard of a copy in its original press. What has become of it?

Well, during my researches I turned it up: the original lines read:

> Mourn genius lost, and lore profound,
> And wit that loved to play, not wound.

The revised version:

> For talents mourn, untimely lost,
> When best employed, and wanted most;
> Mourn genius high, and lore profound,
> And wit that loved to play, not wound.

It was Lord Abercorn (to whom Scott dedicated *The Lady of the Lake*), reading the first proofs with Scott, who had suggested the enlargement of the compliments paid to Fox. This, Oliver Brett's copy, a beauty in original boards, paper label, duly passed to J. K. Lilly, Jr., and is now one of the ornaments of his distinguished Scott collection, which also contains one of the royal paper copies of *The Lady of the Lake* presented by the author to the Princess of Wales, as well as a complete set of the *Waverley* novels in original state.

At any rate, I later uncovered a second copy with the leaf uncanceled and offered it to Van Antwerp, who, his work on Scott being finished, declined its purchase. It went immediately to Carroll A. Wilson, to grace his collection of *First Appearances in Print of Familiar Quotations*, and when I repurchased Wilson's library it went to that of Robert Taylor, where it still resides, only the second copy recorded.

But the refusal of Van Antwerp to purchase *Marmion* gave me an idea. If he wasn't purchasing, perhaps he would sell. The late J. P. Morgan and I had one thing in common, at least—a love for Scott. I knew the Morgan Library had the finest collection of his manuscripts in America, but few of his books. And here was the finest collection ever assembled. It took practically no time at all to convince Morgan's librarian, the formidable Miss Belle da Costa Greene, that I should negotiate for the books on their behalf.

I attempted to do so with no luck. Van Antwerp would not sell. So there the matter dropped and I forgot all about it. Years later coincidence took over. Ordinarily I didn't work at Scribner's on Saturdays, but one weekend a friend asked me to go to a game with him at Princeton, so I went to town to do a little work before we started. The weather turned terrible; my friend called me to say he had a cold, so the trip was off.

About eleven o'clock a gentleman wandered into the store and asked me if I was interested in Sir Walter Scott. When I said yes, he explained that he was a lawyer from San Francisco and in the process of settling an estate. Part of it was a large collection of first editions, presentation copies, etc., of Scott. To my reply that it must be Van Antwerp's, he admitted that it certainly was, and seemed puzzled as to how I knew.

Within minutes I had the Morgan Library director, F. B. Adams, Jr. (who had succeeded Belle Greene), on the phone. Within an hour I had escorted the gentleman from San Francisco there and the matter was settled—Morgan had purchased the Van Antwerp Scotts, Scribner's had an adequate commission, and the lawyer, rid of what he obviously considered a headache, was pleased.

During lunch I asked him how he had come into Scribner's, thinking of course that he had been going through his client's files and come across my correspondence offering to buy it. He replied he had never heard of me before that morning, had never known of the Morgan Library, and knew only of Scribner's as a publishing house. He was in New York on other business, was strolling up Fifth Avenue in the rain, and when he saw our store window full of Scott, thought: *This is the logical place—* which it turned out to be.

The window was full of Scott all right—Scott Fitzgerald, that is. Zelda had just died, and I had put on sort of a memorial show. Only the first name had penetrated my visitor's consciousness, possibly because of the heavy rain.

# Shelley and Keats

I NEVER HAD a great deal of Shelley, though on my very first visit to J. K. Lilly I sold him a respectable (though rebound) first of of "Adonais" (Pisa, 1816) for $3,000, then and now a highish price. I have recounted experiences with Shelley autographs elsewhere, and unless they had an impeccable provenance I wouldn't touch them. I did have one rather morbid piece, though, which was completely authenticated. When Shelley died, Mary kept his heart, which Trelawny had snatched during the cremation, together with locks of the hair of the two children they had lost, in a casket; included also was an autograph notebook of sixty-eight pages lettered: "Manuscript pieces of P. B. Shelley and his Wife, Mary W. Shelley, 1814–1822." Upon the death of Mary the casket was opened and the volume given to Dr. Richard Garnett. It was eventually acquired by John W. Spoor of Chicago, who had a very respectable Shelley collection, and came up in his sale in 1939.

The famed patroness of the Library of Congress, Mrs. Whittall, wanted it badly, largely I believe because she was somewhat casket-minded. At any rate, she already had the manuscripts of the poems Rossetti had buried with his wife, Elizabeth, and later dug up. Remember Dorothy Parker's quatrain?

> Dante Gabriel Rossetti
> Buried all his *libretti*,
> Thought the matter over—then
> Went and dug them up again.

I was told to get the Shelley volume at practically any price, which proved, at the sale, to be $3,900, considerably less than I or the galleries had thought it would bring. They thought so highly of it that they used a reproduction of a page as frontispiece, devoted five pages of fine print and four other illustrations to it, and estimated it at $10,000 up.

The whole sale, as a matter of fact, was a disaster; so much so that after the first session I tried, unsuccessfully, to purchase the remainder from the estate, which didn't endear me for a while to Arthur Swann, long-time head of the Parke-Bernet Galleries. The Rossetti and the Shelley are now at the Library of Congress.

I also bid unsuccessfully for Shelley's very rare pamphlet "The Necessity of Atheism" (Worthington, 1811). Published anonymously, one of three recorded, this resulted in Shelley's expulsion from Oxford. It fetched $9,300 and was bought by the University of Texas, which was promptly in trouble with the legislature for spending state funds to spread atheism among students.

I never did have much other than the usual Byrons for some reason, though I did acquire at this same Spoor sale the only recorded copy of the first state of *Childe Harold's Pilgrimage*, Cantos I–II (London, 1812), with pages 189–190 in two states, canceled and uncanceled, which cost $330 and which I sold Chauncey B. Tinker of Yale for $900. I was wary, however, and still am, of Byron manuscripts, letters, etc. Not only was Major de Gibler, who forged so much Shelley, actively forging Byron in the 1850's, but there was a person in New York City in the late 1920's and early thirties who was really clever at imitating Byron's hand.

It was different with John Keats, many of whose books and manuscripts I have had, some from peculiar sources. Somehow, I know not why, Keats has never attracted forgery the way others have. Incidentally, Robert Burns rates high in this field, though he usually attracted some poor imitators, far below de Gibler in England or Cosey in America, though one ingenious English craftsman was producing excellent Burns in the 1930's.

However, my very first Keats experience began on a low note. Byrne Hackett of the Brick Row Bookshop had sold Jerome Kern a first of Keats's "Endymion" (London, 1818), inscribed on the flyleaf simply "From the Author." Some thought that the inscription was not in Keats's hand, and the volume was withdrawn. This is not to imply that the inscription was wrong. It could well have been written by a friend to whom Keats had actually given this book, or occasionally a clerk in a publisher's office will so inscribe copies sent for presentation or review.

Keats's presentation copies, manuscripts, letters, etc., have never been common, but a fair number did come on the market at not too exorbitant prices in the thirties and forties. At this time Archibald Alexander of Bernardsville, New Jersey, was actively collecting and was a friend of Scribner's. His Baskerville Press collection was notable and his Hemingway remains, to my knowledge, the finest in private hands. He had a special affection for Keats and I supplied him a good many—again, his collection, small but choice, is the best private one I know of and includes several moving letters from Keats to Fanny Brawne.

One of Frank Hogan's most cherished books was the copy of Keats's *Poems* (London, 1817) which was inscribed on the title page: "To W. Wordsworth with the Author's sincere reverence." Inside the front cover is a drawing of a man kneeling, probably by Haydon, and the book is bound in chintz pasted over the boards by Mrs. Wordsworth, who made it a habit to cover books thus with scraps of her dresses. It was a magnificent association of the kind so dear to Hogan's heart.

A well-known book, *Poems* was acquired by the eccentric F. H. Day of the Boston publishing firm of Copeland and Day. Amy Lowell, who knew the volume, concluded that "undoubtedly Keats gave Wordsworth the book one day at Haydon's studio." I understand Day promised to give it to her for her Keats collection. In any event, he didn't, and it was found in his desk drawer when Goodspeed purchased much of his collection. Goodspeed sold it to Hogan, and when part two of Hogan's sale came up, it was the star item, an illustration being used as frontispiece to the catalogue.

I had no customer for this Keats volume but decided I wanted it and purchased it for $9,750. I had at that time Fanny Brawne's copy of *Lamia, Isabella, the Eve of St. Agnes and Other Poems* (London, 1820). Among the "other poems" are "Ode on a Grecian Urn," "Lines on the Mermaid Tavern" and "Ode to a Nightingale." It will be recalled that the publisher's Advertisement (or Preface) to this book explains that "Hyperion" was printed, though unfinished, "contrary to the wish of the author. The poem was intended to have been of equal length with *Endymion,* but *the reception given that work discouraged the author from proceeding.*" In this copy the italicized sentence has been struck through and a note added in ink: "Utterly false. F. B.," thus adding an authoritative piece of evidence to the story of Keats's attitude to the poem. I catalogued the pair for $16,750 and Robert Taylor now has them.

Franklin P. Adams came into the shop one day with a book belonging to Keats which his wife had picked up for nothing in a secondhand bookstall in Madrid. It was authentic and I passed it along to Archibald Alexander. I remember wondering at the time how a Keats got to Spain, but I pursued investigation no further. I found out how later when I was told that a remarkable collection of his works was privately owned in Spain, including presentation copies and books from his library. These were completely unknown up to that time. A little research and a lot of correspondence proved this was true and that they had descended from the family of Keats's sister, Fanny.

She married a Spaniard and became Señora de Llanos and died in Madrid in 1889. The following year Day obtained from the family twenty-one letters of Fanny Brawne around which controversy swirled for many years. But Day obtained no books.

At this time I still had the Keatses previously mentioned but had no objections to having more. Presentation copies of Keats are not exactly common, though one would not imagine so when visiting Harvard's Houghton Library. Prolonged negotiations with the owners eventually resulted in Scribner's securing first editions of both *Poems* and *Lamia*, inscribed and especially bound for Fanny Keats. In addition there were a number of volumes from her library, given her by her brother, including Goldsmith's *Poems and Essays*, sent with a note: "I think you will like Goldsmith."

My favorite, however, was a volume of Collins' *Poetical Works*, inscribed "Miss Keats. The reward of Merit and Industry. Misses Caley's Midsummer Vacation, 1816." Johnny must have been pleased when Fanny received this.

But the greatest coup of all was John Carter's getting the Keats-Haydon correspondence owned by Buxton Forman's son, in 1941. This was catalogued as follows:

> Seventeen autograph letters from John Keats to B. R. Haydon, November 20, 1816, to August 14, 1820. Together with the reverse of correspondence, seventeen autograph letters from Haydon to Keats, March 3, 1817 to July 14, 1820.                    The collection: $35,000

> The Keats-Haydon friendship is too well known to require comment: it was the established, the famous sculptor, Haydon, who took the young unknown Keats, one day in March, 1817, to see the Greek collection newly housed in the British Museum—the famous Elgin marbles —which led him to write, sick with their beauty, his immortal *On Seeing the Elgin Marbles*.

> In the very first letter of the present correspondence, Keats sends Haydon the earliest draft of his famous sonnet: *Great Spirits Now on Earth are Sojourning,* with its praise of Wordsworth:

He of the cloud, the cataract, the lake,
Who on Helvellyn's summit, wide awake,
Catches his freshness from Archangel's wing;

Of Leigh Hunt:

He of the rose, the violet, the spring,
The social smile, the chain for Freedom's sake;

And of Haydon, himself:

Whose steadfastness would never take
A meaner sound than Raphael's whispering.

And in the second letter, he transcribes the same sonnet, at Haydon's request, to send to Wordsworth: "The idea of your sending it to Wordsworth puts me out of breath—you know with what Reverence I would send my wellwishes to him." (Incidentally, Keats's admiration for Wordsworth was unbounded and the copy of his *Poems,* 1817, inscribed to Wordsworth "With the Author's sincere reverence," one of the great association volumes of the Romantic period, is at present owned by Scribner's.) Haydon, however, preserved the sonnet and sent Wordsworth a transcript (see *Correspondence and Table-Talk,* 11, 30).

This letter has another interesting point, The words "Yours sincerely, John Keats" are cut out and copied below with the endorsement: "The original autograph presented Fras. Bennock, Esq. 78 Wood St. for— Longfellow, Esq., the American Poet—Nov. 21st, 1848. Fred W. Haydon." In return Longfellow sent a copy of *Kavanagh,* first edition, 1849, inscribed: "F. Bennock, Esq. With the Author's regards. Boston, May, 1849." The Keats signature is now in the Houghton Library at Harvard. In the remarkable letter of March 14, 1818, Keats includes his *For there's Bishops teign,* seven six-line stanzas, and *Where be ye going, you Devon Maid,* four four-line stanzas.

Aside from the present letters, five others from Keats to Haydon are recorded, viz., Wisbech Museum, British Museum, Pierpont Morgan, Harvard (formerly in the Frank Bemis collection) and one printed by Forman from an original now lost, or at least whose present whereabouts is unknown. The Haydon correspondence is complete except for a single letter which was in the Harris Arnold sale of 1901. This is the last great collection of Keats letters which can ever come on the market. It is, as a matter of fact, larger than the sum of all other privately owned Keats letters taken together. Many great libraries do not possess a single scrap in his autograph.

By far the largest collection of Keats is in the Houghton Library at Harvard, the next is in the British Museum. The present correspondence ranks third. When this is off the market, no individual or institution can ever form more than a scattered handful of fragments of the brightest star—with the exception only of Shakespeare—of English poetry.

There were no takers of any of this material for a number of years. Eventually the Haydon letters were sold to Arthur Houghton, Jr., at a reduced price; the Llanos books were consigned to auction at Sotheby's, where they were purchased by John Fleming for Houghton, and are now at Harvard, where they properly belong.

# Sherlock Holmes

## "The Game's Afoot!"

I CLEARLY REMEMBER my introduction to Sherlock Holmes, which was reading *The Valley of Fear*, probably in 1915, the year of its publication, at which time I was ten. I never knew then that I was reading the true, undiluted, original version—something his compatriots in England were not doing. I only discovered this years later when I purchased its original manuscript.

I became an early, though not a charter, member of The Baker Street Irregulars, having the titular investiture, with the shilling, of "The Golden Pince-Nez," and was editor of the bibliographical department of its *Journal* in its early years. As a dealer I rather specialized in Doyle material (S. H. only), and at one time and another more than half of all of his surviving manuscripts have passed through my hands, and at modest prices by current standards, I must say, though they did show a handsome profit to my firm at the time.

Doyle had a neat, precise hand, and he apparently wrote right off the top of his head, seldom correcting or rewriting. He had a whole story in his mind before he put it on paper.

The surviving manuscripts are mostly still extant only because Harold Greenough, one of the editors of *Strand Magazine*, where they first appeared, saved them. In 1923 they appeared at auction and were largely acquired by William Randolph Hearst. When his collection was dispersed in 1940 I purchased them at an average cost of $100 each and promptly put them back into circulation. Scribner's issued a *Catalogue of Original Manuscripts, and Other Editions of the Tales of Sherlock Holmes, As Written by Sir Arthur Conan Doyle. Together with Important Biographies, Pastiches, Articles, etc., and a Few Extraordinary Association and Unique Items*. This has since, in itself, become a collector's item.

Included among the manuscripts was *The Adventure of Charles Au-*

*gustus Milverton* (with its original title, *The Adventure of the Worst Man in London*), wherein Holmes and Watson commit midnight burglary in the interest of justice. It was priced $450. In 1966 it brought $4,250 at auction at the Parke-Bernet Galleries in New York. Incidentally, this is, as are most surviving manuscripts, from *The Return of Sherlock Holmes*. Only two are from *The Adventures*. One is *The Adventure of the Greek Interpreter*, which I had priced at $850. It appeared in 1966 at Christie's and brought $12,800, purchased by Lew D. Feldman. It was later displayed on Broadway in connection with a musical comedy based on the Holmes saga. The other is *The Adventure of the Speckled Band*, for which Scribner's paid £82 at a London auction in 1934, present whereabouts unknown.

The catalogue wound up with a group of delightful "Association Items," all dreamed up and annotated by myself, with the help of that eminent authority, Vincent Starrett, author of *The Private Life of Sherlock Holmes*. The items themselves were preceded by the following paragraphs by Starrett.

> Without being what is lovingly called a bibliofool, there can be no doubt that Sherlock Holmes was more than a little fond of books. That is to say, he was a reader rather than a collector, less concerned with the misprint on page 38, establishing priority for a certain edition, than with the accurate content of a work. This is doubtless as it should be. However, he was no novice in the field of bibliophily, as we may see from the revelations of Mr. David Randall (in this catalogue), who has clearly shown the detective's knowledge of—and professional interest in—the elaborate forgeries of the late T. J. Wise. He knew a hawk from a hernshaw, a *Queen's Garden* from Regent's Park.
>
> Principally, he was a student of the weird, the wayward and the wonderful, although his interest was largely that of a skeptic rather than a believer. That must have been a remarkable collection of books and pamphlets, resident in his attic, about which he wrote some years after his retirement. The reference is well known: "There is a great garret in my little house which is stuffed with books." If it still exists—and there has been no word of its destruction—one would like to have the cataloguing of it.
>
> Like so many of his admirers, Holmes was obviously a browser in the back-street shops, an Autolycus of the bookstalls, a man instinctively drawn to those wistful-foolish members of the human race called by the directories Booksellers. Old inhabitants will remember that once he assumed the disguise of an old bookseller—what *is* the disguise of an old bookseller?—for good and sufficient reasons. That was in the spring of the year 1894, when the murder of the Hon. Ronald Adair was filling London with fearful joy and poor Watson with despair. At that time,

indeed, Holmes had a little shop of his own—"at the corner of Church Street," he told Watson; a vague enough address, since it is not clear just where at the moment the doctor was living.

No self-respecting bookshelf should be without at least reading copies of the three titles—*British Birds, Catullus* and *The Holy War*—given to the doctor on that memorable occasion. Holmes himself, apparently, was at the time deep in *The Origin of Tree Worship,* an obscure work that has not as yet, I believe, been identified.

His interest in books is well attested. Does he still look forward to all catalogues, in this cottage on the Sussex Downs? I think he will be peculiarly interested in this one, bearing as it does upon his own career, and the careers of some of his associates, in that strange world that was —and forever is—*fin-de-siècle* London. A muster of books that contains the more pertinent writings of the late A. C. Doyle—an authority too often neglected by contemporary Sherlockians; a history of Watson's old regiment—the doctor's own copy, with his signature and a memorandum of purchase; an association volume from the library of Rear-Admiral Baskerville, and Col. Sebastian Moran's *Heavy Game of the Western Himalayas,* to mention only a few, can hardly fail to send his fancy back to days and nights in Baker Street—all but forgotten, perhaps, since that dreadful moment at daybreak, in Sept. 1, 1939, when the world moved from its moorings and became again a wanderer in the void.

One of the items catalogued was:

*An Inquiry into the Nature of the Ashes of Various Tobaccos.*
Tibet: Privately Printed, 1893.                                         $100.
Folio, Second Edition, half green morocco, gilt top, other edges uncut.

A curious volume. The second (and best) edition, as it lists 288 forms of cigar, cigarette, and pipe tobacco ash with numerous plates. The first edition (Camden House, 1880), a not impossible book, is oddly lacking, however (as is the present) from the great George Arents tobacco collection. The first edition, for the record, is entitled *Upon the Distinction Between the Ashes of the Various Tobaccos,* and list only 144 tobacco ashes. The present edition is desirable, also, as an early Tibetan imprint (? the third) in English. It has been said by Thomas S. Blakeney that this work was probably translated into French by M. le Villard; he does not state, however, whether M. le Villard translated the first, or the present second edition. We have been unable to trace any French translation ourselves.

This was a beautiful piece of cataloguing, I figured. But what I didn't figure on was George Arents himself, with his librarian, appearing at Scribner's; he was panting to buy it, rather indignant, as a matter of fact, that I hadn't offered it to him before putting it in the catalogue, hoping he wasn't too late to get it and ordered the 1880 volume when it could be acquired. He was a good customer (his famed tobacco collection is now at the New York Public Library, housed in a handsome room where smoking is not allowed), but without much of a sense of humor. The hoax took considerable explaining, and I sold him books thereafter, but rarely.

But to return to *The Valley of Fear*, which adventure took place from the morning of Friday, January 11, 1887, until the following day. Many competent authorities think this the finest of the Holmes novels; certainly, dealing as it does with the anthracite coal region and the Molly Maguires, it has more interest than most for Americans.

This was my territory, as I was born in Nanticoke, schooled at Shenandoah, Minersville, Wilkes-Barre, and various patches, when there was always, and for all I know still is, loud talk of the "Mollys'" great days.

The Mollys were also, the uninitiated might not know, called the "White Boys" and the "Buckshots." This was from their annoying habit of dressing in white sheets, sneaking up to a lighted window and letting fly with a double load of buckshot at whomever the bodymaster happened to be annoyed with. The results (as in *The Valley of Fear*) were generally fatal and always frightening. I had a certain distinction in my gang, as I not only had a distant relative treated in this manner, but after the event his body was used to stoke a donkey engine and nobody ever saw him again.

On my very first reading I identified the Scowers with the Molly Maguires, and John McMurdo, "not far, one would guess, from his thirtieth year," with famed James McPharlan (McKenna), Pinkerton operative, twenty-nine when he began his investigations. I knew what a bodymaster was, that Vermissa was Shenandoah, and that Mahanoy City was "the ground where the boys are true." Incidentally, a test of one's knowledge of "the region" is one's pronunciation of Mahanoy— *Mock-annoy*, yes. But *Ma-hōney*, and may the breath stick in your throat!

I had always thought of Jake Shafter and his daughter Ettie as Germans. It said so in the book I read: "She was of the German type, blond and fair-haired"; she spoke "with a pleasing little touch of a German accent," and her father with "more than a touch." I had read, recall, an American edition.

When I acquired the manuscript I checked it against an English edition and found scores of variants. There Ettie was Swedish and Jacob Shafter was "the kindly Swedish boarding-house keeper with whom John Mc-

Murdo first lodged in Vermissa Valley." What happened was that the story was finished in 1914, and when English serialization began in *Strand Magazine*, World War I was on and it was patently impossible to have Birdy Edwards marry a German lass, or to have any German depicted as a kindly character in an English publication. This was not vital, however, at the time in America, where Doyle's original characterizations were not changed.

The manuscript itself has had its troubles. Hearst paid $275 for it in 1923. I catalogued it for $900 in 1940 and couldn't sell it. I finally swapped Lew Feldman (of the House of El Dieff) something for it, and he couldn't sell it either. He finally advertised that he was going to break it up and sell individual chapters, which he did, and later laboriously reassembled them!

Of all the Sherlockian material which I have handled, I am fondest of a noble fragment of *The Final Problem*. This is the original autograph of the most memorable letter Holmes ever wrote, and which Watson discovered on the brink of the Reichenbach Falls:

> My dear Watson: I write these few lines through the courtesy of Mr. Moriarty, who awaits my convenience for the final discussion of those problems which lie between us. He has given me a sketch of the methods by which he avoided the English police and kept himself informed of our movements. They certainly confirm the very high opinion which I had formed of his abilities. . . .

Of all the treasures the Lilly Library possesses, I'm not sure I wouldn't rescue this first, should danger threaten. Though Holmes returned after years of wandering in Tibet, he was never quite the same man, as a female fan acutely observed. But even so, there has never been no police like Holmes, as has been remarked.

The location of several important manuscripts is currently unknown but presumed to be Chicago, appropriately enough. The manuscript of *The Sign of the Four* appeared at a New York City auction in 1909 and was sold to a Chicago dealer for $105. *The Adventure of the Speckled Band* appeared at auction in London in 1934 and fetched £82. It was purchased by Scribner's. There is a curious change here between the manuscript and the printed text. In the latter, as any schoolchild knows, the intended victim is Helen Stoner, and Dr. Grimesby Roylott, the poisoner, is her stepfather. However, in the original manuscript Roylott is her father. I imagine this change was dictated by an editor. Scribner's sold this manuscript to the same Chicago dealer mentioned above (since deceased), Walter M. Hill, and it is quite possibly somewhere in that city with the *Sign*.

The second rare book catalogue I issued in 1934 offered the first appearance of *A Study in Scarlet*, in *Beeton's Christmas Annual*, 1887, priced $200. Vincent Starrett says of it: "That lurid paperback of Christmas 1887 is today one of the rarest books of modern times—a keystone sought by discriminating collectors in every part of the world." This is true enough, but the first book edition (London, 1888), illustrated by the author's father, Charles Doyle, is even rarer. The illustrations appear only in this edition, and one glance is sufficient to show why. Though Charles Doyle was, his son tells us, a great and original artist, "more terrible than Blake," illustrating books does not seem to have been his specialty.

A Los Angeles dealer, long since passed from the scene, spotted this in my catalogue and offered it to E. T. ("Ned") Guymon of San Diego, a beginning collector, for $350. Guymon wired Starrett, who was in New York at the time, asking his advice. Starrett came in to see my copy, realized what had happened, and Guymon secured the book from me. Thus began a pleasant association with his renowned collection of detective fiction—so fine and complete that it hasn't any even close competitors. Guymon only recently presented it to his alma mater, Occidental College, and after the first delivery of 2,500 volumes was made, one couldn't even detect that a book had been removed from the library, so double- and triple-stacked were they.

I recently had the pleasurable experience of appraising the books and rehandling many an old favorite which I had sold him. The collection contains not only books but many manuscripts, among them R. Austin Freeman's *The Red Thumb Mark*. Incidentally, the front cover of the book (issued in both cloth and wrappers) has a thumb print on the cover—it is the author's own, as he records in Guymon's autographed copy. There is also all that remains of the original version of Hammett's *The Thin Man*. This was first published in 1932, one year after *The Glass Key*, but was begun well before it, as Hammett's note accompanying the manuscript makes clear.

> In 1930 I started writing a book entitled "The Thin Man." By the time I had written these 65 pages my publisher and I agreed that it might be wise to postpone the publication of "The Glass Key"—scheduled for that fall—until the following spring. This meant that "The Thin Man" could not be published until the fall of 1931. So—having plenty of time—I put these 65 pages aside and went to Holly-

wood for a year. One thing and/or another intervening after that, I didn't return to work on the story until a couple of more years had passed—and then I found it easier, or at least generally more satisfactory, to keep only the basic idea of the plot and otherwise to start anew. Some of the incidents in this original version I later used in "After the Thin Man," a motion picture sequel, but—except for that and for the use of the characters' names Guild and Wynant—this unfinished manuscript has a clear claim to virginity.

Dashiell Hammett

John Carter did the first serious bibliographical study of detective stories in *New Paths in Book Collecting* in 1934. The following year Scribner's issued a catalogue devoted to them, mostly from Carter's collection, which he catalogued and annotated. The title page bore a quotation from Philip Guedalla (often wrongly attributed to Woodrow Wilson): "The detective story is the normal recreation of noble minds."

The issuance of the catalogue was to provide deep disappointment to many collectors who ordered from it, among them Ned Guymon, whose incomparable collection of J. S. Fletcher still lacks *Andrewlina* (London, 1889). It is not Fletcher's first book, as the late John Hayward, commenting on its absence in remarks on the library in *The Book Collector*, said (a rare bibliographical error on his part). *Andrewlina* was preceded by three others. But it is certainly Fletcher's rarest—a fact I did not know when it was priced $6 in the catalogue. No copy has appeared in trade since, to my knowledge. The very day the catalogue was put into the mail a lady walked in, saw the books and promptly bought the entire group. She was not a collector, she explained, she just liked to read detective stories, and here was a whole batch of them she had never heard of. Her husband had something to do with the police department, she confided, and after reading these she thought it would be nice to present them to the department's library.

Some thirty years had passed when I received a call from Harold Graves, my successor at Scribner's. Would the Lilly Library be interested in purchasing this collection? "Yes, of course," I replied, perhaps a little too eagerly and promptly. A price was agreed on and *then* Harold told me the story. The lawyer settling the woman's estate called him to ask if the firm would be interested in repurchasing the collection. It seems they hadn't been touched since she bought them—neither added to, nor subtracted from nor, luckily, given away. What, Graves inquired, would be the price? The lawyer replied that the books were pretty old when she bought them, and thirty years older now. He had found Scribner's original bill in one of them and he would be happy if the estate could get what she had paid for them. Graves was willing. I glance fondly at *Andrewlina* when I pass its way in the stacks.

I keep adding to it and to our Doyle collection on occasion. Gilbert K. Chesterton rather fancied himself as an artist. He was commissioned at one time to do illustrations for an edition of the *Adventures*. Imagine Father Brown doing Sherlock Holmes! Nothing ever came of this, but I once secured a notebook of his with about twenty finished sketches, including the famed Reichenbach Falls episode. They are quite good, indeed, and for good measure some of the *Brigadier Gerard* stories are also illustrated. At any rate, they are a whole lot better than Charles Doyle's efforts.

My early reading was entirely undirected, but I managed to do a lot of it, and there were always relatives around whose libraries had something worth looking into—the places I was brought up in as a youth were too small to have public libraries. As a matter of fact, I first attended school in a Pennsylvania mining patch which no longer exists, in a little red schoolhouse with no library and very few books at all. One teacher taught all classes from first to sixth grade in one room. You were seated according to what class you were in, and your group sat in the first two rows while your grade was in session and then moved back when another class took over, all five or six of them.

This system had tremendous advantages. For one thing, if you were in the third grade and cared to listen, you could easily review what you had been taught, and missed, when in second grade; conversely, you could listen to fourth graders and have a pretty good idea of what you were coming up against next year. At any rate, the system had its merits for me, as, being a sickly child ("I'm afraid he's not long for this world and maybe it's better so"), I never went to school at all until I was past nine. My mother, however, taught me early to read and write (I still can't spell).

But I was a good boy, I am told, and never cried. This was because, it was finally discovered, one of the help was feeding me copiously on paregoric to keep me quiet. Perhaps that explains a lot, in this LSD age. I was never attracted to such experiments, possibly because I got my kicks early and when I became a man put childish things aside. Sherlock, it may be recalled, didn't.

At all events, somewhere I came across a copy of G. A. Henty's *With Clive in India*. This was reading even better than Doyle—for one thing, there was much more of it. Somehow, as birthday, Christmas and other presents, I managed to read my way through practically everything

Henty ever wrote. I was only later to learn that Henty was not only a favorite of Henry Miller, of all people, but also of Sir Winston Churchill, who is reputed to have said that he learned his English history largely from Shakespeare and Henty. I once wrote the great one (Churchill, that is) to verify this, but never got an answer.

Scribner's were Henty's accredited publishers (as they were of Jules Verne, another enthusiasm of mine), and when I came to work for them I kept heavy supplies of his books in stock in first editions. His first novel (not a juvenile) was a three-decker, *A Search for a Secret* (London, 1867). I catalogued, in the thirties, the only copy I had ever seen, for $17.50 and sold it to Morris L. Parrish of Philadelphia, whose library is now at Princeton. Just recently a dealer catalogued (and sold) a copy for $1,250. It is now at Harvard.

I put on a Henty show once in Scribner's Fifth Avenue window which caught the eye of a passing journalist and Henty collector, Pete Martin, then associate editor of *The Saturday Evening Post*. He had, it turned out, *the* Henty collection and had traveled from California (where Henty had visited mining camps) to England to acquire it, searching for heirs, descendants, etc. He had nearly everything, including the author's own copies of many of his books, *A Search for a Secret* among them. We discussed mutual Henty sorrows, notably the double-crossing ways of publishers with books. If you wanted to read *all* of Henty (and who didn't?), it was disillusionment to finally acquire (and pay money for) *A Girl of the Commune*, only to discover you had already read it under the title *The Two Sieges of Paris*, and to subsequently discover that it was also published as *Cuthbert Harrington's Adventures* and as *A Woman of the Commune*, all the same story. Eventually Pete Martin's collection came to rest at the Lilly Library. I reread only recently *Beric the Briton*, and it's still a good yarn.

Another hero of my childhood days was Jules Verne. Here again Scribner's were his main American publishers, and I always had in stock some of his first editions or translations. They were cheap but handsomely bound and thrillingly illustrated. Most of them eventually passed to a homesick Frenchman I had met, maître d' of a famous New York hotel dining room and an avid Verne collector. It used to puzzle my friends how for a good while I often dined at this spot—which even my boss could hardly have afforded regularly—and always received the very best of service and food at what seemed to be absurdly low prices.

Sherlock Holmes would have solved this little problem instantly. Though he once remarked that it was a shame he had to eat at all, because "what your digestion gains in the way of blood supply is so much lost to the brain," still we continually find in the Sacred Writings references to "oysters and a brace of cold woodcock, a pheasant, a *pâté de foie gras* pie with a group of ancient and cobwebby bottles," etc. In any event, my French friend retired recently and returned east, to France. His Vernes, however, traveled west, to Indiana. I no longer visit his hotel's famous room. The hotel has disappeared, but never Jules Verne.

Of course a childhood liking for reading of this kind carries over to adventure stories, science fiction (of which I was an early, though not too ardent, devotee), some Westerns, ghost stories and the like. I was, and remain, an ardent admirer of H. Rider Haggard, and I have had a great many interesting copies of his books, manuscripts, letters, etc., pass through my hands. I have owned at various times among other things the original manuscript of W. W. Jacobs' *The Monkey's Paw*, not inferior in its macabre virtuosity to *Dr. Jekyll and Mr. Hyde*. The price on this was $1,100 and it was around for years. Another favorite (priced $500 and immediately sold) was catalogued as follows:

> STOKER, BRAM.
> The original manuscript notes and data for *Dracula*. [c. 1890.] 79 leaves, 12mo, mounted to 4to.                                    $500
>
> Written in a minute hand, often on both sides of the sheet, on such diverse stationery as that of the Lyceum Theatre, London, and the Stratford Hotel, Philadelphia. Stoker was so careful in constructing his classic that he drew up a diary and time-schedule, as for example:

> May  1—Walpurgis-Nacht. Dead House. Hawker leaves Munich, 8:35 P.M.
> May  2—Arrives Vienna, 6:45 A.M. Leaves Vienna, 8:25 A.M. Arrives Budapesth, 1:30 P.M. Leaves 2 P.M. Arrives Klausenburgh, 3:40 P.M.
> May  3—Seward's Diary.
> May  5—Hawker drove to Castle.
> May  6—Seward's Diary, Castle, etc.
> Aug. 10—Lucy tries to get out. Sea-Captain buried. Sleepwalked.
> Aug. 11—Bat outside Lucy's window.
> Aug. 12—Sister Agatha writes Mina.
> Aug. 14—Lucy at Window, and bat.
> Aug. 17—Boxes to London, Canter. Paterson advised.
> Aug. 18—Mina's diary—Lucy well last night. Boxes arrive, etc.

> So far as we can discover, the final manuscript of *Dracula* is no longer in existence, and the present draft is all that remains in the author's autograph of his conception of the most famous of all vampyre stories.

I have had all of George Barr McCutcheon's *Graustark* manuscripts (now at the New York Public Library), part of Anthony Hope's *The*

*Prisoner of Zenda* (the original of which is now owned by Arthur A. Houghton, Jr.), some Montague Rhodes James ghost stories (one now at Lilly, another at the Pierpont Morgan), among many such.

I was fortunate enough at prep school to have as companion the son of the secretary of that late, great editor of *Adventure Magazine*, by far the best of the pulps, Arthur Sullivant Hoffman. He got advance copies of the magazine and I reveled in the tales first encountered there of Harold Lamb, Rafael Sabatini and Talbot Mundy, among others. I eventually secured a nearly complete run of *Adventure* for the library, primarily, I suppose, so I could reread them. One of the fringe benefits of being a rare book librarian is the chance to buy books with the library's money and read them on the library's time.

# A. E. Housman

I DISCOVERED A. E. Housman in Louis Untermeyer's *Modern British Poets* in 1921. At that time he had published only one book, *A Shropshire Lad* (London, 1896), which I secured in an American reprint and had by heart after a few readings as, I have discovered, did many another.

Housman has always been popular in America though he disliked and derided us. In a 1933 letter to his publisher, Grant Richards, he spoke of "the sham education given at American universities" and described the conduct of someone who wanted to write an article about him as "low, unworthy, and *American*," as if these three adjectives were equally derogatory. Again, "I am told Americans are human beings but appearances are against them." About the only American poet he seems to have approved was Millay. He wrote, in a letter I had, that, "Some things of Edna St. Vincent Millay which I have seen make me think her the best living American poet"; he added, however, that he wished she wouldn't write sonnets.

I sometimes wonder what his reaction would be if he knew that one of the most complete collections of his printed works would end at the Lilly Library in Indiana, and his poetical manuscripts at the Library of Congress. Scorn for the former, I suspect—he wrote Grant Richards about two small errors in *Last Poems* (1922): "No, don't put in an errata slip. The blunders will probably enhance the value of the first edition in the eyes of bibliophiles, an idiotic class"; indignation and outrage at the latter, but more of this later.

There has always been a small group of Housman collectors in America, H. B. Collamore, Seymour Adelman, Fred Adams, Al Perrin and Charles Feinberg among them. First choice of what I had went to Collamore, and there were gems among them, including a unique *Shrop-*

*shire Lad*, probably a trial issue in my opinion, though Carter, his bibliographer, has his reservations. The work was originally printed in five hundred copies, one hundred and fifty of which were sent to America for publication by John Lane in 1897. It was not copyrighted here, as under the manufacturing clause of the 1891 Copyright Act it could not be unless printed here, and was consequently often pirated. Collamore also had the original draft of the famous Preface to *Last Poems*, the original letter to M. Pollet from Housman—the most important biographical document extant—the Grant Richards correspondence about *Last Poems* and much else.

Housman's disinclination for public honors was so strong that he never accepted any. There were in Collamore's collection seven invitations for these honors, six from universities, each with Housman's draft refusal penciled on the verso, all being variations of the same theme. The institutions were the University of St. Andrews, the University of Liverpool, the University of Wales, the University of Glasgow, and the University of Oxford, twice, at dates ranging from 1905 to 1934.

The extreme instance came February 22, 1929, Housman's seventieth year, in a typed letter signed by Lord Stamfordham, private secretary to King George V, offering him the Order of Merit (England's most coveted honor), "in recognition of your valuable work as a Classical Scholar and in the ranks of literature." On the verso of the letter is the draft of Housman's reply, and by return of post, his refusal mailed on February 23.

> With all gratitude for His Majesty's most kind and flattering wish to confer upon me the Order of Merit I humbly beg permission to decline the high honour. I hope to escape the reproach of thanklessness or churlish behaviour by borrowing the words in which an equally loyal subject, Admiral Cornwallis, declined a similar mark of the Royal favour: "I am, unhappily, of a turn of mind that would make my receiving that honour the most unpleasant thing imaginable."

On February 25 Lord Stamfordham replied: "I know his Majesty will appreciate your reasons for this decision and also the grateful and loyal terms in which it was conveyed."

Housman, aside from *A Shropshire Lad*—about a $250 book in first edition, depending on condition—was never an expensive author to collect, and everyone, except specialists like Carter, ignored his prose. In 1941 two groups of his letters to Grant Richards appeared at auction in New York. I purchased both, 128 letters and 31 autograph notes, to which he was addicted, for $1,850, and 37 letters for $400, all ranging in date from 1910 to 1935.

This was more than Collamore wished to take on, so I divided the correspondence into two groups. One relating entirely to *Last Poems* I sold to Collamore for $750. The remainder went to the Library of Congress on an exchange. They had two copies of an extremely scarce and important early American novel, H. H. Brackenridge's *Modern Chivalry: Containing the Adventures of Captain John Farrago and Teague Oregan, his Servant*, 4 volumes (Philadelphia, 1792–97, the third volume, 1793, bearing a Pittsburgh imprint). Furthermore the first volume was a very rare variant without the copyright notice at the foot of the title page, and I had the other.

This set passed to Barrett for $4,500, and everyone was happy except Fred Goff, rare book librarian at the Library of Congress. David Mearns, head of manuscripts, was pleased because he got the letters free, but Fred gave up something and got nothing in return.

One of the nicest and most interesting pieces of Housmaniana I ever had was a poetical commonplace book, a school notebook filled with transcriptions in his autograph of poems ranging in date from Shakespeare to Swinburne, done around 1875. He was partial to the Arthurian verse-writer George Augustus Simcox, largely neglected today, and his long "Si descendero in inferum odes" has some remarkable similarities to Housman's strange poem "Hell Gate" (*Last Poems*, xxxi). The selection, wide as its range is, already reflects something of that melancholy which characterized Housman's own compositions twenty years later. Indeed, the very first quatrain in the notebook, transcribed from Matthew Arnold, whom Housman much admired, might almost pass unremarked in the pages of *A Shropshire Lad*:

> Youth rambles on life's arid mount,
>   And strikes the rock, and finds the vein;
> And brings the water from the fount,
>   The fount which shall not flow again.

This anthology (Seymour Adelman has another) was purchased for $2,750 by Charles Feinberg, part payment, I recall, being in Hemingway manuscripts.

Housman died in 1936, and in 1938 his brother Laurence approached John Carter about the possibilities of selling A.E.'s manuscripts through Scribner's rare book department. This was the logical thing to do, Scribner's being Laurence's American publishers and Carter, with John

Sparrow, Housman's bibliographer. I was delighted. They were purchased for £2,000, the price set by Laurence, and the manuscripts containing Housman's drafts and revisions duly arrived in New York, accompanied by a thorough analysis of their contents made by Carter.

I was unable to sell them. Housman collectors were unused to such a price (or didn't have it, which is possibly why they were Housman collectors to begin with, not Herrick collectors, let us say). I toyed with the idea of breaking up the notebooks and selling the books separately; Lilly, for example, wanted *A Shropshire Lad* but not the rest, and Collamore wanted *Last Poems*, which he, with many others including myself, thinks is the superior volume. But I couldn't bring myself to do it.

Suddenly B. J. Beyer (with whom I remained friendly despite the Lilly episode, recounted later) told me he had a buyer who would present it to a national institution, which was exactly what I wanted. I said he could have the collection for $15,000 and he accepted. Several months later he informed me that through some inadvertence his customer understood that he had *offered* them for $15,000. Could I possibly give him a 10 percent discount from that price, which would hardly reimburse him for the supersalesmanship he had displayed but would at least be something. He then confided that the collection would be given by the purchaser to the Library of Congress and thus belong to THE NATION. Anyone, he implied, except a card-carrying Communist would cooperate.

Well, $13,500 showed the firm a profit, and the collection was going to be kept intact, so I accepted. Beyer had sold it to Mrs. Whittal, a generous patron of the Library of Congress, who duly presented it to them.

A few years later I was doing some research there when Archibald MacLeish was librarian. I remember his taking me into the bowels of the building where I was to work alone for several days. When I asked if I could smoke there he replied, "You are not even allowed to be here." It was on this occasion that I reminded him of the enormous favor I had done his institution by allowing it to acquire the Housman manuscripts for a pittance. "Perhaps," he replied, "you consider forty thousand dollars a pittance, I don't." I never forgave myself, not for the sum Beyer got for them—that was entirely his affair—but for my naïveté in letting him beat me down an additional 10 percent. When I tasked him he replied airily, "We are all entitled to our little white lies." He was a rascal but a bookman, and I admired him for that.

Clause 7 of Housman's will, dated November 17, 1932, reads:

> I DIRECT my said brother Laurence Housman to destroy all my prose manuscript writing in whatever language and I permit him but do not

enjoin him to select from my verse manuscript writing and to publish any poems which appear to him to be completed and to be not inferior in quality to the average of my published poems and I DIRECT him to destroy all other poems and fragments of verse.

Housman left four notebooks, about half the contents of which his brother preserved. Most of the poems were in pencil, with many variant or canceled readings, and these he carelessly erased with India rubber, leaving many of them still legible at that time. The treatment they were later subjected to obscured some of the readings. Housman wrote on both sides of a leaf, and when his brother pasted on foolscap leaves such poems as he thought worth preserving, the pasted-down side sometimes contained material he did not think worth publication. But he couldn't preserve one without the other.

If there was ever a meticulous workman it was A. E. Housman. The smallest kind of printer's error drove him to distraction. When two errors in punctuation appeared in *Last Poems,* he wrote his publisher that he "knew the filthy beasts of printers would do something," and he had only wondered what it would be. And he claimed that he was allowing *Last Poems* to be printed at all while he was alive only because he would still be around to correct the proof. Against the last word in his own copy, now at Lilly, he penciled: "Vain hope!" Error pursued this great precisionist even to his grave. The *Times* of London in its obituary gave his age as seventy-six instead of seventy-seven. And worse was to come. He left a poem "For My Funeral," which was issued in an edition of three hundred copies which were distributed to mourners at the 1936 service, most of whom probably left their copies in their seats. And of all things to happen, the printers of the august Cambridge University Press, remaining "filthy" to the end, set "Ecclesiasticus" where Housman had written "Ecclesiastes." The press made amends by running off a corrected reprint of one hundred copies, thus giving the compleat collector the job of acquiring both versions. Housman must have gazed from Parnassus on these proceedings with frigid disapproval.

The catalogue of the manuscripts John Carter prepared when the collection was offered for sale was prefaced by the statement: "COPYRIGHT. The copyright in any variant readings, superseded readings, early drafts, etc., etc., is (needless to say) retained by the executors. The MSS are sold simply as relics." This note was actually not necessary, as legal copyright in unpublished material, Carter adds, "does not have to be secured or protected; it subsists."

Eventually, though, the manuscripts were soaked off at the Library of

Congress, crepolined (a procedure I abhor in most instances), and some eight hundred lines of Housman's poetry and variant readings were published. I consider this a distinct disservice to Housman's memory and a gross betrayal of trust, and I dislike thinking that it happened here and that I, even indirectly, had any part in it. It is things like this which lead to destruction, not preservation, by people of their private papers, and this was actually one of the episodes which led Hemingway to proscribe any posthumous publication of his letters, an unhappy decision indeed. I do not mean to decry a scholar's right to knowledge of unpublished work, but study of it is one thing while publication against the expressed will of the author is quite another—especially in the face of so clear a clarion call as Housman issued. But I suppose it's all a matter of prestige and getting one's name in print. Somehow I have a distinct feeling, though, that a lot of people who fooled with Housman in this manner wish they hadn't.

It will be recalled that Housman's will directed his brother to destroy all his "prose manuscript writing in whatever language," and this was presumably done—at least little of it remains except stray scraps and bits usually found tucked into some of his books. There is preserved in the Lilly Library some prose, the most characteristic of which is a review of A. Bourgery and M. Ponchont's *Lucian V-X:* "It is presumptuous for editors who understand Lucian and Latin no better than this, to entertain and express opinions upon disputed quotations or interpretations of fact," etc.

But the manuscript of Housman's major work in English prose does survive. This is his famed essay on "The Name and Nature of Poetry" (Cambridge, 1933). He disliked this work and refused to autograph copies. In the Collamore collection is a letter to I. R. Brussel, the American bookseller, dated 7 July 1933, reading:

> I return the copy of *A Shropshire Lad* with my signature added; but I have refused all requests to sign copies of the lecture because I do not think much of it, and wrote it against the grain.

It is one of the many ironies of Housman's life that this should be one of two prose manuscripts of his to survive and that it should bring a sum over twice what his estate received for all his poetical works.

"The Name and Nature of Poetry" is by far the most widely known of Housman's few public lectures, and the manuscript survived because it was given to Mr. (later Sir Sydney) Roberts, then Secretary to the

Syndics of the Cambridge University Press and thus its publisher. It appeared for sale at Sotheby's in 1966, and it was estimated that a bid of between £2,500 and £3,000 would bring it. I wanted it for the Lilly collection badly enough to send a bid of £5,750 for it—far and away enough, I thought—and wasn't even the underbidder! It brought £6,000 and went right back home to Cambridge University, not for cremation, I presume.

The University Press played him false also when printing the lecture, misquoting Shakespeare's "O mistress mine, where are you roaming?" as "O mistress mine, where art thou roaming?" Housman has corrected this in his own copies, English and American, now at Lilly, and at that he missed two other errors the press made (I wonder how his manuscript read?). Shakespeare wrote the line, or at least it appears in our first folio, as, "O mistris mine where are you roaming?" And this happened to a man who noted that accuracy is a duty and not a virtue.

I have one small chunk of what went into building this essay. In a celebrated passage Housman writes: "Poetry indeed seems to me more physical than intellectual. A year or two ago, in common with others, I received from America a request that I would define poetry," and he then elaborates eloquently.

The answer to the letter from America he refers to is on my library wall, and is the first enunciation of his famous definition of poetry.

Trinity College, Cambridge, England. 15 Dec. 1930.

Dear Professor McCote:
   I am afraid I can no more define poetry than a terrier can define a rat. We both recognize the object by its effect on our senses. For instance, if a line of poetry comes into my memory while I am shaving, the hair bristles on my skin, and I have to stop.

It was given me by Collamore when he presented his Housmans to the Lilly Library, and it hangs in my library next to the manuscript of Stevenson's poem "Over the Sea to Skye," a poem which I think (I have no way of knowing) Housman probably liked. At least he liked Stevenson enough to do him the compliment of writing a poem about him, a tribute he paid no other English author. "R.L.S." first appeared in *The Academy* on December 22, 1894. Its next appearance was in Vincent Starrett's anthology *In Praise of Robert Louis Stevenson* (Chicago, privately printed, 1919), and then in a privately printed leaflet of fifty copies done for "the friends of Starrett and Edwin B. Hall" (Yaleta, Texas, 1928), all difficult to acquire.

It never appeared in the two volumes of his poems issued during his lifetime or in the two posthumous volumes issued by his brother. Its first appearance in a work of his is in *The Collected Poems*, edited anonymously by John Carter (London, 1959). Carter's collection is at Lilly, and the flyleaf of his copy bears the note in ink: "John Carter, published on Dec. 1, 1959. 5000 printed, 3000 bound, edited, and the note on the text written by John Carter." Beneath this in pencil is the note:

> This advance copy has the original state of [A3] the contents leaf, omitting the acknowledgements to The Richards Press. The leaf was cancelled before publication (and according to Cape's before review copies went out—but—?) Nevertheless I have not yet (1962) ever seen another copy.

And there is added, in red ink, a later note, "(Nor yet, 1965)."

This ranks, therefore, in rarity with our unique *Shropshire Lad*, so we have the first and the last of his books in their only known copies.

I was in London in 1936 when Carter found out that Housman's library was to be sold, and early one morning he set off to get what he could. Carter, in his talk at the Lilly Library on the presentation of Collamore's collection to it in 1961, relates that:

> Nearly all the books from Housman's own shelves that have ever been on the market derive from one single historic Saturday morning's harvesting in Blackwell's bookshop at Oxford.
>
> Andrew Gow, Housman's closest friend at Trinity, had been in charge of his effects there, and besides distributing in appropriate directions such *rariora Housmaniana* as were found in the closets, had sent bundles of classical offprints to those of us he thought suitable or deserving. It must, I suppose, have been in the early fall of 1936 that he told me the whole remaining bulk of the books on the shelves in Trinity Great Court had been sold to Blackwell's. I at once got on to Mr. King, then the admired if embittered panjandrum of Blackwell's rare book department. He said the books were not even sorted yet, and he didn't know when they would be on sale. No, I couldn't come down and just have a look. No, there was not, nor would be, a list. But yes, since Mr. Gow had said so, he would promise to let me know when they *were* coming on sale. I retired, biting my nails and praying that I was the only person in London who knew even as much as I did—which, allowing for the grapevine, I doubted.
>
> Three weeks later a laconic postcard advised me that Housman's library would come on sale that Saturday morning. A seven o'clock getaway from London in my battered old Chrysler put me on Blackwell's doorstep at 8:55. Six minutes later, I and two unknown characters were in the back room. Were they fellow enthusiasts, or just early risers? I

had no means of knowing. "Where," I whispered urgently, "are the Housman books?"

"Oh, we haven't got them up yet. Were you in a hurry? They'll be bringing some of them presently."

The minutes of my precious start ticked away. In leisurely course, assistants began carrying armfuls of books in and dumping them on the large central table.

Each contained the printed label which Blackwell's had been authorized to affix. Each was priced in pencil (I don't like to think of those prices now). They were in no sort of order: works of literature, history or criticism, volumes of minor poetry, old guide books, Victorian novels, yellowbacks and paperbacks; everything was jumbled together in each successive armful—and every other armful, of course, was on the other side of the table, with the titles facing the other way. One thing seemed odd: there were no classical texts.

One needed to be both lynx-eyed and swiveleyed to pick the grain from the chaff and to make sure that no bit of special knowledge was wasted. One needed to be quick-fingered without the impoliteness of grabbing (this was Oxford, remember, not the Charing Cross Road). One needed to watch not only the incoming books but also the eyes and hands of the competitors. For by 9:30 or 10 o'clock there were a dozen people picking the books over, and a desultory finger could fall on a prize just as fatally as a knowledgeable one.

By now a pile had begun to form behind my "pitch." I have often asked myself since why it was not quadruple the size. But one must remember that Housman collectors were few and far between in those distant days. Also it took a couple of minutes to scan any but the most obviously attractive title—and these were the tiny minority—in case there should be worth-while annotations or some obscure association. Moreover, dons and undergraduates have keen eyes, and Housman's name was honoured in Oxford as well as Cambridge.

By midmorning the back room was full of people, and though the armfuls kept coming, the gamesmanship got progressively trickier. By noon everything was out in the open and we were reduced to gleaning over reaped stubble. At 12:15, in a hurry and a fluster, the first London bookseller appeared (his car had broken down, I learned later). He sized the situation up in one minute flat. He gave me a look of such concentrated venom that I can feel it now. It had been a wearing morning, but a rewarding one.

Yet there was a sting at the tail of it. As I was walking with Mr. King —of Blackwell's (yes, the London dealer's name was King too)—to deal with my purchases, we passed a bay of books in which two very junior assistants sat busy with erasure on the margins of a large stack of volumes which I perceived to be editions of classical authors. "What goes on?" I asked.

"Those," Mr. King replied with his customary melancholy, "are Housman's classical texts. We were only allowed to take them on condition that every single marginal note was rubbed out before they went on sale. The few with ink notes had to be destroyed. The boys are working away at the rest. Seems a pity, doesn't it?"

I agreed that it seemed a pity.

# Mary Webb

I WAS INTRODUCED to Mary Webb by reading A. Edward
Newton and became and remain an admirer of her work—both
poetry and prose. I was influenced, perhaps, by G. K. Chesterton's
observation that "much of the noble work of Mary Webb may be called
the prose poems of a Shropshire Lass," and Housman is one of my heroes.
I don't think they knew each other, yet he was a great influence on her
poetical work. So was Thomas Hardy, on her novels. She dedicated *Seven
for a Secret* "To the Illustrious Name of Thomas Hardy, whose acceptance of this dedication has made me so happy." Yet they never met.

Much has been written of her flower stall in Shrewsbury. She and her
husband would rise at three in the morning and cut the fresh flowers, and
she then walked the nine miles from her home, Rose Cottage at Pontes-
bury, to offer her blooms for a halfpenny a bunch, seldom earning more
than five shillings in one day. Her books earned little more—"out of
fashion," critics said, "not sufficiently in the spirit of our time."

Housman could not have had her in mind in the last poem in *A
Shropshire Lad* (written shortly after she was born), but the opening
lines fit her perfectly:

> I hoed and trenched and weeded,
>     And took the flowers to fair:
> I brought them home unheeded;
>     The hue was not the wear.

On the other hand, she certainly had in mind the closing lines of his
second poem in *A Shropshire Lad:*

> About the woodlands I will go
> To see the cherry hung with snow,

when she wrote:

> Into the scented woods we'll go
> And see the blackthorn swim in snow.

It pleases me to recall that I have had both these poems in their original manuscripts.

When I got into the rare book business I found that Mary Webb had a small but devoted cult of admirers and collectors, and I set out to gather what I could for them. Prices then were quite high, as she had suddenly shot to fame as a result of the praise given her by Prime Minister Stanley Baldwin at a time too late, unfortunately, to do her any good.

Carter bought a fair amount of her books from Elkin Mathews, and I found in Greville Worthington, then a member of the firm, another devoted admirer. Percy Muir, in his autobiography *Minding My Own Business* (London, 1956), writes:

> Greville discovered that Mary Webb's husband owned, and was prepared to sell, presentation copies of all her books inscribed to him, and the thirty books which made up her pathetic library. These were nearly all cheap editions, or rather tattered copies of books she had acquired for a few pence in the market-place where she had supplemented her income by selling bunches of flowers from her cottage garden. There were also a few books given her mostly by not very highly esteemed authors.
>
> What excited Greville most, however, and what caused me most anguish of mind were two manuscripts. One was a fairy story that she wrote when she was thirteen; the other was the manuscript of the novel that she left unfinished when she died, *The Armour Wherein He Trusted*. These two manuscripts had survived only because they were unpublished. All her published manuscripts she had used to light her cottage fire. Mr. Webb was prepared to sell everything of hers that he possessed; and I was shattered by Greville's proposal that we should blue almost our entire bank-balance in acquiring them.
>
> I tried to persuade him to make it a personal speculation, the firm to sell the material for him on commission; but he rightly said that this would not be a satisfactory scheme. Finally I said that I would waive all my objections if John Carter would take a half share in the transaction for Scribner's. John had no higher opinion of her writing than I had; but his appreciation of her reputation among collectors was better informed than mine. We dealt with it jointly, and we both made a good deal of money out of it quite quickly. But that only showed that Greville had been right, and I had been utterly and completely wrong about the whole thing.

I was in London at the time and had an appointment to go with Worthington to visit Mr. Webb, but something came up to cancel my doing so, to my everlasting disappointment. It seemed that on Worthington's arrival Mr. Webb began examining closets, drawers and the like where such of Mary's letters, manuscripts and books which had survived were stored. The more he examined them the sadder he became: he literally wept over a copy of *The Golden Arrow*, her first novel (London, 1916), dedicated "To A Noble Lover H.L.W.," and well he should have. Her last novel, *Precious Bane*, at the start no more successful than its predecessors, was also dedicated to him, though his copy was not inscribed, as she gave it to him personally. Inserted in it, however, was Baldwin's glowing letter to her on his first reading the book, dated "Downing Street, Jan. 14, 1927," well preceding his speech at a dinner of the Royal Literary Fund which struck the effective note of appreciation that led to the great demand for her work which followed.

As he perused these, Webb became more and more loath to part with them, and quite understandably so. Worthington had about given up any hope of obtaining them when the second Mrs. Webb, who had been off somewhere, appeared just at the end of teatime. When she heard that the ragged and tattered remnants of books and papers were worth the modest sum offered for them, she commanded her husband to accept Worthington's offer and "get that trash out of here before the fool changes his mind."

This Mr. Webb did. He must have been a mild man to have put up with Mary, who took some coping with. She never completely recovered from an early illness, either in mind or body, which was certainly not her fault and was expressed in the tragedy of her novels. Creative creatures of any kind are not the easiest to live with, but I have found that authors who frequently change publishers are especially difficult. Mary Webb loved nature, wrote beautifully of flowers, hated injustice, cruelty—and publishers. She did six books for four English publishers from 1916 to 1924.

When I was going over the Scribner files I found a letter written to Charles Scribner by Charles Kingsley, long-time manager of Scribner's London branch. It is dated "16th February, 1926" and should be read with the knowledge that the firm of E. P. Dutton were, at that time, her American publishers. It must also be remembered that this is a letter dealing with Mary Webb in her literary tradings; here she wasn't selling flowers.

> Mrs. Webb. She is living up to the reputation she has here of being thoroughly unreliable and impossible to deal with, to use only the mildest form of language. She told me distinctly that she had broken with Dutton and was returning the advance he had paid her; that the figures I quoted in my cable were what Dutton had offered and would

be satisfactory, that her break with Dutton was owing to her being unwilling to assent to certain clauses in the contract which McCrae had
presented to her. After putting off seeing me and delaying to come down
here when she said she would, she called up yesterday morning to ask
me if I had seen the announcement that "Precious Bane" had been
awarded the Femina-Vie Heureuse prize. I said I had not, and congratulated her, and she then announced that this put a different complexion
on the matter, and moreover that she had just heard that Mr. McCrae
was in town, and she would like to know before she saw him how much
we were prepared to offer. I answered immediately that we were not
making any offer on her book except on the assumption that she had
already broken with McCrae; that she had distinctly told me that she
had done so, and it was on that understanding that we were willing
to negotiate with her, and on that understanding only. She answered
that she had only intended us to understand that she had *made up her
mind to* break with McCrae, which was in distinct contradiction to what
she told me last week, and wanted to know anyway whether we would
be prepared to offer a considerably larger advance and possibly a rising
royalty on her next two books. Evidently her intention was to go to
McCrae and try to get something more out of him on the basis of an
increased offer from us. I replied immediately that under those circumstances we withdrew any offer whatsoever and that we could not consider any further negotiations until she gave me in black and white a
statement that she had broken with McCrae, nor did I assure her in any
way that we were willing to consider any higher terms than the terms
she herself had mentioned previously. She said her publisher here,
Robert Holden, had advised her that she could get much higher terms
now, and that he was going to New York shortly and had promised to
dispose of her rights for her. She has fiddled along with this thing to such
an extent that I should not be surprised if somebody pirated her "Precious Bane" now that it has been brought into prominence.

    The truth of the matter is that she is just a slippery eel without any
conscience or business morals, and I am afraid that anybody who deals
with her is asking for trouble. She double crossed Curtis Brown and
Cape refuses to have anything more to do with her. She told me at the
conclusion of the conversation that after she had seen McCrae she
would call me up, and there the matter rests.

The cream of the lot Worthington acquired, including the manuscript
of the posthumously published, unfinished *The Armour Wherein He
Trusted*, went to Fred Adams for $550. He also acquired for the same
price manuscripts of *Gossip About Shropshire Lore* and *Glimpses of Old
Shropshire*, very important as being sources of *Golden Arrow, Precious
Bane* and *Gone to Earth*, the manuscripts of which had been burned.

    Fred Adams was less interested in Mary Webb's poetry, and I sold
many of these poems to an Indianapolis collector, Benjamin Hitz, including the complete manuscripts of her *Poems* as posthumously published in

1928, some seventy-seven in all, for $875, and much that was unpublished, also. These are now at the University of Chicago. Other things, including a number of books from her library, went to George Matthew Adams, a well-known syndicated newspaper man who had a choice library, mostly of moderns. When it eventually came up for sale I purchased most of his Webb material for the Lilly Library for considerably less than he had paid me.

I have no knowledge of the present location of the dedication copy of *Precious Bane* with the famous Baldwin letter. This read:

> Dear Mrs. Webb,
> I hope you will not think it an impertinence on my part if I tell you with what delight I have read *Precious Bane*. My people lived in Shropshire for centuries before they migrated to Worcestershire, and I spent my earliest years in Bewdley, which is on the border. In your book I seem to hear again the speech and turns of phrase which surrounded me in the nursery. I think it is a really first-class piece of work and I have not enjoyed a book so much for years. It was given to me by one of my secretaries and I read it at Christmas within sight of the Clee Hills, at home. Thank you a thousand times for it.
>
> > Believe me to remain,
> > Sincerely yours,
> > Stanley Baldwin

She was urged to have the letter published in an advertisement but refused.

Seven months later, in October, 1927, she died of pernicious anemia. Only two of her books were in print. In April, 1928, Stanley Baldwin, in a speech at the Royal Literary Fund Dinner, said:

> She died at the early age of forty-six, and I saw no notice in any paper of any kind. I should like to pay a testimony to her for the extreme pleasure she gave me and in the hope that others may share that pleasure who have not heard of her.

Back in print went everything, sparked by a *Collected Edition* with introductions by such notables as John Buchan, Walter de la Mare and others. As Caradoc Evans wrote:

> All her life she had wished for riches, fame, applause, admiration, babies, and pretty dresses, and she got nothing. She is the heroine of a fairy story with a sad ending.

Somewhere, on someone's shelves, rests the dedication copy of *Precious Bane* of surpassing interest. I cannot recall what happened to the fairy story she wrote when she was thirteen.

# Katherine Mansfield

W HILE WORKING on Mary Webb I was simultaneously gathering together what was available of another tragic English authoress, Katherine Mansfield, short story writer and critic. Born at Wellington, New Zealand, in 1888, she was sent to London and attended Queen's College in 1903. Always delicate in health, she died in 1923.

This collection was made for Mrs. Edison Dick of Chicago and is unrivaled. I met her through her husband, who was a budding collector. His interests were then tied in with his business, the Dick Mimeograph Company, and he had the excellent idea of getting together a collection of books based on the various methods of putting ink on paper. I had supplied him a fair number, including the finest known copy of Blake's *Songs of Innocence and Experience* (London, 1789–1794), which is described elsewhere, when World War II broke out. After returning from service in the Navy, Dick lost interest in the collection, and I repurchased most of it from him.

However, he kept, and still has, a few choice things, among them some original copperplates done by William Hogarth, including "Columbus and the Egg," which shows Columbus demonstrating his well-known trick of making an egg stand on its end. Hogarth's satirical tone and admirable comic design have made it one of his most famous engravings. It is found as frontispiece in some copies of his *Analysis of Beauty* (London, 1735). Dick also has the six actual copperplates, each 15 × 12½ inches, of the first and most successful of Hogarth's famous sequences, *The Harlot's Progress* (London, 1732), engraved by the artist himself.

Soon after his marriage in 1729 Hogarth conceived the idea of sequences of paintings on "modern moral subjects," as he called them, in which he aimed at "composing pictures on canvas, similar to representations on the stage." The first of these sequences was his *Harlot's Progress.* The paintings finished, the artist set to work on the engravings, which were advertised for sale in March, 1732. Their success was immediate and tremendous. Subscribers alone numbered more than twelve hundred, and pirated copies circulated in immense numbers. Theophilus Cibber produced a pantomime on the subject at Drury Lane in 1733, a ballad opera appeared in 1735 under the title of *The Jew Decoyed; or the Harlot's Progress,* and the scenes were engraved in miniature on fan mounts. The original paintings were bought by William Beckford, father of the author of *Vathek,* but all except Number 2 were destroyed by fire at Fonthill in 1755.

The complete series of all Hogarth's original copperplates was acquired in the late eighteenth century by Boydell, the London publisher, for his collected edition of 1790. In 1822 this was reissued "from the original plates, carefully retouched by Heath, with letter-press by Nichols" at thirty guineas a copy. Another edition from Baldwin, Cradock & Joy, in fifty-two parts at five shillings a part, came out in 1835–1837; and this again was reissued by Henry G. Bohn.

From Bohn's possession the collection of coppers passed to the original Bernard Quaritch, when, after working with Bohn, he set up in business for himself in 1847. Forgotten in the warehouse for decades, the whole collection was rediscovered early in the present century, only to be broken into by the needs of war—the large majority of the plates being sold for metal in 1916. Of those which survived, *The Harlot's Progress* is the most important and the most decorative series.

These remain unique monuments to one of the greatest of English artists, who was also a pioneer in the production of original engravings as a business proposition. The total cost to Dick was under $1,000.

Jane Dick's dedication to Katherine Mansfield remained constant. She wanted everything and nearly got it. Scribner's were able to obtain for her Mansfield's correspondence with Lady Ottoline Morrell and Dorothy Brett, among others. But the plum was the first editions, letters, manuscripts, and an unpublished diary notebook, acquired from Mansfield's intimate friend Ida Constance Baker. The cache included the manuscript of "Non-Compounders," published in *The Garden Party* (London, 1922) under the title "The Daughters of the Late Colonel." Ida Baker herself was the original of Constanzia in this oft-praised story. There were many unpublished stories: "His Sister's Keeper," dated 1909, and a long story, forty-three pages, "Brave Love," undated. Of most importance was a diary notebook which never has been published, similar to those published in her *Journal*, edited by that unpleasant character, her husband, John Middleton Murry.

Jane Dick collected Mansfield at just the right time, about a decade following her death. While an author is living, friends who have significant material are often unwilling to part with it, in my experience. But as time goes on they become less reluctant. I remember spending a weekend with Franklin P. Adams, famed editor of "The Conning Tower," from whom I purchased some very fine things, but he would not part with anything given him by a living author, among them the dedication copy of John O'Hara's *Appointment in Samarra* (New York, 1934), which I vainly tried to get Scribner's to publish, since it is about my part of the country and O'Hara and I were boys together. It was the same with books inscribed to FPA by Edna St. Vincent Millay and Sinclair Lewis, but when only a short time later they died within months of each other, he then parted with their books.

Among much memorabilia I remember an embroidered desk blotter which Miss Baker treasured; it contained photographs of Katherine Mansfield, an original drawing by her, done in Chelsea, and other intimate mementos.

There was one item Ida Baker did not acquire. Muir knew S. S. Koteliansky, who, with Mansfield, had translated Maxim Gorki's *Reminiscences of Leonid Andreyev* and who somehow came to offer me an old brass bed in which Katherine had slept. I was enchanted but couldn't persuade Edison Dick that it should be added to his wife's collection.

# Cooper and Irving

**M**OST PEOPLE remember James Fenimore Cooper for the Leatherstocking Tales. So do I, but I also remember him because through him I was indirectly taught the cost of caviar and learned (too late) the value of Andrew Wyeth paintings—painful recollections indeed.

The scarcest of Cooper's major novels are his first, *Precaution* (New York, 1820), and his second, *The Spy: A Tale of the Neutral Ground* (New York, 1821), both anonymous. I have had several copies of each, but *The Spy* stands out. Edward Lazare was sent by Harzof to Brooklyn to do a routine estate appraisal of a small library. There was nothing much in it except one book—a copy of *The Spy*, first edition in original boards, uncut and unique thus: the very few copies known then were all in contemporary calf. Eddie related that this was tucked away behind other books, perhaps in the hope he wouldn't spot it—vain wish with that book hawkshaw around.

Besides the unique binding, however, the book was the only known copy inscribed by Cooper—and what an inscription! "To Mrs. Banyer from her Humble Servant the Author, this first copy that has been issued is Respectfully Presented." A very little sleuthing revealed its tremendous sentimental interest.

Mrs. Banyer was the widowed daughter of John Jay, at whose home Cooper spent much time during this period of his life. John Jay was, among other things, head of the Committee of Defense during the Revolutionary War—the secret service of the time—and during this period met Enoch Crane, the Harvey Birch of *The Spy;* and the tales Jay told Cooper about Crane, Cooper rewove into the novel, putting the setting into the familiar surroundings of his home, Westchester County, the "neutral ground" of both armies during almost the whole revolutionary period.

Mrs. Banyer died young, without issue, and the book descended in the family. Lazare found it in the library of her great-grandniece, Miss Julia Pierpont of Brooklyn.

This, I decided immediately, was a book for Frank Hogan, so I telephoned his secretary, Virginia Warren, in Washington (a collector in her own right), for an appointment, only to be told that she and Frank would be in New York the following day for an important meeting. He was staying at a suite at the Waldorf-Astoria and giving a caviar and champagne party that evening. If I could manage to get there before the party was scheduled, however, he could spare me a few minutes: with a book like that and a customer like Frank, that was time enough.

I arrived just after the suite had been set up for the party, and somehow in my eagerness to show Virginia the treasure, I knocked over the caviar, which was reposing in a large salver ensconced in ice. All I could think of was to call room service, get someone to clean up the mess and get a replacement for the caviar before Hogan arrived, which I proceeded to do. There was a gasp at the other end of the phone and a voice said, "You are sure you want another five pounds?" I replied that I did, pronto, and asked to have the bill sent along with the waiter.

Virginia asked casually if I knew how caviar was priced. As I didn't, she then informed me that it was by the ounce, not the pound; that it was weighed before being delivered to the party and weighed after, the host being charged for only what was used. She had no idea what the five pounds' worth spilled over the Waldorf rug would cost, but she advised me that, whatever the price of *The Spy* was, I would be well advised to double my profit before offering it to Frank if I was to come out even on this disaster. I didn't, and she was right.

Frank was fascinated with the book and its story and purchased it for $7,500. At the sale of his books I repurchased it for the same sum and sold it to Lilly. I thus had the pleasure of twice handling the finest known copy of the first American novel to secure international acclaim, and I now have permanent custody of it.

Cooper's first book was *Precaution*, written because, according to some accounts, while reading some boring English novel aloud to his wife one day he remarked he could write a better one and she challenged him to do so. History does not record what novel he was reading, but if it was any worse than *Precaution* it must have been vapid indeed. It is, however, a literary landmark as the beginning of Cooper's career and is an extremely scarce book in first edition. Where found at all, it is usually in contemporary calf, edges trimmed. Fewer than five are known in original printed boards, edges uncut, as issued. I came across one of these somewhere, which I sold to Dr. William C. Braislin of Brooklyn, who had a notable collection of American literature, especially Cooper and Irving. We became close friends and I was a major purchaser at his sale in 1937 where his *Precaution* brought $1,150.

A couple of decades later I was asked by Paul Cooper to appraise the family library at Cooperstown. Much of the archives had been given to Yale, but an appraisal was needed of what remained. As it had already been scanned by practiced eyes, I didn't expect to find anything startling, and I didn't until I came across my old friend *Precaution* in conventional contemporary calf. I glanced at the title page, then at the flyleaf, then froze. It was a presentation copy—again the only one on record. The family were delighted with this discovery, as was I. And the reason for the rarity of both books in inscribed state, aside from the fact that Cooper was not much given to presenting books, is that they were published anonymously and Cooper was at some pains to conceal his authorship.

I once plucked from a dealer's catalogue which was several months old a copy of *Tales for Fifteen: or Imagination and Heart*. By "Jane Morgan" (New York, 1823). This is Cooper's pseudonymous fourth book and one of only three recorded copies. Mine passed to Lilly for $975, having cost less than 1 percent of that figure.

But my Cooper luck did not always hold. N. C. Wyeth illustrated a number of his books for Scribner's, including *The Last of the Mohicans*. I had six of the originals in the shop one time, priced $300 each, when a pleasant young man came in and admired them. He seemed to know something about the artist, and it developed in conversation that he was a relative. He was Andrew Wyeth and did a little painting himself, he admitted. He would like some of the paintings for sentimental reasons, but $300 was beyond him. Would I, he inquired hesitantly, exchange some of them for a few of his landscapes?

I explained why this was impossible. Scribner's was a bookstore, not an art gallery, and the only reason these paintings were here was because of their literary background. We were not Knoedler's, and I am afraid I rather suggested that he sell them his paintings and buy ours. The caviar business all over again, only in retrospect, infinitely more costly.

Ah, well, the pictures wound up being duly appreciated, and that's what's important. I sold them to Waller Barrett, who hung them in the boathouse of his summer home at Lake Placid. When it caught fire, his children, he was pleased to recount, rushed into the place and saved Uncas, Leatherstocking, *et al.* before even trying to extinguish the fire.

I have never had the affection for Washington Irving, nor read as widely in him, that I have for Cooper, Scott or even Henty. I suppose this is because he was stuffed into me at school as a "stylist" along with Addison and Steele, both of whom I can also do without and for the same reason. Style is fine for those who like it—and those who like it usually have it—but it's not, to my overall criterion, primary.

Despite this, however, I have had some interesting Irving books and manuscripts, including that of *The Sketch Book*, as is recounted elsewhere. At the time I knew Dr. Braislin, Philip Blackburn and William Langfeld were doing their Irving bibliography, working partly from Braislin's collection while I was around, so I absorbed some bibliographical knowledge.

Braislin was particularly fond of his set of *Salmagundi; or, the Whim-Whams and Opinions of Launcelot Langstaff, Esq., and Others.* Irving was the moving spirit behind this little cooperative work which was issued in twenty parts, between January, 1807, and January, 1808, and contained whimsical essays mirroring the rise and fall of New York opinion on books, theaters, social life, etc.

*Salmagundi* takes very high rank among the true rarities of early American literature and is bibliographically most complex. It was an immediate success, and when it is found at all the parts are usually labeled "second" to "fifth" editions. It was so impossible a book to obtain otherwise that dealers had taken the convenient attitude that these designations were mere fiction to delude the public as to its popularity and that any parts, no matter how designated, were first editions. Harzof scoffed at this and claimed that at one time or another he had seen all the parts without these reprint designations—though he admitted he hadn't seen them all at one time or in one set. But all existed without these reprint notices, he proclaimed, and he was right.

In any event, Braislin had nine of the correct parts, an unheard-of number at that time. Carroll A. Wilson had a few and was determined to find the remainder. I bought Braislin's copies for him and eventually he succeeded in assembling a complete and correct set. Wilson was then satisfied, but I continued the search and very nearly completed two other sets—one now at the Lilly and the other privately owned. Some idea of their rarity may be gleaned from the fact that I know of only a handful of scattered parts ever being in the trade during my time, and there has been a total of exactly none, except Braislin's nine, sold at auction in the past fifty years. I eventually sold Wilson's set to Waller Barrett for $4,500 along with the only known surviving page of its manuscript.

Next to *The Sketch Book*, Irving's best-known work is *A History of New York, from the Beginning of the World to the End of the Dutch Dynasty* by Diedrich Knickerbocker (2 volumes, New York, 1809). No presentation copy of the first edition is known, probably again because it was printed under a pseudonym. One day there turned up at Harzof's, like "The man Flammonde, from God knows where," Irving's own copy. It had a few miscellaneous notes of no particular moment in his hand but also a lengthy and informative one. This concerned the famous episode of "The Great General von Poffenburg" (General James Wilkinson) and "old Kilderneester" (Colonel Butler), who refused to cut off his queue as ordered and declared "he should be carried to his grave with his eel-skin queue sticking out of a knot hole in his coffin."

Irving annotated this passage as follows:

> The above story is true; General Wilkinson (admirably described as von Poffenburg) actually court-martial'd & broke the heart of the brave veteran, Colonel Butler, who refused to part with his queue, agreably to an order for cropping, without exception, issued by Wilkinson. Col. Butler stated that his queue had been his companion throughout all the battles of the Revolution and he absolutely would not, in his old age, lop off so dear & beloved a friend to please the whims of any Body. The persecution of Wilkinson, actually brought Col. B. to the Grave.

But more was to come. Harzof somehow knew of the whereabouts of the original indictment of Colonel Butler, signed by Wilkinson. A three-page folio document dated "Head Quarter Washington, February 11, 1805. To Col. Thomas Butler, 2nd Infy," it read in part:

> Sir: The following are the transgressions for which you are arrested and must hold yourself in readiness to answer to a Military tribunal.

> Charge 1. Deliberate and continued disobedience of the General order of the 30th April 1801, your refusing the cut of the Hair . . .

> Specification, By refusing to conform the cut of your Hair to the general order of the 30th of April, 1801, as directed in the order of the 1st of February 1804, and contumaciously resisting the Authority of these orders, after you had been tried by a General Court Martial, found guilty of disobedience of the General order . . .

> Charge 2nd. Mutinous conduct.

> Specification. By appearing publicly in command of the Troops, at the City of New Orleans with your hair cued, in direct and open violation of the General order of the 20th of April 1801 . . . thereby given an example of disrespect and contempt to the orders and authority of the commanding General, tending to dissever the bonds of military subordination, to impair the force of those obligations by

which Military men are bound to obedience, also to incite a Spirit of
Sedition and Mutiny into the Army of the United States . . ."

These also passed to Hogan at a price I do not recall, sold in his sale for
a disappointing $2,100 and are now, I think, at the New York Public
Library.

Another inconsequential but charming edition of *Knickerbocker* I had
was an English edition (London, 1821) bound in straight grain morocco
with two contemporary fore-edge paintings of New York scenes. Volume I showed lower Broadway of the period with Trinity Church in the
background, done after an aquatint by William J. Bennett about 1826.
Volume II had a view apparently completely unknown, probably of the
Hudson with Weehawken in the background, though it may be upper
Manhattan from Brooklyn. Fore-edge paintings of American scenes in the
classical period are uncommon, and it was a happy event to find them on
a proper book. I wish I had it back. However, it is Waller Barrett's
now.

John Carter and I really missed a great one on Irving while at Scribner's. After the Richard Bentley collection had been thoroughly gone
over by a number of alleged experts, a pile of debris remained. Gordon
Ray and Carter visited the Bentley house at Slough, looking at the
fragments that remained of this once-great collection. Enough manuscript
material was found to fill a large trunk, and on the assumption that
everything of real interest must have gone long since, a moderate price
for it was agreed on.

The trunk was shipped to Scribner's in New York to await Gordon's
return. I eyed it in the cellar and several times was tempted to open it and
see, for curiosity's sake, what was in it. I didn't and wonder to this day
what would have happened if I had.

It was eventually shipped to Illinois and in due time catalogued. Among
the lot was a mass of papers in a spidery hand of a book titled *Moorish
Legends*. Well, Irving's hand was not well known to the English dealers
and auctioneers, who had all had a chance to examine the lots, and his
name was not attached to it, which probably explains everyone's oversight.

It was the original manuscript of what was eventually published as *The
Alhambra* and is one of the very few complete Irving manuscripts ever to
have appeared on the market. I still don't know what I would have done
if I had opened those crates and discovered it.

I would probably have been as much an ass as I was on another
occasion. Lower Fifth Avenue began to be demolished just before I left

New York. What happens when the big iron ball starts swinging at old buildings is saddening to one who loves them. When the old Breevort was going down, I found one evening several of the stained-glass windows of its old bar (of pleasant memories) lying shattered on the sidewalk. Shaken, I hopped over some barriers, went into what was left of the famed bar and saw that not all had yet been destroyed. Several stained-glass windows were still intact, obviously due for destruction tomorrow. I went home, a matter of a few blocks, to Washington Mews (another beautiful street to be eventually destroyed, rumor has it), changed into old clothes, got a crowbar, proceeded to pry out the remaining stained-glass windows and take them home. I worked all night in full view of Fifth Avenue strollers and cops, took several trips lugging the windows down the avenue (with all that lead they are heavy, believe me), and no one paid the slightest attention.

This is all by way of prelude to Irving. He and later Mark Twain had occupied a charming house on the southeast corner of 9th Street and Fifth. There was a handsome bronze plaque done by Pietro Montana with their faces in relief attached to the building to proclaim this fact, put up by some Greenwich Village association. Valiant efforts had been made to preserve the building, as usual to no effect. (Shrines, I have found, like the Poe House, that of Walt Whitman, and others similar, exist mostly in lonely spots—with no real estate value to speak of. Try preserving one anywhere else—lower Fifth Avenue, for example!)

I watched the ball bouncing as demolition got under way and one evening noticed that the plaque was askew and hanging only by a thread, or more correctly, a bolt. I climbed over the iron fence, juggled the plaque a bit and found it was very loose. I pried a little more and it fell at my feet. I carefully picked it up, took it into the street and put it in the gutter, being careful to cover it with trash. I then went down to the famed Cedar Bar on University Place, a what is now called "beatnik" hangout where some poets of sorts, including Allen Ginsberg, held out (I refused on numerous occasions to purchase the original manuscript of *Howl* at any of numerous prices, an error I now lament). Anyway, when the joint closed I invited several stragglers to come to the Mews for a nightcap. We detoured via 9th Street and Fifth and I "discovered" the plaque, which we carted home.

For some reason or other this act of honorable salvage drew considerable newspaper condemnation—I hadn't noticed them running any fundraising campaigns to save the house. "This," said an editorial in the *Herald Tribune*, "was the act of an unscrupulous vandal." My wife, on reading this, remarked that I should write a "letter to the editor" complaining that my name wasn't spelled correctly.

In a maudlin moment I returned the plaque to some authority, claiming I had found it in the gutter, and I had witnesses. I eventually received due thanks from Carmine de Sapio, got my picture and a write-up in *The Villager,* and the plaque is now embedded in concrete in the huge monstrosity which replaced the charming Irving-Twain home. When in the neighborhood I sometimes take a look at it and retire to the new Breevort for a double martini—one for Irving and Twain and one for the stained-glass windows.

# Edgar Allan Poe

THE GLAMOUR BOY of the American literary collecting scene is unquestionably Edgar Allan Poe. His letters, first editions, manuscripts and memorabilia are the most avidly sought and bring the highest prices. There are writers whose works are rarer (his contemporary, Thomas Holley Chivers, is one) and whose autographs and manuscripts are harder to come by—Herman Melville, for example—but none have that peculiar attraction Poe's works possess for collectors.

In his death, as in his life, controversy rages around him. Usually neglected or abused when mentioned in the immediate decades following his death, in his own country, he was being adored in France and translated by Baudelaire. After Rufus Griswold's vitriolic sketch silenced most American supporters except Sarah Helen Whitman, Poe found several in England, who characteristically quarreled among themselves.

When the collecting of American literature began to be fashionable, in the last decades of the last century, Poe had already worked his fascination, and from the very beginning he dominated the scene. There was a mystery, and still is, about the circumstances surrounding many of his publications which fascinate those interested in such things. This has resulted, to the present day, in dubious Poe attributions, forged manuscripts (the most successful by, implausibly, James Whitcomb Riley), thefts, prison sentences, suicide and, on occasion, happy endings.

The circumstances of the publication of his first book, *Tamerlane and Other Poems*, "Boston: Calvin F. S. Thomas . . . Printer, 1827," remain obscure. The traditional "black tulip" of American literature, absolutely nothing is known about its printing, nor its suppression, and next to nothing about its printer. Its very existence was unknown for many years, and Poe himself ignored his bantling. It is a small booklet of forty pages, $6\frac{7}{8} \times 5\frac{5}{16}$ inches, bound in tan printed paper wrappers. Notices of its publication, but no reviews, are recorded.

It was a juvenile effort if there ever was one. The Preface reads: "The greater part of the Poems which compose this little volume, were written in the year 1821–2, when the author had not completed his fourteenth year. They were of course not intended for publication; why they are now published concerns no one but himself."

This is all we know about it except Poe's only other reference in his second volume, *Al Aaraaf, Tamerlane, and Minor Poems* (Baltimore, 1829), which contains the note to "Tamerlane": "Advertisement. This poem was printed for publication in Boston, in the year 1827, but suppressed through circumstances of a private nature."

As late as 1874, W. H. Ingram, writing on Poe's *Early Poems*, comments that the 1827 volume has "disappeared without a trace," and of the 1829, "it does not appear possible now to obtain a copy." He uses for Poe's *Early Poems* the New York, 1831, edition, with "Second Edition" on the title page, which was dedicated to "The U.S. Corps of Cadets," much to their merriment.

The first copy, and for a long time the only known one, was uncovered by the famous dealer Henry Stevens of Vermont, who was acting as agent in purchasing American books for the British Museum. He bought it, he states in his *Recollections of James Lenox*, from "Mr. Samuel G. Drake as one of the poet's pieces, in Boston in 1859. It was sent into the Museum in 1860 with many other Boston tracts, and was paid for in 1867 for one shilling!" For many years it was considered unique. When acquired by the museum it was in its original wrappers, but these were discarded when the book was rebound!

The next copy was bought for fifteen cents by a Boston bookstore clerk who sold it at auction in 1892 for $1,850. It passed through several owners into the hands of Frederic R. Halsey of New York.

The next copy to appear, at Richmond, Virginia, it is said, also wound up in Mr. Halsey's collection, who thus had two of the three known copies. Halsey sold most of his collection to Henry E. Huntington, retaining one of his *Tamerlanes*. This copy came up at auction in 1919 and brought $11,600. One other copy, "in sheets" (i.e., lacking wrappers), was discovered in 1914 and was bought by W. A. Clark of California.

From 1827 to 1925 four copies of this work were on record. Then Vincent Starrett, grand Cham of booklovers, the Elia of our time, wrote an article for *The Saturday Evening Post* entitled "Have You a Tamerlane in your Attic?"

An old lady living in an attic in Worcester, Massachusetts, did. She dispatched a letter to Starrett, who was on vacation. Never in his wildest dreams had he imagined his article would turn up a copy. After fruitlessly awaiting a reply, she wrote Charles Goodspeed about it. He too took his good time about considering it, but when he did, it was *IT*. One half hour after Goodspeed left the owner's home with the book, Starrett's letter, eager for more details, arrived! This copy of *Tamerlane* passed to Owen D. Young and is now in the New York Public Library. The fascinating story of how Goodspeed handled this deal—a credit to all concerned—is his story, and he has told it well in his *Yankee Bookseller*. The various claims of its having been stolen, etc., are typical of the imposters who have always leeched on Poe.

Within a year the publicity attendant on the Goodspeed-Young copy brought them another, picked up for practically naught at an antique auction sale. This copy, for which Goodspeed paid $20,000, passed to J. K. Lilly, Jr., of Indianapolis, who was up to that time a lover of Poe and a collector of American literature in a small way. Suddenly he was a collector in a not so small way. As he once remarked to me, ruefully, "There is nothing like beginning at the top and working down." One story about this transaction that Goodspeed does not tell in his book is that when Lilly decided to buy it, he was an unknown quantity to them, and father Charles Goodspeed kept him in conversation while son George scurried around to the bank to check Lilly's credit.

My own first opportunity to buy a *Tamerlane*, for $25,000, came in the mid-thirties. It was part of a collection of rare books held as collateral by a Detroit bank, and they wished to liquidate. It was not a recorded copy (by this time several others had been turned up, publicity being what it is), but ever mindful of Starrett's painful experience, I hied me to Detroit. Only to find it was a facsimile! An excellent one had been done in London in 1931, by photograph: indeed, the original prospectus states, "A $15,000 camera has been employed to make the duplicate plates from the original booklet." It is really a first-class job, and to an unsuspecting eye, especially without an original for comparison, is difficult to detect. True, it has the word "Facsimile" stamped on the final leaf in red ink, but not in printer's ink, which is indelible. It can be removed without trace, and a few stainings give it an appearance hard to detect.

It was this that the bank had had passed off on it. It was difficult to convince them that they had been clipped, but eventually the message got through. I don't know what happened subsequently, but I wager that that bank made no further loans on rare books. Few do, even now, as a matter of fact.

One memorable evening C. Waller Barrett invited me to dinner at his home in Garden City and casually handed me a *Tamerlane*. I as casually handed it back with the remark, "That Schwartz facsimile doesn't fool me." I knew, of course, where every *Tamerlane* was, and that no new one had been uncovered, so what else could it be? I also had, or thought I had, a string on every privately owned copy likely ever to be loose. Well, I hadn't. This was the copy owned by Mrs. Sherburn Prescott of Greenwich, Connecticut, sold her by the firm of James Drake and renegotiated by them to Barrett. My big mouth was still the rest of that evening, and I am not sure I have qualified as an expert in Barrett's eyes since then.

My only other chance was just when I was about to leave Scribner's to come to Indiana. Whitman Bennett, the binder and bookseller, came in with a beautiful, authentic copy. It is the most recent, I think the twelfth, to turn up. I was sorely tempted. The price was reasonable, less than $10,000. I didn't have a customer but I wanted the book, just to say I had handled it. I temporized, telling Bennett I'd let him know in a day or so. He took his book, walked across the street and sold it to the Seven Gables Bookshop.

I have had better luck with the mysterious printer of *Tamerlane*, Calvin F. S. Thomas. It is the only book he is known to have printed. The back wrapper carries this advertisement: "Printing. Calvin F. S. Thomas continues to execute Book and Job Printing in all its Branches, including Books, Pamphlets, Catalogues, Cards, Show Bills, Etc.-etc. on the most reasonable terms. No. 70, Washington Street, Boston, Corner of State." Little else is known. He is reported to have been nineteen years old in 1827, to have removed shortly thereafter with his family to Springfield, Missouri, dying there in 1876.

But that Thomas did print labels is certain, for in 1934 three receipts by him for his Boston printing were found by Goodspeed. The best is now in the Lilly Library. It is dated the very year of *Tamerlane* and reads: "Boston, Feb. 19, 1827. A. L. Lowe to Calvin F. S. Thomas, Dr. 70 printing 5000 directions. $15.70 (printing) 6000 labels 62½ $3.75. Rec'd Pay't, $18.75. Calvin F. S. Thomas." Two similar ones, dated the previous year, are also known. One of these I acquired with the Carroll A. Wilson library. So I have had, anyway, two thirds of the printer's known autograph remains. I'd have preferred a "remainder" of *Tamerlane!*

Had Poe written nothing but this first frail volume it would, of course, be valueless. Rarity sans importance equals zero. This would not have been the case, however, with his equally sought-for first separate printing of *The Murders in the Rue Morgue* (Philadelphia, 1843). Fewer copies than of *Tamerlane* are currently known, and they are, in my opinion, equal in commercial value. Certainly where the poetry was bad, the prose was great, and with this one story Poe launched, full-blown, the detective story. It first appeared in the April, 1841, issue of *Graham's Lady's and Gentleman's Magazine*, of the first number of which Poe was editor. It was reprinted in his *Tales*, 1845.

But in 1843 Graham, who was publishing much cheap fiction in paper wrappers, decided to try to capitalize on Poe's fame, or perhaps notoriety is the better word, by issuing "The Prose Romances of Edgar A. Poe—Uniform Serial Edition. Each number complete in Itself." Number I contained "The Murders in the Rue Morgue" and "The Man That Was Used Up," price twelve and a half cents. It must not have been successful, as no Number II ever appeared. So little a stir did it make, in fact, that it was quite unknown until the 1890's, when the late, great bookseller George D. Smith picked up a copy on Cornhill in Boston for fifteen cents, which seems to have been a standard price for unknown Poes. He sold it to Scribner's for $60, who sold it to the New York collector F. W. French for $120. At the French sale in 1901 Halsey acquired it for $1,000. Nice markups right along the line.

The second copy, lacking the back wrapper, appeared at the Frank Maier sale in 1909 and made $3,800. It is now in the Pierpont Morgan Library. It had been discovered by a book scout, Louis Cole, who originally sold it to a dealer for $2, and its story is told in Charles Everett's *Adventures of a Treasure-Seeker;* it cost Maier $1,250.

Stories about the third copy to appear differ considerably. It turned up in a bundle in Dauber and Pine's lower Fifth Avenue bookstore in 1926. Where they got it they claimed not to have known. It was sold for a reputed $25,000 to Owen D. Young. A lot of newspaper publicity resulted, and it is said that a little junk dealer on Second Avenue who felt he had let this treasure unwittingly slip through his hands, having sold it in a bundle for nothing, committed suicide.

The story of the fourth copy has a happier ending, and the facts are verifiable. For years Frank Rosengreen conducted a secondhand bookshop in Chicago on North State Street. One day in 1929, in cleaning out stock, he examined a volume labeled "Miscellanies," in a worn half calf binding, which had been on the shelves for years. It was a typical mid-nineteenth-century conglomeration of orations, prison reports, young-lady seminary doings and the like. But right in the middle of these pamphlets was, of course, "The Murders." It is a small work, only forty pages, and this copy lacked the wrappers; still it was the fourth copy extant. It went to Mr. Lilly at $13,000 to join his *Tamerlane* and growing collection.

A pleasant result was that Mr. Rosengreen was thereby enabled to transfer his shop from Chicago to Austin, Texas, a move he had long wished to make for the sake of his son's health.

Sam Dauber wrote me in 1951 that he had been offered a copy of *The Murders in the Rue Morgue* but didn't have a customer for it. He gave me the owner's name with the understanding that I give him a "finder's fee" if a sale was eventually made. The owner was Aylsworth Brown, who was an employee of Brown University Library. It turned out that he had already offered the book to every conceivable purchaser except Scribner's. He knew more about the history of the book than I did, how many copies there were, at what price they had reputedly been sold, what auction prospects were and so on.

But the one thing Brown wouldn't do was send it to anyone for examination. "To accommodate the numerous requests which have been made by interested people would be to wear it out in the mail to say nothing of the risks undergone by letting it on the loose." No one took the trouble to go to Providence to see it, and for some reason I couldn't visit at that time either, and I finally wrote, in exasperation:

> You know, actually, I think you should present this to Brown University with your compliments. God knows, you seem to have had enough fun out of it by writing so many people about it. You have been getting an education in the rare book business the easy way. One thing you haven't taken into your calculations is an imponderable and very important fact, that you have done what is known in the trade as "hawking the book around." This does more than you would imagine to depress its value. You would be amazed, I'm sure, at the number of letters of yours to various people, like Barrett, which have been referred to me. As I told you, when I wrote you some time ago, I hoped to be in Providence to see the book myself, but I haven't been able to make that trip. However, it has been seen by people whose judgment I rely on, Charles Retz for one, still I would have to see it myself before we could come to any agreement.
>
> What it all boils down to is this: I like the book. I've always been very fond of Poe and done a lot in his first editions. I just purchased, by the way, at the recent Litchfield sale at the Parke-Bernet Galleries, the first edition, first issue, of his *Tales,* 1845, to my mind, the rarest of all his works, for $3300. I'm willing to offer you $3500 cash for your copy if you care to sell it. On the other hand, I think I can get you probably $5000 for it if you want to leave it with me on a consignment basis. Whether I can get it immediately or a year from now, I don't know. Mull this proposition over in your mind and let me know before the end of the year what you decide.

I pointed out in a subsequent letter:

There is one factor in this we have not gone into and that is that Mr. Dauber is the gentleman who first put me in touch with you so I am obligated to give him ten percent of the purchase price which means the book will cost me $3850 and higher than this I do not care to go.

Brown sent the book eventually, and in answer to my query as to its provenance stated:

It has no special dramatic background. It came into my ownership among numerous pamphlets and old books from a family library belonging to my grandfather. I thought somebody might have clipped the story out of some old magazine and thought nothing special of it. Some months ago I shelved a photo-static copy of it supplied by the Huntington Library in our Harris collection. I dug out my copy and compared it and as I was looking it over, our Professor Damon, curator of the Harris Collection, exclaimed "I think you may have something there."

Considering Poe's close, though brief, association with Providence, Rhode Island, this was a quite proper place for the pamphlet to appear. It is also characteristic that a professional librarian should have unwittingly had this treasure in his possession for years before the shelving of a facsimile brought it to his attention! It passed to H. Bradley Martin for $5,000. I was pleased that Scribner's handled the first and last of the twelve recorded copies.

The finest copy by all odds is that in the Library of Congress, the only known inscribed copy. It was found by the eccentric curator V. Valta Parma, uncatalogued, unrecognized, among discards. I saw him sometime after his sensational discovery, which had been widely acclaimed, and remarked, "By God, I wish I had been with you when you found that." To which he replied, "By God, I wish you had too."

The story of the original manuscript of "The Murders" is not without interest. I had a chance, along with everyone else, to buy it, and lost my nerve. I was underbidder, true enough, but that is small consolation.

Its survival and preservation were matters of sheer chance. The story is best told in the words of its first owner.

The original manuscript of Edgar A. Poe's story "The Murders in the Rue Morgue" has a history which may be of interest to admirers of the distinguished author.

I have no data whereby I can fix the exact date at which the manuscript came into my possession, but it was about forty years ago probably in the spring of 1841 at which time I was an apprentice in the office of Barrett and Thrasher (afterwards Barrett and Jones) printers, No. 33 Carter's alley, Philadelphia. If my memory is not at fault Graham's Magazine in whose pages the story first appeared, was printed in the aforesaid office, and the revised proof read in The Saturday Evening Post Office, Chestnut Street above Third—within a door or two of the old Public Ledger building.

After the story had been put in type and the proof read, the manuscript found its way into the waste basket. I picked it from the basket, asked and obtained leave to keep it, and took it to the residence of my father, with whom I then boarded. Here it was put away so carefully that I have no recollection of seeing it for years.

In 1846 my father, leaving me in Philadelphia, removed to Fawn township, York county, and thence, a few years later to Manchester, Md. and Darkesville, Va. In these several pilgrimages, he had, unknown to himself carried the Poe manuscript along with him, folded up in one of the books of his library. Determining to return to Pennsylvania he made sale of his personal effects, and, among a lot of old books offered, was found the Poe Ms! It was at once recognized, rescued from the rubbish among which it had so nearly been lost and forwarded to me—I having in the meantime 1847 removed to Lancaster, Penna. and commenced business as a Daguerreotypist. Twice my Daguerrean rooms took fire, and once (March 8th 1850) almost all my books, papers, pictures and apparatus were consumed—but the Poe manuscript folded within the leaves of an old music book, escaped the wreck.

About the year 1857 (I think it was) a grocery store, occupying the first floor of the building in which were my rooms, took fire and burned furiously. The flames did not reach my books, but the smoke did, and firemen drenched them with water, destroying books, papers and other property, but by rare good fortune the Poe manuscript again escaped all injury except a slight discoloration.

From 1861 to 1864 I was in the army, but on my return therefrom I found the Poe manuscript in the old music book where I had left it on leaving home.

In the Spring of 1865 I took charge of the Swan Hotel, Lancaster. Removing therefrom in 1869, a great deal of rubbish was consigned to the ash pile, the old music book sharing the fate of other worthless articles. My next door neighbor, John R. Watkins, thinking it had been inadvertently thrown away, picked it from the ash pile and handed it to me. On opening the book I again beheld the much-neglected and long mislaid manuscript! Resolved that it should not again be subjected to so many unnecessary risks, I at once had it bound in its present form. J. W. Johnston, Lancaster, Pa., July 26, 1881.

The manuscript was eventually bequeathed, along with much other important material—the original manuscripts of Dickens' *Our Mutual Friend*, André's famous *Cow-Chace* and other first-rank material—to the Drexel Institute of Technology at Philadelphia.

In the early 1940's Drexel got a new president who decided that Drexel, being a technical institution, would be better off with cash in hand than literary manuscripts and forthwith consigned the whole *schmeer* to the Parke-Bernet Galleries for public auction.

This action drew howls of protest from faithful Philadelphians, led by Chris Morley, along with charges of trust breaking, cultural anarchy and its like. But the sale went on in October, 1944. I dearly coveted *The Murders*, of course, and thought there was a good chance I might get it. At this time Lilly and Young were out of the market; Bradley Martin and Richard Gimbel, ardent Poe collectors, were in the armed forces, Koester of Baltimore had expressed lack of interest, and I knew of no public institution liable to reach for it. The consignors had been led to believe it would bring closer to $100,000 than $50,000. I didn't, an opinion partially based on the fact that I was having difficulties disposing of a much greater manuscript—to my mind—Irving's *Sketch Book*, for $35,000 . . . which I eventually didn't get.

Came the sale. The André brought $10,000 to Dr. Rosenbach. It was not the original manuscript, as everyone but he and the underbidder knew. He eventually returned it, and it is entered in *Book Auction Records* as "No Sale." The Dickens brought $17,000 and is now in the Pierpont Morgan Library.

The Poe started at $10,000 and the bidding went slowly. When it reached $20,000 I found myself with only one competitor, Dick Sessler, the well-known Philadelphia dealer. We kept giving each other $500 nudges and at $33,500 I resigned, much to the annoyance of Lew Feldman, who was seated next to me and cheered me on. "Some day, Dave, that's going to be cheap at $100,000," he said. "Keep going." I had a feeling that Dick had a Philadelphia bid and that no matter how high I went I wasn't going to get it anyway. And I was right. Sessler was protecting for the Institute, which bought it and eventually disposed of it to Richard Gimbel at somewhat more than Lew's estimate, I have been told.

The history of Poe collecting is replete with fakes and forgeries. I have mentioned that *The Murders* originally came out in *Graham's* magazine, two years before its appearance in the coveted pamphlet. An enterprising Chicago rogue named Sickles, who used to operate on the fringe of the rare book business, got hold of a copy of the magazine, which is common enough, extracted the story, had a special title page printed, and sold it as an original to a Chicago collector, Joyce, original husband of the famed, oft-married Peggy Hopkins. When the nature of the fake was pointed out to him, he simply refused to believe it. He died possessed of it, though not of Peggy Hopkins. But the city of Chicago does have, appropriately enough (what city deserves one more?), a copy of *The Murders*, at the University.

One of the most skillful of Poe's forgers was the engaging Joseph Cosey, whose nemesis, the New York Public Library detective William Bergquist, has told his story entertainingly in *The Saturday Evening Post*. Cosey specialized in Abraham Lincoln documents, and very good he was indeed. Poe seemed a sort of hobby with him.

We have in the Lilly Library what I think is one of Cosey's major efforts, a manuscript of Poe's short story "Bernice," which originally appeared in *The Southern Literary Messenger*, March, 1835, one of the sixteen "Tales of the Folio Club." It is written in a small twelvemo booklet, binding and paper contemporary with Poe, and is well executed —only Poe didn't write it. But I can't prove Cosey did, either.

Cosey liked to elaborate things, put notes in books in Poe's hand, etc. One charming item we have—and this he did because he told me so—is a copy of *Henry Masterton; or the Adventures of a Young Cavalier* (Paris, Baudry, 1837). The half-title of this bears an inscription in a flourishing hand, in ink: "To M. Edgar Allan Poe on Noel 1846 from Alden Raynard Marsaille. A la Grace de Dieu." Beneath this is: "Edgar A. Poe, Dec. 25, 1846. Richmond." On the verso of the half-title, in pencil, is the notation: "Poe's own book. Given to my dear daughter Adeline. M.S.S.N.Y.— Jan'y 1856. Adeline Stewart." Laid in also is a letter from Poe to N. P. Willis. And as though this were not enough, on page 69 Cosey underlined some passages, such as "I had dreamed I heard a noise, but when I listened all was silence . . . That profound interminable expanse swarming with stars," and wrote in the margin, in Poe's hand, "The Fall of the House of Usher." A beautiful combination!

One of the very earliest, most successful and ingenious Poe hoaxes was that perpetrated by the Hoosier poet laureate, James Whitcomb Riley. There is something ironical in the fact that poverty-stricken Poe was the launching pad for among the most successful, financially, of all poets of all time. Which is just what Riley became, earning and keeping in excess of $3,000,000.

In 1877 Riley was trying to publish his poems in Indiana newspapers with signal lack of success. He believed that if his poems had been written by an author already famous, they would be acclaimed and published.

He wrote a four-stanza poem, "Leonainie," one verse of which is:

> In a solemn night of summer
> When my heart of gloom
> Blossomed up to greet the comer

> Like a rose in bloom;
> All forebodings that distressed me
> I forgot as Joy caressed me
> (Lying Joy! that caught and pressed me
> In the arms of doom!) . . .

He then had an artist friend, Samuel Richards, copy the poem in imitation of Poe's hand, working from a facsimile of "The Bells," on the end paper of a Philadelphia edition of *An Abridgement of Ainsworth's Dictionary, English and Latin, Designed for the Use of Schools.*

Riley then "discovered" it, and it was printed on August 21, 1877, in the Kokomo, Indiana, *Dispatch* by arrangement with the proprietor. The hoax was tremendously successful. It was widely acclaimed as a major Poe poem, both in England and America. The eminent Edmund Clarence Stedman was enthralled. So much so that when Riley claimed authorship Stedman steadfastly maintained it was written by Poe. James Whitcomb Riley was on his way.

The dictionary itself eventually came into the possession of the Cleveland collector Paul Lemperly. This was a "must" book for J. K. Lilly, who collected not only Poe but Riley. For years I tried to get Lemperly to part with it, without success. In desperation I finally went as high as $5,000 in trade or $3,500 cash. No sale. Perhaps I overpressed the owner. It wasn't worth that kind of money to anyone else and we both knew it. Eventually he died and his library came up at public auction in New York, January, 1940. I let it be pretty widely known that I considered this my personal huckleberry and that there wasn't much sense in anyone else's going after it. In any event, I got it for Mr. Lilly for $600.

I wish I had the manuscript of "The Bells," from a facsimile of which artist Richards copied Poe's hand for "Leonainie" (and not badly, either), to put with it, but I haven't. I once had the only extant portion of it known, though, and paid what is certainly one of the highest prices per word for it that poetry ever brought.

The story of the composition of "The Bells" is well known. Poe wrote it at the instigation of his friend, Mrs. M. L. Shew. Two stanzas are extant in his handwriting—varying from the final, posthumously published version. They are headed "The Bells. By Mrs. M. L. Shew," and first appeared in commerce at the sale of the library of C. B. Foot, New York banker and collector, in 1895. The stanzas brought $75, quite a price for the time considering that they have a total of eighty words.

The fragment passed eventually from the collection of Frank Bemis of Boston into the fine collection of Frank J. Hogan of Washington, D.C., and at the sale of his books in 1945 I paid $6,000 for it, or $75 a word. And mostly short words. In the stanzas I had, seventy of the words were one syllable and the longest only four. There are only three hundred and fifty letters in the eighty words, an average of $17.77 per letter!

And Poe got only $10 for "The Raven"! "The Bells" fragment went to William J. Koester of Baltimore. It is of interest to note that until a very few years ago there was much more Poe privately owned than there was publicly. It is within very recent times that the Owen D. Young and W. T. H. Howe collections went to the New York Public Library. This latter, by the way, had the famed dedication copy, to Elizabeth Barrett Browning, of "The Raven," formerly the Wakeman copy. Waller Barrett's collection is now at Virginia, Lilly's at Indiana, Koester's at Texas. Dick Gimbel's and H. Bradley Martin's are the only substantial ones remaining in private hands.

In 1929, in the celebrated sale of Jerome Kern's library, one four-page letter of Poe's, but a very fine one, brought $19,000. This remains the record price for an American literary autograph letter.

Shortly after this sale the late Max Harzof, of the G. A. Baker Company in New York, was sorting out a collection of secondhand books he had just purchased and came across a copy of *The Last Letters of Edgar Allan Poe to Sarah Helen Whitman* (New York, Putnam, 1909). Something made him glance at the Preface and there was an acknowledgment to Mrs. Whitman's heirs, who lived, as she had, in Providence, Rhode Island, of permission to print the letters. That was all the lead he needed. Lazare was put on the trail and shortly afterward the Poe-Whitman collection was his.

It was a most impressive coup—the finest collection by far then remaining in private hands. It had romantic appeal in the highest degree: fifteen love letters from the poet, one of twelve pages; their marriage contract; the only full-length daguerreotype of Poe; scads of correspondence with Poe idolators in the seventies and eighties; a pathetic memento of despair Maria Clemm sent to Mrs. Richmond—Poe's "Annie"—the day after his death: "Annie my Eddy is dead he died in Baltimore yesterday—Annie my Annie pray for me your desolate friend."

Poe's courtship of Sarah Helen had been a wild one. She was addicted to low-cut dresses, enhancing a bosom of which she was quite proud. At one time Poe clung to her dress so tightly, pleading with her as an angel sent to save him from perdition, that the two were separated with a piece of the dress in Poe's hand. This memento, alas, was not saved, but practically everything else was.

The collection passed to Mr. Lilly for only $50,000. One of the letters had a portion, including the signature, cut out with her notation that it had been given to James T. Fields as a souvenir. Years after his purchase Lilly spotted, at Rosenbach's, a copy of the London, 1857, edition of Poe's *Poetical Works*, belonging to Field, with this fragment tipped in. After he purchased it, and only after, he revealed to the Doctor that he had the letter itself.

Lilly had been dealing, at this early stage of his collecting career, with some curious characters. The late dealer Harry Stone of New York was among them. Harry wasn't—at least not very often—deliberately dishonest. His imagination simply took wing on occasion. I should know. I worked for him as cataloguer now and then in my spare time, and he usually complimented me on my accuracy but not, as he delicately put it, my "intuition as to what makes a book sell." He was of Hungarian Gypsy descent, or so he said, and wound up deserting the rare book business for that of early American folk art, in which indeed he was a pioneer. There is an imaginative scope to the art business that books somehow do not allow.

I was amused to find in the Lilly files some revealing correspondence with Stone. He had sold Lilly some important things in the early 1930's, the earliest known manuscript version of *Eulalie*, for example, for $9,500.

He also sold Lilly a copy of, of all books, Sarah Helen Whitman's *Poe and His Critics* (New York, 1860), which he described as an "inscribed presentation copy from Mrs. Clemm to Annie E. Johnson to whom Poe was engaged at the time of his death." Price, $750.

When Lilly pointed out that this was simply not so, Harry acknowledged that he "had been confused in his own mind between Annie Johnson and Annie Richmond" and made a reduction in price, adding that "$250 is a fair price for Annie Johnson not having had the grace to be engaged to Poe." But by this time Lilly had done further checking and decided the book could not have been inscribed by Maria Clemm and returned it to Stone, dryly suggesting he conduct a "private cremation" of it.

About the same time Lilly returned an 1831 *Poems*, commenting:

> . . . unless my eyesight is entirely faulty the "one half front end-paper lacking" is conspicuous by being there. On the other hand no mention is made in your description of the title page from which a generous thumbful has been removed.
>
> I think most of us have particular obsessions when it comes to book buying and my particular one is a perfect title page.
>
> I realize that if I deliberate long enough on an 1831 *Poems,* I may be

out of luck all the way around; however, I can in this case but follow my usual guiding rule: "When in doubt, don't do it!"

Stone soon thereafter ceased to supply Lilly with anything.

I had a lot of fun collecting Poe for Lilly, Koester, Carroll Wilson and others. It is by no means all big-money stuff, although the great books do not come cheap. Poe was a great magazine contributor, and it is still possible to pick up the original appearances of "The Raven," "The Murders," and many of the tales and poems for practically nothing. The trick is finding them.

I once owned what I believe to be the only copy known in its original state, printed wrappers, of "The Mystery of Marie Rogêt," which appeared in *The Ladies Companion*, November and December, 1842, and February, 1843. It cost only $15.

And I was present in Harzof's shop when Jacob Blanck plucked from a pile of junk Poe's own copy of his *Conchologist's First Book* (Philadelphia, 1839), with his notes throughout. I sold this to Frank Hogan and it is now in Bradley Martin's collection. Its authenticity has been questioned, but I stand by its genuineness.

There are also Poe's book reviews to be gathered and, as a hobby, why not a collection of the books he reviewed? No one has done that, that I know of.

And who knows? Perhaps you will come across his own copy of a book he reviewed. I do not know of a single book signed or annotated by Poe, other than his own. Yet he must have had a library!

And if you come across a copy of "The Raven" lacking the last leaf, don't scorn it. It might be the poet's own! It contains his famous poem "To Helen," and there is in the Whitman collection a leaf he tore out of his copy and sent to Sarah Helen. This nugget would have suggested possibilities to Harry Stone. But don't desecrate a perfect copy by tearing out the last leaf and trying to pass it off as Poe's unless you can match perfectly the jagged inner margin of the Lilly leaf.

Poe certainly did work, I am convinced, which is not yet identified as his. There are two very rare books in the Lilly collection which have been attributed to him: *The Philosophy of Animal Magnetism . . . by a Gentleman of Philadelphia* (Philadelphia, 1837) and *English Notes Intended for Very Extensive Circulation . . . by . . . Quarles Quickens* (Boston, 1842). Scholars have not accepted these, but no one has yet explained why the first printing of "The Raven," in the February, 1845, issue of *The American Review*, was signed with the pseudonym "Quarles."

# Audubon Adventures

JOHN JAMES AUDUBON'S *The Birds of America* is our country's most famous and expensive ornithological work. Originally published by subscription at $1,000 a set, its current value is nearing $100,000. Both as art and as science it leaves something to be desired, but Audubon's vivid personal descriptions and his drawings of birds in action have long since overcome professional deficiencies, at least in the public's eye.

The work was first published in England in four elephant-sized volumes, 1827–1838, later in quarto size in America. I had seen the latter but not the former when my boss, Byrne Hackett of the Brick Row Book Shop, East 50th Street, New York City, told me to go to the shop of Gabriel Wells on West 57th Street and bring back the first volume of an Audubon for examination. I walked out into a blistering hot summer day, and when I got to Wells's shop found that what he had was not the quarto I had expected, but the original edition. Now elephant folio volumes are the largest printed: one volume of an Audubon happens to measure 40 by 26 inches, weighs eighty pounds and is damn clumsy to carry.

I hadn't a cent on me for cab or even bus fare, and when I explained this to whoever was in charge of Wells's shop and asked how I was expected to get it to East 50th Street, the reply was "lug it." So I did, down Fifth Avenue, past the University Club at 54th (of which more later) and into Hackett's presence. Only to be berated because my sweaty hands had left marks on the morocco binding! I have no further recollection of what happened to this copy, except that Hackett didn't buy it, and I returned it a few days later, by cab. Somewhere among the hundred copies which survived is one with my latent fingerprints all over the covers of Volume I.

Hackett had a customer for a copy. A young lad residing in New England was to be married shortly, and since he was mad about ornithology, his mother wanted to present him an Audubon folio as a wedding present. Eventually Hackett heard of one privately owned on Long Island by a gentleman well known in social circles and wrote the owner, who answered he was willing to part with it.

Arrangements were made by phone for payment on delivery, after examination, and late one summer afternoon a pleasant young man in a chauffeur-driven car delivered the books, which were collated and found perfect, payment was made, and they were packed and shipped in time for the wedding. I've always been curious about what the bride thought of this present (who first said, "Marriage is for the birds"?). A few weeks later there was bad trouble. The actual owner of the set returned from a European trip to find his Audubon gone—and that's one book that is really hard to misplace, at least all four volumes of it. The next thing the Brick Row knew, the roof fell in. It seems sonny (who I think was a Princetonian) was in a tiny financial gambling jam and, opening Daddy's mail, saw a chance to get a quick $5,000 (which was the going value of an Audubon then), and sold it. Some sort of compromise was eventually worked out, but I don't know what it was.

At that time Audubons were fairly common books. One couldn't exactly say the woods were full of them (that phrase, by the way, first appears in the Preface to Alexander Wilson's *American Ornithology,* 1808, but refers to flowers, not birds), but they were usually available at a price. My next association with a set was a few years later when I was with the G. A. Baker Company. Its head, Max Harzof, had a set he couldn't sell and somehow got the idea of breaking it up and selling the separate prints individually. However, Harzof didn't have a street shop-window to display them in, and somewhere along the line he sold his idea (and his Audubon) to Macy's, who did. It was a successful venture on the part of Macy's print department, and they eventually dismantled several other volumes, thus adding to the rarity of complete sets but incidentally giving a lot of people who could never possess one the pleasure of having at least a plate or two. And, after all, you can only look at one print at a time. I did this successfully at Scribner's with an inferior copy.

I came about this in a curious way. The Mercantile Library Association, one of New York's oldest such organizations, then had their quarters on 48th Street between Fifth and Madison avenues, adjoining the Scribner building. I used to frequent it, and browsing through their card catalogue one day, I found listed a folio Audubon—right in my own backyard! Investigation uncovered it stored away where no one ever looked at it; so why not, I queried, sell it and buy some new books, which proposition was agreeable to them. It was not a really good copy, as it had not been taken care of—many plates were torn and remounted on cloth, etc. Even so, I was happy to give them $4,500 for it. Even in its poor condition, broken up it brought $12,000.

I do not know what the library originally paid for it, but a bookplate, printed on silk (which I still have), reads in part:

> Presented to The Mercantile Library Association by a number of its Members and Friends. The funds appropriated to the purchase of this work have been raised as follows: A *Subscription* in which the amount to be given by each subscriber was limited to fifty cents, was commenced in 1840. At the annual meeting in 1841, it was reported that the sum raised by this subscription amounted to One Hundred and Twenty Five Dollars.
>
> Another *Subscription* was subsequently started at a meeting of Members of the Association which resulted in the collection of the sum requisite for the purchase. The work is accordingly placed in the library this Fourth Day of March, Eighteen Hundred and Forty One.

It remained there ninety-eight years.

My very first purchase of an Audubon was on my first buying trip to London for Scribner's in 1936. I bought it from Gabriel Wells for $4,500 and sold it to a dealer for $6,500, which liquidated the trip's expenses. Travel was cheaper then.

During the next few years I always had an Audubon on hand, it seemed. I remember two especially. I was walking down Fifth Avenue one evening when Whitney Darrow, Scribner vice-president and also, at the time, vice-president of the University Club, came along. Had I ever seen its library, he asked? I hadn't, so he took me through it. It is the best of its kind in America, and is excelled only, among club libraries, by the Athenaeum of London. In a case in a corner of a handsome room I saw an Audubon on display, bearing a card: "Lent to the University Club by . . ." I memorized the name of the lender, found it in the phone book the next day at a Wall Street address and made an appointment.

His story was simple. About twenty years before, his father had died, and in the library was this set of Audubon. He and his wife were living in a small apartment and couldn't possibly house the books. Suddenly inspired, he inquired of the University Club's librarian if he could store them there temporarily, being a member at the time. That astute gentleman agreed. And there they had been ever since. Not only had he forgotten about them, but he had long since resigned from the club. It was like money from home: a check passed hands, he and I went to 54th and Fifth, loaded the books in the service elevator, took a receipt from the rather sullen librarian, and that was that.

Except that Whitney Darrow was bitterly castigated by some members for what happened (he knew nothing about it, of course; I'd seen to that); and I had some trouble getting into the club when I was put up for membership some time later. Though I eventually lived there for a number of years, the librarian always seemed uneasy when I was around.

I had seven Audubon sets over a period of ten years while at Scribner's, costing from $4,500 to $9,000 and retailing at $6,500 to $15,000. Among the finest were the C. T. Church copy, now at the Audubon Sanctuary at Mill Grove, Pennsylvania, and a copy in blue morocco now owned by Paul Mellon.

The copy at the Lilly Library, which I sold J. K. Lilly in 1940 for $15,000, has a curious history. The famed Miss Belle da Costa Greene, the guardian of the Pierpont Morgan treasures, was a good friend to me in many ways. This was lucky, because she could be a formidable enemy. There was always a hint of mystery about her, especially of her nationality. Someone at a dinner party I attended had the temerity, after too many drinks, to put the question direct. She did nothing to enlighten him, merely answering, "I was conceived in Vienna and born at sea."

I got into her good graces by a bit of luck. Somewhere I came across a juvenile work of no distinction except that the flyleaf was inscribed: "J. Pierpont Morgan, on his 12th Birthday, September 7, 1879." I checked and found that this was *the* J.P.M.'s book which he remembered perfectly and was happy to see again. This led to a summons to the library and a pleasant visit. It also led to my being put on his Christmas gift list, which was one pound of imported tea. The last time I saw Miss Greene, just before her death, she was confined to a wheelchair. My attention must have been distracted by something because she suddenly whacked me across the shins with her cane and remarked tartly, "Pay some attention to me; I'm not that goddamned old!"

One day she phoned to say that the library had been offered a folio Audubon but already had one, and would I be interested in acquiring it? Upon seeing it, I was. It was in a binding of contemporary Russia, of no great distinction, but was otherwise a beauty. The plates were brilliant, unspotted and with very large margins, a full half inch over the Cock Turkey's crest. It was also housed in a magnificent mahogany case, especially built to hold it, and a massive affair. It had just been delivered to my quarters when Mr. Lilly came in.

After looking it over he remarked, "I've been turning this down ever since Goodspeed offered me one at thirty-five hundred. The main reason is that I have no place to put it, except under a billiard table. This, like a turtle, has the advantage of its own housing. But that's a pretty large case and it may not go through the door to the library; but if it does, I'll take it." He made his own careful measurements and a few days later I received a telegram: SEND AUDUBON HAVE QUARTER-INCH CLEARANCE.

In 1938 John Carter, my London colleague, achieved a spectacular coup. He bought at nominal prices, a few pounds apiece, somewhere in England, a clutch of original Audubon drawings, all signed and dated 1827. Among them were the "Tufted Titmouse," "Carolina Wren," "Yellow Throated Vireo," "Bluebird," and others. These were sold at prices ranging up to $750 top. What their worth is today I will not hazard a guess.

The Audubon market kept booming as other collectors got into the act, and for a long time little came my way. I happened to be at Lehigh one day and someone asked if I had ever heard of a George Lehmann, who had been an associate of Audubon's. I replied that I had. Lehmann had accompanied Audubon on many of his field trips and did most of the backgrounds for the famous *Birds*. It developed that the Lehmann family was originally from Bethlehem, but the last surviving member was living on a small farm near Pittsburgh, where, my informant told me, the walls were practically covered with original Audubon paintings. I wrote at once, asking details and inquiring if something could be sent along for inspection, etc. Back came a letter stating that this was impossible. The farm was a long way from any post office, it would be difficult to pack the pictures properly, etc. But I was welcome to visit at any time suiting my convenience to examine them.

It "suited my convenience" to be in Pittsburgh a day after receiving the letter. I hired a car and drove to the rural address, which I found eventually after having gotten lost several times—I seem constitutionally unable to comprehend even the simplest directions involving "turn east" (or north); I eventually manage to get where I'm going, but by a circular method, not a straight line.

However, when I finally located the farm and pulled up, a pleasant-looking elderly gentleman with a dog on leash came down the driveway to meet me. He was the descendant of the Lehmann who did the pictures. He was also blind, and the dog was a seeing-eye dog. I was ushered into the parlor to meet his wife (the couple lived alone), who turned out to be completely deaf. It was a curious afternoon. They were a charming couple and I eventually reluctantly departed, with a portfolio full of bird pictures, mostly watercolors, but with also an oil or so. There had been great talk about family legends of Audubon: "Did you know he was a bastard? So many creative souls are," and so on.

Leaving behind a check for $5,000, I hied me back to my lair with my treasures, where the boom descended. None of my pictures, sketches, etc., were signed. And every expert who looked at them, from curators of the American Museum of Natural History to Ralph Shaw Newman, head of the Old Print Shop, unanimously said they could not possibly be Audubon's. *They were too accurate and too good.*

I had handled a fair amount of such material, but I am a bookman, not an art dealer. And I soon found out that though the pictures were beautiful, what collectors would pay for was an admittedly inferior picture, only if it had Audubon's name attached to it.

The question was what to do. I explained the matter to Charley Scribner. I had had a tough enough time purchasing these from the blind-deaf couple, and it would be triply difficult to unpurchase them. Besides, they had needed the money and obviously genuinely believed in the authenticity of what they had, and they were a sweet couple under dire adversity.

Charley said, "Forget it. Salvage what you can and I'll write off the rest." So I sold them as pretty bird pictures ("By Lehmann, after Audubon?"). I thought then and I think now that many of these were Audubon's own drawings despite the experts' opinions. A lot of people have bargains they wit not of and never will.

# Herman Melville

THERE HAS seldom been a once-and-future famous author who was as completely forgotten during his later lifetime as Herman Melville. His most productive period covered eleven years, from his first book, *Typee*, in 1846 to *The Confidence-Man* in 1857. Ten books were done in that time, several being popular successes. After that there were no more novels. There were two volumes of poetry, *Battle-Pieces* in 1866, with some striking Civil War poems, much underrated to this day, and *Clarel: A Poem and Pilgrimage in the Holy Land*, in two volumes in 1876, unread then and unreadable now. Melville wrote of it in a letter I once owned that it was "a metrical affair, a pilgrimage or whatnot, of several thousand lines, eminently adapted for unpopularity." Again silence until two small paper-covered volumes appeared, privately printed: *John Marr* in 1888 and *Timoleon* in 1891, each limited to twenty-five copies.

At Melville's death at the age of seventy-two in 1891 his obituary in *The New York Times* was a scant paragraph, and not a single one of his books was in print, nor any put back in print in America until the mid-twenties. And we have only just begun to dignify him with an adequate edition.

Matters were somewhat better in England. A number of his books had been first published there, including *Moby Dick*, in a three-decker entitled *The Whale* (1851), in a beautiful binding with blue covers and cream backs, with an embossed sounding whale in gold, in striking contrast to the drab, dumpy volume in which it made its American appearance. The text of the English edition differs somewhat from the American and the English is a much rarer book.* Continuing English

---

* His last writing, *Billy Budd*, was also first published in London in 1924 and not in New York until 1928.

interest in Melville is shown by the fact that Constable issued in London in 1922–1924 *The Collected Works of Herman Melville* in sixteen volumes which, though long out of print, remains the first, and to date the only effort of its kind.

The rediscovery of Melville began in 1921 when Raymond Weaver issued his biography. In 1923 E. Byrne Hackett of The Brick Row Book Shop issued Meade Minnigerode's *Some Personal Letters of Herman Melville and a Bibliography*, the first attempt at a bibliography and the first collection of his letters. Melville's letters, manuscripts and association copies are rarer than Poe's, and no even reasonably satisfactory bibliography exists to this day, nor does one of Poe, for that matter.

Because of the Minnigerode work the Brick Row attracted much Melville material. We always had, it seemed, a *John Marr* and a *Timoleon* on hand; I recall Robert Honeyman purchasing a pair for $100—each presented to a niece and with textual corrections by the author. They are now with Honeyman's American literature collection at Lehigh University. No copies have sold publicly since the Hogan copies in 1945, and they are virtually unprocurable now.

Melville very rarely presented books, and then only to his family or closest friends. No presentation copy of *Moby Dick* is known. It is dedicated to Hawthorne, though that copy has disappeared. Dr. Rosenbach had Hawthorne's copy of a later edition only, given him by John Drinkwater, who had purchased it for a few dollars in a New York shop. So there was justifiable excitement one day when the Brick Row acquired what still remains the only known presentation copy of *The Whale*. It was inscribed on the half-title of Volume I: "John C. Hoadley from his friend Herman Melville Pittsfield Jan:6th 1853. If my good brother John take exception to the use of the word *friend* here, thinking there is a *nearer* word: I beg him to remember that saying in the Good Book, which hints there is a *friend* that sticketh closer than a *brother*." On the front end paper is written in Melville's hand: " 'All life' says Okin, 'is from the sea; none from the continent. Man also is a child of the warm and shallow parts of the sea in the neighborhood of the land.' " I have no recollection of where it came from or what was paid for it. It passed to Owen D. Young at a price unknown to me—though whatever it was, it wasn't enough—and is now part of the Berg collection at the New York Public Library.

A good deal of Melville turned up at Harzof's and later at Scribner's while I was around. Harzof could remember Melville slightly, and his friend, the bibliographer Oscar Weglin, used to delight in telling how, as a very young clerk at the shop of John Anderson, Jr., at 99 Nassau, he used to deliver books to Melville at his home on East 26th Street. When Melville died, his widow asked Anderson to purchase his library. He bought a few books, including the remaining copies of *John Marr* and *Timoleon*, and the rest were sold to a Brooklyn dealer for $110 after a New York dealer had offered $100. It is a matter of fact that many of the books from Melville's library which survived have turned up in Brooklyn dealers' shops—I found several there. Brooklyn at that time had a number of very fine bookstores, as well as collectors: Henry Clay Folger, William Chapin, William A. White, Dr. William Braislin, Mrs. Boyle, among many others. It was much more of a book town than neighboring New York at that time, and it spawned, in our time, Sol Malkin, neither buyer nor seller, but a catalyst to both, as publisher of *The Antiquarian Bookman*.

It was Weglin who urged me to keep an eye out for books from Melville's library, and I came across a number, including his copy of Beaumont and Fletcher, now at Harvard. But the *great* finds occurred at Harzof's, right under my nose. A library of miscellaneous maritime books came in, and one of the employees who was sorting it suddenly let out a whoop and rushed up with a copy of Thomas Beale's *The Natural History of the Sperm Whale* (London, 1839), a standard work of no especial importance as a rarity. Unless, that is, it happened to be Melville's annotated copy, which this was. The half-title bore his signature, dated July 10, 1850, and the front end paper had the note "Imported by Putnam for me for $3.38." The book was copiously annotated in pencil by Melville, but someone had erased most of his writing, probably the Brooklyn dealer who bought it—to make it a "clean copy." About seven hundred words in his autograph remained decipherable, and these are most interesting, Melville noting on one illustration of a whale, "The tail part is wretchedly cropped and dwarfed, & looks altogether unnatural. The head is good." Melville mentions this book in the Extracts which preface *Moby Dick*, and it is, I think, the only one of these listed books (ample evidence of his wide reading) of which his own copy survives. So far as I know, no detailed study of this copy has ever been done, and I am sure modern technology could find means to recover most of the erasures.

An even more startling work, discovered by Harzof, was Melville's own copy of the book which was the source of *Moby Dick*—a dumpy twelvemo, lacking pages 123 to the end, of Owen Chase's *Narrative of the Most Extraordinary and Distressing Shipwreck of the Whale-Ship Essex, of Nantucket; Which was Attacked and finally Destroyed by a large*

*Spermaceti-Whale, in the Pacific Ocean* (New York, 1821). Not only was this Melville's copy but it had eighteen pages of manuscript notes in his hand laid in—including his statement that "the reading of his wondrous story upon the landless sea . . . had a surprising effect upon me . . ." Harzof found this in 1932 and it eventually turned up in the Cortland Field Bishop library, where in 1938 I paid $1,700 for it.

At Scribner's my Melville luck continued in both books and letters. From Miss Agnes Morewood, the granddaughter of his brother Allan, I acquired such goodies as the dedication copy of *Mardi* to Allan, Melville's own copy of the English edition of *Redburn* and much related material. I did not get everything she had by any means, however. She parted with what she did rather reluctantly, and some letters finally wound up in the Berkshire Athenaeum.

But what delighted and pleased me most was discovering a two-volume set of *The Poetical Works of Thomas Chatterton* (Cambridge, England, 1842), bound in half morocco. The verso of the flyleaf of Volume I is inscribed: "Herman Melville London Dec. 19th 1849. Bought at a dirty stall there and got it bound near by." The excitement, however, was the inscription in the same position in Volume II. "Herman Melville London Dec. 19th 1849. To my Brother John C. Hoadley Pittsfield, Jan. 6th 1854. Presented in earnest token of my disclaimer as to the criticism of the word 'friend' used on the fly-leaf of the 'Whale.' " Though Owen D. Young was not collecting at the time, he could not resist this at $250, and it is now where it should be, with the "Whale" in the New York Public Library Berg collection.

American first editions of Melville's books when bound in original cloth are not particularly rare—*Clarel* is the scarcest—but some were issued also at a cheaper price in paper wrappers. *Typee* (New York, 1846) is the commonest, followed by *Omoo*, but *Mardi*, *White-Jacket* and *Redburn* are nearly unfindable thus, though I have had them all and sold several to Miss Katherine deB Parsons of New York City, who has a very fine though little-known collection of American literature distinguished by its extraordinarily fine condition, many of the books having been supplied by the late Arthur S. Swann. *Moby Dick* is relatively common and occurs in several colors of cloth, the rarest being red, and with plain or marbled end papers, there being no bibliographical distinction of which I am aware. I have had about twenty-five copies in various combinations. I have never seen a copy in printed wrappers but would not be surprised if one showed up sometime. The book was advertised as to appear in this form, and furthermore a book scout whose word I have no reason to doubt told me that some fifty years ago he had seen a single stray volume—there would be a find!

I have mentioned that Melville letters and manuscripts are very uncommon. I do not know of even a scrap of manuscript which exists of any of his novels, aside from *Billy Budd*, except the famous "Round-Robin" from *Omoo*. This I had in an early draft, differing from the printed version, which was written on the verso of a page of manuscript of *Mardi*. This notable linking of two Melville novels on one leaf is now in the Barrett collection.

I sold many of my Melvilles to Frank J. Hogan and they reappeared at his sale in 1945. Why I passed them up then I cannot now conceive, except that I had been buying very heavily for stock in the sale and was planning to go after the Poes, so I shockingly skipped Melville.

This brings up something originally pointed out to me by Harzof. That is that an item's position in an auction catalogue often definitely reflects the price it brings. "The bargains," Harzof counseled, "are most often at the end of a sale. Then interest flags, most dealers have overbought, people are leaving, attention is distracted, the auctioneer is tired and things slip through." He also shrewdly advised me on "scouting" a bookshop. "Keep to the upper and the lower shelves. What's at eye level has been scanned often enough before. Most people, even the shop-owners, are too damn lazy to climb a ladder or stoop to their knees once the books are shelved, and that's where the bargains are." As usual, he was right, at least in my scouting days. I still try to adhere to his advice, but at my age, bifocals and arthritis do present problems!

Hogan purchased the *Natural History* for $750, the *Whale-Ship Essex* for $2,000. They brought at his sale $1,050 and $2,100, respectively. Both were acquired by the late collector Perc Brown and are now at Dartmouth. The dedication *Mardi*, which I sold for $500, brought $1,150 and is now in the Arents collection at the New York Public Library. A fine series of nine late Melville letters (1884–1888) to James Billson which I had once owned brought $900—bought by H. Bradley Martin. He failed, however, to acquire the copy of *John Marr* presented to Billson. This, a beauty in original wrappers, the only presentation ever sold at auction, brought $800. Martin regrets his oversight to this day, and though he recently acquired a copy, it's a rather scrubby affair, lacks the wrappers, and is shown apologetically. This is a slight blemish only on what is certainly the finest Melville collection ever assembled by a private collector, still and all! He did acquire, for $600 (sold by Scribner's for $500, costing in England $34.50), Hogan's copy of what I consider the rarest of all Melville's works, the original printing of his first book, *Narrative of a Four Months' Residence Among the Natives of a Valley of the Marquesas Islands; or, a Peep at Polynesian Life*, issued in London by John Murray in 1846 in two parts, paper wrappers. The text of this differs from the American (published as *Typee*), which suppressed such vivid passages as the women's visit to the ship.

> What a sight for us bachelor sailors! how avoid so dire a temptation? For who could think of tumbling these artless creatures overboard, when they had swam miles to welcome us? . . .
> Not the feeblest barrier was interposed between the unholy passions of the crew and their unlimited gratification.

Passages such as these, I suppose, did not alarm the British, who, after all, had a long seafaring tradition behind them and accepted such goings-on, but it was too heady stuff for Yankees to read and the original version as Melville wrote it was not reprinted in America until the twentieth century.

The single most important group of Melville's correspondence discovered in recent times is that with the English publisher of most of his books, Richard Bentley. Scribner's acquired these letters for a pittance when they came up for auction in London, along with other Bentley material in 1939. And what letters they are! *Mardi* (London, 1849) had had a bad reception, the powerful *Blackwood's Edinburgh Magazine* lambasting it with more virulence than it usually spent on American books: "Why, what trash is this?—mingled, too, with attempts at a Rabelaisian vein, and with strainings at smartness, the style of the whole being affected, pedantic, and wearisome exceedingly."

This certainly hurt Melville, who wrote (July 20, 1849): "You know perhaps that there are goodly harvests which ripen late, especially when the grain is remarkably strong. At any rate, Mr. Bentley, let us by all means lay this flattering unction to our souls, since it is so grateful a project to you as a publisher, & to me as an author"—and he accepted a cut in the proceeds of his next book, *Redburn.*

On June 27, 1850, Melville wrote of his new (untitled) work: "The book is a romance of adventure, founded upon certain wild legends on the Southern Sperm Whale Fisheries, and illustrated by the author's own personal experiences, for two years & more, as a harpooner."

Bentley did nobly in format by *The Whale*, but it failed completely commercially and was eventually remaindered. On March 4, 1852, the publisher sent Melville a profit and loss statement, the original of which was in the collection. On *Mardi* he lost £68.7.6; on *Redburn*, £76.7.6; on

*White-Jacket* £173.9.6; and on *The Whale*, to that date, £103.4.6, followed by a note "probable eventual loss, £350."

Melville replied with a letter about his forthcoming *Pierre*, asking that Bentley "let bygones be bygones for here we have a *new book*." In one of the saddest postcripts I know of in American letters he suggests that "it might not prove unadvisable to publish this present book anonymously, or under an assumed name—'By a Vermonter' or 'By Guy Winthrop.' " Bentley declined and bluntly informed Melville that if he had "restrained your imagination somewhat and had written in a style to be understood by the great mass of readers—nay if you had not sometimes offended the feelings of many sensitive readers you would have succeeded in England."

The only one who eventually profited a little bit was Scribner's. I bought the letters for $800 and sold them to Harry Levenson, then running the Chaucer Head Bookshop in New York City, for $2,000. They now form part of H. Bradley Martin's incomparable Melville collection, and today any one of these letters could be sold for a sum that would liquidate Bentley's losses and show a profit—or Martin's investment, for that matter.

Melville wrote in all 271 known letters (of which I have had, at one time and another, over 10 percent), and many of them are short and fragmentary. None is more fragmentary than the only known example of his correspondence with W. Clark Russell, the English author of the famous novel *The Wreck of the Grosvenor*. Russell, in 1884, had praised Melville as the highest of the "poets of the deep," and the grateful, lonely, forgotten man dedicated his *John Marr* to Russell as one who "knows the sea, and the blue water of it; the sailor and the heart of him; the ship, too, and the sailing and handling of a ship." Higher praise he could not bestow.

There is in the Lilly Library copy of the first edition of *The Wreck of the Grosvenor* a letter from Russell to an unnamed "Dear Sir," who suggested his doing an article that "should deal with the singular and the original merits of certain great American sea novelists." Russell explained why he was unable to do the article, adding, "Herman Melville dedicated a book to me in 1886. Twenty-five copies only were printed. I never knew Melville personally but exchanged many letters with him."

In the whole of Melville's correspondence only one fragmentary mutilated letter to Russell is recorded. What wouldn't we give for the rest? I have searched widely for some hint of what became of them— even advertising in the Agony column of the *London Times*, but nothing has turned up. Russell left a batch of daughters who married and scattered all over the world. I have heard rumors of the letters' existence stretching from Brazil to Australia, and I only hope that, somewhere, they will be uncovered.

There is one class of "Association books" which I especially like, books annotated by friends (or enemies) of the author who sometimes have information on events he "modified" in the telling; often these throw considerable light on the creative process. Such a book is Harrison Robertson's copy of *White-Jacket* (New York, 1850), now in the Lilly Library, which I sold him years ago for $185. Robertson, according to the Naval Library records, served as captain's clerk on the U.S.S. *United States* from June 8, 1844, at Callao until October 14, 1844, and he thus accompanied Melville on the cruise which is the basis of the book. Robertson has identified many of the characters mentioned by Melville (but not Jack Chase), and has added many penciled notes as to the incidents, e.g., the famous fall from the yardarm is dismissed by the one word "imaginary." The longest note is on the leaf following the title, in very faint pencil, as follows:

> Some of the incidents and characters described in this book occurred on board the Frigate "United States"—in which I returned home, via Cape Horn, in 1844. Other incidents described are either purely imaginary, or happened at some other time & place. The author probably has made his book, not from personal experience wholly, but has patched together scraps picked up from some other person's journal, or conversation—most of the characters & incidents described are grossly caricatured, or exaggerated. H. R.

# Mark Twain

I FIRST READ Mark Twain in the home of an uncle, Charles Randall of Catawissa, Pennsylvania, a newspaper man, editor of *The Catawissa News Item*. He had once worked with Twain on a newspaper in Buffalo and had a good collection of his books. (I wonder now if any were first editions.)

I was occasionally farmed out to him on summer vacations and hung around the printing plant, sometimes being allowed to sort out type, etc. But I didn't like him very much because I once heard him exclaim to my father, "That kid of yours is eating me out of house and home and messes up the shop besides. You should give me board money."

That did it, and that night I started to trudge the twenty or so miles back home. I was picked up the next day, having covered about ten miles in the wrong direction. Uncle Charles told me that Mark had once worked in the coal mines at Shamokin, Pennsylvania, an idea which intrigues me to this day, as I worked there too, but one I have been completely unable to verify.

In New York I became acquainted with Merle Johnson, Twain's bibliographer as well as a specialist in the bibliographies of American authors generally. Johnson's other attractions were a beautiful wife and two even more beautiful daughters. And he had a skinny assistant named Jacob Blanck, with whom I became friends and who knew more about Mark than Merle did, and who eventually completed the revision of Merle's Twain bibliography and then went on from there.

Of all the Twain material I have had, which is considerable, I remember that connected with Tom and Huck best. Chronologically Tom precedes: *The Adventures of Tom Sawyer* was published in 1876; *The Adventures of Huckleberry Finn* (Tom Sawyer's comrade) in 1885. Was there ever so successful a sequel? Usually these are fatal things. *The*

*Memoirs of Sherlock Holmes* do not quite measure up to *The Adventures;* nor *Twenty Years After* to *The Three Musketeers.*

In any event, a fascinating manuscript of *Tom Sawyer* appeared at auction in 1939 and I purchased it for $1,750. Only the famous Preface, the Conclusion and about twelve other pages were in Twain's hand. The remainder was in the hand of two amanuenses, but Twain had made numerous additions, corrections and revisions throughout in his own hand. In many respects it was of considerably more interest than the original manuscript entirely in his hand, which is in the Georgetown University Library.

This was the manuscript from which the English edition was first printed by Chatto and Windus, six months before the American edition appeared. Twain had this copy made for submission to his arbiter and censor, William Dean Howells. The copy is therefore of vital importance in answering the questions of how much Twain toned down "vulgar" passages and how much "suppression" Howells exercised on the book as finally published.

It was considerable. Twain wrote to him:

> There was never a man in the world so grateful to another as I was to you day before yesterday, when I sat down (in still rather wretched health) to set myself to the dreary and hateful task of making final revision of *Tom Sawyer,* and discovered, upon opening the package of MS, that your pencil marks were scattered all along. This was splendid, and swept away all labor. Instead of *reading* the MS, I simply hunted out the pencil marks and made the emendations which they suggested. I reduced the boy battle to a curt paragraph; I finally concluded to cut the Sunday school speech down to the first two sentences, leaving no suggestion of satire, since the book is to be for boys and girls; I tamed the various obscenities until I judged that they no longer carried offence.

Some of Howell's suggestions were perfectly proper and correct. In Chapter III he wrote: "Don't like this chapter much. The sham fight is too long. Tom is either too old for this or too young," as a result of which Twain cut fifty lines from the manuscript, much to its improvement.

There are many other changes between the manuscript and the printed book. "The devil" becomes "Satan," the Thatcher's maid originally drenched the adoring Tom with "foul slop" (changed to "water"), and his "reeking garments" became merely "drenched"; Injun Joe's revenge was to "cut her nose off—and her ears." This was softened (?) to "slit her nostrils—notch her ears."

An amusing change involved the poodle which relieved the suffering of the congregation by sitting down on a pinchbug and went "sailing up the aisle with his tail shut down like a hasp." Howell noted, "awfully good but a little dirty," and Twain scratched out an expressive phrase.

But the most important changes in the manuscript are in Chapter XX, "Tom Takes Becky's Punishment," the deletion of the single allusion to sex in the entire book. This is where Tom sneaked up on Becky Thatcher as she was looking in Professor Dobbins' textbook of anatomy at "a human figure, stark naked," and she, startled, tore the plate. Knowing she would be detected and whipped, she wailed to Tom, "But that ain't everything—it ain't *half*. You'll tell everybody about the picture, O, O, O!*" This and several other passages were deleted—innocent as they seem to us—changed because Howells wrote, "I should be afraid of this picture incident."

Only one presentation copy of the first edition of *Tom Sawyer* is known, Twain being chary with his presentations (until late in life). Harzof used to relate he had bought one from Charles Goodspeed for $10. Harzof couldn't remember what happened to it. In the early thirties J. K. Lilly purchased this copy from Drake for $10,000. It is inscribed: "To C. W. Stoddard from his friend S. L. Clemens, 1877." When he told Goodspeed about it, he dug out a 1909 catalogue and there it was, priced $10. Mark Twain's own copy of the Tauchnitz, 1876, edition, which I had and which is now Lilly's, cost considerably less.

Walter Chrysler, Jr., had a very considerable collection of Twain with many fine books. These were sold at auction in 1954 and included a poorish copy of a first *Tom Sawyer* inscribed on the front end paper: "To Mr. Bartlett from the Author. Oct. 1877." It brought $1,100 and is a genuine inscription; no question about that, only Twain never gave Mr. Bartlett the copy in which that leaf is now inserted. It was originally in a later issue of the book and transferred to a first. I know because I watched the transplantation being done.

There are no serious unsolved bibliographical problems about *Tom*, although there were at least three printings of the book before the date on the title page was changed (the second of which has three issues).

*Huck* is quite another matter and is bibliographically one of the most complex of all American firsts. Should the second numeral 5 in the pagination on page 155 be missing, of the same font, set higher, or slipping? Is the preferred binding cloth? If so, what color, blue or green? And what about the library (i.e., sheep binding), sprinkled edges, versus half morocco, marbled edges? And how about the many states of the

inserted portrait? And so on. Even the English edition presents difficulties: should the sheets be sewn in the conventional manner with thread
or saddle-stitched with wire staples?

Above all, what about the state of the illustration on page 283? It
caused a tremendous ruckus at the time, and no one knows now what
really happened, or ever will. The illustration depicts the scene where
Huck passed as Tom and shows Mr. and Mrs. Phelps facing him. The
caption reads: "Who do you reckon it is?" While the book was in press
the fly on Silas Phelps's trousers was defaced so that the engraving
became ribald. No one knows if this was done by accident or by design,
though Twain was convinced that it was deliberate sabotage, probably by
some disgruntled employee. Others are convinced that the young illustrator E. W. Kemble was responsible. Twain had complained of the
"forbidding and repulsive people" he was drawing and cautioned his
publisher, "You must knock out one of them—the lecherous old rascal
kissing the girl at the camp meeting. It is powerful good, but it mustn't go
in—don't forget it."

By luck the defaced plate was discovered before any copies containing
it were distributed [except advance prospectuses to salesmen], but not
before some 30,000 copies had been printed. In those copies already
bound the plate was redone, the leaf excised and a cancel inserted, a
laborious process. In unbound copies the entire signature was reprinted.
Salesmen whose prospectuses contained the plate were ordered to return
them or face dismissal.

Someone leaked the story to the press and on November 29, 1884, the
following appeared:

### TAMPERING WITH MARK TWAIN'S BOOK

A fortunate discovery, made in the nick of time, saved the first edition of 30,000 of Mark Twain's new book, "The Adventures of Huckleberry Finn," from destruction. Charles L. Webster of No. 658 Broadway,
who is Mr. Clemens' nephew and publisher, was in San Francisco a
few days ago, when his attention was called to the fact that one of the
cuts had been tampered with improperly. He telegraphed at once to
this city and had the publication stopped.

From the New York *Herald*, November 29, 1884:

### MARK TWAIN'S ALTERED BOOK

Mr. Charles L. Webster, nephew of Mark Twain, yesterday offered
a reward of $500 for the apprehension and conviction of the person
who so altered an engraving in "Huckleberry Finn" as to make it ob-
noxious. Mr. Webster said yesterday: "The book was examined before

the final printing by W. D. Howells, Mr. Clemens, the proofreader, and myself. Nothing improper was discovered. On page 283 was a small illustration with the subscription "Who do you reckon it is?" By the punch of an awl or graver, the illustration became an immoral one. But 250 copies left the office, I believe, before the mistake was discovered. Had the first edition been run off our loss would have been $25,000. Had the mistake not been discovered, Mr. Clemens' credit for decency and morality would have been destroyed.

So concerned were Mark and the publisher about the vulgarity and so vigorous was their action that not a single copy of the book with the offending plate has ever been discovered.

Merle Johnson, Twain's bibliographer (an illustrator himself, by the way), relates that he interviewed Kemble, who could throw no light on it, and J. J. Little, at whose plant the book was produced. "He was not at all disposed to discuss the subject, but after insistence on my part he surrendered. 'Oh, well—all right—' and with this he produced a copy of the original plate that had been suppressed. 'This cost me plenty,' was his comment. From that day to this (1935) I have never seen another copy." It was a very expensive prank, as the book, supposed to be published in November to catch the Christmas market, was not issued until March, but at that it did all right, 42,000 copies being sold in six weeks. Yet for all that, the publisher, Twain's nephew, went bankrupt a few years later.

The book was sold by subscription, and traveling salesmen were given a prospectus with a chapter or so of text, samples of binding and blank leaves to note customers' orders. Legend has it that Gill, the Syracuse agent, discovered the marred plate and alerted the publisher. All copies were supposed to have been returned. One day Frank Glenn, a well-known Kansas dealer, produced one that hadn't, and by great good luck this contained page 283 in its defaced state. I acquired this for a modest sum, sold it to Carroll Wilson and eventually resold it to Waller Barrett.

But more and better was to come. In 1885 Mark Twain and George Washington Cable were on a lecture tour together and the publisher sent Mark a set of advance sheets which Twain inscribed and gave to Cable. His daughter showed up with it at the Houghton Library one lucky (for me) day. Bill Jackson, in a rare lapse of judgment, decided against buying it because, as he explained to me later, it just wasn't suitable for display purposes, so he recommended that she bring it to me. I purchased it at once and offered it to Lilly, who refused it for the same reason Jackson did. So I sold it to Leigh Block of Chicago, President of Inland Steel, who was showing signs of becoming a collector and did, but of art, not books.

I later repurchased it and it eventually wound up, with the prospectus, in the Barrett collection. The price progression was $1,500, $2,500, $3,500, $5,000.

Jackson often lamented that he had turned the proofs down, but he recouped in another transaction. Miss Mildred Howells, daughter of William Dean Howells, who lived in Cambridge, Massachusetts, wrote me that she had discovered quite a lot of her father's manuscripts in an attic or somewhere. They had been undisturbed since his death in 1920 and she had found with them an appraisal done at that time by Charles Goodspeed. Would I be interested? I was, of course, but explained that I couldn't possibly put a value on them without examining them and that I was going to be in Cambridge within a fortnight. I arrived and Miss Howells informed me that they had been purchased by the Houghton Library. She had written Jackson the same letter she had written me, and although he was abroad at the time, he had cabled offering to purchase them at twice Goodspeed's appraisal. The fact that he got them for about a tenth of their value is immaterial.

# Stephen Crane

I REMEMBER VIVIDLY the Fourth of July celebrations held in the small Pennsylvania towns I grew up in—bands, speeches in the park, torchlight parades, dances, fireworks, etc. I even heard old men tell tales: Tom Brown, of Minersville, who escaped from Andersonville only to be treed by dogs which shredded his calves, leaving him permanently crippled; an uncle by marriage, Adjutant J. Richards Boyle of the One Hundred and Eleventh Regiment Pennsylvania Volunteers, wounded at Peach Tree Creek, whose father, Major Boyle, was killed beneath the colors at Wauhatchie, Tennessee, prelude to the battle of Lookout Mountain, where every officer of the battalion was killed or wounded; a Harrisburg relative, a member of the famed Pennsylvania "Bucktails," whose duty it was—if Lee broke through at Gettysburg—to drive into the wooden bridges crossing the Susquehanna wagons laden with straw ready to be fired, and he damn near did, on a false rumor that Lee had. I also played as a kid on that field and knew "Devil's Den" as a fine place to dig for spent Minie balls and occasional bones.

The Fourth was an exciting occasion then, and I eventually figured out that, having been born on April 5, I was probably conceived following a Fourth of July celebration (it's nine months to the day)—which would make me much more of a "Yankee Doodle Dandy" than George M. Cohan, who claimed (falsely) to have been born on the Fourth of July. When I once pointed this out to him he agreed, with his usual profanity, that I was right.

In any event, I spent some summers with "Doctor" Boyle, who was then a minister of the Methodist Episcopal Church in the small town of Sinking Springs, Pennsylvania. These were a bore, mostly. I remember asking him once to take me fishing on a nearby pond, where I was not allowed alone, to which he replied that he hadn't time to take from his work. "I," he added, "am a fisher of men—Matthew 4:19." And he gave me, when I went to prep school, a copy of William Jennings Bryan's *In His Image*, with an inscription especially commending Chapter 4, "The Menace of Darwinism." He had, however, a large, though (to me) very dull, library consisting mostly of theology and military history, including a complete set of *The War of the Rebellion.*

This he had used in compiling his chef-d'oeuvre, a history of the One Hundred and Eleventh Pennsylvania Volunteers, *Soldiers True*, which seems to be an accurate work of considerable scholarship and compassion—attitudes I was too young to appreciate. All I knew was that he wouldn't take me fishing, a fact I resent to this day. There were very few novels in the library, but among them were, surprisingly, Crane's *Red Badge of Courage*, thus, my introduction to Stephen Crane. When I asked my uncle what he thought of it, he remarked that it was a good yarn for one who hadn't been there and then added that the best accounts of the Crucifixion were written by nonparticipants. He was a man of parts I was too young to appreciate. I knew, though, he had a locked compartment in his bookcase, which naturally I pried open. The only thing in it I now recall was a copy of Upton Sinclair's novel *Damaged Goods*, based upon Eugène Bricux's play *Les Avariés*. This was my introduction to Upton Sinclair, whom I was to come to know intimately many decades later. I read *Damaged Goods* with eagerness and complete noncomprehension and was disappointed. If it had been on an open shelf I would have paid no attention to it, of course. My total aversion to censorship traces to this episode.

But back to Crane. There appeared in January, 1934, a green-wrapped octavo of thirty-two pages: *Rare Books. The First Catalogue from the Book Shop of David A. Randall. First edition and inscribed copies, mostly modern, together with a special group of volumes from the libraries of, or autographed by, the Presidents.*

This consisted almost entirely of Harzof's stock, together with duplicates and discards given me "on consignment" by Carroll Wilson, David Kirschenbaum, John T. Winterich and a few others. Item 41, by far the most expensive lot in the catalogue, was headed: "Stephen Crane—A Collection of his First Editions and of Craneana."

> The set of first editions of Stephen Crane here described merits the description "complete" more nearly than any other Crane collection that has ever been offered for sale. It is far more extensive than the John Quinn collection, the largest ever to come on the market. Its most noticeable features are a superlative copy of the 1893 *Maggie* (which

though neither "privately printed" nor "suppressed," is as rare as if it had been both) uncut and unopened, a first issue of *The Red Badge of Courage,* the Japan Vellum edition of *The Black Riders* (one of fifty copies, and the rarest volume of American fin de siècle poetry), and a signed copy of *The Lanthorn Book,* of which, according to Vincent Starrett, Crane's bibliographer, "only between ten and fifteen copies bear Crane's signature." The collection is lacking only a few of the leaflets of Craneana which are almost unobtainable and is priced at about what comparable copies of the *Maggie* it contains have been known to bring.

The collection of nearly one hundred volumes was priced $1,750, and it did not sell. The key book was *Maggie,* which a few years before had alone sold well over that figure. What had happened is a curious episode in book collecting history. When a legendary rarity suddenly becomes a common book (or is thought to become so), what is the result?

Suppose the printer of Poe's *Tamerlane* (Boston, 1827) happened one hundred years ago to store away a bundle of the books against future orders which never came. Suppose there were fifty *Tamerlanes* in that bundle, and that it should suddenly be discovered by someone who knew of their value. What would happen to the *Tamerlane* market? To assume that such a bundle exists is, of course, highly fantastic, and to assume that it would be discovered by a book fancier, rather than by a janitor who would dump the whole business into a trash pit, is more fantastic still— but not beyond the broad bounds of possibility.

A real-life approximation of this hypothetical situation occurred in the instance of Stephen Crane's *Maggie: A Girl of the Streets* (New York, 1893), published under the pseudonym Johnston Smith. Crane, unable to find a publisher for his maiden offering, had it printed at his own expense and distributed through the recognized channels for the dissemination of paperbound books. Not quite every copy was returned by the distributors; Crane himself gave away a few. The book became excessively rare, and the resurgence of Crane's fame in the 1920's lent the item a collector luster that was not at all diminished by the sheer unavailability of the book.

The John Quinn copy, sold at auction at the end of 1923, brought $115 despite the fact that it was hardly in the freshest condition. Early in 1925 the same copy sold for $130. Thereafter, although Crane's name appeared regularly in successive auction seasons, no copy of the 1893 *Maggie* reached the rostrum until March, 1930, when a signed presentation copy, the first to appear at public sale, brought the amazing price of $3,700, still the record price for the book.

Behind that figure was an accumulated demand, a concentrated eagerness to own an 1893 *Maggie*, that had perforce been bottled up for five years. *Maggie*, despite her humble origin, had attained more than respectability—she was among the elect of bibliophilic aristocracy.

Two months later—May, 1930—a second *Maggie* visited the auction room, uninscribed, and fetched $2,100. It was the property of Mrs. Florence Coghlan, a niece of Crane.

The result of these previously unimagined figures was that an intensive search for *Maggies* was undertaken throughout the book trade. During the 1930–1931 season three copies reached the block—they sold, respectively, for $500, $775, and $1,125, the last inscribed. Four copies appeared in the 1931–1932 season. They sold, in the order of their appearance, for $550, $230, $85, and $90.

Only the first of these four was in good collector condition. But a consideration that lay deeper than condition, important as that consideration itself is, was responsible for the descending curve. The fear had gripped the book trade, and the world of collectors as well, that a vast trove of *Maggies* had been unearthed and was being doled out too swiftly for the public to digest them. The rumors became quite definite, as rumors have a way of becoming. These fresh *Maggies*, said the rumors, had been found in a soapbox—even a piano box—at such and such a place in New Jersey, in such a corner of an old stable, and there were so and so many copies. The figure was always specific but never the same.

Only one *Maggie* appeared the following season (1932-1933). A re-backed presentation copy, it brought $400. The following season recorded the vending of only a single copy—a presentation that fetched $320. Two seasons earlier the same copy had sold for $230. At the close of 1934 another presentation copy, rebound in cloth, brought $210. It looked as if *Maggie's* good name might yet be preserved.

The panic began to abate. The tide of *Maggies* was definitely slackening. Perhaps the recently discovered copies had been contained in a shoebox rather than a piano box. Reasonable dealers and collectors began to consider the fact that, after all, these presentation copies could hardly have come out of the box; they had obviously been brought to light from as many separate recesses as a result of the $3,700 figure of March, 1930. Equally obviously, there was in all probability some common source whence had appeared some of the uninscribed copies which had also been brought out by the March, 1930, record.

Then in April, 1935, the full story came out. A fine copy of *Maggie* was offered for sale at auction by the Anderson Galleries in New York, and to the usual catalogue description of the lot offered was appended this explanation:

In view of the uncertainty that exists in the minds of collectors and dealers regarding a so-called "large number" of copies that are supposed to have been found, we think it advisable to make the following statement:

From March 11, 1930, to December 5, 1934, eleven copies of this work appeared at public sale in America, three of which were presentation copies; some of the volumes were in very poor condition. Nine of the eleven were sold in these galleries, the first ( a presentation copy) on March 11, 1930, and the last (also a presentation copy) on December 5, 1934. Only two, however, of the nine that we have sold were the property of the owner of the present copy, Mrs. Florence Crane Coghlan.

When Mr. Coghlan came to the Galleries to negotiate the sale of the present copy, we gave it as our opinion that it would be unwise to offer it for sale unless a definite statement was made in the catalogue regarding the exact number of copies still held by him and his wife.

We are informed that they still hold eleven copies and that the present copy is one of the finest, being practically as fresh as on the day it left the printers' hand. The majority of the others are in more or less worn condition, some with the wrappers slightly chipped, and others torn, lightly stained, or with other slight defects.

An arrangement has been made with Mr. and Mrs. Coghlan whereby these eleven copies are to be sold in these Galleries at the rate of two copies each season hereafter until the entire number has been distributed.

In view of the unusual circumstances and the carrying power of the original rumor, the officials of the Anderson Galleries asked Mrs. Coghlan to explain the situation in a detailed statement given over her name. This statement, one of the most unusual in the history of book collecting, merits reproduction here for its fullness and detail:

After the death of my father, Stephen Crane's brother William, in California several years ago, two copies of *Maggie* were sent to my sister Agnes and me by the estate. Not knowing the value, but suspecting that they would bring a few dollars at least, I took them to the Anderson Galleries, where I was congratulated on the possession of these books and they were put up at auction. The result is book history.

Like everyone else, who had ever seen or heard of *Maggie,* I racked my brains to remember any more possible copies in the family library. When our home in Brooklyn was broken up, most of our possessions were stored on my grandfather's farm, and I mentally repacked the books which had been sent there.

As far back as I could remember there had always been a small pile of paper-bound *Maggie*s in our storage room, but when I spoke of this to my mother she said she didn't believe there were any left, as my two eldest sisters had burned them, believing they were "not nice."

However, we took a chance and went to the farm, where our books had been stored in a wagon house for twenty years, and we found the books which the American Art Association Anderson Galleries Inc. are now handling. To my knowledge these are the only first edition *Maggie*s in our branch of the family.

As a result of the restoration of public confidence in *Maggie* which followed publication of this statement, the first Coghlan copy brought $700. A number of copies have appeared subsequently in varying states of condition, and the last one sold at auction in 1949 brought $425. *Maggie* has again become a very scarce book.

My, or rather Winterich's, collection was eventually sold, and by this time I was a Crane "expert" with the help of his bibliographers, Vincent Starrett and Ames W. Williams, and had a few customers, notably H. Bacon Collamore. Collamore had the great good fortune to wander into Goodspeed's one day when they had just acquired the files of the Boston publisher Copeland and Day, who issued *The Black Riders*, and made a tremendous haul. He had pursued Crane for years and had a remarkable collection. In this, as in so many of his enthusiasms—Henry James, D. H. Lawrence, Beatrix Potter and many others—he was way ahead of his times.

Somewhere along the line I met the brother of Robert Barr, the English novelist who completed Crane's unfinished Irish romance *The O'Ruddy*, and through him and others I acquired considerable manuscripts of short stories, presentation copies, etc. The two manuscripts I remember best are *The Battle of Forty Fort* and *In the Depths of a Coal Mine*, both Wyoming Valley tales dealing with "the region." I also came across what I think was the first known copy of *The Pike County Puzzle*, "Camp Interlaken, Pa. August 18, 1894," a parody newspaper written at a camp where Crane was spending some time. He is listed as "Office Boy" and possibly wrote the entire newspaper himself. In the list of "Proprietors" is Cousin Knapp Linson, the young artist who painted the best-known portrait of Crane, which Collamore once owned.

I never did purchase the manuscript of *The Red Badge of Courage*, nor did anyone else who had a chance when it was around for years. As Harzof told me the story, an acquaintance of his, who had bought it originally from David Kirschenbaum, sold it to Dr. Rosenbach for $500 and shortly afterward told Harzof about it. He said it was much too little and advised the seller to get it back. He asked Rosenbach the next day what he wanted for it and the Doctor said $5,000. He had it for years and catalogued it in 1933 for $11,850. It was still around a decade and a half later and he finally sold it to Waller Barrett for $6,000.

I did have, however, the original contract for its publication (this is now at Lilly). It is standard for its times, dated June 17, 1895, and reads, in part:

> A sum of money equal to ten per cent of the retail price of all copies sold provided however that the Party of the Second Part shall not be required to make any such payments until they shall have sold a sufficient number of copies of the said book to reimburse them for all moneys expended in manufacturing and publishing the same.

And no nonsense like an "author's advance." Appleton sold Heinemann the English rights for £35 in "full payment for copyright in Great Britain and Ireland and her Colonies (Canada excepted)."

I had the pleasure of handling much of this Crane material twice, as when Collamore's collection was as complete as he could make it and his interest turned elsewhere, I passed it along to Waller Barrett.

Books from Crane's library are uncommon, for as a journalist he was consistently off to far places and apparently didn't accumulate much of a library. Cora, his wife, however, did. At any rate, I once owned a copy of the first edition of Hardy's *Jude the Obscure* which belonged to her at the time she was proprietor of a brothel. The inner front cover carried the inscription: "Property of 'The Court' Ward and Davis Sts. Jacksonville Fla. Please return to book case in sitting room so that others can enjoy Cora Taylor."

Crane letters are not common, somewhat over two hundred and thirty-five being known. I have had in one way and another a fair share of these. The most substantial group was acquired in a curious way. I had known that much of Crane's affairs in his later years had been handled by Paul Reynolds, one of the earliest and best known of American literary agents. It occurred to me one day to try and trace down the descendants of this Reynolds on the off chance that they might have some Crane memorabilia.

I started looking through the Scribner files. Though they had not published any of Crane's books, the magazine had published some of his short stories and had worked through Reynolds. I found some notes about Crane, including a memo from editor Edward L. Burlingame to Charles Scribner in 1897:

> Although I think Crane did an impressive & on the whole genuinely fine thing in the "Open Boat" (coming in our June number), I don't think he is going to outrun the limits of a sensation. This dangerous piece of literary prophecy will probably recur to you when he is seated on the pinnacle of fame; but he will never consent to sit there; he will insist on standing on his head & waving his legs with a crimson roar.

I finally discovered that the Paul Reynolds literary agency was still around, very active, conducted by his son and situated on the seventh floor of the Scribner building, just over my head!

Right there was a superb collection of Crane letters, twenty-six of them. They were thrilling and pathetic. Crane was constantly beset by poverty and in one letter wrote his agent: "I am all fuzzy with money troubles and last night a writ was served on me by a leading creditor . . . I must have every pennie that you can wrest from the enemy . . . I am going to borrow money from pretty nearly everybody in the world."

I bought these from Reynolds for $400 and catalogued them for $850. There were no takers. After they were around a few years I put them in an auction sale at the Parke-Bernet Galleries and bought them back at $225.

They languished around for more years but did serve one useful purpose. My nephew was at Lehigh and looking around for some sort of thesis for English, and I lent him these letters. He duly edited them, much to Dr. Robert Smith's pleasure, and then returned them to me.

I couldn't get rid of this albatross, and every inventory wrote down the cost another 10 percent. Eventually a young collector with much enthusiasm and little cash got them from me for $325—and still has them. I just recently purchased a good unpublished Crane letter for $750.

When I was in Paul Reynolds' office recently (he is now my literary agent, by the way, and responsible for this opus) I spotted a framed Stephen Crane letter on the wall. Somehow I had criminally overlooked this when I made the original purchase and I pointed out that this belonged with the others I had bought thirty years previously—free, gratis, and for nothing. I couldn't get him to agree with this very rational viewpoint, somehow. The letter is still hanging there and seems likely to remain so. It is typical of Crane's relationship with Reynolds' father (who must often have regretted having become a literary agent; there must be easier ways of making a living), and with his permission I print it here.

> Ravensbrook
> Oxted
> Surry
> Jan. 27th 1899

Dear Reynolds:—

I send you a short story (2000 words) which, first of all, I would like to have you use as a boost for a loan which I am trying to get out of McClure. Dont be too quick to give it to them unless you see this loan in sight. You will be notified in regard to the English rights and date of publication. As to the Harpers, I think that collection of respectable old women has treated us rather badly. I have worked up my English short story market until I can command from six to ten guineas a thousand for the English rights alone. This makes it very essential that when any of the three all-over-the-place magazines buy from us, they must pay big money.

How are you coming on with that other story? Of course I need money and need it badly.

> Yours Faithfully
> Stephen Crane

Crane's last novel was a romantic tale of Irish life, *The O'Ruddy*, done with satiric overtones and deliberately calculated to appeal to a market buying scads of things like *When Knighthood Was in Flower*, *Graustark* and *The Prisoner of Zenda*. Strictly a potboiler, the book seems to have been fun for Crane to do, which is nice to recall. He had little to be cheerful about those last sad months.

He died with it unfinished, and there has always been a hassle about it. Who really finished it, how much tampering was done with it, how much of it was Crane's own work, are unanswered questions. However, the famous Crane exhibition at Columbia University Library in 1957 flatly states that Kipling had been asked to finish it but refused, as did H. B. Marriott-Watson. A. E. W. Mason, author of *The Four Feathers* among other romantic novels, was another approached and seriously considered doing it but dawdled on the job. Another snag seemed to be that Mason, according to a letter in the Lilly Library, insisted that there should be a note at the beginning stating that "the book has been from such and such a chapter completed by another hand."

Finally it was finished by the novelist Robert Barr, who was apparently the one Crane himself wished to finish it, should anything happen to him, and *The O'Ruddy* was published three and a half years after Crane's death as "By Stephen Crane and Robert Barr."

The problem for the Craneologists was to decide how much of the work was Stephen's. They had Cora Crane's (Stephen's wife) statement that he had done twenty-five chapters: the book has thirty-three. Others, notably R. W. Stallman, whose definitive *Stephen Crane. A Biography* appeared in 1968, thought otherwise. He states flatly that "Barr in fact wrote three-fourths of the novel, not just the last chapters," and further comments that "Robert Barr saw to it that *The O'Ruddy*'s authorship included his name," footnoted: "Rightly so since Barr wrote most of *The O'Ruddy*." One couldn't fault Stallman's opinion, based upon I don't know what evidence (none was supplied), and another black mark seemed chalked against Cora's veracity.

By one of those serendipities in which this book collecting game abounds, Donald Klopfer, of Random House, who happened to have read this chapter in draft, remarked to me cheerfully that there was no problem—*he had the manuscript.* And so he had. Where it came from he didn't know: his wife, Florence Selwyn, had inherited it from her father. Would I care to look at it? Would I? It is completely in Crane's hand with a few pages by Cora till about a quarter through Chapter XXV. In his work Barr excluded a few of Crane's paragraphs but did nothing else except finish it. Cora is vindicated.

I remember Wilmarth Lewis once expounding to me at length on "the minor joys of amateur pseudo-scholarship" which occasionally reward collector, dealer and librarian in discoveries faulting the literary salons. I know well what he meant.

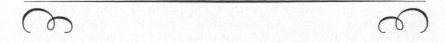

# Edwin Arlington Robinson

SINCE CHILDHOOD DAYS when I first came across Sidney Lanier's *The Boy's King Arthur*, I have been devoted to the Round Table. I am particularly fond of the Tristram and Iseult story and wrote a paper while at Lehigh on the many English redactions of the legend. I subsequently presented Lehigh with a modest collection I had formed.

This was just at the time Edwin Arlington Robinson published the final volume of his Arthurian trilogy, *Tristram* (1927), and I was literally enchanted, when I began work at the Brick Row, to discover that he was an occasional visitor there, a friend of E. Byrne Hackett's, and that I could eventually actually see him and perhaps even talk to him.

Hackett had published the first collected edition of Robinson's *Poems* in 1921 and was about to publish in a limited edition of 250 copies his *Modred*, a fragment deleted from *Lancelot*. He paid Robinson $125 royalty on this, a fact I can prove, as I still have the canceled check Hackett gave me as a souvenir.

The first words I actually ever heard Robinson speak, or rather mutter, were, "Thank you very much, I'm all right." I had come back from lunch and was informed that he was upstairs with the boss. I took a station near the foot of the stairs where I couldn't miss seeing him and waited. Eventually he started down, stumbled, and his lanky length sprawled at my feet, shaken but unhurt. We became good friends, or as good as he would allow a youthful idolator to become, being pleased somewhat by my ability to recite much of his poetry from memory—which I can still do.

He was a star in the book collecting firmament at that time and I find that I once pontificated:

> The first editions of Robert Frost, even making due allowance for the factor of scarcity, which is of prime consideration in any compari-

son of values, have much less commercial worth than those of Edwin Arlington Robinson. Now "time," to use a felicitous phrase of Robinson's, "may have a more reverberant ado" about Frost eventually. In the year 1934, however, the cross-section of the literate reading public represented by the collectors of first editions of contemporary poets is quite clear in its collective mind that time's ado will be about Robinson.

As of thirty-seven years later, I couldn't be more wrong. The last few years Frost has been among the hottest Americans on the market, and Robinson is completely neglected; but this situation will not last, I prophesy: once burnt, stubbornly I return to the candle.

In this same essay ("American First Editions 1900–1933" in *New Paths in Book Collecting*) I referred for the first time in print to "one of the most important of all modern 'proverbial thin sheaves,' Robert Frost's first book, *Twilight*, which appeared in 1894—the collector must resign himself to never possessing a copy unless incredibly lucky, for only one is known and only two were printed."

Louis Untermeyer had told me about this—and that Frost had a copy. I wrote Frost about it and he replied, "the secret that I did such a book got out only by accident. I did call it *Twilight*. I had two copies of it made and bound in leather in 1894 by a job printer in Lawrence, Massachusetts. I have one copy, what became of the other I do not know." He later recalled that he had given it away to a girl in St. Lawrence University. I tried to get Frost to sell his copy but he refused my offer of $400 (I could have gotten $500 for it), which I thought was God's plenty then. After all, I had just sold his first published book, *A Boy's Will*, inscribed by him to Robinson, for $150 (there's an association copy for you!), to Fred Adams, a record for the book at that time.

The subsequent history of *Twilight* is interesting. Captain Louis H. Cohen, of the House of Books, which specialized in first editions of modern literature, and under the able direction of Cohen's widow, Margie, still does, sold it to a notable Frost collector, Earle J. Bernheimer, for a reputed $5,000, in 1940. A decade later Bernheimer disposed of many of his books. I purchased privately a goodly number, including his fine Stephen Vincent Benét collection, now at Harvard, courtesy of B. H. Kilgour, and his Galsworthys, now at the Pierpont Morgan, courtesy of Bradley Martin, but Bernheimer decided to sell his Frosts at auction. So *Twilight* came up and brought $3,500—still the record price for a first edition of a living American author. Waller Barrett was the underbidder and the House of Books the purchaser. It was then sold to a Chicago collector. Barrett was eventually able to acquire it on the very eve of the dedication of the gift of his library to the University of Virginia, but only by purchasing the owner's complete Frost collection. He should not have let it go in its first appearance, he readily admits. Nor should have I!

I rather specialized in Robinson material at this time, selling much to H. Bacon Collamore, who was forming the renowned collection he eventually presented to Robinson's home town, and others. One of the "others" was a quasi-collector, C. C. Auchincloss (known to the trade, and perhaps elsewhere, as "Cold Cash"). He deserves some sort of footnote in bibliographical history, I suspect, for having paid the highest known price for a copy of Wise's fake Reading, 1847, edition of Mrs. Browning's *Sonnets from the Portuguese*, $1,200 from Drake, and being the only collector who, when its true status was revealed, demanded and got his money back.

I was selling Auchincloss some modern literature at the time and pressing Robinson on him. He agreed to purchase as complete a collection as I could assemble, provided I could get Robinson to autograph them to him. I imposed on Robinson's good nature outrageously and he agreed to do so. He was usually sparing with his presentations, unlike Frost. It is, in fact, almost as difficult to get a Robinson book inscribed as it is to get a Frost book uninscribed.

It then turned out that Auchincloss didn't want a mere conventional "Sincerely yours" type signature. He wanted the author to answer pertinent questions about the genesis of the various books, and so on. I agreed to this (there was a modest fee of $10 a volume, as I recall, to be split between Robinson and myself, and this was fair recompense at that time). So I typed, on individual slips, a series of questions which E. A. R. duly answered in autograph—usually briefly. I then tipped these into copies of first editions which I duly delivered to C. C.

This did not please him. He wanted the answers written in the books themselves and proceeded to get them in this manner. He had someone in his concern, who had a fair hand, copy my queries on the end papers of the individual books. He then had Robinson (whom he had never previously met) to a dinner to which I was not invited, and after brandy, had him recopy all his answers in the books themselves! He thus acquired a double set of Robinson's autographs and damn near wrecked my friendship with E. A. R., who was as properly furious as I was humiliated at exposing him to such an ordeal.

Quite nearly three decades passed when I saw a notice that the Auchincloss library was to be sold at the Parke-Bernet Galleries. There, sure enough, were the Robinson books with my pathetically juvenile questions and his answers, duly naked to public scrutiny. I bought most of them back.

As an example of how brash and unknowing a youngster can be and how kindly an elder can treat him, I list here several of the questions and answers. The questions, it will be noted, are verbose; the answers brief but not without interest.

*Modred:*

Q. What was the reason for not incorporating this fragment with *Lancelot* when the latter was published?

A. It seemed out of key.

*The Three Taverns:*

Q. Was the germ of the idea of Tasker Norcross suggested to you through reading Hawthorne's "Christmas Banquet" as is stated by Prof. Cestre?

A. Never read it.

*Captain Craig:*

Q. Amy Lowell said once that "Isaac and Archibald" was the only poem of yours which could be considered completely autobiographical. Is there any truth in this statement?

A. Not much.

*The Town Down the River:*

Q. Was there any reason (other than Horace's advice to poets) that eight years should have elapsed between Captain Craig and this book?

A. My life was rather mixed and uncertain during those years.

*Dionysus in Doubt:*

Q. It has been said that the publication of this book was "ill-advised." Do you feel, even now, that your criticisms of democracy in this poem have been fully justified by the course of events?

A. I should say so—if we call it democracy.

Through Robinson I became acquainted with Lewis Ledoux, a financier, a minor poet and a major authority on Japanese art, particularly prints. He had been a friend and patron of Robinson in the hard days— Robinson had dedicated *Lancelot* to him and had given him a wonderful collection of his manuscripts. I will drop a hint here to collectors, dealers, librarians, etc., about dedicatees: cultivate them! Quite often the author has given them the manuscript of the work in question and they usually have a substantial clutch of other presentations, letters, etc. And very often, authors being as a breed difficult people, dedicatees are no longer on speaking terms with them and are only too happy to cash in. At least I have found it so often enough.

This was not the case with Ledoux, I hasten to add. He refused resolutely to part with his collection during his lifetime and enjoined his estate to keep the collection together in some proper institution.

The collection contained the original autograph rough draft of *Tristram* as well as the final version; the manuscripts of *Matthias at the Door, Talifer,* and other of Robinson's later obscurities. (I once asked him why, in his later years, he didn't write sonnets and lyrics as he once had, and he answered merely, "They don't come that way any more.")

But there was also a great deal of original material from what to my mind is Robinson's finest book, *The Man Against the Sky* (New York, 1916). Here were drafts and final versions of the poems I remember him by: "Ben Jonson Entertains a Man from Stratford," with all its memorable lines. There was also the haunting "Flammonde," "John Gorham," "Old King Cole" and others. It all went eventually to the Library of Congress for $8,750, the gift of Mrs. Whitall, the Ledoux estate getting $7,000.

# Hemingway and the
# Printed Word

WHEN I AM ASKED, or rather challenged, by "constant readers" or professors as to the utility of a modern first edition—"a paperback reprint is just as good; the text is there and that's all that's important"—I answer with a Hemingway story.

Scribner's received a letter in the early 1950's from a German publisher. His story was simple. He was attempting to bring to a German audience representative American literature. Among the translations he published was one of *The Sun Also Rises*. For this he had been hailed before a de-Nazification court and accused of anti-Semitism.

It seems that in the translation he had issued Robert Cohn was a Jew. Was this so in the original edition published by Scribner's in 1926? If it wasn't, he was in real trouble—in fact, he was obviously in trouble already.

The evidence against him, *presented by our own courts*, was a 1949 paperback edition. It had on its front cover the legend, "A Bantam Book, complete and unabridged." The words "complete and unabridged" appear on the back cover; on the final page of text is printed, "This Bantam book contains the complete text of the original edition—Not one word has been changed or omitted." These statements seem to me to be as definitive as English allows.

However, where the German translations would read, for example: "Brett's gone off with men. But they weren't ever Jews," Bantam's read: "They weren't ever steers." *German:* "If she would go about with Cohn and Jews"; *Bantam:* "If she would go about with Cohn and bull-fighters." *German:* "Well, let him not get superior and Jewish"; *Bantam:* "Well, let him not get superior." And so on.

It seemed obvious that this German publisher was insidiously injecting anti-Semitic propaganda into his publications—so "jail" for him!

I never knew the end of this story. Scribner's reported that the paper-back reprint was not what it purported to be and that, of course, the references to Jews were in the original; and took immediate steps to see their reprints were, in the future, untampered with. The affair sent me on a little silent sleuthing, and I found that the Hemingway story was not unique. There was a considerable period during the forties when some-one, somehow, managed to suppress anti-Jewish references in not only his, but other authors' works, J. P. Marquand among them. The words "complete and unabridged, not one word changed or omitted," are just a plain untruth, so far as some paperbacks of that period are concerned. If omissions of such serious nature could be effected without detection, except by accident, how about insertions? Propaganda is a two-edged sword. It is a worrisome thing to know that books are printed which deliberately distort their author's meanings and that such silent censorship can exist. The only refuge for the scholar, or any truth-seeking reader, is a dependence on original sources which libraries preserve. I present this evidence for some enterprising Ph. D. candidate's thesis. Let such a one also investigate, for example, Graham Greene's *The Confidential Agent*. This was, deservedly, a considerable success as a thriller and a smash as a movie. Yet the treatment of certain scenes, characters, motives and ideals differs between the American, English and Dutch editions. And I might note that the Armed Services Edition (New York, 1942) of Housman reprints most of the poems, but with significant omissions, as the admoni-tion in "The Day of Battle" to "Stand and fight and see your slain, And take the bullet in your brain."

I suppose I have had as much Hemingway material in one way and another as anyone else, most of which I couldn't sell, at least not easily. It always puzzled me that this should be so, yet it was. When James Branch Cabell, Edna Millay, E. A. Robinson, Elinor Wylie and so on were being avidly sought by collectors, Ernest was just barely salable. I didn't know why then and I don't know why now.

This fact caused a break between us. In the early 1940's some lad from Yale was sent to interview me about Hemingway by its librarian, James T. Babb, who was an ardent collector of Hemingway's works. The boy wanted to know my idea of the commercial value most Hemingway first editions would have in a hundred years' time. I told him what I con-sidered to be the truth because of the huge first editions issued, which was: "Exactly what they are now, not much over published price; the rarities, his first two works published in France, for example, and a few other limited editions, excepted." Well, the article came out, and as these things have a habit of doing, misquoted me as saying that Hemingway's novels were junk now and would always remain so. This led to a scathing letter from him advising me to keep my pea-picking paws off his reputation and stick to my (obscenity) old and rare. Explanations got me nowhere.

He never accepted criticism gracefully. In the case of Max Eastman, he exploded in Max Perkins' office violently. I was, to my everlasting sorrow, four flights down when this classic erupted, and of all printed versions I have ever seen I incline to credit Eastman's as related in his *Great Companions* as being closest to what I was told at the time. Eastman was, at that time, a Scribner author. He didn't remain one long.

Another Scribner author who fell into Hemingway's disfavor and left the fold was Edmund Wilson. He related the story to me recently while I was trying, unsuccessfully, to extract from him the prodigious journals he has kept since his senior year at Princeton, fifty years ago. He was then doing his famed collection of essays called *The Wound and the Bow*, and Scribner's were to publish it, as they had *I Thought of Daisy* and other Wilson books. One day he was called into conference with Perkins and Scribner about the book, which was already finished, and it was intimated that, perhaps, the part about Hemingway might be modified or, for that matter, even omitted. And so on and so on, with Perkins doing all the talking.

Wilson remained obdurate, and a stubborn "Bunny" Wilson is an immovable object. Finally it came out that Hemingway really objected passionately, and an "either-or" ultimatum was issued. Wilson had, after all, penned the first criticism of Hemingway ever to appear in print, in the *Dial* of 1924, opening: "Mr. Hemingway's poems are not particularly important but his prose is of the first distinction," a review of which he is properly proud. I thought Wilson had said that "to this day I don't know to what Hemingway objected." Reading this statement, Wilson replied: "I do know why because I had a conference with his lawyer: he thought there was a libel on every page. I finally corrected, I think, three erroneous statements of fact."

In any event, Wilson took the "or" and left the firm. He remembers that at the end of the interview with Scribner, the latter said, with his shy, sweet smile, "After all, I had him out to Far Hills for some shooting over the weekend and he's really not very good."

When I asked Wilson the sequel to all this he wrote:

Houghton Mifflin undertook to publish the book, and Hemingway held up its publication by threatening to get out an injunction. It was then that I saw his lawyer and made the corrections. When I wrote Hem. asking to publish his letters in *S[hores] of L[ight]* and referred to the growler he had made about *W & B,* he said that he had forgotten why *Max Perkins* thought it was libellous.

My most vivid early impression of Hemingway is in a room at the Waldorf-Astoria. He was in bed, his leg propped on pillows, clutching a bottle of brandy. A doctor was about to operate on his ankle. The trouble had been that he had tried to show a friend's son how to drop-kick and had stuck his foot through a mirror. There were with him several Spaniards, pretty high in diplomatic and military circles.

The grand idea was for me to return to Spain with Hemingway and bring back to America such treasures, from monasteries, as illuminated manuscripts, incunabula, Columbus relics and so on, to be sold for the benefit of the Loyalist cause. I was, of course, all for it and got substantial promises of backing from Belle da Costa Greene of the Pierpont Morgan Library. Somehow the deal eventually fell through, to my dismay. The State Department's hand was indicated.

I had frequently asked Hemingway for any stray manuscripts and so on which he might have around, with little luck. His habits then were, apparently, to have his final draft typed and sent to Scribner's and destroy the original autograph versions. One day he told me that an ex-secretary of his living in Havana had his original manuscript of *The Green Hills of Africa.* She had typed it for him when he couldn't afford to pay for such a job and had accepted the original in full payment. She was now married and pregnant, and thought the manuscript might be worth something to somebody. It was, to Scribner's, the cost of the baby, doctor, hospital and all. It was, and remains, the only complete, full-length Hemingway manuscript ever on the market. It was written in pencil on over five hundred yellow legal-sized foolscap leaves with heavy corrections, deletions and so on and, invariably, sloped down like the end of a rainbow at the right-hand margins. It was around for years, priced $2,000, without any takers. I finally persuaded Waller Barrett to locate it in Virginia.

When *For Whom the Bell Tolls* was about to be published I inquired if Hemingway had the manuscript of this one and, if so, could I have it and for how much. It seems it was available; he wanted a car, a good car, a Cadillac, no less. This was then not much more than $2,000 again, so I made a deal and sold it, only to have embarrassment on both sides crop up. It turned out that he had given the manuscript to the dedicatee, his wife, Martha Gellhorn, who had no intention of swapping it for a car, even a Cadillac. My only souvenirs of this job are a copy of the advance issue (one of only fifteen done and the rarest of all major Hemingways) in the Lilly Library, inscribed to J. K. Lilly, Jr., by the author, and the original painting which was used as the dust wrapper, which decorates the entrance to my library.

My own copy, inscribed "To Dave Randall to hold for a rise," forms, with the rest of my collection, the basis of the memorial in his high school library at Oak Park, Illinois.

The only inscribed copy of *For Whom the Bell Tolls* which has ever appeared on the open market that I know of was in the Frank J. Hogan sale in 1945, where it brought $90. This was inscribed "To Frank J. Hogan (and he can send me some more Scotch if he wishes) Best always Ernest Hemingway." The story of this is that I had sold the manuscript to Hogan, and when I couldn't deliver it, persuaded Hemingway to inscribe a copy of the advance issue to him, promising that he would get a bottle of Scotch. Instead, Hogan sent him a case! In return for which Hemingway inscribed all his other works for him.

A most amusing, irritating and baffling story concerning Hemingway (and Thomas Wolfe) inscribed books revolves around a Christmas office party at Scribner's where both happened to be present. Some midwestern female collector (that's absolutely all I can remember about her) had sent Scribner's a batch of Hemingway and Wolfe firsts she had collected, in the prayerful hope that the authors would sign them for her. In the gaiety (an advisedly used word) of the occasion, they did. They delightedly wrote full-page inscriptions of the most intimate nature in each other's books, signing each other's names.

These were shipped out next day to the lady, whose name and abode have faded into limbo—for all I recall, she could have been a Hoosier. Sometime—and if it hasn't happened already, it will—some knowledgeable handwriting expert is going to look at the Wolfe books and exclaim, "That's not his autograph." Ditto with Hemingway. And they will, of course, be right.

There have been stories and rumors of trunks of Hemingway manuscripts recovered in Paris, and so on, which may be true. All I know for sure is that the only manuscript of his to be offered at public sale was that of a portion of *Death in the Afternoon*, at the Parke-Bernet Galleries in 1959, which brought $13,000. But that was Texas money.

My favorite of all the Hemingway books I now have care of is *Death in the Afternoon,* which is inscribed to Gertrude Stein in round-robin form: "A bitch is a bitch is a bitch is a bitch. Before the fruits of marriage came, marriage came." I prize this even above our dedication copy of *A Farewell to Arms.*

It was Scribner's custom to produce, not for the trade or for sale but for the personal use of Hemingway and a few others, a very limited advance issue of his books. This was always done by taking the very first run of sheets off the press—usually fifteen or twenty-five—and having them specially bound. This is what happened in the case of *Across the River and into the Trees* (New York, 1950).

Copies exist in several major libraries, catalogued as "first issue of the first edition, before publication." These all contain, on the flyleaf, the following penciled note:

> One of twenty-five copies before the following corrections were made:
> Page 21, line 26: 'Papadopohi' changed to 'Papadoli.'
> Page 86, line 21, second 'how' omitted.
> The blue cloth binding on these copies was experimental.
> The first edition (75,000 copies published Sept. 7, 1950) was in black cloth.
>
> David A. Randall<br>August 7, 1950

This description has also gotten into a standard bibliography, and it is one of the most sought-for of all Hemingway's firsts. No copy has ever yet appeared at public auction.

Well, after I had left Scribner's I ran into the manager of its North River press. "By the way," he said, "I hope I didn't cross you up on Hemingway's *Trees.*" "Of course not," I replied, "how could you?" "Well, you know I had run off the entire first edition when I suddenly thought: 'My God, Randall and his first printing!' So I took some discarded plates we had lying around and ran off a special twenty-five for you and put on a different cloth binding. Betcha never woulda known, hadn't I told you."

I frequently use this story to warn students and bibliographers not to take uncritically any statement any publisher, printer or author makes about any book. This happens to be as foolproof a case as I know. (1) The book is bound in a different cloth than any other edition or reprint. (2) It does have errors corrected in all other editions and reprints. (3) It has a signed statement to this effect by an employee of the firm publishing it, signed and dated a month before the book was issued. (4) The proof sheets contain the errors. (5) It is, therefore, exactly what it purports to be. Q. E. D.

The logic of the reasoning cannot be faulted. But there isn't an element of truth in it. A truly critical typographical eye, knowing the facts, and with an early copy run of the first edition and this "pre-issue" before him, might just possibly detect type degeneration. I can't. Nor can a collating machine. All of which goes to prove an old contention of mine. Bibliography is an art and not a science, and when the boys in the front room begin to try to tell me that, on the basis of a logical sequence, such a copy *had* to precede such another, I remember Papa.

# Wolfe and Fitzgerald

**M**AXWELL PERKINS and I never understood each other. I admired him and I think he liked me. At least, even with all the trouble I caused him on various occasions, he never gave overt signs of actively disliking me. Perhaps he was too gentle to show it. I could never fathom his hold over his authors, more than he could my interest in a book as a physical object, apart from its contents. We would sit sometimes at the men's bar at the old Ritz, or at Cherio's, and I would try to explain this to him, and he would listen. But it never got through. I sometimes wonder if his secret as an editor was mainly his wonderful listening talent.

Editors are seldom antiquarians—at least I never knew but one who was; they are too concerned with next year's books to worry about past achievements. They have, as Scribner editor Roger Burlingame put it, "to tease, cajole, humor, placate and scold angry and brooding men and women who have found a superfluous semi-colon or refused to believe a royalty report or searched the *Times* in vain for an advertisement or been unable to buy a copy of their precious book at a bookstore." Max could never understand my enthusiasm for his own library. He was reputed to have more books dedicated to him than any of his contemporaries—and not all by Scribner authors, by any means. One of the most moving is Thomas Wolfe's:

> To Maxwell Evarts Perkins. A great editor and a brave and honest man, who stuck to the writer of this book through times of bitter hope-lessness and doubt and would not let him give in to his own despair, a work to be known as "Of Time and the River" is dedicated with the hope that all of it may be in some way worthy of the loyal devotion and patient care which a dauntless and unshaken friend has given to each part of it, and without which none of it could have been written.

It was my work habit to take the Third Avenue El to 53rd Street and walk to my office in the Scribner bookstore, passing the motley lot of secondhand pawn and curio shops which then cluttered around the neighborhood. Some were run by acquaintances, and on occasion a book or print of interest would show up in a window. But I never expected to see Max Perkins' library in one of them. Yet that morning, there it was! In a secondhand shop, which was not even a secondhand *book*shop, luckily. First editions of Hemingway, Lardner, Fitzgerald, Galsworthy, Barrie—name them and there they were, many inscribed and some dedicated to Perkins. I rushed in, of course, threatened the proprietor with police action for handling stolen property, ascertained that "only a couple" had been sold that morning since he put them in the window, got his promise to sell no more, and then huffed and puffed to Scribner's and Perkins with the startling news that his apartment had been burgled.

Only to find that it hadn't! He had moved a lot of stuff from his New York apartment to his home in New Canaan. The books? Well, he had told the janitor to get rid of anything left and probably this included the books. His New Canaan home, after all, was full of them anyway, and it was merely a question of space. He couldn't see, really, what the fuss was about, and why my red face? Wasn't it a little early in the morning?

He finally agreed, a little reluctantly, that it was *infra dig* to have these personal dedication and presentation copies being sold all over town. He had no idea of their commercial value and cared less, nor did he have the slightest idea what they had been sold for. But I could go ahead and get them back.

Thus deflated, I returned to the dealer in somewhat of a spot, my bargaining position seriously weakened. He hadn't been handling stolen property and was pretty sore that I had intimated he had. So what was I going to do about it? What I did was to buy the books at a price, it turned out eventually, approximately ten times what they had been sold for—a mere fraction of their true worth, to be sure, but news Perkins received with polite incredulity.

Shortly after Tom Wolfe's death we had a conference about the estate. Despite the publicized Wolfe-Perkins "break," Max was left as his literary executor. Were Wolfe's manuscripts, documents, correspondence and so on worth anything? I assured Perkins they were.

There had been trouble and lawsuits over some of Wolfe's manuscripts while he was alive. These are detailed in Elizabeth Nowell's biography. By coincidence, Wolfe's lawyers were the respected firm of Mitchell and Van Winkle, the Van Winkle who was the collector of sporting books and with whom I had collaborated on a bibliography of the American Robert Smith Surtees, Henry William Herbert, alias "Frank Forester," author of, among scores of books, the classic *The Warwick Woodlands* (Philadelphia, 1845). Though not at all generally well known now, and long out of print, it is prominent enough to be included in the Grolier *One Hundred Influential American Books Printed before 1900*. It was included, I suspect, at the insistence of that great sportsman and collector, the late Harry T. Peters, most of whose renowned collection is now at Yale.

Herbert was, really, a remittance man, a descendant of English peers (the son of the first Earl of Carnarvon), educated at Eton and Cambridge, who, after a colorful career in America, died by his own hand at the age of fifty-one. His works popularized in America the British standard of sport for sport's sake. As Harry Worcester Smith said, "Frank Forester lifted the sport of woodcock and partridge hunting from the shadowy ways of the pot hunter to a position where sportsmen were proud of their dogs and their guns." Besides his numerous sporting works he wrote twenty-five novels, not a single one of which I was ever able to finish, and translated fourteen works from the French.

I once had a letter of his father to him, sending him some money and advising him to invest it in "something good at 10 per cent" and adding he would have sent more if only Americans would get some sense and elect a "safe man," like Henry Clay, President.

I was given authority to dispose of Wolfe's literary remains to the best advantage to the estate. Two conditions were attached to this chore. One was that Scribner's were not to profit in any way from their sale—after all, Perkins was a Scribner vice-president and would stand for no conflict of interest. This ruled out my buying them, which I dearly wished to do. The second condition was that if possible they be kept together in perpetuity in some institution. Modest as Max was, he knew that eventually Wolfe would again come into his own, and that he, as an editor, would be judged largely on his relationship with Tom. He wanted the records kept intact and available.

Curious as it may seem now, thirty years later, Wolfe, at his early death, was not universally admired, or indeed given much chance in many authoritative minds of attracting posterity's attention. The current cult won't believe this, but "listen, my children, and you shall hear."

I remember once discussing Wolfe's eventual place in American letters with Max, who remarked that it was permanently established because "there will always be a new generation of sophomores to discover and delight in him." He also said that he knew from the very start that he, and other Scribner employees, would inevitably figure in Tom's novels, as Wolfe was totally incapable of writing about what he had not experienced.

Stories of the Wolfe-Perkins rift have always amused me. They reinforce my conviction that most biography is fiction. The *Saturday Review* once published an issue devoted almost wholly to the question: "Did Thomas Wolfe Kill Maxwell Perkins?" Swarms of letters were later printed supporting one view or another. Not a single article or letter revealed any gleam of the truth, which was the attitude of Mrs. Perkins, to my mind. Max and Tom used to argue religion endlessly, as their letters attest. Mrs. Perkins' conversion to Catholicism and, probably, Tom's inclination toward Nazism caused sad conflict. None of all this is even hinted at by the "father image" and other explanations so widely advanced.

The sheer mass of Wolfe's corpus, when it was gathered from various spots to a large room on the seventh floor of Scribner's, was appalling. The man was a magpie, an accumulator, who never threw away a thing. There were, in a jumbled heap, some estimated 40,000 pages of manuscript, mostly in notebooks or on the legal yellow paper he used, in pencil. Drafts, short stories, plays, novels and parts of novels, published and unpublished, in drafts, revisions, re-revisions. Mountains of manuscript. Correspondence by the bale and bag. Literally. Letters by the scores were tied with twine and stuffed into laundry bags along with canceled checks, old socks, beer bottle openers, corrected themes from his New York University teaching days, drafts of letters and letters never sent plus every letter he had ever received.

This was but the beginning. There was the library. Textbooks, presentations from contemporaries, torn often, or disemboweled. I suppose when a page or chapter took his attention he ripped it out and stuck it in his pocket for future reference. What scholarly instincts I have were enthralled. Here was treasure-trove indeed. Suppose this had been, say, Swift's library, or Poe's?

The first offer of the collection was to the University of North Carolina. No interest. Next to a parade of libraries. You name them, they had their chances. Again, nothing. For one thing, the bulk was immense and the difficulty, in technical jargon, of "accessioning" it, was going to cost, oh so much. Anyway, no thanks.

The price was $5,000. The basis of the price was that fetched by the original manuscript of *Look Homeward, Angel,* which had sold at public auction in 1936 for $1,750, at, said one and all, a fantastically inflated price because of its having been donated by the dedicatee Aline Bernstein to one of the charity auctions for the Spanish Loyalists. It had been bought by the dealer Gabriel Wells and presented to Harvard as a tax gimmick, said gossip. It was obviously worth a third of what it had brought. So $5,000 was exorbitant.

Eventually an old collector friend, William B. Wisdom, Sr., of New Orleans, heard about the trove. Bill had a good collection of Sherlock Holmes, through which I first met him, a remarkable collection of Huey Long, and other assorted bookish interests. He had known Wolfe personally, admired him immensely and already had a very considerable collection, including a file of the Carolina *Tarheel*, the biweekly newspaper of which Wolfe was editor. He also visited Mrs. Roberts in Asheville, (Margaret Leonard in *Look Homeward, Angel*, Wolfe's inspirational teacher, "mother of his spirit") and acquired their correspondence. It didn't take him long to get the collection, which was eventually sent to him in nine packing cases, two feet high, two feet wide and four feet long. Other shipments followed and Wisdom went on a crusade to obtain everything from family and friends. He succeeded so well that I don't think there is a comparable collection comprising an author's records from the cradle to the grave—at least not one I know of. He recently wrote me that he had acquired "after much pleading in the name of posterity the last x-ray photographs of Wolfe's brain. My argument here was that in the future some vicious detractors might say that Wolfe died of paresis and these highly perishable x-ray plates would prove that he died of tuberculosis meningitis."

Wisdom saw only a small sample of the collection before he purchased it but agreed to take what had already been uncovered with the promise that whatever else might turn up would be his also. Few collectors have seen their judgment justified within so short a time—aesthetically and commercially. The Wisdom collection of Wolfe at Harvard is almost as well known as its Keats collection at this time. One single letter of Wolfe's recently sold for $1,000 to Wisdom.

The very day that the deal with Wisdom was closed I happened to meet Harry Hansen, who was then writing a book column for the *New York World Telegram*, and told him the story. The next day he printed it and the day after that I arrived at Scribner's, late as usual, to be informed that the "fifth floor" was frantically seeking me. In his editorial office I found Perkins, white hat on, a weeping female and her lawyer. Were her letters among those mentioned in that newspaper article? If so, by golly, she wanted them back, or else. While she was there the phone rang and another gal, and another lawyer, were asking for an appointment. I couldn't even tell them whether the letters were there or not. Among thousands? In laundry bags? Unsorted? And even if they were, the women had no legal right to them. They could control publication, but once the letters had been written and mailed they had no power of recall.

But, it seemed, problems were involved. Some of the letters were indiscreet. What about blackmail if some scoundrel at Harvard got hold of them? And other things? Perkins was pretty perturbed about all this and seemed inclined to blame my big mouth for the mess, perhaps properly.

All I could think of was to call Wisdom in New Orleans and tell him the story. It was his property and he was, by location and what I knew of him, a Southern Gentleman. When the situation was explained to him and he was asked to give back to the ladies their correspondence, his answer was a fast NO. When I explained to him that these were probably not really important, were a mere tiny bit of what he had purchased, he replied, "What would you think of someone who destroyed Fanny Brawne's letters to Keats?" On my remonstration that Wolfe wasn't Keats, Wisdom reminded me that that wasn't what I said when I sold him the lot.

Eventually a compromise of sorts was reached. The letters were not returned but were to be segregated and kept apart at Harvard. Came a day when the sorting out was to be done. The letters were dumped on long tables, and it soon became apparent that the principals were searching for, and reading amid weeping and screaming—not their own letters, but *each other's*. The final assorting was concluded by disinterested parties.

A while later Max took me to lunch with Aline Bernstein, a plump and bright-eyed matron whom I had met occasionally in the bookstore and to whom Tom dedicated *Look Homeward, Angel.* Her story was very simple. She had a voluminous correspondence of Tom's and Harvard was asking her to give it to them. Was this the place for them? Indeed it was, I assured her. After all, Harvard had so much that this would fit in beautifully. She had not the slightest objection to being known as Wolfe's Brawne. From the very beginning she had been his brain, she assured me.

Asked if the letters were worth much commercially, I answered they were (Tom's reputation was beginning an upswing). Her reply was that she had always hoped to edit the letters herself—annotating as only she could—but she didn't know when she would do it, and meanwhile they might as well be at Harvard for safekeeping. But *giving* them was another thing.

"Things that are given people for nothing," she observed, "are usually valued at just that." She wanted no money for herself, of course, nor could her name be attached to their sale in any manner—even in a transaction going through Scribner's books. Nor did Perkins wish Scribner's to have any part of it. Eventually the letters were turned over to me and they were acquired by Wisdom for Harvard. I was paid directly, put the check in my account and, after it cleared, sent my personal check to Mrs. Bernstein's favorite charity. All lovely and anonymous. Except that my check went, at her designation, to the United Jewish Appeal.

Now I have not had much experience with fund raisers, but I found out that when, out of the morning mail, a check for a substantial sum emerges from a completely new contributor, wheels turn. I was suddenly deluged with mail, offers of dinners, invitations to banquets—at one of which I was introduced as "our largest contributor from Westchester County"—and asked to match my previous generosity! No one believed me when I tried to tell them the fact—not the truth, that I couldn't—that it was the first and last check they would ever get from me. I was accused of modesty.

There are gaps in the Bernstein-Wolfe correspondence. These are accounted for, she explained to me at Armonk when I went to get them, by the fact that Tom, in one of his rampages, tossed everything of his he could lay his hands on into the fireplace. These letters had survived because they were in a chest under her bed.

Some have been published, but not unexpurgated. A typical salutation, as I recall, was, "My heavy-breasted grey-hair Jewish bitch, I love the stench of your plum-colored arm-pits," and descended from there. Tom was not a nice boy. She once remarked to me that falling in love with him was akin to a Japanese maiden's deliberate jump into a volcano. She knew it was to be fatal but couldn't resist.

She gave me, as a souvenir of our experiences, two letters, with the admonition only that I not part with them during her lifetime. One was a letter she wrote Tom on his birthday but never mailed. The other was a seventeen-page fragment of a letter he had written her. Here they are:

Armonk, N.Y.

Dear Tom –
    I cannot let your birthday go without sending you some word. I have read in the paper that you have finished and delivered your book to

Scribner's, and I hope to see it soon. I have always, beside me at my bed table, the copy, the first one, of *Look Homeward Angel*, that you gave me on your birthday, Oct. 3, 1929. It is a wonderful book, and I believe you received just praise for it. I have often been tempted to destroy your written* inscription in my anger at you. But it sounds so good and true, if you could see it you would burn, at least you would if you had the power to feel humanly. Our lives were so closely woven, for so long, that you are still part of my tissue.

I have been ill for a long time, and finally I am forced to stop my work. I have two more plays coming on, but they are in such shape that my assistant can finish them. I wish you would go to see Judgment Day, it is exciting and I think would interest you. I enjoyed working on it, and it was a fine experience working with Elmer Rice. I have to take to my bed, after moving down to New York on Monday. I am so depressed about it, for it will be a long time until I can work again, but I am going to write, there is so much to say. I have written again the stories that you refuse to return to me, and I hope someday to have them published. It is an experience that should not go unrecorded. But that will be a long time, and I would first ask your consent, only you choose to behave like a God on Olympus and will make no utterance to me. You also behave as though I had injured you, instead of an opposite state of affairs. After all, it would not have hurt you to read my story, the story of the child that still lives in me, and that I first wrote for you.

I have heard you rail against the world and people, I have heard you curse their selfishness and cruelty, it is all so easy to do. It is not easy to be honest, nor kind, nor faithful, that is for a man.

Look into yourself Tom, on your birthday. Add the sum of yourself, and think well what it totals. The world is in a bad fix, and to me the outlook is dark, but the only reform can come with the reformation of the individual in himself, and not in the State.

You were born with a great talent, and many people envy you. I know you are not to be envied. The very use of the talent itself is such agony and I know the bitterness of your soul.

I know we will never speak with each other again, I hope we never will. Nevertheless, you are still in my heart of hearts, and I can only wish you well.

Aline

Tom's letter to her:

Paris Wednesday night
Dec. 1 (1930).

My Dear:—

I came here from London on Sunday; I am staying right in the heart of Paris, thirty steps from the Rue St. Honoré, and seventy or eighty

---

* *Look Homeward, Angel* has the printed dedication, "To A.B." The copy he gave her, now at Harvard, is inscribed:

"To Aline Bernstein on my twenty-ninth birthday. I present her with this, the first copy of my first book. This book was written because of her and is dedicated to

from the Madeleine. The place is called the Hotel Burgundy: it is in the
Rue Duphot just across from Prunier's, the great fish and lobster place.
I have a good sized room at the back, perfectly quiet, for thirty francs a
day. And I have dined and wined myself sick these three days past—
at Webers, the Regency, Sams and A La Fontaine Gaillon, where we
went two or three times.

I got a letter from you today—sent on from Oxford. It was the first
in two weeks—the longest I have ever had to wait for one, although I
know you have waited longer for mine, and after I cabled to New York
the other day I found two cables from you—one probably in answer to
my own.

Your letter is bristling again with news of the theatre—I set my teeth
into my lip and bear it, although it seems you never learn what you do
to me, even though, at dull times, and drugged times, and bored times,
and mad times I have written you in bad, dull, dreary letters, which
nevertheless contain some of the most extraordinary things that have
ever been written in letters, all out of my desire to reach your head
or your heart with a particle, a filament of what I am and what I feel.
You must know by now that after what has happened to me these last
few months the theatre is the last thing I want to hear about: at the
present time in particular, to mention it is like rubbing salt pork in a
bleeding wound—I want to forget it. My few last days in London I spent
in going to crook plays and mystery plays and a jolly play about Pepys;
and my delight here in Paris will be in revues and farces. I lose myself
wholeheartedly in these things now; I get a great comfort in simply
being made to laugh, or amused, and I have begun to look at these
bright gimcracks again with the wonder of a child: I forget any heart-
beat I might ever have felt for my lost kingdom in watching and believing these silly little pieces with all the happiness of an amateur, for
getting whatever nonsense about technique and probabilites I might ever
have known. And one of the great horrors of New York that I have is
hearing again about the O'Neills and Howards and Romains and Wer-
fels, and having you bring me again the horrible yellow cover of the
Theatre Arts to show me pictures of your sets with a wise article kicked
together with all the jargon I know and despise so well. You mustn't,
that's all, and if you tell me, after what has passed between us, and after
I have come back 4000 miles to you, that you must, that it is your life,
I will say prayers to your God to water with his tears the shrivelled seed
that is your soul (Yes, in spite of the S. 'S, I'll do it)

But, believe me, my dear, I don't mind hearing about your part in it,
and I believe no one is so proud as I am of your successes. Only, I have
sometimes wished, when I was so sore and bitter over my own dreary
failure, that you wouldn't beat me over the heart so unmercifully with

---

her. At a time when my life seemed desolate, and when I had little faith in myself, I
met her. She brought me friendship, material and spiritual relief, and love such as I
had never had before. I hope therefore that readers of my book will find at least part
of it worthy of such a woman. Thomas Wolfe. Oct 3, 1929

notoriety. After all, it's a triumph I could enjoy over a ten year old boy, of intelligence and sensitiveness, but I couldn't do it, and you are just as far beyond (and above) me as I am beyond a ten year old child.

Thursday (Rather Friday)

It's three o'clock in the morning, I went to La Chauve Souris tonight, Cutey-cutey-cute Stuff   Are any of you any better than Cute Stuff. I am Nothing, but are you   Do you remember when you saw me on the boat how you told me that Joyce's Exiles was "the greatest play that had ever been written," You did you know   It was because you didn't know me, I am sure you would not have stomach to say it to me now But you are such a fool to show off so to me   Why do you degrade your self so? You are beyond all that. And your friend the tall woman who has been your Procuress told me someone had written a book about her or spoken of her in it. And in your last letter you spoke of Pygmalion, and of the glorious things in it   It hurts me and worries me just as when the Playhouse woman tried to tell me how much was "in" the Spanish play   I'm afraid you're exulting again or someone who gets printed has talked to you, I looked at Shaw recently   They have bound him with myrtle in New York, but I'm afraid he's Cute Stuff too   I remember Pygmalion—It's a funny play but he's one of the Little Fellows the world—believe me—has been full of them   Why didn't you read the Gulliver's Travels I gave you over   You would see what I mean   We must begin as children again   Swift was simply terrific Do you know you boast of being a self made woman "without education" You have done this certain times   And two or three times you remind me maidenly that I have twit-twit-twitted you with "getting things done"   You are coyly definitely proud of it.

I have the contempt of people such as you because I do not get things done, but for 16 hours a daye I broode upon my spirit  –

Sunday Morning 2: AM

My Dear: I got a letter from you this morning; it reassured and calmed me unmeasurably   You know I am beyond reason when I do not hear from you—I have been terribly disappointed because I have had only two letters from you since I left Oxford. You make a great mistake when you are busy on a show (or in some less honorable affair) and do not write me often. I take it bitterly to heart; even in these past weeks when the treachery that has made your whole life stink has crept in again, you should have written me again and again about it, describing in the grandest manner the Beautiful Thing that has happened which you had never known as a Young Girl; and which now has come to you to your Little Hour of Life I notice with deep emotion that you have "given yourself to me in your mind"—oh good good good! I will be content. All flesh is as grass—You are faithful in all the immortal parts— you may open your legs to everything under 80—to all the Nice Young Men what does it matter.—I am promised the most satisfying union of intellectual concubinage. I may lie with your mind, no matter who and what lies with your baser parts.

Oh my dear, at the hearts core I can never again really blame you—never never. Terribly these two years gone have I learned mercy: in my heart a great flashing gem has hardened slowly out of pain. I was thinking today how all my life I have held some loved thing against my life until one day I saw that the beloved thing had gone, that there remained a lovely and imperishable image, and that somewhere far belived, and far below in the tropic and abysmal filth of life moved something wretched, leprous, walled in its own pollution out of which, nevertheless, this image had come. And do you know that my images are unbroken—all, all unbroken.

Sunday Night

My Dear:—I'm trying to get away to Strasburg and then to Germany tomorrow. I'm depressed about the book—I haven't touched it in two weeks. And travelling now I don't know how much I'll get done. I went to the Louvre this afternoon and to the opera tonight to hear *Faust* Oh weary weary weary! The ultro folly of this soup they call grand opera struck me for the first time—ten swords, and the Devil in red tights, and a Hell-scene full of Degas ballet dancers.

I have begun to be a-weary of the sun—and there's no sun. I want to ask you certain questions which I cannot escape You say you hope I am there for New Years, but that you must pass it with your family in order to avoid hurting their feelings. Do you not feel this thing at last deserves a certain amount of openness? Do you not think if I came back, that there should not be some attempt made to lift and enhance the quality of our relation? Are you not bothered at times by the thought that your life may become merely greedy and selfish and ruinous to another's, that—all sins admitted—you may wreak out a grievous wrong on much the highest spirit you have ever known simply by celling it in the dungeons of clandestine adultery—with all the others

You have never met or answered this fairly or　(end of letter)

Other Wolfeian episodes included a sad one with John S. Terry, who had graduated from the University of North Carolina in 1918 and become an English professor at New York University. He was editor of *Thomas Wolfe's Letters to His Mother* (Scribner's, 1943) and aspired to be his official biographer. He was a cripple, dragging himself around on crutches with the help of a sort of major-domo chauffeur, when he left his Brooklyn home at all. Perkins allowed him to borrow some of Scribner's (and Wisdom's) Wolfe material, and when I tried to get it back several years later, Terry denied ever having had it. This entailed police-protected visits to his Brooklyn home where he existed in incredible squalor—he had threatened to cane Perkins and brain me—and eventually we got our manuscripts back.

A gayer acquaintanceship was with Belinda Jelliffe, whose autobiography, *For Dear Life*, Scribner's had published in 1936—and a remarkable book that one is. She had battled her way from a wretched North Carolina farm, in true Horatio Alger fashion, through backbreaking and menial jobs, to a position as a trained nurse in New York. Her first remembered prayer was "Please, God, send me some books." She ran away from home with fifty cents and her spare clothes on her back so she could get more learning than was possible in rural schoolhouses. She eventually married Dr. Smith Ely Jelliffe, the well-known psychiatrist who, she once carefully explained to me, found her much more of a problem than any of his paying customers and was so fascinated that, she not being able to afford his fees, he married her. That, she remarked, was really taking your work to bed with you.

It was inevitable, of course, that she meet and know Wolfe in New York, and her stories of him were hilarious. She gave him his first typewriter, which he never learned to use. She had some correspondence, books and so on of his, which I eventually acquired for Wisdom and Harvard. She was one of the few people I know who was intimate with Tom and escaped unhurt. Her background was similar and she was too gay a soul to be browbeaten by the likes of him.

The last time I saw Wolfe was on a Saturday afternoon when he came into the store pretty plastered—an awesome sight—to cash a check. I couldn't do it, strictly against orders, but I offered to lend him what I had. He refused this, reeled down the aisle, bouncing customers off each elbow, shouting, "Randall is a crook, Randall is a crook," until he disappeared out onto Fifth Avenue. In a minute he reappeared, looked over the startled ensemble and remarked, "God damn it, you're all crooks," and left.

The next estate settlement Max and I were involved in was Scott Fitzgerald's. I was introduced, in Max's office, to an impressive and amusing gentleman, the Honorable John Biggs. He must have been amusing to have been Scott Fitzgerald's roommate. The impressiveness came from his being a Federal Judge, no less, and noted as one who had slapped a $7,000,000 fine on a corporation and, furthermore, made it stick.

The immediate problem was removed some four decimal points to the left. The Judge was executor of Scott's estate—such as it was—and one of its few assets then was his library—his manuscripts, letters, books and so on. An offer had been made, and Biggs, knowing nothing about such things, sought expert advice. Was the offer fair and one which he, as a prudent executor, should accept?

I could not give an offhand opinion as I would have to see the material. But for a preliminary opinion even a casual checklist would suffice. The Judge had it. Sadly inadequate, but something. The offer was for $750.

Without looking at Max I said to the Judge, "Scribner's will give you now a check for $3,750. If, and I find it hard to believe, you were offered that paltry sum, whoever made it was either a fool or a knave, if not both. After I see the library the price may go up but—$3,750 of now."

Well, it seemed that the material was mostly in Judge Biggs's home in Wilmington, Delaware. I could see it there, but, Max explained, not to purchase it for Scribner's. That old devil again: a conflict of interest. We were all one family, and, as a matter of fact, Judge Biggs had written a fascinating first novel which Scribner's had published years before, and he was working on another. Zelda, Scott's widow, needed every cent which could be raised. That was what mattered.

At this time, the whirligig of taste being what it is, Fitzgerald was on a downbeat. He had even been dropped from the current edition of Merle Johnson's inclusive book collector's *vade mecum, American First Editions*, and it was pretty impossible to get lower than that.

A visit to Wilmington revealed, in the Biggs's garret, just among casual items, as I recall, a Joyce *Ulysses* inscribed with a sentiment that Joyce wished he could write with the feeling for words Fitzgerald had. Manuscripts, scenarios, letters, diaries, peacocks' tails, doctors' reports of Zelda's condition at various times—material of the most intimate nature.

For $750 yet! It turned out that the offer had been made by the Princeton University Library. When I pointed out to the then librarian, Julian Boyd, that, in my opinion, the heirs were being robbed, I was reminded tartly that Princeton was not a charitable institution, nor was its library established to support indigent widows of, and I quote, "second-rate, Midwest hacks" just because they happened to have been lucky enough to have attended Princeton—unfortunately for Princeton.

When I inquired of the librarian if he would care to go down in Princeton's history as one who refused to purchase Fitzgerald's library, he allowed he would—rather than as one who was remembered as "squandering" funds on purchasing it.

I wasn't particularly surprised at this attitude. I had had to force-feed Princeton into obtaining Ray Stannard Baker's notable Woodrow Wilson collection—now one of its glories. A vivid spot during this sordid transaction is my remembrance of a weekend spent with Baker at his home in Amherst. We had just gotten into the Second World War, and spent one long evening listening to him recall Wilson-Versailles and the high hopes which had vanished, somehow.

At that time, though, the name Wilson was a nasty one at Princeton—perhaps the only thing he and Fitzgerald had in common, except a love of America. Perhaps it still is. Certainly Princeton stretched things a bit in naming their library.

Yet they got the Fitzgerald collection eventually, for free, after much fussing, including their ukase that no books were to be purchased from Scribner's while I was employed there. Considering the intimate Scribner-Princeton relations over more than a century, this was a considerable accomplishment on my part, as I figured it. Scott Fitzgerald's daughter gave the collection to them.

Perkins always told me that Fitzgerald was the greatest potential talent he ever worked with. This sounds like something from a Hollywood column, but I think I know what he meant. I was lucky when the fairies passed out gifts—the urge for creativeness was omitted. Perkins was patient, as his marvelous letters attest, with an author's struggle to achieve, but he couldn't sympathize with those who wouldn't continue the struggle and kept putting things off till tomorrow. He remarked to me, just before he died, "These people think they will exist forever." His admiration for the fall and rise of Fitzgerald was unbounded.

There has always been speculation as to who "discovered" Scott—Tarkington is one candidate, Henry van Dyke another. It really was the Irishman Shane Leslie. The first intimation anyone at Scribner's had of Scott's existence was a letter of May 6, 1918.

> 2127 Leroy Place
> Washington
> May 6, 1918

Dear Mr. Scribner,
    I am sending you the MS of a book by a Princeton boy a friend of mine and a descendant of the author of the Star spangled banner. He calls himself the descendant of Benedict Arnold in his autobiography in the approved style of modern youth! I have read it through and in spite of its disguises it has given me a vivid picture of the American generation that is hastening to war. I marvel at it's crudity and its cleverness. It is naive in places, shocking in others, painful to the conventional and not without a touch of ironic sublimity especially toward the end. About a third of the book could be omitted without losing the impression that it is written by an American Rupert Brooke. I knew the poetic Rupert Brooke and this is a prose one, though some of the lyrics are good and apparently original. It interests me as a boy's book and I think gives expression to that real American youth that the sentimentalists and super patriots are so anxious to drape behind the canvas of the Y.M.C.A. tent. Though Scott Fitzgerald is still alive it has a literary value. Of course when he is killed it will also have a commercial value. Before

leaving for France he has committed it to me and will you in any case
house it in your safe for the time? If you feel like giving a judgment
upon it, will you call upon me to make any alterations or perform whatever duties accrue to a literary sponsor.

Without tying you down in any way, accept our best thanks in advance as well as my apology for intruding upon your good will yet
again—

Yours faithfully
Shane Leslie

Perkins' reputation as an attractor of young talent was not hurt by
Fitzgerald's association with him—a fact he was the first to admit. Here
are some, to my mind, sound observations of Scott's on Wolfe and
Hemingway and himself, taken from letters he wrote Perkins.

1307 Park Avenue
Baltimore, Maryland
March 11, 1935

Mr. Maxwell Perkins
597 Fifth Avenue
New York, New York

Dear Max:

The second annoyance to you in two days—pretty soon I'm going to
be your most popular author. (By the way we had sort of a Scribner
congerie here last night. Jim Boyd and Elizabeth came to supper and
George Calverton dropped in afterwards. Your name came up frequently
and you would have probably wriggled more than at Wolfe's dedication.
To prolong this parenthesis unduly I am sorry I mentioned Tom's book.
I hope to God I won't be set up as the opposition for there are fine
things in it, and I loved reading it, and I am delighted that it's a wow,
and it may be a bridge for something finer. I simply feel a certain disappointment which I would, on no account, want Tom to know about, for,
responding as he does to criticism, I know it would make us life long
enemies and we might do untold needless damage to each other, so please
be careful how you quote me. This is in view of Calverton's saying he
heard from you that I didn't like it. It has become increasingly plain to
me that the very excellent organization of a long book or the finest per-
ceptions and judgment in time of revision do not go well with liquor. A
short story can be written on a bottle, but for a novel you need the
mental speed that enables you to keep the whole pattern in your head
and ruthlessly sacrifice the sideshows as Ernest did in "A Farewell to
Arms." If a mind is slowed up ever so little it lives in the individual part
of a book rather than in a book as a whole; memory is dulled. I would
give anything if I hadn't had to write Part III of "Tender Is the Night"
entirely on stimulant. If I had one more crack at it cold sober I believe it
might have made a great difference. Even Ernest commented on sections
that were needlessly included and as an artist he is as near as I know for

a final reference. Of course, having struggled with Tom Wolfe as you did all this is old hat to you. I will conclude this enormous parenthesis with the news that Elizabeth has gone to Middleburg to help Mrs. White open up her newly acquired house.)

> 1307 Park Avenue
> Baltimore, Maryland
> April 15, 1935

Dear Max:

You don't say anything about "Taps" so I gather it hasn't caught on at all. I hope at least it will pay for itself and its corrections. There was a swell review in *The Nation;* did you see it?

I went away for another week but history didn't repeat itself and the trip was rather a waste. Thanks for the message from Ernest. I'd like to see him too and I always think of my friendship with him as being one of the high spots of life. But I still believe that such things have a mortality, perhaps in reaction to their very excessive life, and that we will never again see very much of each other. I appreciate what he said about "Tender Is the Night." Things happen all the time which make me think that it is not destined to die quite as easily as the boys-in-a-hurry prophesied. However, I made many mistakes about it from its delay onward, the biggest of which was to refuse the Literary Guild subsidy.

Haven't seen Beth since I got back and am calling her up today to see if she's here. I am waiting eagerly for a first installment of Ernest's book. When are you coming south? Zelda, after a terrible crisis, is somewhat better. I am, of course, on the wagon as always, but life moves at an uninspiring gait and there is less progress than I could wish on the Mediaeval series—all in all an annoying situation as these should be my most productive years. I've simply got to arrange something for this summer that will bring me to life again, but what it should be is by no means apparent.

About 1929 I wrote a story called "Outside the Cabinet Maker's" which ran in the *Century Magazine.* I either lost it here or else sent it to you with the first batch of selected stories for "Taps" and it was not returned. Will you (a) see if you've got it? or (b) tell me what and where the *Century* company is now and whom I should address to get a copy of the magazine?

I've had a swell portrait painted at practically no charge and next time I come to New York I am going to spend a morning tearing out of your files all those preposterous masks with which you have been libeling me for a last decade.

Just found another whole paragraph in "Taps," top of page 384, which appears in "Tender Is the Night." I'd carefully elided it and written the paragraph beneath it to replace it, but the proof readers slipped and put them both in.

> Ever yours,
> Scott

1307 Park Avenue
Baltimore, Maryland
April 17, 1935

Dear Max:

Reading Tom Wolfe's story in the current *Modern Monthly* makes
me wish he was the sort of person you could talk to about his stuff. It
has all his faults and virtues. It seems to me that with any sense of
humor he could see the Dreiserian absurdities of how the circus people
"ate the cod, bass, mackeral, halibut, clams and oysters of the New
England coast, the terrapin of Maryland, the fat beeves, porks and
cereals of the middle west" etc. etc. down the "pink meated lobsters
that grope their way along the sea-floors of America." And then (after
one of his fine paragraphs which sounds a note to be expanded later)
where he remarks that they leave nothing behind except "the droppings
of the camel and the elephant in Illinois." A few pages further on his
redundance ruined some paragraphs (see the last complete paragraph on
page 107) that might have been gorgeous. I sympathize with his use of
repetition, of Joyce-like words, endless metaphor, but I wish he could
have seen the disgust in Edmund Wilson's face when I once tried to
interpolate part of a rhymed sonnet in the middle of a novel, disguised
as prose. How he can put side by side such a mess as "With Chitterling
tricker fast-fluttering skirrs of sound the palmy honied birderies came"
and such fine phrases as "tongue-trilling chirrs, plumbellied smoothness,
sweet lucidity" I don't know. He who has such infinite power of suggestion and delicacy has absolutely no right to glut people on whole meals
of caviar. I hope to Christ he isn't taking all these emasculated paeans
to his vitality very seriously. I'd hate to see such an exquisite talent turn
into one of those muscle-bound and useless giants seen in a circus. Ath-
letes have got to learn their games; they shouldn't just be content to
tense their muscles, and if they do they suddenly find when called upon
to bring off a necessary effect they are simply liable to hurl the shot
into the crowd and not break any records at all. The metaphor is mixed
but I think you will understand what I mean, and that he would too
save for his tendency to almost feminine horror if he thinks anyone is
going to lay hands on his precious talent. I think his lack of humility
is his most difficult characteristic, a lack oddly enough which I associate only with second or third-rate writers. He was badly taught by
bad teachers and now he hates learning.

There is another side of him that I find myself doubting, but this is
something that no one could ever teach or tell him. His lack of feeling
other people's passions, the lyrical value of Eugene Gant's love affair
with the universe—is that going to last through a whole saga? God, I
wish he could discipline himself and really plan a novel.

I wrote you the other day and the only other point of this letter is
that I've now made a careful plan of the Mediaeval novel as a whole
(tentatively called "Philippe, Count of Darkness" *confidential*) including the planning of the parts which I can sell and the parts which I

can't. I think you could publish it either late in the spring of '36 or early in the fall of the same year. This depends entirely on how the money question goes this year. It will run to about 90,000 words and will be a novel in every sense with the episodes unrecognizable as such. That is my only plan. I wish I had these great masses of manuscripts stored away like Wolfe and Hemingway but this goose is beginning to be pretty thoroughly plucked I am afraid.

# James II Memoirs—
## An Odyssey in the Midi

THE ANNOUNCEMENT in 1951 that Charles Scribner's Sons had acquired the lost "legendary" Shuckburgh copy of the Gutenberg Bible from a member of the British royal family caused interest in other than purely bibliographical circles. Press associations carried the story, articles were written and interviews given, and offers of "family treasures" swelled to full flood from all continents.

It was as a direct result of this publicity that a young French girl residing in New York telephoned one day to inquire about the value of some minor first editions of Robert Browning, Lord Tennyson and Walter Savage Landor. The value of minor works of these poets was minor then and indeed remains so today, but she had called upon the recommendation of a friend who had seen the Gutenberg story, and courtesy required that I look at them; besides, Mademoiselle had a most attractive voice, and currency restrictions being what they were at the time, even a few American dollars would be useful to a foreign visitor.

The first book examined, the Browning, was inscribed by the author to Walter Savage Landor, as was the Tennyson volume. The books by Landor himself turned out to be his own copies of his own works, annotated throughout in his waspish style and of considerable bibliographical interest. They were purchased immediately, upon mutually satisfactory terms; promptly a suitable home was found with Chauncey Brewster Tinker, and they are now with his collections at Yale.

One's immediate reaction to material of this nature (if, that is, one is interested at all) is naturally: "Where did it come from?" and "Are there any more at home like you?" The answers were that they came from the family library in France, which was a large one, that other similar material *might* be there, that these particular ones had been brought to America as they seemed the most likely to be salable here, and that Mademoiselle was descended from Walter Savage Landor, which satisfactorily explained their provenance.

"Visions of sugarplums" danced immediately, of course, but it turned out that the library was in a somewhat inaccessible spot, the castle was closed, there was no one locally capable of making even the briefest kind of inventory, and so on. Nor could John Carter, my London associate at Scribner's, go to France at that time. Perhaps later!

Desultory meetings and correspondence evaporated as Mademoiselle left New York. And some research revealed that much else of Landor's library had appeared on the market over the past decades, indicating that it was not nestling in France *en bloc*—it seemed questionable indeed if much else were there of the type of material which had been brought to New York.

In 1954 I happened to be going to England and the Continent on a rare-book hunting expedition, and my companion on the trip to France was to be Percy Muir of the firm of Elkin Mathews, famed British antiquarian bookseller, long-time friend and wonderful traveling companion, whose knowledge of French booksellers, French books and, in short, France, was (and is) encyclopedic. It is an advantage for an American to be able to consult with someone who knows the customs of the trade on the Continent, as they order so many things differently.

And this was not the first joint Scribner-Mathews collaboration. A notable earlier one had brought out of Germany and to America the original autograph manuscript of Mozart's Symphony in D Major (the so-called Haffner Symphony), as recorded earlier.

The forthcoming trip recalled, of course, the memory of the Landor library, and some sleuthing found the daughter living in Paris and married to the son of a famed Irish-American author. Arrangements were made at last to visit the castle, in the Midi, where Mademoiselle's mother was now in residence.

We took an overnight train from Paris to the Midi, where we were met by the Countess, and a charming weekend followed. Only there were no books; or, to be more exact, there were no books of the type I hoped for. The library was very large, cluttered, ill-lit, of course, and contained many works of the kind which, in England, would constitute a "gentleman's library"; but of true rarities, none. It had obviously been scanned before by someone with a practiced eye. Only one book of real value turned up in the whole course of search, uncovered by Muir, after having been overlooked by me (who was supposed to be the expert on Americana). That was the rare first edition of Henry D. Thoreau's first book, *A Week on the Concord and Merrimack Rivers* (Cambridge, 1849), in fine condition and inscribed, furthermore, by Thoreau to Landor. This the Countess parted with reluctantly, obviously disappointed that nothing of importance (aside from the French works with which she would not part) had been uncovered. As I recall, most of its pages were unopened. This, at any rate, would pay round-trip train fare from Paris, I can only excuse myself for my dreadful oversight by explaining that the drab little volume, in the typical brown cloth most American books of its period are bound in, nestled obscurely as the last book on an ill-lit shelf in a wooden bookcase exactly its shade. But even this protective coloration failed to deceive Muir, obviously a man to have on your side. This volume took a long voyage home and, curiously enough, returned eventually to the very town in America from which it had been sent a little over a hundred years before.

I was particularly annoyed about my oversight because in this book Thoreau recounts the saga of my favorite of all my ancestors, Hannah Dustin, born December 23, 1657, at Haverhill, Massachusetts, daughter of Michael and Hannah (Webster) Emerson.

Indians raided the town on March 15, 1697, killing or capturing forty of the inhabitants. Hannah's husband and seven of their other children escaped but she, her nurse and week-old child were captured. Hannah saw her house in flames as the Indians started their march northward and one of them snatched her baby and brained it by knocking it against an apple tree.

After several days' march through the snow and without shoes, the party reached a small island (now called "Dustin's") at the confluence of the Contoocook and Merrimack rivers, a few miles above Concord. The captives were to be stripped and forced to run the gauntlet. The Indians fell into a drunken stupor, anticipating the fun, and Hannah and another captive lad killed ten of them, only a squaw and a small Indian boy escaping.

Part way back to Haverhill it occurred to Hannah that her story might be doubted, so sending the others on she returned and herself scalped the ten savages, of whom she had personally killed nine, the boy one. For the loss of their property and for her exploit, the General Court awarded her £25.

Cotton Mather gives the classic account of this story in his *Magnalia*

*Christi Americana* (1702), having had the story from Hannah herself. The date of her death is unknown though she is supposed to have outlived her husband who was still alive in 1729. Somehow the blood seems to have thinned since then.

The castle was very old and had somehow (probably from its rather isolated position far off the traditional invasion routes) managed to escape the desolation of the wars from the Middle Ages through the twentieth century. Among its proud traditions—and they are many—is the fact that Richard the Lion-Hearted had visited it. The library and many other rooms had plenty of important and interesting documents connected with its long history—on the walls, in closets, cupboards, etc.—but most were connected with the family and were not to be parted with under any circumstances, understandably.

The evening before our departure I went prying around some of the plentiful old closets, as is any bookman's habit, partly to see if something hadn't been overlooked and partly to prove to Muir that, by golly, I was as good a needle-in-a-haystack hunter as he was, when, on top of a large pile of seventeenth- and eighteenth-century books and documents, I chanced to pick up a manuscript. Had it been at the bottom of the pile, I would never have reached for it. I opened it in the middle, and it seemed obvious that, being in French, it was another document with which the family would not part, but something made me glance at the title page. This, I thought, required some consideration, so I returned to my rooms and meditated on it, skimming through with my faulty French.

The book, 145 folio pages, written on both sides, was bound in blind-tooled calf without lettering. The title page read, in part, "Campagnes Tirées mot pour mot des mémoires de Jacques Stuart Poulors Duc d'York, et depuis Roy d'Angleterre Jacques Second," etc. Bound in were four folio leaves, written on both sides, headed "Preface du Cardinal de Bouillon," and an attestation, with seal, dated 1734. There was a bookplate of Turenne d'Aynac and name "M[arqu]is de Turenne d'Aynac" written on the flyleaf.

It was obvious what it was, but I was hazy as to its true importance. Though not particularly well informed in this period, I was familiar with Winston Churchill's *Marlborough*, a work Scribner's had issued in America. I particularly recalled his vivid chapter on James II's memoirs, the romantic tale of the attempt to smuggle them from France to England, their destruction at Saint-Omer during the French Revolution and the subsequent controversies over the authenticity of various texts. Churchill discusses the fate of the original English memoirs as follows:

There is no doubt about the existence of the Memoirs nor where they lay during the whole of the eighteenth century. On the outbreak of the French Revolution the Scots College tried by various channels to send these historical treasures to England for safety. In 1793 it is believed that a Monsieur Charpentier finally undertook the task. He was arrested at Saint-Omer, and his wife, fearing lest the Royal Arms of hostile England on the bindings might be compromising, first buried the volumes in the garden of her house, and later dug them up and burned them. Thus ended the travels of the Memoirs, the only original memoirs "writ in the King's own hand."

Reading the Cardinal de Bouillon's Preface was enough to explain the reason for the existence of this manuscript in this particular spot.

The next morning, with Muir accurately translating, we discovered that the Preface was in the hand of Samanuel-Theodore de la Tour d'Auvergne, Cardinal de Bouillon, nephew of Henri de la Tour d'Auvergne, Vicomte de Turenne, the French Marshal. In the year 1695, while in exile in Saint-Germain-en-Laye, King James II of England made the acquaintance of the Cardinal, who was the nephew of the great French soldier. The King related to the Cardinal many stories of his own experiences as a young man serving in the French Army under his uncle, most of which were unknown to the Cardinal. He therefore humbly requested the King to attempt a record of these facts. To this the King replied that he had already written memoirs of his early years, that he would extract from these all references to the Marshal together with his experiences in the Low Countries down to the Peace of the Pyrenees and the Restoration of his brother Charles II to the throne of England and would have these translated into French for presentation to the Cardinal.

On January 27, 1696, James sent for the Cardinal, took him into his private apartments and presented him with this manuscript, with the injunction that it was to be shown to nobody during the King's lifetime.

This injunction was faithfully observed by the Cardinal, not only during the life of the King, but during his own lifetime also. It was only in the year of de Bouillon's death, 1715, that he wrote the Preface to this manuscript, giving its history and adding his intention to bequeath it to the next in seniority in the family of Turenne, with the hope that it would remain in the possession of the senior member of his family from generation to generation in perpetuity.

The Cardinal's heir was his nephew, Henri-Oswald de la Tour d'Auvergne, Comte de Turenne, who inherited from the Cardinal not only this manuscript, but the whole of his very considerable library. This library was eventually dispersed, but the manuscript remained in the family.

It has been remarked above that King James promised the Cardinal a translation of only those parts of his memoirs that would be of interest to him. It emerged from the certificate of authentication, however, that this manuscript is in fact a verbatim of the King's original English memoirs.

The certificate of authentication, bound between the Cardinal's Preface and the body of the manuscript, was prepared for and given to the Cardinal's nephew. It is signed by five officials of the Scots College of the University of Paris, where the papers of James II had been deposited by his order. The most important of the signers is Louis Inesse, who uses the French form of his name, originally Lewis Innes. He succeeded Robert Barclay as principal of the Scots College in 1682 and devoted himself to the preservation and arrangement of the records in the college library. He was one of the five members who acted as James II's cabinet at Saint-Germain after the King's return from Ireland in 1690.

The certificate reads:

> These Memoirs of the late King James II of Great Britain conform to the original English Memoirs written in H.M.'s own hand which, in accordance with a minute signed by his hand, are preserved in our said college. And we, the aforesaid, certify further that the present manuscript, revised and corrected by the said King James, translated by his order, given by his hand to the late Cardinal de Bouillon on January 27, 1696, and written in the hand of Dempster, one of the Secretaries of his said Majesty, confirms in fact, circumstances, reflexions, and generally in every way (the turn of style and method of relation excepted) to a second translation of the same English Memoirs, made by order of the late Queen of Great Britain, signed in her hand, sealed with her Seal bearing her arms, countersignd by My Lord Caryl Secretaire d'Etat on November 14, 1704, and given on January 15, 1705, by the said Louis Inesse to S. A. R. the Cardinal de Bouillon, to be used in the Histoire du Vicomte de Turenne . . .

This was a discovery indeed, but what could be done about it? I thought from the first that the family could be persuaded to part with it on the theory that it had really little French interest at all, being merely the secondhand record of an Englishman who later became King. But we were leaving for Paris the next day, and how to persuade the owner of this (I had not yet revealed the discovery), arrange for the innumerable details (assuming she were willing to part with it) and so on was a puzzler. It also seemed vital for it not to go through the normal channels of our London office, as once in England, I was afraid an export license might be denied us upon grounds that it was a "national treasure"—which has happened to lesser items. The problem was solved in the simplest manner. I returned to London and left Muir to attend to the details. His account from *The Memoirs of James II* follows:

Randall's discovery of the James II manuscript, coming after our experience in purchasing the Thoreau book, was not discussed at once with the Countess. I was convinced that it would be wise to await a psychological moment at which to broach the subject.

The moment arose soon after a late supper on our last evening at the chateau, when the Countess announced that we must inspect the countryside by moonlight from the battlements. We climbed a spiral staircase in one of the towers, and as we emerged into a kind of loft under the roof we found the floor covered with an amazing variety of receptacles. There were buckets, baths, chamberpots—even a bedpan or two. Our hostess explained that this was a precaution against a repetition of the experience during the previous year's rainy season, when water had streamed through the roof and brought down ceilings. She reminded us of the water-stained walls in the rooms below, which were indicative of the intensity of the flood.

As we emerged onto the roof, the Countess pointed out that all the lead was porous and needed replacing. She had had an estimate for renewing it, but it was a sum entirely beyond her means to provide.

"And you had hoped, perhaps," I suggested, "that Landor's books might provide for the possibility."

"Yes!" she said. "But you have removed that foolish idea from my head. I am sure your valuation is an honest and accurate one. But the money would go nowhere. Perhaps you will still find something, somewhere in the house, that will keep a roof over my head."

"We have," I said. And at three o'clock in the morning, on that moonlit roof, I told her what we had found. I was not surprised to learn that she had no idea of the existence of the document; and its nature had to be described to her in detail. She wanted to see it at once and we went down to examine it. She was quite indefatigable and would have sat up the rest of the night poring over it and discussing it. I finally succeeded in persuading her to retire to her bedroom with the manuscript, and we were able to sleep for a few hours.

The next morning Randall announced that his schedule required that he return to London immediately, so that, while I was able to stay, he was forced to leave with the great purchase still uncompleted. The Countess was torn between reluctance to part with a family document and anxiety about the roof. She had decided that her daughter must be consulted about the manuscript. It was a part of her inheritance and she must make the decision.

"But without a proper roof," I said, "neither this manuscript nor anything else in the chateau may be worth inheriting."

"Of course, you are right," she answered. "You will see her in Paris on your return there. She is a very sensible girl. She will see the point. But if she says I am not to sell I shall be glad."

I had to leave without a decision and without the manuscript, although we did agree to abide by the daughter's future decision. A further condition was made. If we did buy the manuscript, a complete facsimile in a copy of its original eighteenth-century binding was to be made and given to the Countess at our expense.

Since the daughter did approve the purchase, there was a second journey to the chateau, when I did acquire the manuscript.

The delivery of the manuscript to America occurred just prior to my leaving Scribner's to become librarian at Indiana University. It became my first major addition to that collection and was published by the Indiana University Press in 1962, with an Introduction by the well-known historian Arthur Bryant. A curious sidelight was the revival of an effort to get James II (of all people) sainthood!

# George Washington—
## Father of His Country and of Governor Posey of Indiana?

**T**HE FIRST TIME I ever came across the question of the paternity of Thomas Posey (soldier of the Revolution, lieutenant governor of Kentucky, senator from Louisiana, and governor of Indiana Territory) was a dozen or so years ago while glancing through *A Collection of the Writings of John James Ingalls. Essays, Addresses and Orations* (Kansas City, Missouri, 1902). The late Senator Ingalls' speeches are not particularly favorite reading matter of mine, and the only reason I ever opened the volume was because I was endeavoring to trace the earliest appearance in print of his sonnet "Opportunity." This has been called the finest sonnet written by an American; it is indisputably the finest sonnet written by an American senator. A reference to Washington as the father of Posey struck me as curious, but I immediately forgot it in the excitement of finding "Opportunity" in this volume, though this is not, I later discovered, the first printing of the poem.

In going over a lot of old correspondence of the firm of Charles Scribner's Sons with authors and would-be authors, I came across a file of "nut" letters, of which every publisher receives his share. These varied in degrees of madness, and I am quite sure that if I had never read Senator Ingalls' remark about Washington, Frank Abial Flower's letter would not have made the slightest impression. But the very first words of that letter, "The MS. of General Posey, Son of General George Washington," rang memory's bell, and I laid aside the letter for future investigation.

The first rumor to reach print concerning Posey's paternity probably was a correspondent's note in the *Cincinnati Commercial* about 1873. "Some ten years ago a correspondent of the *Cincinnati Commercial* started the story that Governor Posey was a natural son of George Washington, but the romance did not take root. Had he been Washington's son, begotten in wedlock, he would have honored his father's name." These curious sentences are in William Wesley Woollen's *Biographical and Historical Sketches of Early Indiana* (Indianapolis, 1883). *The National Cyclopedia of American Biography* states that "His [Thomas Posey's] mother was Elizabeth Lloyd of a family of high social standing, but except that little is known of his origin. He is said to have been the natural son of George Washington." These, with Ingalls' denial, are the only references in print I have come across. None of the standard lives of Washington I have consulted even dignify the story by a denial, and *The Dictionary of American Biography* merely says that Posey was "born in Fairfax County, Va., and grew up as a country boy with few educational advantages. At the age of nineteen he removed to the Virginia frontier."

There is evidence, however, that Washington knew and associated with Posey in the early 1750's. *The Diary of Col. George Washington for August, September and October, 1774*, in *Annual Report of the American Historical Association for the Year 1892*, records his entry of Aug. 17, 1774: "I rid to Doeg Run, Muddy hole, Mill, & Poseys Plant[ns]," with the footnote:

> Posey's Plantation refers to a farm which Washington bought of Capt. John Posey, lying below the mouth of Dogue Run on the Potomac. In 1753, by Act of Assembly, a ferry from Posey's farm to the plantation of Thomas Marshall in Maryland was authorized to be established. . . . In 1769, Washington bought this farm and united it under the Mount Vernon management as part of the Dogue Run Plantation. Capt. Posey at the time, reserved the ferry and the ferry house with 12 acres which, however, he sold to Washington in 1772. . . . Capt. Posey is believed to have served with Washington in the French and Indian Wars. He was the father of Col. Thomas Posey of the Revolution.

In *The Diaries of George Washington 1748–1799* (Boston, 1925) we find that "Washington contributed to the education of several children of his various friends. Thomas Posey, son of his neighbor, Captain John Posey, was one of these." And "Amelia (Milly) Posey, daughter of Captain John Posey. She seems to have been considered in the light of a ward of Mrs. Washington."

Read in the light of these facts, the following letter from the Scribner files may not be as completely crazy as it first appears and may possibly be worth someone's investigation.

August 28, 1906

My dear Sirs:

The MS, "General Posey, Son of George Washington," about which I recently wrote but which you stated you had not received, has come to hand. Being in haste to catch a steamer, Col. Dickinson sent the pkg to your house by a messenger. As no one in your office was inclined to sign the messenger's receipt book, the pkg was returned and has just now reached me.

The attempt to send this MS to your house was due to Judge Watson, chairman of the U.S. Com'n to Codify the Laws, because he stated that relatives or clients of his had been particularly well treated by you, and he regarded the work as important.

The attempt having failed, I am led to ask you whether you believe the character of the work is such that you would like to examine it with a view to publication.

While natural and truthful, the most offensive part of the MS is its title. It may suggest a mere scandal; the text itself, however, is not at all scandalous—and that, perhaps, is its greatest weakness; the tightest of tights on the billboards but long skirts on the stage.

The poorest and most unsatisfactory part of the book is the Introduction. I never could write a Preface. Having the title and the Introduction may enable you to decide whether you wish to read the entire MS, and for that reason, in order to save time, I take the liberty of enclosing a carbon copy of the prefatory remarks.

This Introduction, too, will be offensive to many. I did not want to make explanations or pleas in the body, the historical portion of the work, and so gave such facts in the Introduction as seem to me to be necessary to a correct view of a pregnant episode in the life of Washington.

In the text the fatherhood of Washington is not dwelt upon nor seasoned. Neither is the fact that he was the father of another noted son, of a son by an Indian woman, and of 21 mulattoes of African blood.

The work is designed to be purely historical. It contains much Revolutionary and Colonial matter never before offered to the public, including letters by Washington, Posey, Wayne, Madison, Jefferson, Judge John Marshall, etc., etc.

It is written in the style of my Life of Stanton, recently published, tho the last chapter of that was put at the front to please the publisher.

There are over 100 pictures to be used as illustrations. I will send them if you shall decide that you would like to examine the MS.

One of the blood descendants of Washington, a bachelor of culture and wealth, spent over 30 years and more than $50,000 in trying to disprove the story that his family was of irregular origin. While prosecuting this attempt he became aware of the fact that I knew the family secret and had hunted out information about Posey as part of my series of illustrations of the fundamental laws of heredity. When he was compelled to give up defeated he came in disguise to my house and confessed and said that if I would not disclose where I found the matter he would turn over to me family papers and material that never could be secured by an outsider.

Of course I agreed and he remained a guest in my house till I had taken copies of everything. He permitted me to retain many papers in the original.

This person died suddenly this summer, and I then attempted to send my MS to your house as above explained.

When published I think my MS should be put out in the highest style of the printer's art because Washington stands at the head of all American historical characters; Posey, tho the fact is not known, was not far below or behind him, so far as comparisons are possible.

I also think that the price should be moderate—the MS is not large—for the tendency of the day toward low prices in all printed matter.

Very Respectfully Yours
P.S.—Wil it b konsidrd treson 2 put out a bok not spelt ala rusewelt?
Frank Abial Flower.

Scribbled at the top of this letter is Charles Scribner's penciled annotation: "Discourage and return Introduction," and the reply was a brush-off.

In reply to your letter August 28 we beg to say that our hands are now so full of other pressing matters that we cannot offer you any special encouragement to send us your manuscript, "General Posey, Son of General Washington," which you are good enough to bring to our attention. From what you tell us of your work we foresee with reasonable certainty that we should be unable to make you an offer of publication, and we feel therefore that we had best spare you the delay of a protracted examination.

Now first let us consider the author. Flower was certainly an eccentric but he was not a nonentity. He was well known enough to have made *Who's Who*. According to it he was a publisher, editor and author and was born at Cottage, Cattaraugus County, New York, May 11, 1854. He was the author of: *Histories of Fond du Lac County, Wis.; Waukesha County, Wis.; City of Milwaukee, Wis.; History of the Republican Party; Life of M. H. Carpenter; Outline History of Wisconsin; Industrial Wisconsin; Old Abe; Eye of the Northwest; Plan of International Co-operation; International Deep Waterways; Life of Edwin M. Stanton*. He wrote three reports as Commissioner of Statistics of Wisconsin as well as many leaflets, pamphlets, magazine articles and reports.

When all this is put together, several points stand out which seem significant to the writer.

(1) A manuscript was once in existence which attempted to prove that Washington was Posey's father, and two apparently responsible citizens, a Colonel Dickinson (at present not further identified) and a Judge Watson, knew of it, and the latter "regarded the work as important." While it does not necessarily follow from this that the work *was* important, it is significant that it was thought to be so by a lawyer trained in evaluating evidence and able enough chairman of the U.S. Commission to Codify the Laws. This was probably David Kemper Watson, who was born in Madison County, Ohio, in 1849, and was the author of numerous monographs on legal history.

(2) Flower was far from being a totally inexperienced author. He had numerous books published and many of them, for example, his work on Stanton, involved historical research.

(3) The story of the "blood descendant of Washington" who "spent over 30 years and more than $50,000 in trying to disprove the story that his family was of irregular origin . . . was compelled to give up defeated . . . came in disguise to my house and confessed," seems altogether too incredible a yarn to have been invented out of whole cloth.

(4) Flower claimed to be in possession of hitherto unpublished documents. It is highly unlikely that anyone would make such a claim unless he actually had such documents (either genuine or fake), as no reputable publisher would dream of issuing the book without checking the actual source material. And Flower did offer to send for inspection "over 100 pictures."

The question is: What happened to Mr. Flower's manuscript? He died in 1911 and it may have been destroyed. Equally possible, it may still be extant.

If it is found, Scribner's would like another chance to examine it! It may reveal, as Mr. Flower stated in his letter, "a pregnant episode in the life of Washington."

Since the above notes were written another lead has developed. There is some slight evidence (*vide* Flower's biography in *Who's Who*, 1910–1911) that he either published or contemplated publishing a book on *Suppressed Colonial and Revolutionary History*, but diligent research has failed to uncover a copy. It is not registered at the Library of Congress. It may have been privately printed by the author, but where is a copy? And, more important, where are the original documents the author claimed to have owned? As Sherlock Holmes would say, "The Game's Afoot!"

# Thomas Jefferson
## and the Declaration of
## Independence

O NE OF THE KEY documents of American history is, of
course, the Declaration of Independence. On July 2, 1776, the
Continental Congress formally resolved "that these United
States are, and of right ought to be, free and independent states," and
from July 2 to July 4 they discussed Thomas Jefferson's "rough draft" of
a justification to the world. From the beginning we have celebrated the
anniversary of the adoption of this immortal document rather than the
earlier day on which independence was voted.

On the evening of July 4, Congress, acting as a committee of the
whole, approved the Declaration and ordered that it should be printed
and copies "sent to the several assemblies, conventions, and commanding
officers of the continental troops that it might be proclaimed in each of
the united states and at the head of the army." The printing was entrusted
to John Dunlap of Philadelphia, and the Committee of Five ordered to
"superintend and correct the press."

There is no record of how many copies of this first broadside were
done, but Michael J. Walsh, the great Americanist of Goodspeed's,
located only fourteen in his census, done in 1949. These copies belonged
to: American Philosophical Society; Library of Congress (three copies,
one imperfect); Harvard; Massachusetts Historical Society; New York
Historical Society; New York Public Library; Public Record Office,
London; Yale; Historical Society of Pennsylvania; and three, surprisingly,

privately owned—the John Hinsdale Scheide, Roberts Harrison and Henry Flynt copies.

I, and, of course, others, had approached these owners for possible purchase with negative results. I was particularly covetous of the Henry Flynt copy as it was accompanied by a remarkable letter from John Hancock to Governor Cooke of Rhode Island, reading as follows:

> Philadelphia July 6th, 1776.
>
> Sir,
>     Although it is not possible to foresee the Consequence of human Action, yet it is nevertheless a Duty we owe ourselves and Posterity in all our public Councils, to decide in the best Manner we are able, and to trust the Event to that Being who controls both Causes and Events, so as to bring about his own Determination.
>     Impressed with this Sentiment, and at the same Time fully convinced that our Affair may take a more favourable Turn, the Congress have judged it necessary to dissolve all Connection between Great Britain and the American Colonies, and to declare them free and independent States, as you will perceive by the enclosed Declaration, which I am directed to transmit to you, and to request you will have it proclaimed in your Colony, in the way you shall think most proper.
>     The important Consequences to the American States from this Declaration of Independence considered as the Ground and Foundation of a future Government, will naturally suggest the Propriety of having it proclaimed in such a Manner as that the People may be universally informed of it. . . .

A mouth-watering combination indeed!

Henry Flynt, the well-known New York lawyer and an old customer of mine, who lived in Greenwich, Connecticut, had quietly gathered a very distinguished group of letters and documents of the Constitutional period, of which this was a part. A born antiquarian, he had become interested in the restoration of Deerfield, Massachusetts, perpetuating old homes as shrines for students of American culture.

He called one day and inquired if I was still interested in the Declaration and the Hancock letter. Was I! Well, a price was mentioned and agreed on and I drove to Greenwich from my home in Larchmont on a Saturday to get the documents, Scribner's check in my pocket. When I asked Flynt what had changed his mind about selling, he replied that he had recently been made chairman of the board of trustees of Deerfield Academy. As a gesture, I presume, he had offered to present the Academy with these documents, and the authorities had gently intimated that they would prefer their value in cash. Flynt was rather annoyed, I gathered, and quite properly. While I was drinking a silent toast and thanking God for such knuckleheads, the documents were produced and I handed over the check.

It wasn't, my friend immediately pointed out, certified. I replied that, after all, it was signed by Charles Scribner. If I had signed it, that would be something to worry about. The next question was, where was I taking it? The answer was, home for the weekend and then to Scribner's on Monday. Was it insured in transit and while in my home? Negative answers. Well, suppose my house burned? To this I replied I was living in the old George Palmer Putnam house, which was nearly as old as the Declaration itself and hadn't burned yet.

All this did not suit Mr. Flynt's legal mind, and he suggested mildly that he keep the documents, bring them to Scribner's himself on Monday, insured all the way, and that I then present him with a certified check. There being no alternative, I agreed.

Sunday, my house burned. I would not say that on Monday Mr. Flynt was the most pleased man in seven states, but I certainly remain grateful to him. My commission on this deal went for house repairs. I told this story some time afterward to Ian Fleming, the British bibliophile and newsman, who wrote it up in his column. Somehow, the *Reader's Digest* picked it up and paid *him* for it.

In any event, the document and the letter are in the Lilly Library on permanent display—surrounded by Carroll A. Wilson's copies of *The Pennsylvania Magazine* for July, 1776 (edited by Thomas Paine), which is its first periodical printing; *The Genuine Principles of the Ancient Saxon, or English Constitution . . .* by Demophilus (probably Samuel Bryan), Philadelphia, 1776, its first printing in book form; *The Remembrancer; or Impartial Repository of Public Events. Part II* (London, 1776), its first printing in England, and (acquired from Richard Wormser) *The Pennsylvania Evening Post* of July 6, 1776, the first newspaper printing and the form in which "We, the people" first read it.

Bookish things have had a curious way of happening to me in two's. While I was doing a bit of free-lancing and straightening out my affairs between leaving Scribner's and going to Indiana, I happened to be in Chicago and stopped in to see Harold Tribolet, the well-known binder and restorer of R. R. Donnelley and Sons. There was a package on his desk, wrapped for mailing, and, justifiably proud of a superb restoration job, Tribolet unwrapped it to show me. He laid before my incredulous eyes a completely unknown and unrecorded fifteenth copy of the Philadelphia, Dunlap, 1776, broadside Declaration. It had come to him mutilated and he had done a masterful job of matching paper and ink in its restoration.

When I recovered sufficiently to speak quietly I asked him if he felt free to tell me who owned it. Certainly, he replied, it had been sent in by the old book firm of Tuttle, of Brattleboro, Vermont. The question was, did they still own it or had they sold it "as is" and had the repairing done for the owner? A phone call revealed that they had not sold it but were willing to. They meant to use it for the cover of a forthcoming catalogue, but if I wanted it for a price—exactly one tenth, it turned out, of what I had paid Flynt a few years before—it was mine.

This, of course, was a natural for Waller Barrett. Jefferson was its author and there was no copy south of Washington. What better home for it than the University of Virginia? There remained only the matter of price, which was finally settled, not at $10,000 as *The New York Times* reported, but at a figure which exactly covered the down payment on the modest home in Bloomington I still occupy.

I am not an ardent Jeffersonian—had I lived in those times I believe I'd have been a Hamilton man, myself—but somehow a fair amount of material by and relating to Jefferson has come my way. I am reminded of Millicent Sowerby, who compiled the great catalogue of Jefferson's books for the Library of Congress which was financed through a Lilly grant. British-born and still a British citizen, she queried me plaintively once as to why Jefferson so disliked the English. "Good God," I remarked, "haven't you ever read the Declaration of Independence?" And she blandly replied that she hadn't and furthermore had no intention of doing so!

We have in the Lilly Library a remarkable Jefferson letter, to Elbridge Gerry, dated May 13, 1797, with one fascinating sentence in it. "The second office of this government," Jefferson remarks, "is honorable and easy. The first is but a splendid misery."

By all odds, the finest Jefferson book I ever had, certainly the most desirable conceivable, was his own copy of *The Federalist*, two volumes (New York, 1788), annotated by him. This originally came from the sale of his library at Washington in 1827 and has changed hands but once since then. It is now in the possession of Rudy Ruggles of Chicago, who also has one of the three surviving original manuscripts of the *Essays* which comprised it, as well as what I consider the finest letter John Jay ever penned—a very long explanation of how the Constitution came to be formed and accepted.

Of almost equal interest, now in the Lilly Library, is Jefferson's copy of the *Acts Passed by Congress, 1789* (New York, 1789), containing the first printing of the Bill of Rights. A small folio, in original calf, it bears on the front cover a label "The Secretary of State" and inside an inscription presenting the book to him by George Washington—our first President to our first Secretary of State! It has Jefferson's usual marks of ownership, was also in his sale and bears one autograph correction. The printed phrase "cruel or unusual *imprisonments*" is corrected in his hand to read "cruel or unusual *punishments*," as it now stands.

There cannot have been many copies presented by Washington to members of his cabinet, of whom there were only four. Fate handed me another of these, however. The label on the front cover of this reads "Chief Justice of the United States" and on the title page, in Jay's hand, is: "9 Decr. 1789, presented by the President of the United States to John Jay." This is now part of the Edward L. Doheny Memorial Library at Camarillo, California. I may add that John Jay did not correct the passage which Jefferson did.

The most interesting of Jefferson's books is his *Notes on the State of Virginia*, which went through many editions and laid the foundation of his high contemporary reputation as a universal scholar and his present fame as a pioneer American scientist. Its full title is *Notes on the State of Virginia; Written in the Year 1782, for the Use of a Foreigner of Distinction, in Answer to Certain Queries Proposed by Him*. It was privately printed in Paris in 1784, in an edition of two hundred copies, none of which was for sale, though some were given to friends with strict injunctions to secrecy. It is a bibliographically complex book, and the Lilly Library is fortunate in having it in all its variants.

Of the two hundred printed I have had five at one time or another, two of them presentation copies, and the only surviving portion of the original manuscript, now at the University of Virginia. The most important of these copies, presented by Jefferson to Franklin, I sold to Edgar Monsanto Queeny, then head of the Monsanto Chemical Company and author of *The Spirit of Enterprise* (Scribner's, 1943), who later presented it to Herbert Hoover.

The *Dictionary of American Biography* says of Jefferson's book:

Persuaded that public service and private misfortunes were inseparable, Jefferson retired to his neglected farm, his cherished books and his beloved family, convinced that nothing could again separate him from them. He took advantage of the leisure forced upon him by his fall from a horse to organize the careful memoranda about Virginia which he had made over a long period of years. Arranging these in the order of the queries submitted in 1781 by Barbé de Marbois, secretary of the French legation, he somewhat corrected and enlarged them during the winter of 1782–3, and at length printed them in France in 1784–5.

Unpretentious in form and statistical in character, this extraordinary, informing and generally interesting book may still be consulted with profit about the geography and productions, the social and political life of eighteenth-century Virginia. With ardent patriotism as well as a zeal for truth, Jefferson combatted the theories of Buffon and Raynal in regard to the degeneracy of animal and intellectual life in America and he manifested great optimism in regard to the future of the country but included "strictures" on slavery and the government of Virginia.

The presentation copy in the Lilly Library is inscribed by Jefferson in the third person:

> Th: Jefferson having had a few copies of these notes printed to offer some of his friends & to some estimable characters beyond that line, takes the liberty of presenting a copy to Mr. Febrone as a testimony of his respect for him. Unwilling to expose them to the public eye, he asks the favor of Mr. Febrone to put them into the hands of no person on whose care & fidelity he cannot rely to guard them against publication.

In 1786 Jefferson added three appendices to the unused sheets. The Lilly Library copy of this has all three, including *An Act for Establishing Religious Freedom Passed in the Assembly of Virginia in the Beginning of the Year 1786.* This is only four pages, yet it was entirely his work and gives him high rank among those who have championed man's intellectual and religious freedom. On the simple stone over his grave at Monticello Jefferson is described as he wished to be remembered: as the author of the Declaration of Independence and the Virginia statute for religious freedom, and as the father of the University of Virginia. This copy bears the contemporary bookplate of Richard Taliaferro, of a well-known Virginian family. Both copies had been acquired by Mr. Lilly from Scribner's on two different occasions, ten years apart.

In one of those delightful, implausible serendipities which make collecting so fascinating, Warren Howell of San Francisco told me just recently that he had acquired several Jefferson letters he thought I would be interested in. When I saw them, I was. One was a letter from Jefferson to Febrone (actually, M. Fabroné; Jefferson consistently misspelled his name).

> I take the liberty of presenting you with some notes giving an account of the country which once hoped to account you among its citizens. They were written—while our country was wasting under the ravages of a cruel enemy and whilst the writer was confined to his room by an accidental decrepitude. Less than this added to his want of talents

would account for their errors and defects. Sensible of this he does not make them public, having printed a few copies only to present to particular persons. . . .

This seemed treasure enough to add to the Febrone copy. But more was to come. In another letter to Febrone, Jefferson

asks your assistance in the following case. There is in the state of Virginia a family of the name of Taliaferro, which has always supposed itself of Italian extraction. The original name is probably Tagliaferro. They are informed that there is a district of country not more than four or five leagues from Florence which bears that name. They therefore conjecture that their family came from Tuscany and that their coat of arms (leurs armes) may be found in that country; especially if there be there a Herald's office where such things are registered. . . .

The odds against two letters, casually offered, fitting exactly the two books owned, are pretty astronomical.

My experience with the Virginia Declaration of Rights had for me a less happy ending than the one with the Declaration of Independence. Formulated by George Mason and adopted by the Virginia Convention on June 12, 1776, it preceded by seventeen days the adoption of the constitution which made Virginia an independent state. It was a model for other state constitutions and vitally affected the first amendments to the Federal Constitution, the Bill of Rights.

James Lewis Hook was a Pennsylvania dealer, specializing in historical material, government documents chiefly, but with side excursions into a wide variety of Americana, sport and literature among them. I had frequented his father's shop in Harrisburg, Pennsylvania, when I was a schoolboy there and remained a customer of his through the years. On one visit to Philadelphia I went to his home, which was also his shop, to see what was new, and he laid before me Mason's original notes for the Convention. A very hot item indeed. How hot, I was soon to discover.

It should, of course, have been in the Virginia State archives. But it obviously wasn't. Hook knew little of its history except that it had been brought back to Pennsylvania by a Civil War soldier as a souvenir. So far as we could reconstruct its provenance, it was probably this: when the fall of Richmond became imminent, the priceless Virginia archives were loaded into wagons and sent West, over the mountains. Some made it, some didn't. These notes were presumably fished out of some ditch by a literate Pennsylvanian, and Hook now had them—by honorable purchase.

The question was, what were we to do with them? I was convinced that they should be in Williamsburg, and Hook gave the volume to me, on approval, at $5,000, profits above that to be divided. Williamsburg expressed interest but wanted (1) proof of its genuineness and (2) a clear title. I was certain of the first and had no particular qualms about the second. Our government has been notoriously slack, lax and indifferent to its historical records—read Mary Benjamin's hair-raising account of their slaughter in Washington during the Civil War in Chapter XII, "The Importance of the Collector," in her *Autographs: A Key to Collecting.*

To satisfy Williamsburg I took my documents to the Virginia capital, Richmond, for examination and verification, a mere formality, I had been informed. This turned out to be a mistake. So long as the notes were in New York, or Pennsylvania, or outside the state of Virginia, it seems, the state would have had considerable trouble replevining them—and probably wouldn't have gone that far. But, once back in their clutches, they had me, and Hook, hooked.

It seemed that the Old Dominion never surrenders title to anything without an act of legislature, a fact, I believe even J. P. Morgan ran up against in the case of Washington's will. All the state would do, it turned out, would be to recompense Hook for what he had originally paid for the manuscript. This they honorably did—and they got a bargain at $100. Hook never trusted me with an item "on approval" again. He was a close friend of Cecil Byrd, however, and just before Hook died Cecil purchased from him a most curious broadside, *Hieroglyphics of John Bull's Overthrow*, place and publisher unknown, but probably upper New York State, 1812, which contains the first known printed reference to "Uncle Sam." Till Hook uncovered this, the Library of Congress copy was considered unique.

# Thirteenth Amendment— Lincoln

THE APPEARANCE of an article about me in *The Saturday Evening Post* of March 22, 1952, by *Post* editor and book collector Pete Martin, with the attention-getting title, "He Finds Fortunes in Forgotten Corners," attracted considerable mail—some five thousand letters within a matter of weeks, from all over the world. Mostly these were offers of old family Bibles, "first additions" of McGuffey Readers, trivia and trash of all kinds. Mostly these were answered by form letters, but the few that appeared to have remote possibilities of any kind of value were further explored.

An exasperating factor in all this is that many notable books and historic documents have been reproduced in more or less exact facsimile; some many times and long ago. If something has been in someone's family "for generations," the owner invariably assumes that he has inherited a "priceless treasure" but one upon which he has put a price—generally a damn high one. It is a ticklish job, and an unrewarding one, to convince him that what he has is worthless. No one cares much for the bearer of bad news, and his motives are always questioned—obviously he is trying to rob them. The owners seldom stop to consider that the true originals of their precious documents are probably in the Library of Congress, the Public Records Office or some such official depository. The best, though not the polite, solution is simply to ignore such communications.

And yet there is always that offbeat chance! For not all historical documents are where one expects they should be, and some exist in more than one copy, and great-grandpa may just have emigrated from Scotland with a first edition of the Kilmarnock Burns. The possibility has led many people on many fruitless journeys, myself included.

So when a letter arrived from a Miss Wormley, of Washington, D.C., stating that she had a manuscript of the Thirteenth Amendment, signed by members of the House and Senate and by the President, I sent out a form letter in reply. That should have ended the matter. But back came an answer intimating that I did not understand the importance of the document in question. I replied that I thought I did, and what the lady had was unquestionably a reproduction, of which many had been made. I suggested that as she was a resident of Washington, D.C., all she had to do was take it to the Library of Congress and David Mearns, of the manuscript division, would speedily verify my opinion.

Miss Wormley's reply was that she was old and infirm and seldom left her home. And she added that her copy could not possibly be a facsimile or reproduction of any kind since it had been in her family's possession since 1865. I could see it at any time I was in Washington, but she did not care to entrust it to the mail, as it was in a heavy oaken frame, glassed, and so on. And there the correspondence ended. If she wouldn't go to the trouble to even consult the Library of Congress, in her own city, this seemed to me pretty solid proof that someone already had, and that what she possessed wasn't what it was purported to be.

About a year later I happened to be in Washington with nothing much to do, and her name suddenly popped into my head. I found in the phone book a Miss Imogene Wormley. She answered my call in a pleasant, cultivated southern voice and identified herself as the owner of the document, recalled our correspondence and made an appointment to have me see it at ten that evening.

When I left my hotel and gave the cabbie the address he looked at me curiously and said, "Are you sure you know where you're going?" On my reply that that was the address, he shrugged and took off. A while later we arrived in a rather dilapidated part of town, but at the correct address, and he said that perhaps he'd best wait till I came out. It was hard to get cabs that time of night in that part of town. I agreed. Ten minutes at the outside should do it.

When I rang, the door was opened by an aged but stately Negro woman who introduced herself as Miss Imogene Wormley. I was ushered into a spotless parlor, and Miss Wormley, who was arthritic and walked with a cane, explained to me that the document was on the second floor, under her bed, and asked if I would mind going up and getting it.

It had hung in the parlor for years, she explained, but had begun to be sun-faded, so she had stored it in the one place in the house where it would be adequately protected. I dragged it out and downstairs, and when I got a look at it, even through the glass which had been criss-crossed with adhesive tape to prevent breakage, said to myself, "Good God, this is real!"

The obvious question was, how did it ever get here? What was Miss Wormley's title to it? She made me some coffee, frequently replenished during the next few hours (I had dismissed the cab), and told me her family history. A more gracious, entertaining and intelligent hostess I have seldom met, nor one with a more interesting background. Had I ever heard of her grandfather, she inquired? In answer to my negative response she shyly said that she thought perhaps I might have, as he was in the *Dictionary of American Biography*, which Scribner's published. This was startling news to me, who had vaguely assumed that only Booker T. Washington and Crispus Attucks, of their race, had made those eminent pages. Certainly few of my ancestors, including my grand-fathers, had.

Her grandfather, James Wormley, became a hack driver for his father, a free Negro, who kept a livery stable in Washington and secured most of the trade of the capital's two chief hotels, the National and the Willard. In the course of his trade he met and became friendly with many prominent politicians. After an adventurous fling in California during the gold rush of 1849 and a later stint as a steward on a Mississippi River steamboat, he returned to Washington to become attached to the house-hold of Charles Sumner, the "great Abolitionist."

Wormley's later career was spectacularly successful. After the war he opened Wormley's Hotel, at H and 15th streets, for more than two decades distinguished for its international clientele. He became steward of the Metropolitan Club when it was first opened, and in 1868 he accom-panied Reverdy Johnson to London to act as steward at the American legation. With an indescribable dignity and pride Miss Wormley told of her family's dedication to the problems and welfare of the Negro, and of how they were educated and trained to serve their people. She and her sister had spent their lives as elementary schoolteachers; a nephew had been the first Negro to be commissioned from Annapolis, another had been an Ohio State senator, another a successful New York attorney, and so on, in a revealing roll call. Such, briefly, is the Wormley clan.

To return to the Thirteenth Amendment. Manuscript copies signed by some representatives and senators are not too uncommon. But copies signed in addition by Lincoln are. And Miss Wormley's had Lincoln's autograph.

On February 1, 1865, the House passed the Thirteenth Amendment, ending slavery or involuntary servitude except for punishment for crime, by the necessary two-thirds majority, the Senate having passed the same resolution the previous year. The occasion was recognized as historic, to the extent that Speaker of the House Schuyler Colfax surrendered the chair in order to descend to the floor and have his vote recorded in favor and, on returning to the chair, accepted a motion for adjournment.

In the atmosphere of general congratulation and celebration which followed adjournment, a small number of souvenir copies were drawn up in addition to the official engraved copy which now rests in the National Archives. Various members of the government appear to have carried these copies among their friends to obtain signatures of those who had voted for the amendment. Most of the known copies have relatively few signatures and almost invariably lack Lincoln's, as does the official copy. This is because the President's signature is not required to authenticate a constitutional amendment, nor is his approval legally necessary, the Constitution thus placing the constitutional process of amendment beyond the power of Executive veto.

I knew that the Library of Congress had a fine copy, signed by Lincoln, which had recently been presented them by Arthur A. Houghton, Jr. Before leaving, I asked Miss Wormley if I could take her and her document to the Library of Congress to compare signatures the following afternoon. Miss Wormley was reluctant, never, she told me, having been "on the Hill." But I insisted that she go, especially to tell David Mearns her story and also get disinterested advice about the value of her manuscript. It was a delightful afternoon. Her copy turned out to be exceptionally fine, being signed by thirty-three senators, one hundred and fourteen representatives, the four authenticating officers of Congress (Colfax's signature appearing twice, once as Speaker and again as Representative), and President Lincoln.

And Miss Wormley told of the family tradition: that Charles Sumner, on the day of the amendment's passage, February 1, 1865, gave this, his personal copy, to his servant James Wormley, as a token that his people were forever free. She further explained that she had always hoped to present it to Howard College but had finally decided that a more practical solution was to sell it, not for personal profit, but to aid her relatives' children to attend college. This was arranged to everyone's satisfaction, and the Sumner-Wormley copy of the Thirteenth Amendment—probably the copy of the greatest human interest—is now on permanent exhibition in the Lincoln Room of the Lilly Library.

I acquired another, less dramatic copy with fewer signatures of the

Thirteenth Amendment for Mrs. Nicholas Noyes of Indianapolis, who was forming a small but choice collection of American historical autographs. This included a fine set of the signers, including Button Gwinnett, of the Declaration of Independence. I also acquired for her, from the Oliver R. Barrett Lincoln collection, a unique copy of the Emancipation Proclamation, signed by both Lincoln and Seward on January 1, 1863—suppressed because of an error. The manuscript draft was sent to the State Department to be engrossed. After it was signed someone noted an error in the subscription. It read: "In testimony whereof I have hereunto set my name," etc. But this phraseology was used by Lincoln to proclaim treaties that had been ratified by Congress. His independent proclamations always read: "In witness whereof I have hereunto set my hand," etc.

I bought this for Mrs. Noyes for $18,000 and it joined her Bancroft copy, the fourth known draft (of five) of the Gettysburg Address, which I appraised at $100,000 when she gave her collection to Cornell. She later remarked to me, "If I had known Joe Lilly was going to give his library to Indiana, I'd have given them my collection, also."

I have had uniformly bad luck with this famed Address. Curiously enough, though five various manuscript drafts are known, there were, until recently, only three copies of its first printing extant. This was in a sixteen-page pamphlet, The Gettysburg Solemnities. Dedication of The National Cemetery at Gettysburg, Pennsylvania, November 19, 1863, with the Oration of Hon. Edward Everett, Speech of President Lincoln, etc., published at the Washington [D.C.] *Chronicle* office, 1863.

When the great exhibition of books representing "Printing and the Mind of Man" was held at Earls Court in London in July, 1963, rightly considered "the most impressive collection of books of this kind ever gathered under one roof," I was charged with arranging the American loans. The only privately owned copy of the Gettysburg Address was owned by a friend, Carl J. Haverlin, who agreed to loan it only if it were sent by sea, not air. It was also arranged that my library would purchase it on its return. Everything else, sent by air, returned safely. This, sent by sea, disappeared on its return. So now there are two.

In the fall of 1965 there was a great deal of newspaper fuss made over the "discovery" in the files of the New York State Historical Association at Cooperstown, New York, of a manuscript describing the autopsy on President Lincoln by his family physician, Dr. Robert K. Stone. There has been much controversy about the wound that killed Lincoln. The murder weapon was a small Derringer pistol, and a single shot was fired at the President's head from about two feet away on the evening of Friday, April 14, 1865. He died without regaining consciousness at seven twenty-two the next morning, and the autopsy was performed about noon in his own bedroom at the White House.

There was great confusion about the shooting and the autopsy. How did the bullet hole come to be in the left side of Mr. Lincoln's head, since Booth approached from Lincoln's right side? Could his life have been saved given modern medical techniques? Did the probing of the wound with unsterile fingers contribute to his death? And where did the bullet end up—above the left or the right eye? The statements of the two doctors who reached him first contradict each other completely.

I have no intention of getting mixed up in disputes between Lincolnists —these can be ferocious matters. What I did have, twenty years ago, were the original notes now at Cooperstown. I bought them at a Parke-Bernet sale in May of 1949 for $160, and through Paul Cooper they were placed in the Historical Association, to be "found" after the assassination of President Kennedy. There are remarkable similarities in the fatal woundings by John Wilkes Booth and Lee Harvey Oswald, but recent examination of the evidence by Dr. John K. Lattimer of New York City seems to prove conclusively that even with modern medical and surgical techniques, Lincoln would not have survived Booth's shot.

# Hitler-Marx-Lenin

I WAS EARLY fascinated by Hitler—probably because I knew Kurt Ludecke well, who was his secretary in the very early days managed to escape the purge and get out from the whole mess alive, and whose book, *I Knew Hitler*, Scribner's had published. I used to spend endless hours drinking coffee with him and listening to his yarns as to how, implausible as it was, the whole Nazi gang of no-goods took over an entire nation and indelibly changed history.

*Mein Kampf*, Ludecke assured me, was unquestionably the most important book published in the twentieth century, and Hitler meant every single damn word he said in it; and Kurt knew—he'd been in prison with him and helped write part of it. This meant, to me, that I had to have the first edition. Getting one at that time (this was the early thirties) was quite a chore. The book was first printed in Munich in 1925 (a second volume in 1927) and even on the Continent had become very expensive and difficult to acquire. The reason was that everybody in Germany who could possibly get one, did. Possession proved one had been in at the beginning—a good party member from its origin, rather like forty-niner California society ratings. There had been in addition to the regular trade edition a special edition of five hundred numbered copies, some signed by Adolf. These were absolutely unobtainable at that time.

But through Kurt, and from refugees, I managed to get three sets of the regular edition. Two I promptly sold—one to Lilly, another to Edgar Queeny: the former is now at Indiana, the latter Queeny gave to the Hoover War Memorial Library. The third hung around a while, and one day I decided to put it up at public auction. The reason wasn't financial— I simply wanted to see what it would bring under the hammer (I had sold my copies for $250 each), and its exposure might flush out other customers for material of this type. This is common practice.

I had absolutely no idea of what a storm I was brewing. The book was put into a miscellaneous sale at the American Art Association Anderson Galleries scheduled for December 10, 1936. Hitler was on the move at that point, and suddenly things began to happen. Auction galleries were at that time staid, stodgy and somnambulant places where anything louder than a nod or a whisper was a scream. Mostly they were used for the dispersal of estates, and their resemblance to funeral homes was marked. This was before television!

Suddenly the Anderson Galleries found itself picketed. I still don't know how it all started, but unexpectedly there were demonstrations, remonstrances, threats and whatall. The directors got in touch with me at once and demanded I withdraw the book. This I refused to do. It smacked, to me, too damn much of Hitler's own tactics. Scribner's and I had a perfect right to sell any book printed without committing ourselves to agreeing with its thesis. Start that and where do you end?

The consignment of the book had been anonymous, but it didn't take long for Scribner's ownership to "leak." A swastika was scratched on our Fifth Avenue window. And so on. Charley Scribner backed me every step and the book was sold as advertised. I was told the event would make the front page of *The New York Times*. It didn't. The front pages that day were cluttered with a more newsworthy item, Edward VIII's abdication. But the Hitler story did get a couple of columns on the inside, as follows:

The New York Times, Friday, December 11, 1936

POLICE GUARD SALE OF BOOK BY HITLER
First Edition Bought for $250 by Scribner's Consigner,
in Test to Fix Its Value.

2-Volume Work is Rare

Gallery Gets Protection After Receiving Protests
and Threats of a Demonstration

Under police protection, a copy of the first edition of Adolf Hitler's "Mein Kampf" was sold at auction for $250 yesterday afternoon at the American Art Association Anderson Galleries, Inc. This was said to be the first copy of the two-volume first edition of the book to be offered at auction either in this country or in Europe.

Threats of a demonstration during the auction led Hiram H. Parke, president of the auction galleries, to ask for police protection. Two plainclothes men were in the auction room during the sale and two patrolmen were on duty outside the entrance. Bidding began at $50 and quickly reached the final figure.

The successful bidder was Charles Scribner's Sons. Although the name of the consignor was not announced in the catalogue of the sale and the galleries declined to reveal it, a report in circulation that Scribner's had offered the book for sale was not denied by that firm.

### Wanted to Know Its Value

David Randall, head of the rare book department of the Scribner bookstore, said that, since the book had never come up at auction and its true market value could therefore be only guessed at, it was put up at auction so that public bidding could determine the value.

He denied a report that a lack of interest on the part of private buyers had caused the book to be placed on auction, saying that the firm already had sold privately two copies of the work.

Before the auction the American Art Association Anderson Galleries, Inc., received telegrams of protest requesting that the book be withdrawn from sale. Among those received was one from John Haynes Holmes, another from the Anti-Nazi department of the American League Against War and Fascism, and another from Harry Schaffer, Commander-in-Chief of the Jewish War Veterans of the United States.

Apprehension about a possible demonstration at the sale arose yesterday when persons well-known to the galleries telephoned that they had been informed of such plans. At 4 o'clock, immediately before the two-volume work was offered at auction, Mr. Parke read a statement.

"Since the publication of the catalogue, we have received telegrams from certain organizations and private individuals requesting, on different grounds, that this item be withdrawn from the sale," it said. "Upon receipt of these communications, I got into touch with the consignor of the item who is, in fact, one of the most reputable booksellers in the country, and advised him of the receipt of these messages of protest.

"As we are in this matter merely his agents, I laid the matter before him and requested his instructions. This gentleman, who is the consignor not only of this item but of other lots in the sale, informed me, first, that he had himself recently sold two copies of the book and that he knew of the existence of several others for sale in this city, and second that he desired us to proceed with the sale of this book.

"We, therefore, wish to inform the audience that our position is this: First, that we are the agents of the consignor and under contract with him to carry out his wishes wherever possible in respect to the sale of his consignment, and second, that the company never has assumed and will not assume a position of partisanship in respect to any material that it may offer at auction.

"Such a position is upon our part entirely untenable, and the association cannot as a whole take any other standpoint in respect to goods offered by it at public sale."

I hadn't had so much fun in a long time. I promptly put the book in our front window along with firsts of Paine's *Rights of Man*, Marx's *Com-*

*munist Manifesto, The Federalist Papers*, an early printing of the Magna
Carta and similar material. And, that night, a brick was tossed through it.

One thing the whole episode did was make Scribner's rare book department a sort of clearinghouse, for a while, of such Hitler material as came
on the market on this side of the water. I had some pretty dramatic stuff
pass through my hands. And I was never able to convince more than one
single collector that it was really important. I was, and remain, firmly and
unswervingly convinced that part of the job of dealers is to preserve the
sources of history. And the time to preserve them is when you are around
to get them. I am historical-minded enough to remember that Napoleon,
once only a name to scare kids with in England, became not too many
years later that country's most collected historical figure. And the same is
true of everyone connected with him—marshals and so on. It's going to
happen with Hitler.

Hitler books just came to me. One acquaintance of mine was among
the detail sent to pick up Göring for the Nuremberg trials. When the rest
of the boys were getting souvenirs of radios, pistols, wristwatches and
other swastika-decorated stuff, my friend looked over the library, took
the copy of the first edition of *Mein Kampf* (the limited one) which
Hitler had given Göring, and, asking his superior officer if he could keep
it, was told, "Hell yes, but why don't you take something valuable?"

The most important books were a clutch from Hitler's personal library.
These were rescued from the burning Braune Haus by an American
lieutenant who was, in addition to being in the task force fighting
through it, a book collector. There are six books, described in Scribner
catalogue 137, as follows:

### HITLER'S PERSONAL LIBRARY

HITLER, ADOLF. His personal copies of:

(1) *Mein Kampf*. Munich, 1925–7. 2 volumes, 8vo, First (Limited)
Editions, the former bound in white vellum, the latter in full red
morocco. Autographed by Hitler.

(2) *Mein Kampf*. Munich, 1938. Special edition done for Hitler's
fiftieth birthday, given him, signed by various party members, including
Meissner. 8vo, full blue morocco.

(3) Rosenberg, Alfred. *Der Mythus des 20 Jahrhunderts*. Munich,
1938. 8vo, First Edition, original black cloth. Inscribed on the fly-leaf
to Hitler by Rosenberg and dated Munich, July 23, 1930.

(4) Mjoelnir, Dr. Goebbels. *Das Buch Isidor*. Munich, 1928. 8vo,
First Edition, original black cloth. Inscribed on the fly-leaf to Hitler
by Goebbels and dated August 12, 1928.

(5) Röhm, Ernst. *Die Geschichte eines Hochverräters*. Munich,
1928. 8vo, First Edition, original black cloth. Inscribed on the fly-leaf
to Hitler by Röhm and dated August 3, 1928.

(6) Ford, Henry. *Mein Leben und Werk*. Leipzig [n.d.]. 8vo, Fifth Edition, original grey cloth. Inscribed to Hitler: "Mit allen besten Wünschen für 1924. Ernst Hanfstaengl."

Hitler's own copies of *Mein Kampf* are the most important in existence. His copy of Rosenberg's *Myth of the 20th Century*, which was the Nazi bible, is similarly vital. The other volumes, presented him by Goebbels, Röhm, etc., are of course unique. The most important portion of Hitler's library which can ever come on the market. Together with letters to him, etc. Further details upon application.

The collection $4,500

The most dramatic document though, was the proclamation of the Franco-Prussian War, signed by Kaiser Wilhelm and eventually given by Hess to Hitler as a Christmas present. Its description in the same catalogue was:

THE DECLARATION OF THE FRANCO-
PRUSSIAN WAR—SIGNED BY
KAISER WILHELM. LATER GIVEN
BY HESS TO HITLER

WILHELM, KAISER. The Proclamation of the Franco-Prussian War, signed by Kaiser Wilhelm. Bound with the broadside printing of the same, beginning: "Nous, Guillaume, Roi de Prusse, faisons savoir ce qui suit aux habitants des territoires occupés par les armées allemandes," etc. Bound together, folio, white vellum with the imperial Austrian crest, in black, with a special title page, printed in gold and blue, autographed by Rudolf Hess, to Hitler.                              $2,750

The specially printed title page (in gold) reads (translated): "To the Führer, Christmas, 1938, in which year he twice overran borders in order to bring back German territory into the Reich (signed in autograph) Rudolf Hess."

A printed colophon recites the history of this dramatic document. Given by Bismarck to the famous General Stieber, it passed from Hess to Hitler, as recounted above, as a Christmas present.

Nobody wanted these when I had them. One day a person I had never heard of then, and haven't since, bought them, explaining that he thought that someday they would be of historical value, and having suffered from Hitler, he thought it fair that he should buy them and eventually present them to the Brooklyn high school his children attended. That's all I know about whatever happened to the books; the document was purchased by Robert Honeyman, who gave it, along with other notable material, to his, and my, alma mater, Lehigh University.

I have also had a fair amount of Russian literature and political material. This came about in curious ways. I had read a lot of Russian literature—

in translation, of course—and being interested in political theory, I had at least heard of Marx and Lenin. This all fitted in well with Scribner's background. They had published some of the earliest translations in English of Russian novels; Tolstoy was introduced to America by Scribner's with *The Cossacks* in 1878, and they also printed the first collected edition of his works. Some Scribner, I believe, had an official connection with our embassy in Moscow, and the firm became enthusiastic about Russian literature. Right down the line, and to the present time, there have always been Russians around Scribner's. During part of my stint there the manager of the bookstore was Nicholas Wreden, a remarkable lad, who had authored *The Unmaking of a Russian* (New York, 1935), and the current and long-time manager is Prince Igor Kropotkin, head of the Orthodox Church in America. Nick had dramatically escaped from Russia after the revolution—along with Alec Gard, the famed ballet cartoonist—in a stolen submarine which landed in England. Alec was then doing all the caricatures for Sardi's restaurant, which were still there the last time I was, the only pay for which he ever got was one meal and two drinks a day, free. Like Hervé Riel—"that he asked and that he got, nothing more."

Through them I got to know a fair lot of White Russians, many of whom had books I wanted, or ways of getting them. Among these was Mark Aldanov, the great Russian historical novelist in exile, whose smash success, *The Fifth Seal* (New York, 1943), Nick translated. John Carter also had substantial connections, and so, in one way and another, I acquired some first-class Russian works. First choice of what he wanted, chiefly literature, went to Lilly, most of the rest to B. J. Kilgour of Cincinnati, who was just beginning his great collection, now at Harvard. And a lot went to F. B. Adams, Jr., then in private industry and scouting for material for his "Radical Literature in America" hobby.

One of the most interesting books I ever had was an edition of Maxim Gorki's *The Lower Depths* (Petersburg, 1920) inscribed by him: "This book tells the truth about the Russian people, about the way they preach without considering the consequence of their sermon, about the way they console one another without faith in the power of consolation, and pretend to love without knowing how to love. In the end each one of them wants only one thing: leave me alone!" The copy is signed and dated October 10, 1920. It now belongs to the eminent Swiss financier Martin Bodmer of Geneva, who has assembled what is without question the greatest private library put together in our century.

A particularly interesting collection was that of Serge Diaghileff. This, incredibly enough, had been stored for years in the cellar of a small Paris hotel, where he died, as security against his unpaid bill. The Scribner brief catalogue description of it follows.

A collection of scores, orchestral parts and manuscript material from the library of Serge Diaghileff and in use from 1909 until 1929 by his *Ballets Russes*. Preserved in 26 cloth boxes. $7,500

It would be difficult to exaggerate the influence in the history of music, the theatre, the pictorial arts and cultural taste in general of Diaghileff's *Ballets Russes*. The present collection of full scores, orchestral parts, piano scores (used by choreographers and conductors) and manuscripts, comprises the major portion of the surviving musical library of Diaghileff himself. Many of these volumes have the markings of a succession of famous conductors; while members of the orchestra would record on their parts the date and theatre of performance in Paris, Monte Carlo or Buenos Aires. Some show corrections or additions in the autograph of their composers, others choreographic notes by Fokine or Massine. Prokofieff presents the MS of *Le Fils Prodigue,* Auric the first edition of *Les Matelots,* to Diaghileff. Stravinsky corrects the unpublished MS. score of *L'Oiseau de Feu.* Massine annotates his own principal dance for the first ballet he ever designed. And so on.

The importance of this astonishing collection is twofold. Its romantic or sentimental appeal, as the most intimate of all souvenirs of a historic company and a man of genius, needs no stressing. But it has also unique features of interest for the musician, the historian and the practising choreographer. *Le Lac des Cygnes* shows the actual rearrangement of the score from the earlier versions to the Diaghileff version in use today, and represents the transition from the classicism of Petipa to the romanticism of Diaghileff's first master choreographer, Fokine. The collection abounds in supplementary and corrective manuscript material, largely unpublished. The notes of the choreographer or conductor preserve, as nothing else could do, the classic tradition of the performance of the golden age of ballet.

I was unable to sell it *en bloc,* and it was finally dispersed piecemeal.

Reasonably soon after the Hitler fuss, Carter managed to get a remarkable collection of Lenin material, all published before 1917, and I splashed it in our windows. The Commies and their dupes, of course, had been behind the Hitler episode, and I was showing impartiality.

One of the items included was the true first edition of *The Communist Manifesto* (London, 1848)—a damn rare book. A note in the window read:

With one-sixth of the habitable world actually governed by Marxian doctrines and with the rest of the world increasingly agitated over the possible spread of communistic social orders, an acquaintance with their fundamental principles becomes every day more essential to the understanding of world history and the forces behind the ever-sharpening clash between fascism and "the Left."

All this led to a visit to Scribner's from the editor of, and a reporter from, *The Daily Worker*. They couldn't understand how capitalist Scribner's had such material. I explained that as a dealer in old and rare books I was interested in political and philosophical movements and such source material as I could lay hands on from a historical point of view. I then gave them a catalogue of the Lenin material to look over. After a close reading the editor exclaimed, "Who the hell wrote this?" I modestly and inaccurately admitted authorship, explaining that Nick Wreden had done the Russian translations but that I was responsible for the bibliographical notes and the general tone. "But," they both protested, "this follows the party line exactly." "And why shouldn't it?" I asked, trying to look mysterious and haughty. Nick immediately took his cue from this and went off into some convincing story in Russian, during which our visitors became extremely warm and friendly indeed.

They left thoroughly convinced that we were both part of some apparatus or ring which had penetrated the publishing world. What they didn't know was that the catalogue had been prepared for Scribner's by two British Communists, one the most expert bibliographer in this field, and the other equally well known as a political theorist, and both high-ranking party members, one at that time the secretary of the British party itself. I am the only rare book dealer who ever had a favorable editorial written about him in *The Daily Worker*. The Lenin collection was sold eventually to B. L. Kilgour and now forms part of his extensive collection at Harvard.

Now these newsboys were not easily duped. Material of the type I had is not easily come by. Of the original printing of the *Manifesto* itself, in both its issues, there are but fourteen copies known, four in America, three of which I have owned.

Original documentary sources of the Russian revolution are hard to come by. The Preface to the Scribner Lenin collection explains why:

> To understand Lenin's contribution to the modern world it is necessary to know what he wrote; but this is no simple matter. The modern Russian editions of his works have been edited in an atmosphere of polemic; their editors have been inclined to select and annotate with their eye on current controversies in Russia. The selections translated into other languages have been determined by the requirements of Com-

munist propaganda abroad rather than any elucidation of Lenin's own development. Their translation has sometimes been incompetent and sometimes tendentious. The only scientific avenue to Lenin's writings must be a complete collection of the first editions in their original language.

But this again is not easy. They were for the most part issued by illegal organizations, banned by the police, distributed from hand to hand among the workers in Russia. Some were hectographed, some printed on single sheets, in small pamphlets or in the pages of periodicals. They were printed in secret in Russia, or abroad on flimsy paper to be smuggled over the frontier pasted into the linings of trunks or dumped in waterproof wrapping in the Black Sea. Some have been entirely lost, and others have survived only in single copies. The only considerable collections exist in Russian museums; and these have been derived to some extent from Lenin's immediate circle, but more largely from police archives. These museums have a monopoly on such sources of supply, and nearly all first editions of Lenin are thus of very real rarity.

The present collection is a truly remarkable series, and it is improbable that it can ever be equalled outside Russia. It contains all Lenin's work of major importance published before 1917. In the absence of any complete bibliography it is not possible to say exactly how many pieces are not here represented, but it is thought that only one book (*The Development of Capitalism in Russia*, 1899) is missing, besides some smaller pamphlets. The most useful substitute for a comprehensive bibliography of Lenin's first editions is *Russkaya Politicheskaya Literatura Zagrantsei, 1883–1905* (*Russian Political Literature Abroad*, Paris, 1913. 4to green wrappers), which was edited by L. B. Kamenev. A copy of this is included with the collection: but it does not include works published either secretly or legally in Russia, and does not come down later than 1905. It has been supplemented from the notes to the first edition of the *Collected Works in Russian* (Moscow, 1924–1926).

The works by Lenin listed below have been arranged according to the date of their composition. Care has been taken to note the first as well as the most accessible appearance of each piece in English; . . .

Here is the note on the very first item, *The Law of Factory Fines:*

Workers of the World, Unite! Explanation of the Law on Factory Fines. Published by 'The League of Struggle for the Emancipation of the Working Class.' Geneva, Press on 'The Union of Russian Social Democrats.' 1897.

Small 8vo. 106 x 151 mm., original grey wrappers, printed in black, 48 pp.

The Second Edition. The first edition was printed illegally in St. Petersburg in 1895 on the secret press of Narodnaya Volya (The People's Will), which was a terrorist organisation. This is the first work by Lenin printed outside Russia, and his first work which has survived in its entirety. (Of the hectographed *What are the Friends of the People and How They Fight against the Social Democrats* [1894] only parts I and III have survived.) Russian *Collected Works* (1st Ed. vol. i.) Not yet translated into English. Written in 1895. The best account of the writing of this pamphlet is in N. Krupskaya (wife of Lenin), *Memories of Lenin*, London, 1930, vol. i, pp. 10–11.

In this pamplet Lenin first demonstrated the essential relation between the immediate economic demands of the factory workers and the political demands of the Social Democrats. It is his first pamphlet addressed to the as yet unconsciously political elements in the urban proletariat.

They were sure right about all this following the party line!

# Sir Winston Churchill

WINSTON S. CHURCHILL'S American publisher during the 1920's and 1930's was Charles Scribner's Sons, and the great man had himself been a frequent visitor to the New York store. He was never a collector's favorite until well after 1950—then, zoom! What was particularly sought after was his first and only novel, *Savrola*, published in both London and New York in 1900. I found that the American edition was published on February 3, 1900, the English not until ten days later. It was, with Scribner's, a standard $15 book in either edition before the Churchill boom. The most recent copies to appear at auction brought £160 for the American edition, £120 for the English.

This romantic story of derring-do in a South American republic, à la Richard Harding Davis, has a curious plot: the hero rescues the republic from a fate worse than death—dictatorship. Local color was supplied from Churchill's war correspondent experiences in Cuba. At one point just after the war I nearly succeeded, with the aid of dramatist (and Henty collector) Talbot Jennings, in selling it to Hollywood, with Churchill's consent, only to have the deal killed at the last moment, I was reliably informed, by some mogul's decision that, "The hell with Churchill, he's anti-Semitic." An inferior version was eventually made abroad.

In any event, I became something of a Churchill specialist, finding his unrecorded first book appearance in *The Risings on the North-West Frontier* (Allahabad, 1898), which included dispatches written by him at the age of twenty-four as special war correspondent, which later formed the basis of his first published book, *The Story of the Malakand Field Force* (London, 1898).

There has been controversy about this book; his bibliographer, Frederick Woods, relegates it to "Appendix IV" with a disparaging note to

the effect that though "the status of the book is apparently still a controversial matter . . . facts seem to disprove the attribution of the book to
Sir Winston." He further states that he thinks he is right "in saying that it
was relatively unknown until it appeared in the *Times Bookshop Exhibition* celebrating Sir Winston's eightieth birthday" in 1954. Perhaps it is
this statement which prejudices me. I was publicly offering the book a
decade before then, catalogued thus:

> [CHURCHILL, W. S.] The Risings on the North-West Frontier
> (compiled from the Special War Correspondence of the "Pioneer").
> Allahabad: Printed and Published at the Pioneer Press, 1898. 8vo,
> First Edition, original red cloth, with leaf of Errata tipped in before
> title-page and map preceding introduction.                          $45
>
> Churchill is referred to in Appendix IV, page xx, at line 11 seq.:
> ". . . he [General Jeffreys] has praised the courage and resolution of
> Lieutenant Churchill of the 4th Hussars, correspondent of the *Pioneer*
> newspaper with the force, who made himself useful at a critical mo-
> ment." The reference is to the action described in *The Story of the
> Malakand Field Force* [London, 1898]. A more extended account of
> Churchill's personal experiences may be found in *A Roving Commission*,
> Chapter XI, "The Mahmund Valley."
>
> This compilation includes dispatches written by Churchill at the age of
> 24, later forming the basis for his first *The Story of the Malakand
> Field Force,* in which he mentions the fact that his letters were re-
> printed in a London paper but does not mention the *Pioneer*. In *A Rov-
> ing Commission,* Chapter X, however, he clearly indicates his authorship
> by saying that he "had been commissioned as war correspondent by
> the *Pioneer* while his mother had arranged that his letters should be
> published simultaneously in London by the *Daily Telegraph.*

I was particularly anxious to get hold of a Churchill manuscript but
was told that this was impossible. He was acutely conscious of his place in
history, I was informed, and every scrap of paper of his was being saved,
to be given eventually to the nation.

Just after the end of the war, while my London colleague, John Carter,
was working with the British Information Services in New York, Winston Churchill came to America. He was to have a dinner with Charles
Scribner, but I knew better than to ask Scribner to intercede for me in a
matter such as this. He never allowed his personal friendships to collide
with his business.

However, Carter promised to attempt what he frankly said would be
the impossible. In due course and without any fuss I received a fifty-page
carbon copy of a typescript of a Churchill speech. It was not everything I

wanted but it was more than I had really expected and it was interesting in its own right. And it was, furthermore, the copy of his most notable postwar effort, the famous "Iron Curtain" speech delivered at Fulton, Missouri, in 1946. So far, good. But then I made an error. It has always been difficult for me to keep my big mouth shut. I could have disposed of it without publicity, but I was planning on issuing a catalogue of fifty distinguished books and manuscripts, featuring the Shuckburgh copy of the Gutenberg Bible, the original printing of the Declaration of Independence and other extremely interesting material, such as General Ross's original manuscript maps detailing the march of the British army in August, 1814, on Washington, which led to its burning of the Library of Congress; the declaration of the Franco-Prussian War, signed by Kaiser Wilhelm, later given by Hess to Hitler as a Christmas present. So I included the Churchill document. It was listed as follows:

### CHURCHILL'S MOST FAMOUS
### POST-WAR SPEECH

CHURCHILL, WINSTON S. Speech at Westminster College, Fulton, Missouri, 5 March 1946. Original typescript, with corrections. 50 leaves, text on rectos only. $550.

There are over seventy differences between the typed version and the published speech (pp. 93–105 of *The Sinews of Peace,* a copy of which accompanies the typescript). The large majority of the changes can be seen in the making in this corrected typescript which shows the greatest orator of our time at work. But there are also two of three points at which can be observed in uncorrected form.

Preparations for Mr. Churchill's epoch-making speech at Fulton were studiously informal, as befitted the ostentatiously informal character of the occasion. The draft of the speech was typewritten according to Mr. Churchill's normal formula, viz. on small octavo sheets of blue paper, heavily paragraphed for his characteristic delivery. Of this draft, on which Mr. Churchill worked at the British Embassy in Washington the night before he left for Fulton, there was made, in addition to the original, one single carbon copy. As Mr. Churchill, in the course of rehearsing the speech, added his own final polishing and corrections, these were taken down in shorthand, by his secretary. One sheet only of the fifty was so heavily corrected as to need re-typing (viz., sheet 6). The remaining sheets carry pencil corrections and additions as taken down from his dictation.

These were then immediately typed on Mr. Churchill's own top copy, from which he delivered his actual speech. This annotated carbon copy, therefore, although it contains nothing in Mr. Churchill's own writing, remains slightly the more "original" of the two original typescripts of the Fulton speech.

This typescript was given privately to a member of the staff at the Embassy in Washington, in order that he might prepare from it an unofficial abstract for communication to the press. It remained in his possession until purchased by Scribner's.

The catalogue was issued and the Churchill document was purchased by an old friend, Robert Honeyman. Nobody bought the Gutenberg, but almost everything else went (at the present writing, though, Scribner's still has one item left in stock).

Then one day Dan Longwell, another old friend, came in. Where, he wanted to know, was the Churchill document? When informed it was sold, he insisted that I get it back, if at all possible. *Life* magazine, of which he had been editor for many years, was issuing Churchill's *Memoirs*, and he himself had a notable collection for which he needed this manuscript. As an added incentive he planned on presenting it eventually to Westminster College. Honeyman, an amiable person, agreed to this. It wound up eventually at Columbia University.

A few weeks later Charles Scribner summoned me to his goldfish bowl of an office on the fifth floor and, as I entered, requested me to close the door behind me. This was ominous. It was and continues to be a Scribner tradition that all doors are open at all times, literally.

Handing me an official-looking letter, he said, a little wearily, "You got me into this; you get me out." It was a letter from Churchill, written in a towering rage. Somehow, I never did know how, he had heard about the sale of the manuscript and was displeased. "Waste-basket scavengers" was one of the mildest epithets he applied to us. He reminded Charles of his long friendship with the firm, of the recent advice he had given him, and so on. Heads, by God, were going to roll, and I could already see mine under the desk. Incidentally, Charles explained to me Churchill's "recent advice." The publishing rights to his *Memoirs* were up for grabs and the competition was furious. "Stay away from it," Charles told me Churchill had advised him, "nobody is going to make money out of it but me."

All I could do was write Churchill the exact truth as to how (but not from whom) it was obtained, the price given, £100 ($280), and stress the fact that no one had dreamed of improper behavior, etc. I also mentioned that John Carter had been the moving spirit behind Scribner's presenting him the original manuscript of Arthur Hugh Clough's poem "Say not, the struggle nought availeth." Churchill quoted this in one of his most famous speeches, given at England's darkest hour in 1941:

> Say not, the struggle nought availeth,
> The labour and the wounds are vain,

> The enemy faints not, nor faileth,
> And as things have been they remain.
>
> If hopes were dupes, fears may be liars;
> It may be, in yon smoke concealed,
> Your comrades chase e'en now the fliers,
> And, but for you, possess the field.
>
> For while the tired waves, vainly breaking,
> Seem here no painful inch to gain,
> Far back, through creeks and inlets making,
> Comes silent, flooding in, the main.
>
> And not by eastern windows only,
> When daylight comes, comes in the light,
> In front, the sun climbs slow, how slowly,
> But westward, look, the land is bright.

Scribner's had the original manuscript, which was in a letter from Clough to the poet William Allingham. This Scribner's gave Churchill, "as a token that the principle of 'lend, lease and give,' extends beyond material aid to those intangible weapons of the spirit which are the common armament of two free peoples." Carter presented it to the Prime Minister personally and had the pleasure, during a solitary audience, of hearing him read it aloud from the manuscript.

That was the whole story, and what did Churchill want? Back came a three-word answer—"Half the profits." This he received, but he never discovered, luckily, that I recouped for my firm much more than this by selling our correspondence.

There is an amusing bibliographical problem involved in an edition of his *A Roving Commission. My Early Life*, which Scribner's first published in 1930. It was published the same year in England as *My Early Life—A Roving Commission;* why the change of title I could never understand. In any event, Scribner's reissued it in 1939, with an Introduction by Dorothy Thompson. Churchill is described on the title page as "First Lord of the Admiralty" and needed a shove to get him before the American public, who wouldn't have recognized him from Adam's off-ox. The best the dust jacket blurb could produce was approval of him, in a *Saturday Evening Post* article, by Vincent Sheean.

Anyway, since late in 1929 it has been Scribner's habit to put a capital letter *A* under the copyright notice on the verso of the title page to indicate a first edition. If that is not present, the book is a reprint (usually). But in this particular case there was a *double* capital under the copyright, i.e., *AA*. This was later brought to my attention by a Churchill collector who inquired "How so?" Well, I asked around and was informed by those who knew about such things that this was normal procedure. After all, it was a new edition with a new Introduction, hence, the new material had to be copyrighted, hence the double *A*.

This was nice, reassuring, logical and right out of headquarters, and I so reported. Some months later I met a girl at a party somewhere who was working for Scribner's, at the press. She was Bryn Mawr, I recall, and I simply happened to mention this anomaly. "Oh, I remember," she replied. "I was asked about that. I put in those double *A*'s. *The page looked prettier that way.*"

For one who has spent his entire adult life with the printed word, I have a skepticism about it all. I have seldom known a story, of which I knew anything firsthand, which received any newspaper treatment that remotely resembled the truth. And I double-check reference books and bibliographies where possible. Scribner's poured a lot of money into a large reference book: *American Authors and Books 1640–1940*, 858 double-column pages. After others worked on the book for years, I was asked to look it over just before it was to be issued. I recall writing an eighteen-page, single-spaced report of errors. The original issue of this reference work is hard to find. It was promptly remaindered—even before being published—and now has a cancel title page, bearing another imprint. At the bottom of the spine of the cover there is a pasted-on label which, if peeled off, will reveal Scribner's stamp.

This fiasco sort of shook my faith in reference books generally, and I am not too happy about being able to prove myself a really dead bastard in print. The official family genealogy, *Randall and Allied Families. William Randall (1609–1693) of Scituate and His Descendants* (Chicago, 1943), has only one serious defect I know of—it omits me. My brother is there, I'm not. Officially I'm a bastard.

When I became a librarian I was made aware of the fact that *The National Union Catalog* of books, issued by the Library of Congress, is the ultimate source of all librarians' information on dates, titles, births, deaths, publishers, anything. I found the entries: "I. Randall, David Anton, 1905–1946. II. Lilly, Josiah Kirby, 1861–     ." In two lines the Library of Congress managed to make three errors. They cut me off in 1946, the year of J. K. Lilly's father's death, and they confused him with his father, whom they had still alive and in his advanced nineties. All official, by golly, and embalmed in print.

# Carroll Atwood Wilson

CARROLL ATWOOD WILSON'S collecting career spanned two decades, from 1925 to about 1945, when he became seriously ill. He was one of the first Rhodes scholars, from Williams, and in the same group as Christopher Morley. Wilson was, his Williams classmate Philo C. Calhoun recounts:

> A hardworking, full-time practicing lawyer, charged with the guidance of all the immense business and philanthropic interests of the family of Guggenheim, officer in half a dozen corporations, trustee of as many great charitable foundations. During most of his life his home was a modest downtown New York apartment.

He was by no means a wealthy man. "All my life," he once said to me, "I have made an adequate living, but I have never been able to accumulate any capital." At his death, nearly half his estate consisted of the value of his library—this cannot be said of many collectors.

His copy of Trollope's *The Warden* (London, 1855) has his penciled note on the end paper: "The purchase of this book began my serious book-collecting. I bought it as a birthday present to myself in May, 1925, and thereby opened the door to some of the pleasantest hours of my life." How vigorously and successfully he pursued his avocation is shown by the fact that Michael Sadleir, in the Preface to his unrivaled *Bibliography of Trollope* (London, 1928), said of Wilson: "His energy, enthusiasm and generous collaboration have so greatly contributed to this Trollopian record that I feel his name would more properly appear as co-author than recipient of thanks." And the same could be said of Richard Curle's *Collecting American First Editions* (New York, 1931), but wasn't.

Wilson immersed himself in bibliographical matters, *The Colophon*, the Grolier Club, and especially the Bibliographical Society of America (he was chairman of its committee on publications). His most important work with the latter society was his insistence, against no inconsiderable opposition, on its sponsoring the massive *Bibliography of American Literature* (New Haven, 1955–   ). The second volume, compiled by Jacob Blanck, is dedicated to his memory.

Wilson did some writing but not too much. He did his own catalogue of his incomparable collection of Samuel Butler, given to Chapin College at Williams (I can still hear him reciting, after a few of his excellent bourbons, "O, God, O Montreal"); a few papers here and there and not too much else. He worked long and hard on a bibliography of his beloved Gilbert and Sullivan, of whose works he had a great collection, but could not be induced to publish it.

"I am not," he once quipped to me, "going to publish a bibliography only to open one of Scribner's or some other dealer's catalogue, and see something listed triumphantly as 'Not in Wilson' and priced, therefore, at almost triple what I can offer." The bibliography was nearly done—I have seen it myself—but it has unaccountably disappeared, a great loss indeed, especially as no even reasonably adequate bibliography exists and the complex work will have to be done all over again.

Not that he was ungenerous with information. As John Carter wrote, "Wilson's preferred method was to open the shelves of his library and the stores of his knowledge to other workers. And this he did to such generous effect that any recent bibliographer in his field whose preface did not contain a tribute to his assistance could almost automatically be suspected of negligence."

Wilson's first love was the New England authors, Alcott, Emerson, Hawthorne, Holmes, Longfellow, Lowell, Thoreau and Whittier, and his collections were unrivaled in their time. He also had good collections of Irving, including that great rarity, *Salmagundi* (New York, 1807–1808), in parts; fine Melvilles and good Poes, but these collections "jest growed." His two main English author collections besides those mentioned were of Thomas Hardy and Anthony Trollope, and he also had the best collection in America of H. Rider Haggard.

My favorite of Wilson's remarkable Longfellows remains *The Hanging of the Crane* (Boston, 1874). It was privately printed for Longfellow's personal use—only four copies are known, a fifth was lost in the mails in transit to Owen D. Young—and was long considered the rarest and most valuable of Longfellow's first editions.

Longfellow had written at the top of the first page of this copy: "*Pendre la crémaillère*, to hang the crane, is the French expression for a house-warming, or the first party given in a new house." It also had corrections in his hand. No copy had ever appeared on the market, those recorded being in Craigie House or public institutions.

Two ladies came into Harzof's one afternoon in the early thirties and showed him this copy, which was in the original envelope in which it was mailed, addressed in Longfellow's hand to his second cousin: "W. O. Bartlett, Esq. N. York Sun Buildings, New York. By Adams & Co.'s Express. To be delivered immediately. Paid." They did not know where it came from, but they were related to Bartlett somehow; this had turned up in some papers, and they had nothing else. Harzof asked them what they wanted, and when the answer was $25 he paid them. As soon as they were out the door he hailed me, explained what he had and said, "Get your friend Wilson on the phone. Ask him for five hundred dollars!" I got Carroll and told him what Harzof had; he replied, "I never thought I'd see that. How much is it?" I answered $1,000, and he told me to hang on to it and that he would be around immediately after work to pick it up. It was a major investment for him in those times but he knew, none better, what he was being offered. In the thirty-five intervening years no other copy has been uncovered.

Amid general jubilation in the shop the door opened and the two ladies reentered. Approaching Harzof apologetically, they stated that perhaps they had made a mistake in selling him this item. They had told a friend about it and had been advised that they were foolish because "probably the stamps were worth that much." Harzof graciously removed the stamps and presented them to the ladies, who departed delighted. In the Wilson catalogue you will find this with the notation: "In the original wrapper (stamps removed) in which it was mailed."

Now, had the ladies asked Harzof, who was hard-boiled but perfectly ethical, what the pamphlet was worth, he would unquestionably have offered them at least several hundred dollars. Had he offered them $25 knowing what it was worth, it would have been unethical, if not illegal. But there was nothing wrong in accepting their offer. This is why dealers, unless they know their client, are reluctant to make an offer but insist the owner state his price. If they don't want to do this they can always put the item up at public auction and take what comes. Another reason that dealers are reluctant to make offers is that all too often the owner wants only what amounts to a free appraisal or a figure which can be used in offering the item elsewhere at a higher price.

Also, and this has happened many times, when the dealer offers a fair and substantial sum, he is met with the reply: "My, I didn't know this was worth that much. I'll just keep it, as it won't ever be worth any less eventually, will it?" It damn often is.

Perhaps the assiduousness with which Wilson put things together is best represented by his copy of Laurence Hope's *The Garden of Kama and Other Love Lyrics from India Arranged in Verse*, third edition (London, 1903). He also had it in its first edition (London, 1902) in his "Familiar Quotations" section, as it contains the first appearance of her best-remembered poem, "Pale hands I loved beside the Shalimar."

> Inscribed "To Thomas Hardy with sincerest thanks for the hours and hours of pleasure he has given me by his works Laurence Hope," and with Max Gate book-label.
>
> Enclosed are two cards and a t.l.s., signed with the author's real name, Violet Nicolson, to Hardy, a long letter from her solicitor, with full explanation of her suicide and the spiritual reason therefor, and an a.l.s. from Gosse to Hardy, revealing that on the very day she died he and Hardy were discussing her poems.
>
> Also inserted, the original draft of MS of Hardy's obituary notice of Laurence Hope for *The Athenaeum*, Oct. 29, 1904, some 300 words, much corrected, a beautifully written tribute to a poet and poetry which he clearly valued very highly. This tribute appears without signature, and it is not generally known that Hardy wrote it. I have noted the few slight differences between this MS and the final form, a type-written copy of which accompanies this.
>
> With these also is the a.l.s., 2 pp., signed "Thomas Hardy," dated Max Gate, Oct. 23, 1904, to the editor of *The Athenaeum*, showing that Hardy to a certain extent solicited the opportunity.

After Wilson's death in 1947 the problem of the proper disposal of his library came up. The estate could have sold it at auction, but it was not the kind of library susceptible to this treatment. It contained some remarkable rarities, true enough, but also a great mass of material which would bring very little "under the hammer" and would be very expensive to catalogue, as a tremendous lot of "bundling" would have to be done. It also seemed criminal to break into fragments collections of related fragments he had so carefully assembled.

Scribner's finally purchased it with an agreement to keep as much of it together as possible and also to publish his major opus, a catalogue of the collection on which he had worked for many years.

This eventually appeared in two stout volumes with the rather cumbersome title: *Thirteen Author Collections of the Nineteenth Century and Five Centuries of Familiar Quotations* (Privately printed for Charles Scribner's Sons, New York, 1950), edited by Jean C. S. Wilson and David

A. Randall, priced at $50. It still remains a monument to Wilson, especially as it prints, often for the first time, many important letters and especially his notes. These have been retained *ipsissima verba* and give some of the personal flavor of the man. The volumes lack, however, an index, which makes for hard going in many instances. Never, never (or hardly ever) do a reference book without an index. It is rather akin to the Bellman's map in *The Hunting of the Snark*, "a perfect and absolute blank."

We managed to keep the majority of the American collections together. The Emersons went to Duke University, the Whittiers, appropriately, to Swarthmore College, which has a fine antislavery collection. The rest went mostly to Waller Barrett and are now in his great collection at the University of Virginia.

The Hardys and Trollopes were broken up but found proper homes: the major Trollopes with Bob Taylor and the Hardys with Fred Adams, Philo Calhoun and Colby College. This all would have pleased Carroll very much. His wife kept his Gilbert and Sullivan at the time, planning on eventually finishing his bibliography. This never eventuated, and just a few years ago they were acquired by Scribner's and purchased from them by me for the Lilly Library.

# Frank J. Hogan

I FIRST MET Frank J. Hogan in 1937 in his law offices at Washington, D.C. He was already well known as a collector of Elizabethan material and was expanding his interests to English and American literature of all periods.

He was a feared trial lawyer who had made his reputation defending Edward Doheny of the famed Teapot Dome scandal. I remember his patiently explaining to me how he secured the acquittal of Doheny on charges of offering Albert B. Fall, Warren Harding's Secretary of the Interior, a $100,000 bribe to lease some California oil lands to a drilling company while Fall was being convicted of accepting the bribe on the same evidence. I didn't understand, but then I haven't "the legal mind," as I speedily discovered at Harvard Law School.

I had sold Hogan some books indirectly and finally had an appointment to meet him. I arrived on time with a bag full of books, to be told that he was "in conference" but would see me shortly. About an hour and a half later I was in the men's room when the loudspeaker squawked: "Mr. Hogan will see Mr. Randall." I rushed to the waiting room, picked up my bag and was escorted into his plush office. He was seated behind a large desk, his secretary at one end. I sat at the other and began showing my wares. Hogan said never a word and I began to get nervous. Finally I brought out a nice copy of the first American edition of *Hamlet* (Boston, 1790), the earliest of Shakespeare's plays to be printed in America.

His first words were, "I like that, what do you want for it?" When I replied $250 he said, reflectively, "You know, I think we can do business. But the next time you come into my office, would you mind buttoning your fly first?" Then he added, "Go right ahead now. Don't mind Virginia. Will you take a hundred and fifty dollars?" All I could say was "Christ, yes. Anything to get out of here."

He later explained that he was sorry to have embarrassed me, but it was simply the lawyer in him. "I can't help taking advantage of any weakness I spot in a person I meet for the first time, and, boy, did you leave yourself wide open!"

Hogan was in the true Horatio Alger tradition. Born in considerably less than affluent circumstances, he was a sickly youth, a self-educated, self-made man, and at the climax of a brilliant legal career was president of the American Bar Association. He did not come to book collecting until his middle fifties, guided to it by Mrs. Doheny, but once his interest and curiosity were aroused, he was insatiable.

At heart a witty, sentimental Irishman, he loved association items and had, among many such, the copy of Keats's *Poems* which the poet had given Wordsworth, the original manuscript of "Auld Lang Syne," a notable Poe collection, the original manuscript and drawings of "Old Mother Hubbard" and kindred treasures. He was extremely fond of quotations and formed the collection on which Merle Johnson based his bibliography *You Know These Lines*, which is dedicated to Hogan. He was particularly proud of the original manuscript of Longfellow's "The Village Blacksmith," which he eventually presented to the Library of Congress, among other gifts.

He once considered leaving his library to his alma mater, Georgetown University, through whose law school he had worked his way, eventually graduating with the highest marks made up to that time. I was unwittingly one of the main reasons he didn't. Georgetown had been given somewhere along the line manuscripts of *Tom Sawyer* and *The School for Scandal* (which exists in several versions). I wanted to see them, and Hogan said he did also and drove me out to the library. Whoever we consulted didn't even know they were there—let alone where—and it took nearly an hour's search to discover them somewhere in the cellar, tied up with string and covered with dust.

My association with Hogan was tragically brief. He was suddenly stricken with deafness (a sore affliction for a trial lawyer) and then Parkinson's disease.

His will stated:

> I had thought of bequeathing my valuable books and collection of autographs and literary manuscript material, including my collection of first and rare editions of English and American literature, to some institution to be permanently kept together as a collection, but this idea I have abandoned in favor of a plan that will accomplish their dispersion among those coming after, who will experience, as I have felt,

a profound happiness and satisfaction in possessing these precious monuments of human thought and progress. There is something sacred in the
spiritual and intimate companionship of a book, and I do not deem it
fitting that these friends of many happy hours should repose in unloved
and soulless captivity. Rather, I would send them out into the world
again to be the intimates of others whose loving hands and understanding hearts will fill the place left vacant by my passing.

There were those who demurred from this decision. I didn't.

In an interesting codicil to his will, typical of the realism which he
displayed in both his professional and his collecting career, he further
stated: "The drastic changes which have occurred in our national econ-
omy due to war conditions require me to take into account the ever-
narrowing opportunities for disposing of such material, and for that
reason I do not wish my executors to be required to force the material
upon a scanty and unwilling market." He then conferred upon his
executors "full discretionary power to dispose of the material free of any
limitation as to time" (though not as to method).

The trustees insisted on an immediate sale, against my violent objections, which I put in print. In a *Publishers' Weekly* article, November 24,
1944, about the first session of his sale, the American literature, I wrote:

> The past auction season or so and certainly the present one, so far,
> at least, has not been notable for high, or even moderate, prices fetched
> by the type of literary material Mr. Hogan collected. Certain types of
> books have sold well, true enough: French books (as witness the
> Crowninshield sale), classic literature (Kalbfleisch), color-plate books
> (suitable for breaking up by print dealers), and press books, are
> examples. But the records show that literary material, especially Eng-
> lish, and particularly the more valuable items, has been forced upon,
> as Mr. Hogan foresaw, "a scanty and unwilling market." One needs
> only to recall the Howard Sachs sale in February to confirm this. And
> certainly a $90,000 gross for the Drexel Institute literary collection
> (including $5 fetched for the family Bible of the generous donor of that
> collection, George Childs) could not have led to any dancing in the
> streets by that Institute's misguided board of directors. There is
> probably no time in the past twenty-five years, in our opinion, that that
> particular sale could have been scheduled with less advantage to every-
> one concerned.

And I concluded, "if the market, through no fault of its own, can't at
the moment absorb material of the highest quality, it certainly shouldn't
be forced to attempt what is bound to be disastrous."

Frank had been an officer of the Riggs Bank at Washington, D.C.,
and as I was sort of consultant on his library I remember a Riggs trust

officer expostulating to me that he had always thought of Hogan as a sane, sober, reliable citizen and suddenly found that "he put nearly three quarters of a million dollars in some goddamn old books."

I had estimated that his American literature session would bring $200,000. It brought $202,000, pleased the Riggs people and established with them my *bona fides* as an appraiser. It was sold on January 23–24, Scribner's were major purchasers and the estate netted a considerable profit on books Hogan had purchased from the firm, which gratified me. With very few exceptions all of our purchases were for stock. And I repurchased or underbid to over my selling price every book he had bought from us. These included Coopers, Irvings, Melvilles, etc., as detailed elsewhere in these pages. One minor book I was particularly pleased to get was the first appearance in book form, in Sarah Josepha Hale's *Poems for Our Children* (Boston, 1830), of "Mary Had a Little Lamb." This was a beautiful copy, rare in original printed wrappers, and brought $650. Its original appearance in a magazine, *The Juvenile Miscellany*, earlier in the same year, is reasonably common.

The second session was held April 23–24, 1945, and comprised Hogan's English literature of the eighteenth and nineteenth centuries. This sold moderately well, and my estimate was again just on the nose. I acquired from this such goodies as Samuel Johnson's *Proposals for Printing by Subscription the Dramatic Works of Samuel Johnson* (London, 1756), one of three copies known, $600, now in the Hyde collection; Keats's *Poems* (London, 1817), $9,750. This is now in the Robert Taylor collection. I happily repurchased, for $3,250, the original manuscript of "Old Mother Hubbard," now in the music collection of Broadcast Music Incorporated, courtesy Carl Haverlin. I also purchased for $1,300 a superb association copy of Charles Lamb's *Elia* (London, 1823). It was inscribed "Mr. Lamb presents his respects to Mr. Munden and begs his acceptance of a volume, at the end of which he has ventured a faint description of the pleasure he has received from Mr. Munden's acting. 20 Great Russell Street. Covent Garden."

Joseph Shepherd Munden was one of the most famous actors of his generation. As Lamb's essay on him is the only one upon a contemporary included in the volume, it seemed to me it could be called, without too much stretching of the imagination, the dedication copy. Or so I claimed when I catalogued it. It now belongs to Robert Taylor, who, I think, agrees with me.

I also acquired the earliest known manuscript by Burns of "Auld Lang Syne" for $3,900. This was an old friend whose story is told earlier in this

book. At the very tail of the sale was a copy of the excessively rare
Bristol, 1798, edition of Wordsworth's *Lyrical Ballads* with the first appearance of Coleridge's "Rime of the Ancyent Marinere" among its many
other claims of being a seminal volume. I didn't intend to purchase this
but I did, out of pique.

I knew that Indiana University, with which I had been doing some
small business, had a resplendent Wordsworth collection but not this; few
places have it, as only about a dozen copies are recorded. I solicited their
bid and was given one which I thought might bring it. Just the day of the
sale I was notified to disregard it, as a member of the library staff was
attending the sale and would bid for the university. That tore it. It wasn't
the loss of a small commission that mattered; that was of no moment. It
was that here was a book I had never handled and dearly wished to. It is a
matter of some prestige and more pride for a dealer to purchase at
auction a work of this quality, particularly when it is in the library of a
friend. I decided to buy it against any opposition and got it for $2,700 and
eventually sold it to Indiana. I never dreamed then, nor did they, that
eventually it, and I, would both become Hoosiers. It is always wise for
librarians and collectors to collaborate with dealers, especially in the
tricky field of auction commissions.

The third, final and vital session of the sale comprised "Rare Early
English Literature" and was held April 24–25, 1946. This being a field in
which I had not sold Hogan much, I shied away from prophecy and
didn't plan on any extensive purchases. Suddenly lightning struck.
Mitchell Kennerley invited me to lunch and sprang a stunner. He had a
client, he confided, who wanted to purchase the Hogan Elizabethiana *en
bloc*, if possible. It wasn't possible, contracts for public sale already
having been made (though this is how the Elizabethan Club at Yale
acquired its notable collection).

Well, then, would I, acting as Kennerley's agent, purchase at the sale
every important item, including all the Shakespeares, up to a total of
$500,000? The answer to that was a quick yes, provided, of course,
Scribner's were assured of the solvency of his principal. This was resolved satisfactorily—it was Barbara Hutton. I had known her as a plump
and pleasing teen-ager who came into Scribner's occasionally, wrote and
privately printed poetry but who never showed any book collecting
instincts. Mitchell explained that his son was an old friend of hers and had
persuaded her to take up collecting as a hobby—starting at the top.

As Kennerley's feuds with the Parke-Bernet Galleries have been notorious, he couldn't bid himself and didn't want to, as a matter of fact. He

wanted his connection to remain completely unknown. He had far-reaching plans for Barbara.

He was a very persuasive person and I agreed, a decision I came to regret. Hogan had been a most generous buyer from Dr. Rosenbach and they were close friends. It was at the Doctor's that he concentrated on Elizabethan literature, in which field he spent considerable sums for those times.

Hogan had the famous Earl of Rosebery first folio of Shakespeare, which had sold in 1933 in London for £14,500 and was a beauty. It cost him over $80,000 (much more than he anticipated) because between the time he bid on it and the time he paid for it the pound had gone up.

He also had a spectacular copy of Spenser's *The Faerie Queene*, which Rosenbach described as "Spenser's own copy presented by him to his future wife with the only verses known in his hand—the most romantic volume in the history of English literature." For this, with Francis Meres' *Palladis Tamia* (London, 1598), an important book containing contemporary references to Shakespeare, he paid $46,000. And there was a great deal else, indeed. All this I was to acquire, sweeping through the sale like a prairie fire with practically unlimited bids on everything. It was a bookseller's dream.

With this deal in my pocket I was compelled to turn down some attractive bids from other customers. This is always a thorny problem to a dealer and one I was never able to solve to anyone's satisfaction, even my own.

I was put on a spot once when what is the only known presentation copy of Whittier's "Snow-Bound" came up for auction, in the rare white-cloth binding. Carroll Wilson gave me a bid of $500 on it and Parkman D. Howe, also a Whittier collector, sent me a bid of $600 which I only received after the sale, through a Scribner error. I bought the book for $260. Both collectors wanted it badly and almost wound up not talking to each other or to me. Carroll got it and left it in his will to Howe, who still has it. All such disputes are not settled so amicably.

A day or so before the sale Kennerley called me in obvious consternation and asked me to meet him at our usual spot—the men's bar at the old Ritz. When I got there he had a drink ready for me, and while I was working on it he confirmed my fears: the deal was off. Barbara was leaving the United States to go abroad, divorce Cary Grant, remarry, build a home in Tangier and settle there. I could understand how with all this going on, her thoughts were not on Elizabethan poetry.

This complicated things for me. The sale was imminent, I had no customer bids, I had bought heavily for stock in the other sessions and I still had most of these purchases. I couldn't plunge too heavily for stock again, particularly in a field in which I did not specialize. There were two books I badly wanted, however, the first of *Pilgrim's Progress* and the first of the *Canterbury Tales*. Lilly had neither of these, but he was not in the market at the time.

Hogan had purchased these from Dr. Rosenbach, who had them on consignment from the Charles W. Clark estate. Together with the *Compleat Angler, Gammer Gurton's Needle* and Shelley's *Refutation of Deism*, Hogan paid $69,000, "the biggest sale Dr. Rosenbach had made in years," his biographers report.

I was undecided on which to attempt to purchase: *Pilgrim's Progress* or the *Canterbury Tales*. I finally chose the latter, which turned out to be a first-water mistake. The *Pilgrim's Progress* was a "made-up" copy. As is stated in the Winterich-Randall *A Primer of Book-Collecting:*

> The substitution or insertion of a signature or a page is in most cases frowned upon by the cognoscenti, and properly, yet the grafting of wanting leaves from a hopelessly imperfect copy has the sanction of long tradition, and is certainly as respectable a procedure as the patching of a Tudor bedstead. But the book has to be rare and costly to lend the procedure the dignity it has acquired, and the fact of substitution must, of course, be proclaimed and not concealed. And thereby what would be at worst a fraud and at best a total destruction of sentimental and commercial value in the instance of a *Scarlet Letter* or a *Raven* or a *Way of All Flesh* becomes an accepted bibliophilic convention where a Caxton or a Shakespeare folio or a *Pilgrim's Progress* is concerned. It all sounds suspiciously like class legislation, and it is.

Hogan once stopped me when I was about to examine this book in his library with the story that the Doctor had enjoined him not to allow anyone to open it because it was in its glorious original binding. "Damn it," the Doctor said to Hogan, "you have let someone open this. The hinges are getting tender." I thought the Doctor was worried because the inserted leaves might drop out. When proofs of the Hogan catalogue were circulated, the book was catalogued as "perfect," which it wasn't (though Hogan never knew that), and the description was revised at my insistence. The story behind all this is not without interest. It shows among other things how publicity on rare books can uncover unsuspected copies.

On June 30, 1921, there was sold at Sotheby's, carefully and accurately described, two imperfect copies of the first edition of *Pilgrim's Progress*, both in original calf and one with the original blank leaves, which, put together, would make a perfect copy. They were bought by Quaritch for £2,500. The price apparently flushed out another imperfect copy (lacking six leaves of sig. M), sold also at Sotheby's on June 20, 1922, also to Quaritch, for £2,010. A fourth, very imperfect, appeared at Sotheby's, July 22, 1921, sold to Meredith for £500. Imagine four copies at public sale within thirteen months! These copies were "melded" and the better one passed to Clark and then Hogan, who was delighted to get it.

I passed it by at the sale because, for one thing, I didn't want to be accused of deliberately denigrating it to buy it cheaply (as has happened), and I thought I knew where I could eventually get another copy. It brought $8,000 and is now in the Library of Congress.

I was eager to purchase the *Canterbury Tales*, however. This was printed at Westminster by one W. Caxton in 1478, the first substantial book of poetry to be printed in the English language and of legendary rarity. Of the dozen extant copies none was privately owned in America at that time; only four copies were owned by institutions, Huntington, Folger, and two at Pierpont Morgan, all imperfect. Such institutions as Yale, Harvard, Princeton, New York Public and Library of Congress did not possess as much as a single leaf of the first printing of this earliest glory of English poetry. This was the last copy to come on the market during my lifetime, I assumed.

I thought I would go to $20,000 or perhaps a bid or two higher, but I got it with surprisingly little competition for $13,000. I catalogued it for $20,000 with no takers and several years later forced it on a reluctant Lilly for $18,500.

A decade and a little more passed when the Lilly Library acquired an infinitely superior copy with a noble provenance—the Heber-Bright-Ashburnham-Bennett-Pierpont-Morgan-Poole copy. What happened was that the Morgan Library disposed of their duplicate to Hans Kraus in a deal involving their acquisition from him of the famed Constance Missal, and he sold it to Poole, who had a notable array of early *Canterbury Tales* printings.

Meanwhile the *Pilgrim's Progress* I thought I might acquire had vanished and I was left with two *Canterbury Tales*, no *Pilgrim's Progress* and no chance of ever getting one. My grief is somewhat assuaged by the fact that the Hogan copy sold in the Lilly duplicate sale for $47,500 and is now at Brick House, destined for Yale.

The rest of the Hogan Early English sale was a rather sad story. The Bunyan was Item 15, the Chaucer Item 21, and they pretty much set the tone of the sale. The glorious first folio sold to a private buyer for

$50,000, *The Faerie Queene* for $6,000 to another private buyer, Raymond Hartz (this had long been a suspect book, whether justifiably so or not I don't know), the Meres' *Palladis Tamia*, $4,200. On only eight books which cost Hogan nearly $200,000 the estate netted about $75,000.

Hogan greatly admired Dr. Rosenbach and trusted him completely. In negotiations over the Rosebery first folio of Shakespeare, he wrote the Doctor that he "would be willing to blindfold my eyes, stop up my ears, have my mouth gagged and follow *your* judgment." I felt at the time that this devotion was ill repaid.

Withal, Hogan had as much sheer fun and pleasure in collecting and exhibiting his books as anyone I ever knew, and his approximately one-third loss on his investment he would have cheerfully written off to friendships. Still, I should have bought more, and what a chance Barbara Hutton missed. She has had other husbands but will never have those books!

# M. L. Parrish

ORRIS LONGSTRETH PARRISH was a small, always immaculately dressed man from a socially prominent Philadelphia Quaker family. He had been somewhat of a dandy in his youth, enough so to have left Princeton in his freshman year by request, I have been told, and to later scandalize proper Main Liners by his association with Lillie Langtry. "She was," he once remarked, "the most beautiful and most completely *un*moral woman I have ever known." "Sometime," he added, "I must show you her letters to me." He never did, and I wonder what happened to them.

He had a lovely home, Dormy House, which he built overlooking the Pine Valley Golf Club in New Jersey, when the course was being built. An ardent golfer when the game was young in America, he was stricken with some disease just when his home was completed and never played the course. When he recovered he was left with a severe limp and always walked with a cane.

He was a close friend of Carroll Wilson, and of Michael Sadleir, whom he visited in England every year for book scouting trips in the provinces, and was prominent among Philadelphia collectors. In the decades between the world wars Philadelphia was full of important collectors and dealers— a distinction it no longer has, at least to the same extent—and through Parrish I met most of them. If I offered him a book he had or one he didn't want, he would frequently phone one of his friends and sell it for me.

And he allowed me free and generous use of his library. He read his books carefully, with a proofreader's eye, noting every discrepancy and sometimes discovering important variants, which he allowed me to announce. On weekends when I occasionally visited Dormy House he would retire at eleven and leave me alone in the library, and often when dawn was breaking I was still there (I was young then), and Morris, going out to his bird-watching, would shoo me to bed.

He began collecting in 1913, attempting first to round out a set of Dickens his mother had given him. Then he bought Thackeray and Trollope (in those days, as now, Trollope was largely out of print, and one had to buy first editions if one admired him enough to want all his minor works). Gradually the idea of forming a library of Victorian fiction grew, and at Parrish's death, thirty-one years later, Dormy House in Pine Valley housed the finest collection of Victorian novels in mint condition ever assembled in this country. Mind that word "novels." Parrish was allergic to poetry. He had much of it, fourteen copies of variants of the first edition of the Brontës' *Poems* and many extremely rare and little-known examples of the occasional poetry of Thackeray, Bulwer-Lytton and Stevenson among others. However, though they were included for the sake of completeness they were not much loved or read. Parrish would have been happier, and in some cases—notably Bulwer—so would their authors, if they had never been published.

The principles which guided the formation of the Parrish collection were condition and completeness. The books had to be in as nearly published condition and the author collections as complete as possible. But condition—"Parrish condition" became a trade byword—was a *sine qua non*. Many, many titles at Dormy House were the third, or tenth, copy he had owned.

The glory days of his collecting had passed when I met him, and I suppose his library was then 85 percent complete. Though possessed of substantial means, he was not a man of wealth; his brokerage firm had suffered in 1929, and he had slowed his pace. This was fine with me, as I was able to scout out rare "fillers" he could appreciate at prices he could afford and which showed my firm, usually, a large return on a small investment. And it is this material which transforms a "collection" into a library.

Anyone with sufficient cash can buy a *Pickwick Papers* or *Vanity Fair*, in parts, or *Barchester Towers*. But try and find Thackeray's *Jeames's Diary or Sudden Riches* in the original wrappers (New York, 1846); Stevenson's *The Master of Ballantrae* (New York, 1888) or Barrie's *The Wedding Guest* (New York, 1900) in their Scribner copyright editions, or Trollope's *The Struggles of the Firm of Brown, Jones and Robinson* (New York, 1862), all of which I supplied—regardless of price—and you begin to realize what Parrish accomplished in a half-lifetime devotion to Victorian literature.

He also had a good collection of American authors: Emerson (including Dickens' copy of *Essays, First Series* and a presentation copy of *Second Series*); O. W. Holmes, Longfellow, Whittier and especially Hawthorne. There was that great Hawthorne rarity *Fanshawe*, heading a collection lacking only "The Carrier's Address to the Patrons of the Salem Gazette" for January 1, 1838—though he did have its commoner companion piece for 1839. But his heart was never really in these collections. For one thing the books were not very attractive to look at, certainly compared with his Victorian three-deckers, and Parrish, like Sadleir, liked books as physical objects. He rarely had slipcases on his books (pamphlets excepted), and if you were foolish enough to show him a book in its dust wrapper, he would take the jacket off and toss it in the wastebasket, from which you had to rescue it.

He only collected Americans, really, to please Carroll Wilson, I suspect. He decided to get rid of them and to put the proceeds into his beloved Victorians. The trouble was he hadn't enough to make a sale, so he approached me about the problem. Scribner's had some very nice things which would bolster his material and between us make quite a splash. He owed us a considerable sum at this time and we had other things he badly wanted. So we decided on a combined sale under his name. All proceeds were to go to him, and whatever the Scribner material brought was to be used to liquidate his current bills and apply to future purchases. Some lawyer agreed this was perfectly proper (Parrish bought the books from us for a dollar or something), so Parrish sent his books along to the Parke Bernet Galleries and sent me a couple dozen of his bookplates to paste into what Scribner's were consigning.

All went swimmingly until proofs of the catalogue arrived. A suddenly agitated Morris summoned me to Philadelphia and explained to me what was bothering his Quaker conscience. These Scribner books had never really been his, were not the sort of things he would have collected to begin with, and it just wasn't right to have it appear as though they were. He seemed particularly distressed because I had consigned the first two editions of *Leaves of Grass*, the work of a man whom he never would have invited to dinner and whose books he would not have admitted to his shelves. I protested that the first edition had pasted in it the very rare Emerson broadside praising Whitman, and Parrish already had a fine Emerson collection and approved of *him*. Also that the second edition was a presentation copy, one of only two recorded, and there were other works of distinction he should have been proud to own.

Well, it seemed I had included Carl Sandburg's first book, *In Reckless*

*Ecstasy* (Galesburg, Ill., 1904). Who was he? The Mark Twains were all right, but how about those Elinor Wylies? Who was she? Maybe these were authors of consequence, but he didn't know. He was not well read in modern literature, he confessed, because he couldn't find time to read it—there was so much Victorian literature he either hadn't read or was anxious to reread!

The upshot was that on Thursday, March 3, 1938, at 8:15 P.M. there was sold at the Parke-Bernet Galleries, 742 Fifth Avenue, *First Editions of American Authors. Property of Morris L. Parrish, Dormy House, Pine Valley, N.J. Together with Some Important Items from Another Owner.* I had, meantime, spent several evenings at the galleries patiently soaking off the Parrish bookplates from the Scribner consignment I had so recently carefully (and strongly) pasted in.

The sale was not much of a success and only redeemed from total disaster by the purchases of Walter Chrysler, Jr., who was collecting American books at that time. Among his purchases of works Scribner consigned was one of six copies done on India paper of Twain's *The Prince and the Pauper* (Boston, 1882), inscribed to Koto House, adopted daughter of Edward House, a journalist friend of Twain's since the "Quaker City" days. It brought $1,450. It was to this sale that I consigned the finest collection of Stephen Crane letters extant and bought them back for $225. The first copies to appear at auction of Baum's *The Wonderful Wizard of Oz* (Chicago, 1900), and Sandburg's *In Reckless Ecstasy* brought $300 and $85, respectively. The first *Leaves of Grass* with the Emerson broadside brought $1,150, the second, inscribed, $145.

In an article I did for *The New York Times* on Parrish and Hogan after their deaths, "The Adventures of Two Bibliophiles," I wrote:

> The ultimate disposal of his library perplexed Mr. Parrish in his later years. It was very valuable and he was not an extremely wealthy man. But he knew what he had created—the time, the effort, the traveling and the incessant searching that had gone into its formation. Few of his books had been bought at auction or came from famous collections. They had been acquired by searching bookshops in America, England and the Continent, over thirty years, and with the cooperation of collectors and dealers the world over. The library could never be duplicated; he was not willing to see it dispersed, no matter what the advantage to his estate. He was not a college graduate, though he had attended Princeton briefly, and it is to Princeton, finally, that he has left his library.

This was in complete contrast to Hogan's decision on his library, and both men were correct. I attended their funerals, which occurred within a short time of each other, and again there was a vivid contrast. Parrish's simple Quaker ceremony was quickly over, but Hogan was buried from Washington Cathedral with bell, book and candle, and that ceremony took over two hours. There was a most impressive gathering of all sorts of prominent people, and I couldn't help thinking, a little irreverently, what a spot to hold his auction! Hogan was very high among Catholic laity, a Prince of the Church, I think. When I once remarked to him that I supposed such distinction did not come easily he answered, "It cost more than my library did and gave me much less satisfaction."

I was surprised at Parrish's decision to give his library to Princeton. He offered it to them once with the sole stipulation that they physically reproduce the actual room in which the books were housed at Dormy House. They cheerfully agreed to this, provided he would pay for it as well as give them the books. This annoyed him and for a while he thought of selling the collection to Scribner's, but nothing came of this. It was finally given to Princeton, and in building their Firestone Library the university did an almost exact replica of the library room, in which the books are arranged as Parrish had them.

# Michael Sadleir

I FIRST MET Michael Sadleir on one of his last trips to America, in 1936. He was already a legend to me, the famed collector and bibliographer of Anthony Trollope, an acknowledged expert on Victorian literature, friend and mentor of John Carter as well as of Carroll A. Wilson and Morris Parrish. He was also a publisher, head of Constable and Company, and an author—his true friends tactfully never mentioned his novels if perchance they had read them. Not so, of course, his biographies and essays: *Things Past*, for one, is a fascinating book, to be put on the same shelf with Chapman's *Portrait of a Scholar*.

I was living at the time on 10th Street just off Third Avenue, at St. Marks-in-the-Bouwerie. This was then the center of the secondhand bookshops whose shelves Sadleir eagerly pillaged. It was also the center of a great American art—killed by the late Mayor "Little Flower" La Guardia—burlesque. Sadleir was enchanted and was a regular visitor to the Irving Place. I did not know at that time of his expert knowledge of Victorian low-life, which eventually blossomed in his best-remembered novel, *Fanny by Gaslight*.

I later visited him several times in England and was awestruck by his choice collection of Victorian fiction and particularly by the immaculate condition of the books. Sadleir's account of the formation of his collection is engagingly told in his "Passages from the Autobiography of a Bibliomaniac," the most complete and delightful account of the formation of a fine library I know of, always excepting Wilmarth Lewis' *Collector's Progress*, though that is a book; Sadleir's, an essay.

The "Autobiography" prefaced his two-volume bibliography of his own collection, *XIXth Century Fiction*. In reviewing this in the London *Times Literary Supplement*, Carter commented: "It is given to few book collectors to exert a decisive influence on the technique as well as the taste of their age . . . It is one thing, and a very fine thing, to assemble a great collection in the classic tradition or in the prevailing manner. It is another thing, and a much rarer one, to change the whole climate of book collecting. And that is exactly what Sadleir did."

After Sadleir's bibliography was published, Carter alerted me that he was considering disposing of his collection but warned that we hadn't much of a chance as Sadleir wanted it kept together, and anyway it had to be offered to the nation first. Sadleir records what happened next.

> In 1948, for various reasons, a domestic house-move was resolved; and the new home chosen might, with luck, hope to accommodate about one-sixth of the collection. What next? The books could go into store (as indeed they did for a couple of years) or in whole or in part they could go to auction (which would mean breaking up into at least two thousand pieces an entity which could never again be brought together) or they could be disposed of en bloc to an Institution. In my own country the first opportunity to acquire the books was secured by law to the Copyright Libraries (The British Museum, The Bodleian, Cambridge, and Scotland) and to these great Libraries the collection was duly offered. Two high officials of the British Museum came to inspect it; and, on their own behalf and that of their privileged colleagues, decided that the Copyright Libraries were not organised to house or display a mass of novels, of the great majority of which they, by Statute, had received copies at the time of publication and still possessed. I should like to acknowledge the ready generosity with which, not desiring to acquire the books themselves, these British Museum officials at once recommended to the Board of Trade that I be given permission to offer the collection in the United States.

The copyright libraries passed up a fantastic opportunity. If the "high officials" mentioned dreamed that any one of their institutions, or all of them combined, possessed anything remotely comparable to the Sadleir collection in any way, they were mistaken. The copyright libraries, if they had the books at all, had them in rebound, shabby, imperfect and generally totally unacceptable copies. Here was a glowing opportunity to secure for the nation a resplendent glory, and they passed it by. It's the old story of dealing with uncomprehending officialdom—pearls before swine. It was not a matter of price, but simply of apathy on their part. I recall this and many similar instances when I periodically read letters in the London *Times Literary Supplement*, for instance, of America's "arrogant and purse-proud attitude" which enables us to "purchase from other countries part of their cultural birthright." Generally speaking, the reason things leave England's shores is simply English lack of interest in what they have when they have it. Take it away from them, preserve it, put it to use and they wail like banshees. I don't notice the Elgin Marbles leaving England's shores and returning to the nation "part of whose cultural birthright" they are. But of course Byron in "The Curse of Minerva" (London, 1812) disowns Elgin:

> England owns him not.
> Athena, no! thy plunderer was a Scot.

Nor do I ever recall any great breast-beating by the British I have known about depriving us of our "cultural birthright" by wantonly putting the torch to all of Washington, including the Library of Congress, in 1814.

In point of fact I have never met an Englishman, the better historians and bookmen excepted, who knew this happened or even that there was a War of 1812! The library was at that time in the north wing of the Capitol. The assistant librarian succeeded in hauling away several wagon-loads of archives but no books. As an indication of how highly the books were regarded, I might mention that fines for failing to return any on the date due were $3 per day for folios, $2 for quartos and $1 for octavos.

In *l'affaire Sadleir* somebody, in this case two somebodies, blundered and Scribner's had their chance. But the collection was not easily sold. It should have gone to Princeton, where, meshed with Parrish's books, the combination would have been forever unmatchable. I did my best but could not prevail against the Princetonian counterparts of the English dolts.

The trouble was not that the library authorities then there (things have changed now) were anti-book, though that entered into it. It was that they rather resembled those admirable characters in *The Wonderful Wizard of Oz:* the Scarecrow who had straw instead of brains in his head, and the Tin Woodsman who had no heart. Unlike them, however, the Princeton officials arrogantly refused to recognize their deficiencies, even when kindly pointed out to them by as amiable a soul as myself.

I am reminded of the conclusion reached by Randolph Adams—a great librarian and historian (a rare combination)—in his iconoclastic essay "Librarians As Enemies of Books":

> Book collecting and the building-up of great libraries is as much a
> matter of the heart as a matter of the head. The man who is all heart

and no head would be a very bad librarian. But the man who is all head
and no heart is a very dangerous librarian.

In the case of Sadleir and other institutions, the problem of duplication
raised, as usual, its ugly head, so, one way and another, things hung fire.
My second choice for a home for the library was the University of
Illinois, principally because Gordon Ray was then there. He knew
Sadleir, had visited him on occasion and fully appreciated the scholarly
potentials of the collection. But there were difficulties in arranging
finances—the price then was about $100,000. UCLA knew about the
collection, as its press had published Sadleir's bibliography in America. Its
imaginative librarian (who had both head and heart), Larry Powell,
wanted it but was also faced with problems of finance.

One December day I received a phone call from Larry. Was the Sadleir
collection still available? I assured him it was. The pound, by the way,
had gone down just at this time, so the price in American dollars was
considerably reduced. He told me excitedly that he had just been informed by some fiscal authority that a sufficient sum was available provided the transaction could be closed before the end of the year. Only—
and here was the catch—one of their regents, who was not a collector but
who had heard of Dr. Rosenbach, insisted that that eminent authority on
Victorian literature write a letter recommending its purchase and authenticating its value. I remember asking Larry if he had holes in his head
and hung up.

It happened that there was a meeting that afternoon of a committee, of
which I was a member, of the Bibliographical Society of America, dealing
with what turned out to be Jacob Blanck's bibliography of American
literature, and I jokingly told the story. Immediately all present agreed
that the collection should come to America and wired everyone concerned their approval.

There was Larry on the phone the next day. The telegrams were all
fine, but the trouble now was that none of those who urged its purchase
had actually ever seen the books. The reluctant regent agreed that Dr.
Rosenbach never had either, so I could forget about him. Could I get an
endorsement from someone who had seen them: and right away, not just
next week; yesterday would have been preferable.

There was one such person, Gordon Ray, who had recently examined
the collection critically with an eye to eventual purchase. An appeal to
him brought a prompt and generous response. Rather than take a risk of
losing the collection for America, he urgently advised that UCLA acquire
it, and that is where it is now. With Fred Adams I had the pleasure of

delivering an address at the dedication ceremonies which recorded its installation on November 13, 1952.

Of all the collections I have had in my bookseller days which I wish were now at my library, Sadleir's takes pride of place. Others have been much more valuable but none more admired.

# C. Waller Barrett
# and Other Americanists

LONG ABOUT 1938 I sensed that a new collector of American first editions was in the market. The collecting world is a very small one, and any new influence registers as infallibly as a minor quake does on a seismograph. The firm of Thoms and Eron, 89 Chambers Street, began buying at public auction some pretty good books to which they had no right. They were old and respected dealers, true enough, and I had done much business with them. But their forte was the hard-to-get, out-of-print type of thing—*Encyclopaedia Britannica*s and the like. On occasion, however, they had some good first editions and other rarities, picked up in the normal course of trade, and they had, being close to Wall Street, some pretty substantial clients. But they were not specialists in the field of American literature. That they would suddenly begin purchasing at auction items they would not normally stock—taking some away from me, to boot—meant only one thing. They were acting for a client.

The salesman for T & E was an old whiskey-drinking, poker-playing pal of mine, Vanover. At that time their chief customer was Walter Chrysler, and I had funneled a fair amount of books to him through them. Chrysler was considered difficult to deal with, and I was happy to act through an intermediary. But Van confided to me that the recent purchases were not being made for Chrysler, and he also added that the new collector was very enthusiastic, serious and loaded!

I could, given time and through normal channels, have found out who this was. But I decided on a different approach which would, I hoped, make him come to me. There were due at an upcoming sale at the Parke-Bernet Galleries some duplicates consigned by the New York Historical

Society, among them the very rare first edition of the very first book of America's very first professional man of letters, Charles Brockden Brown. The book was *Alcuin* (New York, 1798), an essay, really, on women's rights and of no intrinsic importance but still a milestone in our culture. I had searched for it for years (the Lilly Library still doesn't possess it).

A few months before, Van had bought several of Brown's early novels, and I was pretty sure his man, if he was a really serious collector, would go after *Alcuin*—a copy had not appeared at public auction since 1916 and one hasn't since. So the evening of the sale I picked a spot where I could see Van bidding, determined to take the book away from him regardless of price if he went for it. Surely enough, he did, and I matched him bid for bid, finally getting it for $550, a fairly high price then, for despite its rarity (its only virtue) it was not everyone's cup of tea. Van, assuming I had bought it at that price for a customer, never even asked me what I wanted for it.

A while later the phone rang and a pleasant voice identified itself as C. Waller Barrett, of 20 Church Street, President of the North Atlantic and Gulf Steamship Company, and inquired about the book. Did I have it, and if so, how much did I want for it? He further explained (he has learned better since) that he had been in Havana at the time of the sale and had not had a chance to see the volume but had wired T & E to purchase it, carefully mentioning no price—i.e., an unlimited bid. Van's imagination had run out at $550. I've often wondered what the book would have brought if it hadn't.

I was at Barrett's office within the hour, and though I could have probably doubled my cost, the book changed ownership at a nominal 10 percent commission to Scribner's, and one of the most satisfactory of all my dealer–customer relationships began.

Incidentally, this ploy is not always successful and it once backfired on me, disastrously. A great collector of sporting books, a casual Scribner customer before I became manager, never became a considerable buyer from us directly, possibly imagining that we were high-priced—and, I may add, with some reason, especially on the English colorplate books, Alkin, Surtees *et al.* I eventually placed many rarities in this collection through Ronald MacDonald, the bookbinder, though little directly.

In 1945 the very fine collection of sporting books formed by Alfred Maclay came up for auction. One of the scarcest works in it was:

> The Sportsman's Companion; Or, An Essay on Shooting, Illustriously
> shewing in what Manner to fire at Birds of Game, in various Directions
> and Situations; And, Directions to Gentlemen for the Treatment and

breaking their own Pointers and Spaniels, and the necessary Precautions to guard against many Accidents that attend this pleasant Diversion; With Several other useful and interesting Particulars relative thereto, [Never before Published]. By a Gentleman, Who has made Shooting his favorite Amusement upwards of Twenty-six Years, in Great-Britain, Ireland, and North-America. New-York: Printed by Robertsons, Mills and Hicks, 1783.

A fully descriptive title, and typical of its times. The copy was not the finest in the world: it had some foxing in the text, and the binding, though contemporary, was not original. But it was the only copy which had shown up during my career, of the first edition of the first American book on sport—the Godolphin Arabian of its kind. And I wanted it. Not to read, just to have. I was the bibliographer, after all, of Henry William Herbert (Frank Forester), who first popularized in America the British standard of sport for sport's sake. And I had handled, with the single exception of sporting specialist Ernest Gee, as many American sporting books as anyone in the country. But not this one. Fewer than five copies were recorded and probably this was the last to be offered.

The customer attended the sale and bid on the book which was knocked down to me at $2800. On leaving the sale I thought I saw a fine chance to get Scribner's off the "high priced" hook by offering it for a mere 10 per cent over cost so I proceeded to do so. That was an error as the collector apparently thought I had deliberately run up the price, or something, and refused its purchase, to my puzzlement. I mentioned this to Harry Peters (who I think then had the only other known copy in private hands) and he replied that I simply hadn't priced it high enough but he was probably kidding me. In any event I did no more business directly with that customer and for a long time I never knew why. Probably I should have waited for the possible client to have approached me—as was the case with Barrett. John Carter in his *ABC for Book Collectors,* written with wit and authority, has a most perceptive article on auctions—any auctions—detailing the many hazards to which a bidder is subject, not the least of which are psychological. The book eventually passed into Paul Mellon's notable collection of sporting books.

Incidentally, Mrs. Donald Hyde relates, in an account of the "Four Oaks Library," how she and Donald had an argument with me, on our first meeting arranged through their great friend Randolph Adams, over commissions, all of which ended happily.

Following the sale of *Alcuin* I became for a while Barrett's partial auction representative and semi-adviser. I say "partial" and "semi-" as he never has been a one-dealer customer and has always had a mind of his own. His purchases during this initial period included some English books, but the emphasis was increasingly on the Americans. During the war, of course, being in shipping, he directed his energies elsewhere, but his interest never flagged. He was wisely feeling his way, and though it was easy to sell him ten books for $100 each, the purchase of one book for $1,000 took a lot of salesmanship on my part and soul-searching on his. It was quite an event when he eventually purchased from me the finest American literary manuscript I ever possessed—or anyone else, for that matter—the major surviving portion of Washington Irving's *The Sketch Book*, including the immortal "Rip Van Winkle."

I acquired this from Boies Penrose of Devon, Pennsylvania, who had inherited it. I have always been a firm believer in putting things where they belong, a feeling which, in part, consoles me for the Tom Wolfe collection's being at Harvard and the Scott Fitzgerald at Princeton—instead of at Indiana University. And I resent the fact that George Barr McCutcheon's manuscripts, which Scribner's once owned, including *Graustark* and *Brewster's Millions*, are at the New York Public Library and not in Indiana. Strangely enough, I seem indifferent to the fact that *Peter Pan* and *The Old Wives' Tale* are in Indiana and not in Kensington Gardens or The Five Towns.

As the obverse of the coin, I also believe firmly in taking away from people things that don't really belong to them, or which they are not possessed by, and putting them with those who will properly appreciate them.

It didn't take me long (after I found its location) to persuade Penrose, who had no particular liking for Irving anyway, to part with his manuscript. Not that he wasn't a bookman. He was and is an excellent one. His forte was not American literature, however, but the study of the exploration and exploitation of non-European areas by Europeans during the fifteenth and sixteenth centuries. He was ardently collecting Ptolemys and other geographical literature of the Renaissance, and such books come seldom these days and come high. The money acquired from Irving went into material which culminated in his *Travel and Discovery in the Renaissance, 1420–1620* (Harvard University Press, 1952), a jewel of a book.

Having gotten my manuscript I promptly trotted off to place it where it obviously, properly and inevitably belonged: the New York Public Library. Irving had been its first president, they had a permanent exhibit of his works on display, American literature first gained international recognition from his work, and so on. Briefly, no sale. Worse than that, no interest. At any cash price. The New York Public Library simply wasn't interested. I couldn't understand their attitude then and can't now. I desperately wanted this to be put where I knew it belonged. So I tried another tack. The New York Public Library has four copies of the famous folio edition of Audubon's *Birds of America*. Even they can exhibit only one at a time. So I proposed a swap of the Irving manuscript for one of their stored copies. And again was turned down flat—the reason this time was that the copies, all being gifts, were unavailable for anything except storage. I shouldn't have expected anything else, I suppose, but I was shocked at their total lack of elementary understanding or interest. Librarians!

The next try was the Irving home at Sunnyside, New York, which the Rockefellers had restored as a public memorial. It had lovely grounds, a charming home and nothing else. I could be, and obviously am, wrong in expecting in a restoration something besides brick and grass. Such a setting should, if possible, enshrine the relics of the heart which created it in the first place. Again, no sale. Though in this case it was not because a price was too high, but too low. If it was upped, and a kickback arranged—who knew, I was informed by an underling. This used to be a fairly common pattern in certain collecting circles but one, luckily, I never had to employ, Scribner's being what they are.

In any event I was left with my treasure. It always surprises outsiders, I think, to hear that glamorous items are difficult to sell—for hard cash money. It would seem as though if one had a truly superb piece that a solvent concern really needed, the sale would be automatic. " 'Tain't so." And that's one of the things that makes the business so fascinating. The manuscript was eventually exposed to a considerable public in a *Life* magazine article, with no takers, and finally appeared in a Scribner's catalogue as follows:

IRVING, WASHINGTON.
Original autograph manuscript of the surviving portion of *The Sketch Book* (including *Rip Van Winkle,* complete). 196 leaves, 4to, written mostly on one side in ink, making 200 printed pages of the first three parts of the first edition. Bound in a large 4to volume, full brown morocco, comprising:

Part I   *Directions to the Printer.* 1 leaf.
        *Title-page.* 1 leaf.
        *Prospectus,* dated London, 1819. 1 leaf.
        *The Author's Account of Himself.* 7 leaves.
        *The Voyage.* 15 leaves.
        *Roscoe.* 17 leaves.
        *Rip Van Winkle.* 38 leaves.

Part II  *Title-page.* 1 leaf.
       *English Writers on America.* 21 leaves.
       *Rural Life in England.* 17 leaves.
       *The Art of Book Making.* 17 leaves.

Part III  *A Royal Poet.* 20 leaves.
       *The Country Church.* 13 leaves.
       *The Boar's Head Tavern, Eastcheap.* 27 leaves.

                                    The collection, $35,000

This is all that is known to exist of the manuscript of *The Sketch Book* with the exception of a single page, formerly in the possession of William R. Langfeld, Irving's bibliographer, bought at the sale of his library by Scribner's, and now privately owned.

Irving was in England when he conceived and wrote *The Sketch Book* and he intrusted his old friend, Henry Brevoort, with its publication in America. Their correspondence, now in the Yale University Library, gives a detailed and minute account of its publishing history. It is unquestionably due to Brevoort, also, that this precious manuscript has been preserved. Apparently only the manuscript of these first three parts was sent to him, hence it was all he could save. Irving wrote him on Aug. 2, 1819: "I forward Sketch Book No. 4 to my brother E. Irving." This has been lost. Later Irving wrote Brevoort: "I shall send no more manuscript to America until I put it to press here," so it seems most likely that the final three American parts were set up from English sheets and that the manuscript was not preserved by the English publisher, Murray, or by Irving, if Murray returned it to him.

*The Sketch Book* holds a most important place in American literary history. *The Legend of Rip Van Winkle,* of course, is immortal and has always been recognized as the characteristic and abiding production of its author. *The Sketch Book* itself is the volume by which Irving is best known today among readers on both sides of the Atlantic. The book was translated into almost every European tongue, and for many years it served, and still serves, in France, in Germany, and in Italy as a model of English style, and as a textbook from which students are taught their English.

Furthermore, it was the first American literary effort to gain international renown, and can be termed the fountainhead of our modern literature without which the hard row of our early writers would have been much harder indeed. . . .

This, one of the most distinguished American literary manuscripts in existence, and probably, at least historically, the most important, has been privately owned since its publication, was recently purchased by private treaty by Scribner's and is now offered for the first time for public sale.

The manuscript was around quite a while before Waller Barrett acquired it at a sharply reduced price.

A very great influence on Barrett's planning and thinking at this time (though I did not know it till later) was the late Carroll A. Wilson.

Wilson's collection of the chief New England authors was exhaustive. With comparatively limited funds, but with unbounded enthusiasm, energy, knowledge and work, he formed remarkable collections of them.

I like to think I introduced Wilson and Barrett, though of this I am not sure. Certainly they saw a lot of each other, particularly toward the close of the war (Carroll died in 1947), and it seems to have been in his pleasant bachelor book-lined penthouse at 2 Horatio Street that Waller received his vision. And a ridiculous vision it was, if he had asked me, which he didn't. Inspired by what Wilson had accomplished in a limited field and with a few authors, Barrett decided to emulate over the entire field of American literature, no less, from the Federal period to the present.

When he started, intensive collecting of American literature had been going on for a half century and notable collections were at Yale, Harvard, the Library of Congress, Huntington and the New York Public, among many others. But there was nothing substantial south of the Mason-Dixon line, certainly nothing comparable to Barrett's vision. It seemed incredible that at this time substantial collections of the manuscripts and rarities of Walt Whitman, Twain, Brockden Brown, Frost—you name them—could still be gathered in quantity and quality to form a library of American literature, the peer of any in our country, even given substantial resources and dedicated purpose. Yet that is exactly what Waller Barrett has accomplished, and in about the short space of fifteen years. The results, for all to see, are at the University of Virginia.

I do not know when the transformation of Barrett from a private collector, with a private collector's passions and pleasures in his books (which he has never lost), to builder of an institutional scholarly research library, came about. Such patterns are rare in collecting history. There are, on the one hand, the Folgers, who apparently determined very early along to build a great library and eventually give it to the public and were completely uninterested, often, in even seeing what they had purchased; the other extreme is a Lilly, who, having given his collection, retired completely from book (though not other) collecting and left the future direction to other hands. The private collector who, relatively early in his career, gives his library away and then continues avidly to augment it personally, is a *rara avis* indeed.

The change in Barrett's collecting came, I think, when I purchased the Wilson library for $100,000. Wilson had collected his favorites, which included besides the Americans, the English authors Hardy, Trollope, and Gilbert and Sullivan, "in depth." Which meant not only the first editions but association copies, books from their libraries, magazine appearances, reprints of bibliographical interest, variant bindings, etc. Such collections, built up with loving care and knowledge, should not be casually dispersed. But they are not easily sold to collectors. The main reason is that few true collectors like the idea of acquiring *en bloc* someone else's preformed library. It deprives them of the pleasure of piece-by-piece acquisition.

J. K. Lilly, Jr., for example, was seldom a bulk buyer (his Riley and Wallace archives are conspicuous exceptions, and these simply because they were Hoosiers). He preferred single acquisitions, personally selected. I remember very well when Scribner's had purchased, from Percy Muir, a complete collection of first editions of the works for which the Nobel Prize had been presented. It was no mean collection, nor easy to acquire, as many of the works represented were first published in obscure scientific journals, in many languages, and difficult even then (this was 1939) to acquire and practically impossible now. When I offered it to Lilly he turned down the collection, though not the idea, saying: "Let's get them all, but not in a mass. That takes the fun out of acquiring them." Eventually he did get most of them—though not all. The original collection is now one of the cornerstones of the Buffalo Museum of Science.

One Saturday afternoon Waller appeared and we discussed matters. There were lovely Longfellows I knew he wanted. What finer volume is there than the very first printing of *Tales of a Wayside Inn* (Boston, 1863), in which appears "The Children's Hour," descriptive of his playtime with his three daughters—"grave Alice, and laughing Allegra, and Edith with golden hair"—especially the copy, as Wilson's was, which Longfellow gave Alice, who was ten years old in 1863? The book was accompanied by a letter to his cousin, dated October 22, 1853, reading:

> Fanny has a daughter, born this morning a little before sunrise! And when the sun did rise, a splendid rainbow arched the West, right opposite the window. May it be a beneficent presage to the little girl!
>
> Alice looks upon the baby in dignified silence. She thinks it is one of those dolls that squeak when you press their bodies. Charley says "Santiclaus!" and Erny, "That's some of Mrs. Sumner's doings, I know."
>
> Such, dear Emmeline, is the present state of the household. Fanny is very well; and all things look auspicious . . .

Observe that, as yet, "Edith with golden hair," just born, has no name.

Thoreau's *Walden* (Boston, 1854) was the copy he had given his mother, the Holmes collection was incomparable then in private hands (though matched now, I imagine, by Parkman D. Howe's), and the

Melvilles were unusual, including among the letters one to—of all people —Havelock Ellis. Of the beautiful Hawthornes, one of the most interesting, typical of the way Wilson collected from various sources his "ensembles," as he liked to call them, was his *Scarlet Letter* with related documents. The following is Wilson's own description of it:

THE SCARLET LETTER. A Romance. With 4 pp. of advertisements, dated March 1, 1850. Boston 1850.
All the distinguishing points of the first edition are present.
At page 3 of this book Hawthorne writes:
"In my native town of Salem, at the head of what . . . was a bustling wharf,—but which now . . . exhibits few or no symptoms of commercial life; except perhaps, a bark or *Brig* . . . *discharging hides;* or . . . *a Nova Scotia schooner, pitching out her cargo of firewood.* . . ."
About 1925, when I started collecting, and searched for something of association interest for this book, I acquired the enclosed customs and landing receipt, signed by Hawthorne as surveyor, of the—
"*Sch.[ooner]* Linus," from "Digby, N.S.," whose cargo is "Twenty three Cords *Wood*."
This was excellent, but, still searching, NINE YEARS LATER, in 1934, I acquired a like Hawthorne-signed receipt, for the—
"*Br.[ig]* Granite," whose cargo was:—
"Fourteen thousand Ox Horns; Fifteen hundred Web S. *Hides*; One Hundred Dry Lining *Hides*; Fourteen Hundred Dry *Hides*; Thirteen Bales *Hide* Cuttings; Two Bales Dry S. *Hide* cuttings."
It will be observed, from p. 5, that any congestion of shipping came "usually from Africa or South America," and that the Br[ig] *Granite*, appropriately enough, is from "R. Grande," *i.e.*, the Argentine.
On putting these two together, I got the thrill that comes only to a collector who seeks that he may find. The date of the receipt for the Nova Scotia schooner with its firewood was *May 30, 1848;* that of the South American brig with hides, *June 2, 1848.*
Could there possibly be another such coincidence? Can there be any doubt, from these two dates, that these two items in the summer of 1848 are the actual source (and the signed source) of this passage in the 1850 book?

In any event, I explained to Barrett that these collections could not be broken up, that they contained large quantities of material no one but the most ardent specialist would want, and so on. After all my considered reasoning with him, aimed primarily at explaining why he couldn't have his coveted plums, he casually crossed me by taking the whole pudding! How much, he inquired, would the entire Alcott, Hawthorne, Holmes, Irving, Longfellow, Lowell, Melville and Thoreau collections, plus some other oddments, come to? I put a price of somewhat over two thirds of the cost on them, and he accepted on the spot. I suddenly realized I was coping with a man who was no longer collecting individual items per se, but one who was pursuing an idea: the grandest, and rarest, form of collecting. Carroll Wilson would have been proud of his friend and ecstatic at what had happened to his own library. And I have my personal satisfaction in having a small hand in one of the great collecting ventures of our times.

For a while I was worried lest Barrett was going over his depth—it has happened. So I warned him to, perhaps, go a little slowly, only to be reminded, "Your job is to get me the books: mine, to pay for them." And that was the end of that conversation.

A few years later I was contemplating doing a book and needed time and a vacation. Barrett suggested that my wife and I might find it pleasant to go on one of his freighters to Venezuela—a six-week round trip. We had previously been on much shorter ones to Cuba and knew what we were getting into. No passengers were carried at all, so we had to sign on as supercargo, at a wage of $1 each. But we both loved the sea, the chartered vessels were Scandinavian—the current one Swedish—and the bunks adequate for sleeping. And meals with the captain invariably began with aquavit for breakfast, which suited me fine.

It was a pleasant trip, a cargo of cars going down, a few days at fabulous Caracas and then a trip some three hundred miles up the Orinoco to take on a load of iron ore for the return. This was ill-loaded and we had a pretty rough return, which effectively prevented my doing much writing. We were due to dock in Philadelphia New Year's Day. The projected book hadn't been going very well and I was fed up with it. What I had written was in a carton under our bunk, with other junk in it. New Year's Eve at sea was quite an affair, what with Swedish punch and all, and when we turned in I thought: The hell with the book. It's no good anyway, and since it's the new year let's make a new start. So I pitched the carton out the porthole.

Next evening when we made Philadelphia the customs men and so on came aboard and I was asked for our passports. In a sudden, blinding flash I realized where they were. God knows how many fathoms deep now, down Cape Hatteras way! They were in the carton I had blithely pushed into the sea.

Well, this was a pickle, and no doubt about it. In the first place it was a holiday and I couldn't get in touch with anyone I knew to vouch for me. And in the second place the officials involved took a very dim view of my story. The going price for an American passport in Venezuela, I was frigidly reminded by high authority, started at $1,500. And a more implausible story of how ours were lost had apparently never passed over any State Department desk. In the end, I guess, it was my honesty which won our freedom. Or Barrett's intervention: I never knew which.

At any rate, after being locked up overnight we were let loose the next day, after interminable document signing and so on. All I really know is that I had a hell of a time getting my passport back, and Barrett never again invited me to take a slow boat of his anywhere.

I seem to be born to bad travel luck. I always forget that in France, for example, you present your ticket at the end of the railroad journey. I somehow always mislay or lose mine before then.

A few years ago I was visiting, in Geneva, Switzerland, the world's greatest book collector, Martin Bodmer, to whom I had sold much American and English literature, including the very rare "London, 1865" *Alice's Adventures in Wonderland*, which is the only copy on the Continent. On the flight back to New York the man seated next to me was a handsome Englishman, traveling on a diplomatic passport and obviously a VIP. It turned out in our conversation that he was going on diplomatic business to the embassy at Washington and that we had mutual friends both there and in London. And, to make things more congenial, he had definite bookish interests and had authored several plays. He was the tenth Earl of Bessborough, and it turned out further that his wife was a New Yorker, Mary Munn, some of whose family I knew, though I did not know her. She was to meet him later, he explained, because having been together in one near-fatal air crash, they now always traveled in separate planes for their child's sake.

We stopped in Gander about three in the morning, and never having been there, I decided to look around. We would be on the ground, I was told, about an hour. At that time there isn't much open except the bar, where I soon found myself with one amusing Australian. We bought each other a couple of drinks and talked away till I suddenly realized that considerable time had passed. No flight announcement had been made, though signs said they would be. Still I thought I had better stroll out to see where my plane was. Where it was, was up in the wild blue yonder, headed for New York—with my baggage, containing some pretty valuable books, most of my money, my passport, my clothes, but not me.

It couldn't have happened. The planes are supposed to have all passengers checked in before taking off, but, somehow, nobody checked. And the public-address system in the bar, it turned out, had not been connected. Mishaps like this don't bother me much—I've lived through too many—but I was flying BOAC and it seemed to trouble them. At any rate, I was put on standby for the first available seat on the first available plane. Half a day or so later, having had my fill of Gander, I was shoved onto another BOAC with assurances that my belongings would be at Idlewild, with the proper profuse apologies.

This time my seatmate was a petite American girl to whom I was soon relating my story. She turned out to be Lady Bessborough. As we came down the ramp at Idlewild, arm-in-arm, her husband, there to meet her, exclaimed, "Good God, I've heard of fast work, but nothing to match this!" My most recent meeting with them was when he escorted the Grolier Club members through the House of Lords library and we had tea on the terrace.

I even had trouble getting to Bloomington the first time—I flew from New York to Indianapolis, loaded with baggage, and then took a Greyhound bus southward. There was a stop at Martinsville and I left for refreshments. Suddenly I heard a noise and saw the taillights of my bus, with my baggage and, I may add, some books of considerable value. There were no taxis, no bus for another several hours, and there were people waiting to meet me at Bloomington. Phone conversations eventually straightened things out and I arrived, sans baggage, late as usual. The old routine over again, I mused, taking up my new duties.

# *J. K. Lilly, Jr.*

I FIRST MET J. K. Lilly, Jr., in 1932 under distinctly disadvantageous circumstances, to be much aggravated later. Harzof's best customer was William D. Breaker of Brooklyn, a broker of some kind (that's all I know about him), who over the years had been guided to a considerable collection of fine first editions of literature, and especially American history. Suddenly Breaker needed fewer books and more cash and approached Harzof to get it for him. Harzof did his best, explaining to me that had it not been for Breaker, "I'd still be a secondhand book peddler." This was when the "old and rare" was beginning to feel the pinch of the Depression. Oddly enough, in retrospect, it seems to have been about the last business to feel its economic pressure, but when pressure was finally applied bookselling was also among the last to recover.

As I recall the episode, Harzof explained to me that I was to go out to Indianapolis with a bag full of Breaker books and beard Lilly. It would be no use for him to write Lilly about these, he explained, as that would give J.K. a fast chance to say no without seeing them, and he couldn't go himself (he seldom stirred off Manhattan)—come to think of it, he had certain Nero Wolfe qualities.

And even that early in his collecting career, Mr. Lilly was totally disinclined to purchase a book he hadn't personally examined. So I was to entrain for Indianapolis, present myself at Lilly's office without advance warning but with such samples of the Breaker goodies as I could lug in a suitcase, and return with some cash—at least enough to justify the trip's expenses and enable Harzof to prove to Breaker that, Depression or no, his books could be sold.

I wound up in Indianapolis on a miserably hot day in the early summer of 1932, determined that if I ever got out of Indiana alive I'd never return. I checked into the Claypool Hotel and went to the Lilly offices, satchel in hand. Miss Armington, his long-time secretary, reminded me recently that I "staggered in."

What I did not know then was that there was an old-time subscription-set salesman operating out of Pennsylvania, named Randall, whom Gabriel Wells used occasionally as an agent. Even among that brazen breed Randall was distinguished for—perhaps the best word is audacity. He had gotten mixed up in an ugly way with J. K. Lilly, Sr., over some Stephen Foster manuscripts, had sold J. K. Lilly, Jr., some dubious portraits done by Poe, and barely escaped prosecution.

So Lilly, Jr., was scarcely well disposed toward a Randall, when I presented my card at his office. Only the fact that I represented G. A. Baker induced him to see me. When his files were turned over to the library I found my card, filed away in his methodical manner. On it I had scribbled, "Dear Mr. Lilly: could you grant me an interview at your convenience? Regarding a most desirable collection of privately owned books of great importance." When he asked, carelessly, if I came by any chance from Pennsylvania, I answered, honestly, "for generations." Further conversation developed, luckily, that I was from eastern, not western, Pennsylvania, and that I had never even heard of the "other Randall." Lilly's prep school had been Hill School in Pottstown, Pennsylvania, where I had many acquaintances, so we were soon on a friendly basis.

Unfortunately the Breaker library was composed largely of historical Americana which Lilly at that time was not collecting at all—nor had he the remotest intention of doing so.

Looking back on this first meeting, the book I most regret his not taking is that monument of New England printing and basis of New England theology, the so-called "Cambridge Platform"—*A Platform of Church Discipline gathered out of the Word of God and agreed upon by the Elders: and Messengers of the Churches assembled in the Synod at Cambridge in New England.* Printed at Cambridge by S.G. in New England and are to be sold at Cambridge and Boston Anno Dom: 1649.

Not merely are only eight copies known, but this was one of two copies (the other being at John Carter Brown) which Wilberforce Eames considered the first issue. The asking price was $5,000. Harzof had impressed on me the rarity and importance of the book. "It is more significant by far than the Bay Psalm Book," he counseled me. But Lilly was not collecting Americana. "I am too late to take up that field," he said. The book eventually wound up in what was left of Breaker's library in a sale at the American Art Association Anderson Galleries, April 7, 1937, where it brought $3,750. It was acquired by Thomas Streeter of

Morristown, New Jersey, and in 1967 brought at his auction $80,000, the second-highest price ever paid for an American book, the highest being the $151,000 for the Bay Psalm Book. Personally, I'd rather have the "Cambridge Platform." Incidentally, it may encourage collectors to know that at the time Lilly thought he was too late to form a significant collection of Americana, Streeter was just beginning his, which will, when finally dispersed, probably double the previous highest American auction sale of a library.

Among other great treasures Breaker had was a magnificent Eliot Indian Bible (Cambridge, 1663) in its original calf binding by John Ratcliffe with a provenance tracing back to its origins, including its ownership by Ezra Stiles, a famous New England book collector, president of Yale and clergyman (in order of historical importance). This I could not sell for $3,500 and it went, at Breaker's sale, for $2,700. The most recent copy sold at public auction in 1966 fetched $43,000 and was vastly inferior to Breaker's, with no provenance, rebound, and lacking three blank leaves.

Luckily Breaker did have some very good literature, and on that first visit Lilly purchased six items. I have Baker's bill for them.

| | |
|---|---:|
| Milton. *Paradise Lost*. First issue, original calf. 1667. | $5,000 |
| Shelley. *Adonais*. 1821. Morocco. | 3,000 |
| De Quincey. *Opium Eater*. 1822. Original boards. | 750 |
| Lowell. *Conversations*. Inscribed. | 375 |
| Longfellow. *Outre Mer*. Two parts, inscribed. | 2,000 |
| Tarkington. *The Guardian*. | 90 |
| | $11,215 |

The bill is dated June 10, 1932. Thus began a friendship which culminated, a quarter of a century later, in "The Lilly Library, Indiana University, Bloomington, Indiana. David A. Randall, Librarian," an event then beyond either of our wildest imaginings.

Of that first purchase, the Milton was a truly great copy, certainly the equal of any known. It is the "first title" with Milton's name in sloping capitals and is the McMillin-Norton copy, which had last sold in 1918 at $2,000, up to that time the highest price it had ever brought.

From the very beginning of his collecting career Lilly's appreciation of quality and condition was keen. He turned down my offer of the Breaker set of the first five editions of Walton's *Angler* (formerly M. D. C. Borden's) because of the rather gaudy bindings: inlaid pictorial, of piscatorial design, in Riviere's best manner. He remarked that he would prefer to wait for a set in original bindings. I reminded him how rare the book was in any state and he replied, "Fishermen and collectors are patient souls. I'll wait." In the spring of 1940 Carter cabled me that the Arthur Gilbey collection of books on angling was coming up for sale at Christie's and it had *the* pedigree set of Walton, all five volumes issued in his lifetime (London, 1653–1676), in their original bindings, the first having the musical notation on page 216 turned in and intact (it is usually cropped) and the third a presentation copy, one of only two of any edition of the *Angler* recorded thus. Carter estimated they would bring upwards of £2,500; we decided to try for them and we got them. The London *Times Literary Supplement* commented:

> The price of the first five editions of Walton's "Compleat Angler" at Christie's on April 29 was a great disappointment. Expert opinion had estimated that they would bring well over £2,000; your correspondent expected £3,000, which was perhaps, over enthusiastic. They brought £800 at the Ashburnham Sale in 1898 and they are not the kind of books that are less fashionable now than they were then. They have gone to America for £1,600 and somebody has bought a great bargain. One hears a great deal these days of the perplexities of investors, many of them compelled to sell their American holdings and not sure how to reinvest the proceeds. It is a pity that so few of them are knowledgeable about books. There could be no more certain or profitable lock-up for capital appreciation than these books at this price. They were very fairly described in the catalogue, with the possible exception that some would have put the linings inside one or two of the covers slightly later in time than the cataloguer. Certain it is that no finer set, nor any set nearer in condition to the editions as Walton saw them (these five are all the editions that appeared before his death), can have survived.

Lilly eventually acquired them for $11,500.

My second visit to Lilly was almost my last. Barnet J. Beyer was a well-known dealer in New York at the time and had somehow acquired two very important items, a group of eighty-one manuscripts of Walt Whitman (mostly from *Calamus*) and a manuscript transcript in her own hand of Anne Bradstreet's *The Tenth Muse, Lately Sprung up in America* (London, 1650), the first volume of poetry to be published by an author residing in America. These were priced at $83,750 and $100,000, respectively, at that time (Beyer's prices fluctuated with the stock market). He somehow talked Harzof into sending me with him and his manuscripts to Indianapolis to tempt Lilly. I was against the venture as I knew these would not appeal to him, but I was overruled. Lilly was polite, as always, but not interested, and I returned to New York, leaving Beyer, who claimed to have other business in the Midwest. I didn't hear from Lilly again for several years, getting merely courtesy replies to my letters.

It was only when I became associated with Scribner's that he told me what had happened. After I had left, Beyer returned the next day and tried to sell him a collection of pornography. Now it was good stuff, of its kind, some with exquisite eighteenth-century French copperplate illustrations, but Lilly was simply not the sort of person to whom these should have been offered. I became associated in his mind with this unfortunate episode. I don't think I ever would have seen him again had I not been employed by Scribner's. Guilt, or innocence, by association!

My first Scribner catalogue, "Familiar Quotations," caught his attention and he ordered generously from it. From there out all went well. He liked to collect by lists, the Grolier and Newton "Hundreds" for example. This was not because of lack of imagination—he had God's plenty of that—he simply used these as springboards. He came into Scribner's one day with Asa Don Dickinson's *One Thousand Best Books.* This was simply a distillation of all other "best book" lists. "Don't you think it would be fun to try and get all of these in their first appearances in their original languages and perhaps their first English translations?" he inquired. I did not disagree and eventually we acquired a very high proportion of them.

His collecting interests were beginning to broaden. He already had most of the conventional seventeenth-century to twentieth-century English and American literary landmarks and was beginning collecting key books in science, medicine, books that had influenced thought and works of that ilk. He began to think that he had perhaps put too much into his Poe collection and he had other doubts.

In May, 1938, Carter alerted me about a forthcoming Sotheby sale. I wrote Lilly:

> I know you are not adding to your library at present, but there is coming up in London shortly an absolutely mint copy of the first edition of *The Little Minister,* presented by Barrie to Thomas Hardy. This is something very special and should by no means be missed. Would you care to have me bid on it?

Back came the jesting reply:

> *The Little Minister* sounds very tempting but at present I may not consider bidding upon it unless you will take over my Poe's *Tamerlane* at $25,000!

I replied:

I'm sorry you decided not to go after the Barrie presentation to Hardy of *The Little Minister*. However, I'm going to buy it myself for stock if it doesn't go too fantastically high. [The book was purchased by Maggs for £225 and eventually passed to Lilly for $1,550.]

I'm afraid I can't at the moment move your *Tamerlane* at $25,000 but I can sell your *Paradise Lost* for at least $15,000 (for which, if you remember, you gave me $5,000) if you wish to have me do so.

This seemed to me to be a golden opportunity for Scribner's. Lilly had written me on April 28, 1938:

I have recently come to the conclusion—or, at least, I may be approaching the conclusion—that my book collecting activities have been to date entirely too catholic.

You will recall that we had some conversation along this line, I think, in fact, upon the occasion of our last visit together. At that time some discussion was entered into regarding the formation of an American collection involving, largely, the 19th Century. Would you care to enlarge upon this theme and give me the benefit of any thoughts you might have in this connection? [From these discussions came, through Lilly's subvention, plans for the *Bibliography of American Literature*, edited by Jacob Blanck, one of the monumental bibliographical undertakings of our time.]

Should I decide to make such a change in my future collecting activities, how do you suggest I might best dispose of my British and Continental books? Do you suppose that over a period of time you could place the manuscript of "Peter Pan" and other items involved in a manner to admit of my getting substantially my costs out of same? I realize, of course, that certain items would have to be disposed of at considerably less than they cost me but, on the other hand, there should be certain items that could be disposed of in advance of costs. If I could get my costs out of the material, I would then be free to proceed along the line suggested earlier in this letter.

You are so familiar with my collection that I should appreciate your giving the matter earnest consideration and then advising me.

I had replied:

This is scarcely a matter to be decided by mail, or discussed by mail either. I think that I had better come out to Indianapolis for an evening's talk any time suiting your convenience—I can do it any time after this weekend—such an undertaking as you have sketched needs clarifying and planning before it is even begun.

I alerted Carter to the possibilities, and he wrote Lilly a letter that eventually proved very important to his future book collecting.

Randall has written me that you are considering a change of direction, and a limitation of scope, in your library. It is a feeling which I imagine comes over many collectors when they realise that their collection is becoming a library with a capital L.

There is, however, one department of your library which I hope very much that you will decide to continue with, and that is the field of Continental first editions. I was much impressed with the ones you have, and I was also particularly pleased to find them there, because it is a subject in which I myself have always been interested. I have enjoyed sending over books of this character, which have ultimately found their way on to your shelves, and have looked forward to sending you similar material in the future; but quite apart from such personal feelings, it does seem to me that it would be a thousand pities to disperse the nucleus of a collection already distinguished, and capable of expansion into something really significant. There are very few collectors in your country to-day who are paying the proper attention to first editions of the masterpieces of Continental literature, and in that fact, as well as their intrinsic interest, lies the importance and value of this department of your library.

I hope you will forgive me for airing my views, but I take a real interest in your library, and I should be very happy to think that your affection for this part of it was strong enough to induce you to continue it as a side line to your main aims in the future.

Lilly needed no advice to go cautiously. He wrote me May 9:

Before you make a jaunt to the western country, I should like to have a little more time on the book collection problem.

It would not do to make a move now that I would likely be sorry for later and I had better take plenty of time before doing anything!

These matters rested until I spent the following Fourth of July holiday at the Eagle Crest Library discussing bookish matters. Lilly decided to dispose of part of his Poes, to begin with, keeping the *Tales, Raven, Grotesque and Arabesque*, and a few other pets. On my return to New York I wrote him as follows:

I've gone over your Poe collection. As it stands (from the cards I have) the cost to you is $118,000. There is collateral material, I imagine, which was not on the cards (the presentation *Eureka*, etc.). The total cost of the entire collection is, I judge, around $130,000. Now I think there is a good chance of selling it *en bloc* and I would like to try and do so. It would be a mistake, I am convinced, to break up the collection by selling separate items, as—say, the *Tamerlane*—unless as a last resort. If you want me to, I will be glad to try several people on the collection. As I see it, it should be salable at around $100,000. The more I go over the autograph material, the better it seems, especially the Whitman lot. These are worth today what you paid for them. The big losses come on the *Tamerlane* (cost $25,000. Worth today $15,000), the *Murders in the Rue Morgue* (cost $13,000. Worth today only about $5,000), *Animal*

*Magnetism* (cost $2500. I have one for $250). And I can't conceive of those Poe portraits being worth anything like the cost—$8,715, and there is, of course, that questionable letter. These losses are the important ones, and taking them into account, I think the $100,000 price I mentioned, not an unreasonable one. So, if agreeable, I'll start and see what I can do.

Lilly stopped in New York in August for a day on his way to his summer home, Red Oaks, on Cape Cod, at Falmouth. He inquired if I was about to bail him out of potential bankruptcy by selling the Poes and seemed slightly perturbed when I told him I had a strong nibble from a Baltimore collector. I could give him a definite answer in a few weeks, as it was merely a matter of settling on a price. He hesitated, and with a salesman's intuition I felt it was not my Baltimore fish trying to get off the hook, but my Indianapolis bait!

On September 19 I wrote Lilly inquiring if he would accept $125,000 for the collection: "My commission would come aside from this, from the purchaser, not from you." I was not really surprised to receive his immediate answer, dated September 21.

> This will acknowledge your letter of September 19.
> At the risk of your putting me down as completely insane, I may only say regarding the Poe collection that I am unable to arrive at a figure! If I must plead guilty to being slightly balmy I think you will simply have to consider my condition as one general to all book collectors —otherwise they wouldn't be book collectors! Really, when it comes right down to turning the green go-sign on Mr. Poe and his works. I can't bring myself to do it at this time.
> As you have already spent considerable time on this subject I will honor any modest bill forwarded—me to be the judge of what is modest!

To which I replied:

> Your decision about the Poe collection didn't come as an entire surprise to me, and I certainly don't think you're completely balmy—at least you're not any balmier than the general run of book collectors, not to mention dealers. And in many ways I'm glad you decided not to sell, even though I might have made a substantial commission on the deal.
> It's terribly hard to give up something one has spent so much time and effort on, as you have with your Poe collection. It can never be duplicated, as you well know, and some day I have no doubt that I will be able to get you a really staggering offer. There is no charge, of course, for the little work I did on the collection.

So nothing came of that, nor of tentative plans to dispose of other of his book collections. He could not bring himself to part with what he had collected so he simply kept them (luckily for Indiana University), without adding much to them, and took off on other book collecting ventures.

Lilly did very little collecting during the war but returned to the fold in 1946, his main interests then being medicine, science and Americana. He purchased from Henry Stevens, Son and Stiles, a small but exceedingly choice lot of Americana formed by the German Baron Hardt, headed by the famous Rome editions (the first Latin printing) of Columbus' letter announcing his discovery, printed by Stephen Plannck, 1493, both the "Ferdinand" and "Ferdinand and Isabella" editions, a fine run of Jesuit "Relations" and much more, for $75,000. Scribner's never specialized in this field, though we did supply him with some fine things, including Richard Hakluyt's *The Principal Navigations, Voyages, Traffiques & Discoveries*. This was a proper copy with the first state of the Molynaux-Wright map without the inscription concerning Sir Francis Drake and the Straits of Magellan, and very rare thus for just under $5,000.

In the last half decade of his book collecting career Lilly concentrated especially on the classic books in the history of medicine and science, from the beginnings down to the present time. But what were they? Everyone knew some of the great books and traditional rarities. Picking fifty or so would be easy—getting them, quite another matter.

What was needed but was not available was guides for the discriminating collector who was forming a personal, not a research, library. Since these did not exist, Lilly characteristically decided to have them created. He wanted them objective, wryly relating that he once requested a famous dealer to recommend a list of important works on another subject only to find that 95 percent of the books suggested were reposing on the dealer's shelves. The choices finally fell on W. R. LeFanu, librarian of the Royal College of Surgeons of England, who compiled a list of *Two Hundred Key Books in the History of Medicine and Surgery*. I. Bernard Cohen, then managing editor of *Isis*, did the same for science.

Though these books were not then as available and as cheap as they had been a generation before, still they had not anywhere reached their present rarity, popularity and price. Lilly was lucky in his timing—collector's luck, if you wish. One could still reasonably expect to have an offer of several decent copies of most desiderata within, say, half a decade while, to use a felicitous medical phrase of Gordon Ray's, when writing recently of nineteenth-century literature, "prices had not yet been inflated to the point of dropsy."

Lilly's entire expenditure on his medical collection was scarcely double the price of his first edition of Poe's *Tamerlane* (Boston, 1827), which was $25,000. Indeed, fewer than five books in the collection cost into four figures. Had he attempted to do in the decade following 1955 what he accomplished in the decade before then, it would have been proved impossible.

It might be mentioned that, though he was a generous buyer and seldom questioned a price if he wanted a book (though he often returned things on the grounds of condition), Lilly invariably collected within a strict budget. He never gave a blanket order for any books on any list to be purchased as they appeared. His dealers, therefore, had to exercise discretion in the spending of funds allocated to them. In practice this meant that they offered him the uncommon books—those unlikely to appear on the market reasonably soon again—first. Generally it was on these books that a higher profit could be obtained, while the more common books which (one thought then) would always be available were often not offered at all—they could be sold next year if real rarities could not be obtained.

For example, in September, 1953, I sent ten desirable medical books for Mr. Lilly's consideration. With the letter was enclosed a clipping from an English dealer's catalogue offering a set of Richard Bright's *Reports of Medical Cases* . . . (1827–1831) for £450—Lilly having purchased his set a few years before for $485 (a copy sold recently at auction for $3,500), a gentle reminder to the collector as to the moderation of Scribner prices.

Back came a typical answer.

> This is a somewhat tardy reply to your letter of September 26 but I waited until the medical books came in and were collated before replying.
>
> You will recall that earlier in the year I wrote you what my budget with the Scribner Book Store for 1953 would be. I have to report that with the present receipt of the ten medical books forwarded, we are now right on the button so please don't ship me anything else this year or at least not until after December 15 and then only with the proviso that the invoice may be settled during the first week in January of 1954. In this connection, I wish to proceed with the medical book want-list to the tune, as we go into the new year, of a budget of $10,000 so please don't commit me to any outlay beyond this sum until you hear from me further on the subject which may probably not be until late in 1954!
>
> In view of the above I may not presently consider the other item mentioned in your letter of September 26.
>
> Thank you so much, indeed, for your good offices—past, present, and future.

Lilly was always bibliographically minded. As early in his collecting career as 1930, when he was concentrating on Poe, he wrote the Library of Congress requesting:

> full information concerning bibliographies available of works of various authors. At the present time I will be particularly interested in obtaining a complete bibliography of the works of Edgar Allan Poe. Is there a catalogue available of bibliographies issued by the Library of Congress?
>
> Also, I would like to have complete information concerning library cards and request a catalogue of those available if this is supplied.

He received an answer: "There is a complete set of our cards in the State Library at Indianapolis."

A few years later Lilly became interested in American juveniles, especially the works of Harry Castlemon, a childhood favorite, author in the 1860's of "The Gunboat Series": *Frank Before Vicksburg, Frank on the Lower Mississippi*, etc. Finding that there was very little bibliographical information available, he set out to remedy this in a characteristic manner. He wrote the Library of Congress asking

> whether or not it would be possible for the Rare Book Department to receive a fund annually which could be applied toward the employment of a research man and toward defraying expenses incurred in connection with assigned work. If American Juvenilia (including Castlemon) could be one of the first items on the program, this would be very pleasing.

A grant was made of $6,000 a year for five years, anonymously. Immediately everything began to go wrong. The curator of rare books, V. Valta Parma, hired as bibliographer Gustav Davidson, described in one recommendation as "short story writer, essayist, novelist, poet, dramatist, musical critic, radio script writer, etc." But he was not a bibliographer. Lilly was a little annoyed, explaining to me that he "didn't like having him learn that business at my expense." Then, too, Parma took the view that most of the funds were for the purchase of books and proceeded on that assumption. Lilly mildly protested that "the big end of the grant should be used for compensation and travel charges and only occasionally to purchase books."

A health faddist, Parma took to sending Lilly great bunches of some rare seeds for which he claimed mysterious medical merits. If only the Lilly Company could isolate the effective element everyone would live forever, or at least to one hundred. In the spring of 1938 he wrote Lilly: "The letter from your Research Division reporting on the seeds arrived in due course and is another of those matters which I should have acknowledged promptly. It is probably not surprising that the X element in the seeds did not show up."

Most of 1938 was occupied by Parma in getting himself publicity, gleefully reporting his speaking engagements at Columbia University, among others, on the project: "I believe that next Sunday Winchell may mention it in his broadcast and also in his syndicated column." All of which was complete anathema to Lilly, who also began to suspect that no one with any competence in even elementary bibliography was doing any work and so expressed himself. He never suffered fools gladly.

In June in 1939 some sort of explosion occurred, of which I have no firsthand knowledge, and Davidson was dropped as bibliographer. He wrote Lilly complaining that the whole undertaking had been mismanaged from the start, and that his superiors referred to it slightingly as dealing with "baby books," and considered the idea "inconsequential and a waste of money," and sent bitter letters to Lilly, who by this time was regretting his philanthropy. All he wanted was a competent bibliography of children's books. He never, to my knowledge, except once, intervened in any way with any grant he made and was infinitely distressed by having distasteful personality problems inflicted on him.

At this point Archibald MacLeish succeeded Herbert Putnam as Librarian of Congress and asked me among others to suggest an adequate bibliographer. There was one at hand, Jacob Blanck, whom Lilly knew of through his work on Mark Twain, and also as the author of a recent (1938) bibliography of the best-loved American children's books, *Peter Parley to Penrod*. Blanck accepted the appointment a little dubiously, because after the job was done, where would he go from there? He needn't have worried. Lilly wrote MacLeish, "I am delighted about the appointment of Jacob Blanck to the bibliographical post. If he does a good job, and I have no reason to believe he will not, in this assignment, perhaps we may provide some future work assignments for him after the juvenile bibliography is completed."

By 1941 Jake had completed *Harry Castlemon, Boy's Own Author. Appreciation and Bibliography* (New York, R. R. Bowker). Lilly was so pleased with this and with Jake that in 1942 he asked him to come to Indianapolis to help Dorothy Russo finish her bibliography of James Whitcomb Riley, which the Indiana Historical Society was doing under his sponsorship. With Jake's departure from the Library of Congress nothing further was done about the juveniles, so far as I know. But this disaster in no way diminished Lilly's enthusiasm for bibliographical enterprises. In E. Millicent Sowerby's "Compiler's Preface" to the first volume of the magnificent *Catalogue of the Library of Thomas Jefferson,* issued by the Library of Congress, there is a line: "First of all, our appreciative thanks are due Mr. Josiah K. Lilly, Jr., of Indianapolis, Indiana, through whose interested consideration this Project was supported."

He had already set his sights higher. He had long been aware of grave deficiencies in the bibliographies of major American authors, especially Poe. There were few competent author bibliographies, most of which were outdated, at that time; checklists like P. K. Foley's and Merle Johnson's about did it. Lilly decided something should be done about this, and he had discussed possibilities of a "Big Book" with Blanck, i.e., an ambitious project Blanck had suggested.

In the fall of 1943 I spent the Labor Day weekend with Lilly at his summer home. He had originally planned to have the Foley-Johnson work revised and enlarged under the auspices of the Library of Congress. The fiasco the juvenile project had ended in, however, changed that plan and he now had another. Briefly this was to underwrite the compilation of a definitive series of bibliographies of American literary figures, akin to what Evans and Sabin had done for American history. He had discussed this with Blanck, who was enthusiastic. I suggested that the work should be administered by the Bibliographical Society of America, and Lilly asked me to approach them. Thomas Streeter was then president and appointed an ad hoc committee to consider the possibilities. This comprised Carroll A. Wilson, chairman; James T. Babb, then acting librarian of Yale; Clarence S. Brigham, director of the American Antiquarian Society; William Jackson, director of the Houghton Library at Harvard University; and several others, including myself. It ran into trouble at the start. Bill Jackson was not enthusiastic (his heart belonged to *The Short Title Catalogue*) and at that time he only approved the grant with an eye on the future, writing Lilly: "What you propose is a good one to show whether or not the Bibliographical Society can do it to your satisfaction and that of scholars generally. If the Society proves its efficiency in this one, then perhaps you may be interested in other things later." Lilly was distressed at this lukewarm attitude and considered dropping the whole idea. Eventually Jackson became so enamored of the work that the entire project found a permanent base in the Houghton Library, from which it currently operates. There was another rumpus when the Society came to name the permanent committee to administer the grant.

Lilly wanted a diversified committee composed of other than librarians and public officials, and he tentatively suggested including a collector (his choice was Fred Adams) and a dealer, myself. When the committee was finally selected I was not on it, nor was Fred.

Librarians objected because I wasn't one of the fraternity and was "in trade" besides. Some dealers resented the fact that I would, supposedly, be privy to information on newly discovered "points," "issues," etc., from which I would reap a fortune while some influential collectors at that time regarded any dealer (except their special tamed pet) as a natural enemy.

Lilly was annoyed at this attitude and the efforts of "effete Easterners," as he phrased it, to dictate. In any event I am told he intimated "No Randall, no grant," and I was back on the committee, of which I am the surviving member. On Carroll Wilson's death a few years later, Fred Adams succeeded him as chairman. Jake Blanck carries on his monumental job and the fifth volume of the *Bibliography of American Literature*, the half-way mark, has just been published.

Despite his continuing purchases in his now restricted fields, J.K., I had the feeling, was becoming less interested in his books and much more in other collecting fields. Increasingly he talked more of stamps, gold, paintings, etc. In the fall of 1954 while we were doing some fishing he casually asked if I were indissolubly wedded to Scribner's, adding that he was giving up book collecting and was puzzled about the disposal of his library. If he was not going to add to it, he didn't want it around, so would I consider going in business with him with his library as my stock? I replied, a little shakily, that I had no contract with Scribner's but I certainly had an obligation to talk the matter over with them. They generously urged me to accept with their blessings, and I went to Indianapolis for further conferences. These resulted in my doing a careful inventory of costs, current values, etc. It was a bookseller's dream; the finest private library in America and the most diversified ever assembled was mine, all mine. Eventually we had a conference with his lawyers and financial advisers and the roof fell in. He had, of course, been doing extensive buying all through the Depression, and values had increased so much that it was impractical to sell it, as taxes would be too high. It would be cheaper to give it away! This seemed nonsense to me and I never could understand it, but there the big ugly fact was, and I descended suddenly from cloud nine.

It was Lilly's own idea to give the collection to Indiana University, which he had never even visited, "if they would accept it." He knew of the great concentration of books on the East and West coasts, and though there were many fine university and other collections between, there was

nothing of the quality and depth he had formed, nor was there ever likely
to be. And he was, after all, a Hoosier.

Next came the question of a curator, and Lilly asked me to consider it.
I had been in the business for over a quarter-century and thought that
was enough. I had had some years of commuting (from New York to Cos
Cob, Connecticut, then an hour and a half each way from door to door),
apartment living, Long Island living, club living, a private home in the
heart of New York—all of which made a beautiful university campus seem
infinitely attractive. Besides, I had gone into my profession in the first
place because I liked to be around books which, individually, I could
never have aspired to. But the trouble was (or so I rationalized), someone was always buying them and taking them away just when we were
becoming friends. Here I could get them and keep them—and what a lot
of old friends I had to begin with. I never regretted my decision.

After J.K.'s death I was inordinately pleased to receive from Fred
Adams a letter that read in part: "I got a nice autograph note from Eli
Lilly in which he said that his brother Joe told him not long ago that his
book gift to Indiana University was the most satisfactory thing he ever
did."

Perhaps I can end my account of our relationship by quoting from an
article I wrote for the *Antiquarian Bookman* about Lilly after his death,
entitled "America's Quiet Collector."

> It should be emphasized that while doing all this collecting he was
> leading a busy business life. The year before he left for France, in World
> War I, he entered the family pharmaceutical business, which was just
> beginning an era of great expansion. He then wrote a personnel policy
> for the company that is still regarded as a very model of its kind: "The
> greatest business problem today is the human problem of labor and the
> wise handling of employees," he stated, at the age of 23, fifty years ago.
>
> He projected this view into his collecting. He made his errors and mis-
> judgments; he was used (and misused) on occasion; deceits, fakes, forg-
> eries and misplaced confidences caused heartaches and regrets. But he
> loved what he was doing and persisted in doing it despite betrayals. He
> was a fast student and he hit hard in whatever direction he spent his
> energies. When one famed dealer misrepresented something to him
> (through ignorance, not fraud), Lilly dropped him, later remarking, as
> he had in another case, "I didn't intend to let him learn his busines at
> my expense."
>
> I can speak from firsthand knowledge only of his library. Others have
> assembled more important collections of some of its segments, but taken
> as a unit it is by far the greatest, in any way you define that adjective,
> assembled by anyone in his era. There are, I have been told, individual

collections of stamps, coins, paintings, and perhaps guns, which are individually superior to any of those assembled by him. And there are those who have spent upon such pursuits much more money. But there has been no one who even approached his combined achievement or who so completely realized his own vision of what he desired to accomplish. It should be mentioned incidentally, that through five vital years, 1941–1946, during which time he would normally have been at the height of his collecting career, he bought nothing. I can only speak for bookmen, but these years spanned the A. Edward Newton through the Frank Hogan sales, when an enormous amount of things of the type that interested him came on the market. I assume this happened in other fields. In any event, he bought nothing, on principle.

The public knowledge of any of a dozen of his avocations would have made him well-known had he cared for such fame. He simply didn't. His expressed philosophy was "You have done something worthwhile when you have taken something that is ugly and replaced it with something beautiful." He quietly accomplished a multitude of such transformations. And just as quietly he surrounded himself with the best he could find of the objects which expressed the ideas he loved. He was the *beau idéal* of the perfect collector.

# Index

## About the Author

DAVID A. RANDALL has been involved in book collecting and bookselling for forty years. After schooling at Lehigh and Harvard Law, he learned the rare book field by working for various experts. Then, after having his own bookshop in New York for a few years, he became manager of the Rare Book Department at Scribner's in 1935, a position he held until 1956, when he became Librarian of the Lilly Library at Indiana University. He has been a frequent contributor of bibliographical articles to *The Book Collector, The Colophon, Publishers' Weekly, The Baker Street Journal, The Antiquarian Bookman,* etc., and was co-author with John T. Winterich of *A Primer of Book Collecting*. He was also co-author with Jean C. S. Wilson of *Thirteen Author Collections of the Nineteenth Century and Five Centuries of Familiar Quotations*.